D0914998

JUSTICE WILLIAM J. BRENNAN, JR.
Freedom First

JUSTICE WILLIAM J. BRENNAN, JR.
Freedom First

Roger Goldman with David Gallen

Carroll & Graf Publishers, Inc.
New York

Collection and original text copyright © 1994 by Roger Goldman and David Gallen

First Carroll & Graf edition 1994

Carroll & Graf Publishers, Inc.
260 Fifth Avenue
New York, NY 10001

Library of Congress Cataloging-in-Publication Data

Goldman, Roger L.
    Justice William J. Brennan, Jr. : freedom first / Roger Goldman with Davin Gallen.—
1st Carrol & Graf ed.
        p. cm.
    ISBN 0-7867-0069-6 (cloth) : $24.95 (Canada $33.95)
    1. Brennan, William J. (William Joseph), 1906–   . 2. United States. Supreme Court
—Biography. 3. Judges—United States—Biography. 4. Judicial opinions—United
States. I. Brennan, William J. (William Joseph), 1906–   . II. Gallen, David. III.
Title.
KF8745.B68G65   1994
347.73'2634—dc20
[B]
[347.30735]
[B]   94-6417
                                                                                     CIP

Permissions

The publisher gratefully acknowledges the following for permission to reprint:

Jeffrey T. Leeds and *The New York Times Magazine* (October 5, 1986) for "A Life on the Court"

Owen Fiss and *The Yale Law Journal* (March 1991) for "A Life Lived Twice"

Nat Hentoff and *Playboy* magazine (July 1991) for "The *Playboy* Interview"

William J. Maledon and *Arizona State Law Journal* (Winter 1990) for "Justice William J. Brennan, Jr.: A Personal Tribute"

Thurgood Marshall and *Harvard Law Review* (November 1990) for "A Tribute to Justice William J. Brennan, Jr."

Abner J. Mikva and *Harvard Law Review* (November 1990) for "A Tribute to Justice William J. Brennan, Jr."

Daniel J. O'Hern and *St. John's Law Review* (1991) for "In Honor of William J. Brennan, Jr."

E. Joshua Rosenkranz and *Nova Law Review* (Winter 1991) for "Dear Boss: A Law Clerk's Tribute to Justice Brennan"

Virginia A. Seitz and *Judicature* (February/March 1991) for "Recollections of Justice Brennan"

Peter L. Strauss and *St. John's Law Review* (1991) for "Justice Brennan"

Nina Totenberg and *Harvard Law Review* (November 1990) for "A Tribute to Justice William J. Brennan, Jr."

Byron R. White and *The Yale Law Journal* (March 1991) for "Tribute to the Honorable William J. Brennan, Jr."

I gratefully acknowledge the helpful comments of Stephen R. Felson on earlier drafts of the book, the research assistance of Anthony W. Horvath and Kathleen Casey, and the encouragement of Dean John B. Attanasio and Professor Eileen Searls of the St. Louis University School of Law.

This book is dedicated to my mother, Miriam Goldman, the most professional of volunteers, who has given thousands of students the opportunity for higher education, without ever seeking the recognition she so richly deserves.

—Roger Goldman

Contents

Part I
Reflections on Justice William J. Brennan, Jr.

Part II
The Jurisprudence of Justice William J. Brennan, Jr.

Contents

Part III
The Opinions of Justice William J. Brennan, Jr.

Part I

Reflections on
Justice William J. Brennan, Jr.

In October 1986 William J. Brennan, Jr., began his thirtieth year as a justice on the Supreme Court. Earlier that year, in the summer, Jeffrey T. Leeds, who had been serving as a law clerk to Justice Brennan for the 1985–86 Term, had the opportunity to converse on the record with Justice Brennan about his life on and off the Court over the past three decades. The piece that follows was first published by The New York Times Magazine.

A Life on the Court

Jeffrcy T. Leeds

Shortly before 10 tomorrow morning, as the United States Supreme Court begins its 1986 October term, Justice William J. Brennan Jr. will leave his chambers, turn right, then left, toward the small locker-lined robing room. There, he will slip his black judicial robe over his suit before crossing the corridor to await, along with his colleagues, for 10 o'clock precisely to arrive. At that time, a short electronic beep will sound, followed immediately by the sound of the marshal's gavel. Brennan will pass through the red velvet curtain that divides the anteroom from the courtroom to take his place on the mahogany bench just to the right of the Chief Justice, the seat traditionally occupied by the Associate Justice with the greatest seniority. Tomorrow will mark the beginning of Justice Brennan's 30th year on the Court. He is 80 years old and very fit, in part as a result of daily sessions on his exercise bicycle.

Only two Justices appointed in this century, William O. Douglas and Hugo L. Black, have sat on the High Court longer than Brennan. During his tenure, he has written not only leading, but landmark, cases. And yet, despite his colorful personality, his long tenure and the enormous impact he has made on American life, Brennan remains, like all of the Justices, relatively unknown to most people.

3

This is not because the public or the press has lacked curiosity. It is the result of the traditions of the Court. With the exception of the intelligence agencies, no institution in American political life operates with such secrecy. The Court's decision-making meetings, known as conferences, are closed not only to the public, but to the staff. Arguments before the Court are not televised nor broadcast on radio. Internal rules and procedures are unpublished and are unknown even to those who appear regularly before the Court. Appointed for life, Justices do not attend political meetings, make speeches on behalf of candidates nor appear on Sunday morning newsmaker shows.

Moreover, even when Justices are publicly criticized, their practice is to remain silent. The public is rarely given a glimpse of why they think the way they do. Three weeks ago, for instance, an official of the Justice Department attacked Brennan. In a speech at the University of Missouri School of Law, William Bradford Reynolds, the Assistant Attorney General for civil rights, said that "the Justice has allowed his liberal orthodoxy to shape his jurisprudence," and described Brennan's "radical egalitarianism" as a "major threat to individual liberty."

Not surprisingly, Justice Brennan declined to answer the charges or comment on this particular attack. But, to judge from his more general comments below, he finds remarks such as Reynolds's puzzling. He takes a long view of these matters and says that, in time, he might even be thought of as "Brennan the right-winger."

From July 1985 through July 1986, I served as one of four law clerks to Justice Brennan. The clerkships are one-year appointments made by the Justice to recent law school graduates. In addition to his secretary and messenger, the four of us comprised the Justice's entire staff. Our job involved being research assistants, sounding boards, writers of memos and drafters of opinions, as well as staplers, collaters, brewers and bringers of coffee.

Justice Brennan's law clerks are especially fortunate, because of the man's command of the Court's history and the access he affords to his younger colleagues. He is also easily the warmest member of the Court, famous for his charm, always linking arms with his colleagues or reaching out for a hand or a shoulder. The Brennan clerks are given a much greener light than the clerks of some other Justices to talk about cases. He told us we were free to discuss his views with other law clerks. We were also in a good position to tell him what we thought the views of the other Justices might turn out to be. He said to us, "I take help from wherever and from whomever I can get it."

When I first met him, the Justice noted that I was born in 1956, the year he was appointed to the Court by President Dwight D. Eisenhower. Brennan has participated in more than a quarter of the cases decided by the Court in this century. Including dissents and concurrences, he has written more opinions than any other Justice in the history of the United States with the exception of Douglas. "His footprints are everywhere," says Judge Abner J. Mikva, a judge on the United States Court of Appeals for the District of Columbia Circuit and a friend of Brennan. "His influence can be felt in nearly every area of the law."

"Everything I am," the Justice told us, "I am because of my father." William J. Brennan Sr. had emigrated from County Roscommon, Ireland, in 1893 and settled in Newark. He stoked fires at the Ballantine brewery there and later became a labor leader and an elected public official in Newark. William Jr. was born in Newark in 1906, the second of eight children. As Justice Brennan tells it, his father became particularly friendly with some very prominent lawyers and asked them often to his house. "He watched them and decided he was going to make a lawyer of me, by golly," the son says.

Brennan Jr. was an honor student at the University of Pennsylvania's Wharton School. He completed Harvard Law School on scholarship after his father died, graduating in the top 10 percent of his class. In 1928, while at law school, he married Marjorie Leonard, with whom he eventually had three children. She died in 1982. The following year, Brennan married the former Mary Fowler, a woman then in her 60's and his secretary for more than 26 years. Brennan has eight grandchildren.

Upon receiving his law degree in 1931, he began practicing with a Newark law firm, becoming a partner in 1937. Five years later, he resigned to accept a commission in the Army and served until 1945. He then returned to his firm as a name partner. In 1949, Brennan again resigned from private practice, this time to accept the nomination of Gov. Alfred E. Driscoll, a Republican, to a judgeship on the New Jersey Superior Court. One year later, he was elevated to the Appellate Division of the Superior Court, then, in 1952, to the New Jersey Supreme Court, where he remained until President Eisenhower appointed him to the Supreme Court of the United States.

I asked Justice Brennan if his father would have been surprised to see him as a Justice. "No," he answered, "he would have expected it."

Justice Brennan, perhaps better than any living person, understands the workings of the Court. Accordingly, in recent years his law clerks have sought—and generally failed—to persuade him to share his views by giving interviews to the press. "I write them, I don't explain them," has been his standard response to these requests, echoing almost every judge's conviction that written judicial opinions need no embellishment.

But as the Justice's 80th birthday and his 30th anniversary on the Court approached and the requests from the press mounted, we law clerks sensed he was beginning to change his mind. In late June, as the work of the Court tapered off, I asked him to discuss with me on the record his work as a Justice and his life on and off the Court. He agreed, stipulating that the interviews would appear in a question-and-answer format.

Shortly before we began the first of our summer conversations, President Reagan nominated William H. Rehnquist to be the next Chief Justice and Antonin Scalia to be a new Associate Justice, the first since Sandra Day O'Connor was appointed in 1981. Would this lead to a dramatic shift in the direction of the Court? To what degree do a Justice's personal views inevitably determine his or her vote on a particular case? What, finally, is it like to live a life on the Court?

QUESTION: You are often described in the press, and have been attacked by members of the current Administration, as the Justice on the "extreme left." Are you at all surprised to find yourself labeled that way?
ANSWER: Quite honestly, I don't understand it. Anyone familiar with what I have done here, the opinions, and anyone with historical perspective, would have to know that I am not on the extreme left. It does make me chuckle. I have never gone as far as the extreme left on the Court, let alone the country. How would you characterize Justices Black and Douglas? We didn't see eye to eye in so many things. They were, I suppose, far to the left of me.
Q: It doesn't bother you?
A: No. People have short memories and times change. Maybe one day, someone will talk about Brennan the right-winger.
Q: When you sat in the Oval Office with President Eisenhower back in 1956 and heard him offer you the job of an Associate Justice on the Supreme Court, did you think: This man doesn't know what he is letting himself in for?
A: Never gave it a thought. Very frankly, the difference between the responsibility of this Court and the responsibility of a state supreme court—particularly in those days when we hadn't yet extended the Bill of Rights to the states—is just vast. Enormous. There is nothing that

you do that prepares you for this job. Even Felix Frankfurter used to say that his lifelong study of the Court never really prepared him for this job. You simply cannot study it from afar and expect to know it. You simply cannot know how you will respond to the legal issues as a Justice, as opposed to a law professor, or a judge on a court of appeals or even a state supreme court. I know that was certainly true of me.

Q: Burger is gone, Rehnquist is Chief Justice. Scalia is an Associate Justice. Is the Court—and the country—about to experience momentous change?

A: That's a hard, perhaps even impossible, question. It's been observed that in terms of personnel, a conservative has been replaced by another conservative, and that, for that reason, there may be no change in terms of votes in individual cases, assuming, of course, that Chief Justice Rehnquist votes in the future as he has in the past. However, in an institution this small, personalities play an important role. It's inevitable when you have just nine people. How those people get along, how they relate, what ideas they have, how flexible or intractable they are, are all of enormous significance.

Q: What kind of a Chief Justice do you expect Justice Rehnquist to make?

A: I'm not sure what value predictions have, and, of course, we will know soon enough. But I do think that Bill is not going to be a loner to the extent that he has been one. I think the figure that appeared in the press was that he had dissented by himself in 54 cases. I think you will see less of that. This means he may have to moderate some of his positions. My guess is that he is going to do it.

Also, with the extra work that goes with being Chief Justice, he may have to stop writing books and give fewer speeches. Didn't I see that he was in a play this year? His acting career may also be in jeopardy.

Q: What about Antonin Scalia? Do you know him?

A: We've met. He's delightful. If what they say about him is true, he will be great fun to have as a colleague. But I would rather not speculate. Like everybody else, I will wait to read his opinions.

Q: In addition to being thought of as a great liberal, you seem to have the reputation of being the "playmaker" of the Court, the consensus builder who somehow manages, in case after case, to get five votes for very liberal opinions. Do you think that is accurate?

A: I have always had an uneasy feeling about that. I don't know if it is completely accurate. I don't think I do anything differently. What do we do in these chambers? We have an opinion to write. We think about it, and then we talk about it and then write it, and we circulate it, and we get suggestions, and perhaps we make some changes, and then we end up with five votes. What is so special about that?

Q: I suppose the success rate has been special.

A: Perhaps. Doesn't that mean only that we are doing our work well? Writing sound opinions that are persuasive to at least four others?

It really isn't very mysterious or complex, what we do. Just look at how we work in these chambers. We debate the issues, the merits, and when it comes time to write, we discuss the various possible approaches. We ask about some of the approaches. Will this be rejected by Lewis Powell or Harry Blackmun? Will Thurgood agree with this? Has John Stevens written any cases which may suggest how he is thinking and about which we should be aware? What does Sandra think? You try to get, in advance of circulation, a sense of what will sell, what the others can accept. And you write it that way, and when it works out—and maybe you have suggestions that come in and perhaps you make substantial revisions—but when it works out and you have a Court, you are delighted.

I don't think what I did when Earl Warren was here is any different than what I did when Warren Burger was Chief or what I intend to do now that Bill Rehnquist is Chief. That is the job as I see it. The implication about the "play-maker" phrase that I reject is that you go running around the building talking, shaking hands, putting your arm around everyone. Only once did I go around and talk to everybody, and that was on the Nixon tapes case. I thought that case, in the context of the times, called for the kind of opinion we had in 1958 with *Cooper v. Aaron*, a critically important desegregation case, with everybody signing the opinion to emphasize the fact that we were unanimous. And I went around to see everyone and tried to sell that idea, and, of course, it was a complete failure. Nobody agreed. Not one. So, I suppose it is a good thing I have not tried to do business that way over the years. If I have been successful, it is because of the advance preparation, the hard work, the careful thinking that we try to do in here.

Q: The play-maker reputation generally seems to go hand in hand with accounts of your relationship with Earl Warren. Do you remember your first impressions of him?

A: Oh yes. My first impression was that he and I weren't going to have any difficulty in getting along.

Q: Isn't that something of an understatement?

A: As things developed, yes. But not as a first impression.

Q: Where and when did the first meeting take place?

A: The very day I learned that I was to be named to the Court. Herbert Brownell, who was the Attorney General at the time, had shuttled me from the White House to the Department of Justice and then back to the White House to be introduced to the press. After the press conference, Brownell said we ought to get down to the Supreme Court and meet the Chief Justice. And so Brownell, Bill Rogers and I came here. We had a lovely lunch, and that was that. The Chief and I made a date for me to come back to meet the others. That was a famous day, when Warren took me upstairs to Room 317. He opened the door, and it was pitch dark, and then he turned on the light, and there were all my new colleagues huddled around a television watching the opening game of the 1956 World Series. The Chief introduced me to each of my new colleagues, and they each shook my hand, and then someone said "Put out the lights," and they did. And that was my introduction to the Brethren.

Q: When did you realize that you and Chief Justice Warren were going to have a special relationship?

A: Our relationship just developed, just grew, from the outset. From the very beginning we did a lot of things together, particularly in sports. We were both very sports-minded, especially about football and baseball, and we often went to games. Then, with some frequency, we would dine at one another's homes, but generally little was said about the Court. As far as Court work was concerned, we began to compare notes on cases, and that finally led to a weekly meeting on Thursdays, here in chambers, before the conferences. He would sit just where you are sitting now.

Q: Why did he come in here to your chambers? After all, he was the Chief Justice.

A: He believed in the old adage that he was Chief among equals. He fought like the devil against increasing the disparity between what he got paid as Chief and what the Associate Justices received.

Q: Was your relationship off the Court an intimate one?

A: We were very close, personally, but I think probably the closeness was largely judicial. Black always was further from us, and Douglas was even further. It's funny. I suppose we just gravitated together. We had more of the same approaches to the cases than the others. Their analyses were not quite the same as ours, they were a little bit more extreme, as we were just saying, than ours. We were just kindred spirits on many of the issues that came to the Court.

Q: Give me an example of how Black and Douglas were extreme.

A: Well, we were all for the same results. And more often than not, we did agree on the analysis, but as for the First Amendment area, for example, Black's and Douglas's position was that when the Constitution directs that Congress shall make "no law" abridging freedom of speech, that means *no* law, and this was something that neither the Chief nor I could accept. In our view, there were limits. And this extreme view of Black and Douglas carried into the libel area and obscenity area and religious area. Very often we could all agree on a case, but sometimes we couldn't. In the *New York Times* case, for example, neither Black nor Douglas could join, because it didn't go far enough for them.

Q: If someone had asked you in 1963 or 1964 who your best friend was, would it have been Earl Warren?

A: Well, that is interesting. Somehow, he was always the Chief Justice. In the sense, it might not have been something that he would have wanted, but it was there anyway. There has to be a distance between yourself and the Chief Justice. He was always the Chief, the Super Chief.

Q: Did you call him the Super Chief?

A: Yes, but not to his face. I think I first used it in an appreciation of him in the Harvard Law Review. I just called him "Chief."

Q: Not "Earl"?

A: Never. That is just not the way it ever is. Once Bill Rehnquist is confirmed, he will never be anything but "Chief" to me.

Q: What made Earl Warren so great a Chief Justice?

A: He had everything. He was hard-working, he knew how to work with people. He was marvelous with people. He would take approaches that would often escape my eye. He was just extraordinary.

Q: Should the Chief Justice be a leader with respect to jurisprudence?

A: I think the old expression is the "massing" of a point of view, of a Court—of ensuring at least five votes for an opinion, and, on those cases that require it, of seeking and getting nine votes, a unanimous Court. Of course, John Marshall was the great master of that technique. Earl Warren was also. I suppose, in a sense, it is less doctrinal than it is institutional.

Q: How did Warren do that? Did he go to the other chambers to sound out the others?

A: Oh yes, he did it all the time. Of course, some Justices are more receptive to visits than others. You know that my door is always open, but that is not true throughout the building. And of course, Bill Douglas was often not even *in* the building—or in Washington, for that matter.

Q: *What was Douglas like to work with?*

A: Well, his great mistake, Bill's, was his insistence—and he repeated it time and time again—"I have no soul to worry about but my own." This was always his justification for his conduct as a Justice. He was not a team player ordinarily.

Q: *Was that something he would actually say—about his soul?*

A: Oh, yes, a good number of times he said that, when walking down the hall or talking one-on-one in his chambers or mine.

Q: *And you would argue with him and tell him that he was wrong to take that view?*

A: Yes, and I wasn't the only one that would do that. I am sure.

Q: *What else does it take to be an effective Chief?*

A: A conviction that you have to be fair in the assignment of opinions— this ensures good feelings all around—and an extraordinary capacity for persuading others to a point of view.

Q: *What do you think the historical assessment will be of Chief Justice Burger's performance as a Chief Justice? Many people feel that he lacked some of the qualities you describe as important.*

A: Yes, I am afraid that is the contemporaneous assessment and will be the historical assessment as well.

Q: *Many have observed that Rehnquist is very personable. Will this be to his advantage as Chief Justice?*

A: It's to all of the Justices' advantage.

Q: *But not to Rehnquist especially?*

A: It's hard to know what that would mean. It's not as simple as there being two sides on the Court, or even a case. I think people are very wrong who think that is the way it is.

Q: *Certainly, that's the way the Burger Court was often characterized.*

A: I think if you look at a lot of important cases and areas—abortion, free speech, the religion cases—the votes did not align the way a simple approach would expect.

Q: *Still, didn't the Burger Court depart from the Warren Court?*

A: Perhaps in terms of direction and momentum, yes. But the times changed also. Of course there have been some erosions in some areas, for example the Fourth Amendment right not to be subject to unreasonable searches or seizures, but I don't think it's very accurate to speak of the Burger Court having unraveled the work of the Warren Court. Some important decisions affirming personal liberties came down during Burger's years. The abortion decision was not a legacy of the Warren Court, but the Burger Court. The first case to strike down the death penalty in a number of states came out of the Burger Court. Also, important cases involving the separation of church and state—prayer in school in particular—and the affirmative-action cases this past term.

Q: In 1967, when Warren was Chief Justice, you did not write a single dissent, and you averaged roughly four a term during his tenure. This last term alone, you wrote 26 dissents. Was the changeover to the Burger Court very dramatic in terms of your role as a Justice?

A: No. I feel so strongly about that. This Court is final on constitutional matters. Outside of overruling itself, only constitutional amendments can change the constitutional interpretations that the Court renders, and because of that fact, I have always felt that a member of this Court is duty-bound to continue stating the constitutional principles that have governed his decisions, even if they are in dissent, against the day when they may no longer be in dissent. It has happened so often in the history of the Court, and must continue to happen, that views that represent the minority position come to be understood as correct. That is why I continue to dissent on the death penalty and in other areas, and I am going to continue to do so because I am duty-bound. So the job hasn't changed. I still work hard to interpret the Constitution as I believe it must be read. The Court has, of course, changed, and the results in some cases have changed. They will change again.

Q: Was the changeover personally disruptive?

A: It was an inevitable change. It had to be. In a sense, it became a bigger challenge and it made the occasions when you managed to have the majority of your colleagues agree with you sweeter than it had been. We have certainly continued to prevail in many important areas. In other words, there is room for the old dog.

Q: You were the first Democrat appointed to the Supreme Court by a Republican since Benjamin Cardozo was appointed by Herbert Hoover. Did anybody in the Eisenhower Administration grill you about your politics or your judicial philosophy before you were offered the position?

A: Oh, there was no grilling at all. Not a single question was asked.

Q: No one asked you any questions about politics or policy?

A: No, although the press did ask. When Jim Hagerty picked me up to take me to the press conference where my nomination was to be announced, I was asked, "Did you vote for Eisenhower in 1952?" I was able to say that I wasn't eligible to vote in 1952, since we had moved to a new county in 1952, and under New Jersey law you had to be a resident of the county where you wanted to vote for six months before you could vote. Well, I was then asked, "If you had been eligible to vote, would you have voted for Eisenhower?" I said, "I really can't answer that—I don't know."

Q: Do you believe the period we are going through now is different, in the sense that the Administration really does have a specific agenda in terms of judicial appointments?

A: I think it was different then. My experience, as far as I know, was also the experience of those who followed—Stewart and Whittaker in the Eisenhower days. And Justice Harlan, who had preceded me, never suggested to me that there had ever been any question of any kind. Of course, this isn't to say that the only concern was with the quality of the mind or the legal training. But probably there was less concern with specific results in specific areas.

Q: How does a new Justice learn the ropes and develop a style? I know that Felix Frankfurter was your professor at Harvard. When you first came to the Court, was there any effort on his part, or anyone else's, to win you as an ideological ally?

A: Well, the interesting thing about Felix specifically is that he was absolutely superb in doing this without your being conscious of it. His chambers were next to mine, and he used to come in with some frequency, and he would tell me much about the great giants that he had known and worked with and what brilliant contributions they had made. He made conversation, he flattered you, he made you feel that it would be an honor to be associated with him and his crowd of giants.

Felix also worked socially. I recall he had a dinner at his home for me, and the guests were Dean Acheson and John Lord O'Brian, and I heard much in the discussion after dinner over brandy about the role of the Court and the role of the Justices. I recall particularly the story that Acheson told of how Justice Brandeis, for whom he had clerked, on one occasion asked him to footnote an opinion which was to come down on Monday. And Acheson footnoted the opinion, and Monday came and Brandeis did not announce the opinion. Acheson was amazed, of course, and asked the Justice afterward what had happened. Brandeis took the opinion and pointed to a footnote that cited two cases, state cases, that Acheson had discovered and cited in the footnote. Brandeis said, "I looked at those cases and they won't stand for the proposition for which they were cited.'' And Acheson said he was grateful he wasn't fired. The main reason for telling this story, I realized later, was to communicate that you had to be that meticulous about what you produced sitting on this Court. Felix wanted me to understand that.

Q: Did he finally give up on you?

A: I suppose we reached an understanding. We always were good friends. He never stopped or gave up trying to persuade me in individual cases, but he knew that I would not, could not, accept his approach across the board.

Q: Were you aware of a change in yourself sometime after you arrived?

A: I must say, I wasn't conscious of the change, although I suppose I did change. It is hard to say why it happens. All I can attribute it to is what I suggested, that when you have actually to discharge the responsibility—not just think about it or talk about it—things go a lot differently. Everyone thought Felix Frankfurter would be a flaming liberal when he came, and there was a lot of reason to think he would. And yet, when he got here, his conscience wouldn't let him, because of his conviction that the judiciary should not be resolving many issues that, in his view, should be decided by the legislative or executive branch. Talk about disappointing a President—certainly Felix disillusioned F.D.R.

Q: Do you think Justice O'Connor is changing, jurisprudentially?

A: I think she has, but I don't think it is a satisfactory answer to say she has moved to the left, which I read or heard somewhere. A change in a new Justice is so often a product of the significance of this responsibility—of being a Justice—and it is something that you simply have no idea of until you get it. And when you get it—I don't care who has appointed you—there come issues that no matter what may be the popular, or the Administration's or anyone else's view, in conscience you find that you can't resolve the issue in that way. The Constitution requires a different resolution, and that is pretty obvious to you. It is just so important that all Federal judges are independent, not the voice of any Administration. As a Justice feels more comfortable here, the judicial independence tends to put some distance between the political people who were so excited, initially, about the appointment.

It is very interesting, Sandra fitted in so quickly, more quickly than I had expected. She ceased immediately to be ''the first woman Justice'' and became just another Justice, and quite a fine one. Moreover, she is delightful.

Q: The Administration aside, Justice O'Connor may have disappointed

some women who were hoping for more unequivocal support for the abortion right.
A: Even so, but the fact that there is a woman makes women generally feel a little more comfortable. I think everyone is better off ultimately when a Justice is truly independent-thinking.
Q: There has for many years been a so-called "Catholic seat" on the Supreme Court, and the same used to be said about a "Jewish seat." Since Abe Fortas left the Court in 1969 there has not been a Jewish Justice. Do you think it is, beyond the symbolic value, important to have ethnic and cultural diversity on the Court?
A: I do indeed, I think there ought to be, although I think it has got to be done very carefully. There ought to be diversity in many respects: localitywise, for example. Not everyone should come from the East or the West. There ought to be diversity in political persuasions. There ought to be a black, a woman, and, of course, religious diversity. These are all segments of our pluralistic society, and I think people are a little more comfortable when they see a broadly representative group. It is more than a symbol. People bring different experiences and insights to their work. I believe that when President Reagan nominated Justice Scalia, there was an express acknowledgment that his Italian heritage was a factor in the appointment.

Of course, it is also true that individuals turn out to be disappointments to an ethnic group. I have been a disappointment to some Roman Catholics. Father Andrew Greeley wrote a piece in which he said that if the Roman Catholics who played a role in the Brennan selection had had any idea he would turn out the way he did, he would have never been appointed.
Q: How important was your religion to your appointment?
A: It has been reported that Eisenhower was looking for a Catholic, and, even more important, in order to emphasize the nonpartisanship of his Administration, a Democrat from the Northeast. You have to remember that the 1956 elections were coming up.

Eisenhower was also asked directly how he came to appoint me, and he said—well, we asked everybody who would be the best man for the job. We asked our friends in California, and they said Bill Brennan of New Jersey. We asked our friends in the South, and they said Bill Brennan, this fellow up in New Jersey. We asked Senators, Governors, business leaders and union men, and they all recommended this Brennan fellow.

Q: Have you ever had difficulty dealing with your own religious beliefs in terms of cases?
A: No. That is very interesting. I really crossed that bridge in my confirmation hearing when initially the committee unanimously said it was most inappropriate to ask me whether, as a Catholic, I would follow the Constitution. But then they did ask me. And I had settled in my mind that I had an obligation under the Constitution which could not be influenced by any of my religious principles. As a Roman Catholic I might do as a private citizen what a Roman Catholic does, and that is one thing, but to the extent that that conflicts with what I think the Constitution means or requires, then my religious beliefs have to give way. And, as I say, I settled that in my mind and that took care of it.
Q: If the Constitution were being rewritten now and you were given the responsibility to decide whether there would be a right to abortion, what would you do?
A: I would say that, in this society, nobody can dictate for everyone else what must be done with respect to the most intimate choices, private choices, family decisions, that individuals face. I would adhere to what we have said. And I don't know that I could ever agree that the right to privacy that is protected by the Bill of Rights should not be a part of a fundamental charter of a civilized society.
Q: What is the most difficult decision you have had to make as a Justice?
A: A couple of cases, and, I suppose, particularly the school-prayer cases. The 1963 *Schempp* opinion is some 80 pages long. The position I finally took a long time to come around to. In the face of my whole lifelong experience as a Roman Catholic, to say that prayer was not an appropriate thing in public schools, that gave me quite a hard time. I struggled. And of course I've said some things I wish I hadn't. I've had 30 years to make mistakes.
Q: Such as?
A: Oh, I prefer to correct myself in opinions, and I have. After all, I've also had 30 years to make those corrections.
Q: Was there a case or line of cases that have been singularly disappointing not to prevail on?
A: I don't know whether to prevail on, I do wish we had found a solution to the definitional horror of obscenity. Perhaps it has been my fault; this has been a very difficult issue which we seemed to have not gotten quite right.

Q: You seem to possess an abiding faith that the most difficult problems are susceptible to legal resolution.

A: I certainly believe so. We must never give up trying, because how are we going to have an ordered society unless the problems are re-dressable somehow by law? I don't mean necessarily law as pronounced by the judges. Major problems can be as effectively addressed by the Congress, as it demonstrated in Title VII of the Civil Rights Act.

Q: Where do you think that faith of yours in the law comes from?

A: I can only suggest, I don't know if by osmosis, but I surely came away from law school with that. I don't know if I started with it. It is what is so magnificent about law.

Q: You have been a lawyer for almost 60 years. Have you ever awak-ened in the morning and wondered what it would have been like to have tried something else?

A: Never.

Q: Always happy with the choice?

A. I would have loved to have been a great quarterback.

Q: A play-maker perhaps?

A: Oh, I don't know. On my team, plays could have been called by consensus.

Q: Only 10 other Justices in the history of this country have served 30 years, as you will, beginning this term. Is it a particular time for reflection?

A: No. It is another term with a lot of work to do.

Writer and columnist Nat Hentoff interviewed Justice Brennan for Playboy *magazine in 1991. "The Justice breaks his silence,"* Playboy *announced: "For the first time since his retirement, Supreme Court Justice William Brennan delivers the closing argument on his colleagues, the Constitution and what the country faces."*

The *Playboy* Interview

Nat Hentoff

Sitting across from him in the chambers he still has at the Supreme Court, it is difficult at first to realize that this short, decidedly informal man with so playful a wit was the most powerful and influential Supreme Court justice in the history of the nation.

William J. Brennan, Jr., is entirely without pretentiousness. The ordinary city councilman takes himself more seriously than Brennan does. But the justice who retired on July 20 of last year after nearly 34 years on the Court—always took his job very seriously. He has described that job as requiring him to protect the dignity of each human being and to recognize that "every individual has fundamental rights that Government cannot deny him."

Accordingly, his many landmark decisions on behalf of the individual against the Government led New York University law professor Norman Dorsen to say that "we would be living under a very different Constitution if Justice Brennan were not on the Supreme Court."

Brennan greatly expanded and deepened First Amendment rights for the press, for teachers, for students, for book publishers, for moviemakers and for civil rights organizations. More than any other justice from the 18th Century on, he successfully broadened the rights of criminal defendants. No jurist, for example, has taken more seriously the Fourth Amendment's prohibition of illegal search and seizure by the police.

18

Brennan was an insistent leader on the Court in strengthening civil rights laws, including affirmative action, and no justice—including Sandra Day O'Connor—more successfully ensured women equal protection under the law. Symbolically, he was the first justice to often interchange pronouns in an opinion. Even if a case involved only males, he would use "she" in parts of his writing. "Why should males," he explained, "be the only illustrious participants in whatever events we're talking about?"

Brennan was also responsible for the reapportionment of every state legislative system in the country, thereby ending the power of rural legislators to allot fewer votes to big cities than to their own less-populated areas. A devout Catholic who goes to Mass every Saturday, he was unyielding in defending Thomas Jefferson's wall between church and state, a position that drew protests from bishops in his own Church and from many other denominations. Furthermore, Brennan was a formidably consistent supporter of a woman's right to an abortion.

He suffered defeats through the years and most regrets his inability to get a majority of the Court to abolish the death penalty. Capital punishment, he insists, is a violation of the Eighth Amendment's declaration that "cruel and unusual punishment" is unconstitutional. Says Brennan, "Even the vilest criminal remains a human being possessed of common human dignity."

Even during his last years on the Court, when he was in the minority among conservatives, Brennan won a number of decisions—such as the ruling that deemed flag-burning protected by the First Amendment—because he was so persuasive, so deeply knowledgeable about the Constitution and so nonconfrontational. He was liked as well as respected by everyone on the Court.

I have never known anyone who loved his work more. A couple of years ago, we were walking out of the Supreme Court building, Brennan holding me by the elbow, and he looked around the marble hall and said, "It's just incredible being here—I mean the opportunity to be a participant in decisions that have such enormous impact on our society!"

When he suddenly retired last year because of the effects of a stroke, I wondered if he would ever recover—not from the stroke so much as from leaving the Court. "This is the saddest day of my life," he told a friend of mine.

When I talked with Brennan, it was clear that his was not going to be a passive retirement. He was considering offers from law schools to teach, and, indeed, later, with his doctors' approval, he accepted an invitation from New York University Law School to spend time in residence over the next four years.

He has also been approached by Georgetown University Law School and other institutions. "It'll be a lot of fun," he said.

His mind, however, was still on the Court. In previous conversations, he had stressed his disappointment at the way the Court was covered by the press—at the inaccuracy of the reporting and the placing of decisions out of context. He had not changed his mind.

"I'm afraid," he said, "that most of your colleagues in the press simply don't do a good job." A key exception, he said, is Linda Greenhouse of *The New York Times:*—"She's a whiz."

He kept returning to the failures of the press, because although the Court makes decisions affecting millions of Americans, many have only the dimmest notion of the content of those decisions and of how they were arrived at. And that, he thinks, is the fault of the press.

"What I would like to see," Brennan said, "is that important cases are covered from beginning to end, from before they get to the Court to the final result. But what you get in most papers are a few lines about whether there was a reversal or an affirmation of a lower-court decision."

I reminded Brennan that one way more people would understand and become involved in the drama of the Court would be to have oral arguments before the justices seen on TV. C-SPAN has offered to carry all oral arguments in their entirety.

Brennan believes strongly that those arguments should be televised. When he was on the bench, however, most of his colleagues refused to allow cameras in the courtroom. They preferred that the Court do all its work in isolation. Since he left, there has been no indication that the justices have changed their minds.

I asked Brennan his appraisals of certain justices, past and present. He was unusually candid, perhaps because he is off the bench. We began with William O. Douglas, a passionate defender of the individual against the Government and often Brennan's ally.

I quoted New York University law professor Burt Neuborne, who said there had not been much staying power in Douglas' work. "When he retired," Neuborne said, "Douglas left behind no legacy that transcended his death. By contrast, Brennan's influence is great and lasting."

Brennan did not comment on his own legacy, but of Douglas, he said, "There's too much damn truth in that appraisal. His last ten years on the Court were marked by the slovenliness of his writing and the mistakes that he constantly made. He seemed to have lost the interest that was so paramount in everything he did when he started on the Court. It's too bad."

"He had a quick mind," I said.

"Yes, but it ran away with him," Brennan answered.

Thurgood Marshall and Brennan voted similarly much of the time—they were always in agreement on death-penalty cases. I was a little hesitant when I asked Brennan his reaction to the judgment of some Court reporters that Marshall can't keep up with the other justices in terms of the quality and quantity of his work.

"No," Brennan said, "I don't think that's a fair appraisal at all—especially in the areas that are his particular interest. Of course, all of those are sort of racial interests. In those areas, I don't think there's anyone in the country who can match either his experience or his expression of his experience. When he does put himself to it, the resultant product is just as good as it used to be in his trial days, when he was regarded—and with justification—as one of the ablest trial lawyers in the country."

I asked Brennan about Sandra Day O'Connor and my sense that she can be a good deal more impassioned than her image as a cool, self-contained jurist.

"She can and does get quite passionate," Brennan said. And he mentioned *United States* v. *James B. Stanley*, which resulted in one of the most appalling decisions in recent Supreme Court history—though it received very little press coverage. Brennan thinks that that case still deserves a great deal of attention.

In 1958, James B. Stanley, a master sergeant in the Army, had answered a call for volunteers who were to test the effectiveness of protective clothing and equipment against chemical warfare. He and the other volunteers were cruelly deceived. Secretly, the Army doused them with LSD to find out how the drug worked on human subjects. In Stanley's case, the drug produced hallucinations, periodic loss of memory and incoherence. Also, according to the Court record, Stanley would occasionally "awake from sleep at night and, without reason, violently beat his wife and children, later being unable to recall the entire incident." His marriage was destroyed.

Years later, when Stanley found out what had been done to him by the Army, he sued for damages. Speaking for a majority of the Supreme

Court, Antonin Scalia said Stanley had no redress, because military discipline and decision making could not be called into question without the entire military regime being disrupted.

O'Connor was furious in dissent, attacking the Army's conduct as being "far beyond the bounds of human decency." The Constitution, she said sharply, guarantees even soldiers due process of law.

Brennan remembered his own dissent in Stanley very well. He emphasized that after the Nuremberg war-crimes trials, the United States Military Tribunal established the Nuremberg Code, which prohibits medical experimentation on unknowing human subjects. Yet the U.S. Supreme Court was putting its awesome imprimatur on similar experiments by its own Armed Forces.

So angry was Brennan that he ended his dissent with, "Soldiers ought not be asked to defend a Constitution indifferent to their essential human dignity."

Reliving that case with me, Brennan said, "Wasn't that an outrageous case? It was incredible! Some of us were so shocked by it when it came down that we were fearful it had started a trend. But, thank God, it hasn't shown its head again—not yet, anyway."

Capital punishment, however, shows no sign of disappearing. In all of our conversations through the years, Brennan has said that "the evolving standards of human decency will finally lead to the abolition of the death penalty in this country."

With more and more executions taking place, I asked him why he remained optimistic.

Brennan laughed. "Maybe because it's the way I want it to come out. I just have a feeling. Do you realize that we are the only Western country that has not abolished the death penalty? I can't believe that the leader of the free world is going to keep on executing people. I don't know when the change is going to come. I've never suggested it's going to be next week or five years from now. But I am absolutely convinced that it will happen. When I start doing some writing, I'm going to have quite a bit to say about capital punishment."

I told the justice that a recent Amnesty International report had revealed that 31 prisoners in 12 states in this country were "under sentence of death for crimes committed before they reached their 18th birthday." And this nation is one of only four—including Bangladesh, Iran and Iraq—that execute juvenile offenders.

"Isn't it horrible to be in that company?" Brennan said. "Good God!"

The Court also decided, I noted, that a retarded person can be executed.

"That's right," he said. "That's even worse. Well, I still believe that eventually, we'll become more civilized. It would be horrible if we didn't. I wish there were more people arguing in the opposition."

Except for Thurgood Marshall, there are—with Brennan gone—no other absolute opponents of capital punishment are on the Court. "Well," said Brennan, "people on the Court can evolve, too. I give you the opinion for the Court by the Chief Justice in the *Hustler Magazine, Inc.,* v. *Falwell* case."

Larry Flynt had a fake ad published in *Hustler* in which the Reverend Jerry Falwell and his mother were depicted, with Falwell saying that his first sexual experience was with his mother in an outhouse. Both were drunk. ("I never really expected to make it with Mom, but then, after she showed all the other guys in town such a good time, I figured, 'What the hell!' ")

A lower court awarded Falwell $200,000 for intentional infliction of emotional distress, but the Supreme Court unanimously reversed the decision—with William Rehnquist writing a passionate defense of free expression. "At the heart of the First Amendment is the recognition of the fundamental importance of the free flow of ideas and opinions on matters of public interest and concern.")

In the past, however, Rehnquist had not been one of the Court's most able defenders of free speech. Nor did landmark opinions by Brennan, such as *New York Times Co.* v. *Sullivan,* make it any easier for public officials and, later, public figures to win libel suits. But in the Falwell case, Rehnquist actually embraced Brennan concepts he had previously criticized.

However, in the 1989 flag-burning case *Texas* v. *Gregory Lee Johnson,* a year after *Hustler* v. *Falwell,* Rehnquist did a serious reverse with regard to the First Amendment. Said Brennan, "If there is a bedrock principle underlying the First Amendment, it is that the Government may not prohibit the expression of an idea simply because society finds the idea itself offensive or disagreeable." Rehnquist sternly disagreed. A parody of Falwell and his mother having sexual intercourse in an outhouse was one thing, but disrespect for the symbol of American freedom must be punished.

I asked Brennan how much give-and-take there is at the conferences during which the justices tentatively decide how they will vote on a case they've just heard argued. Did he and Rehnquist, for instance, get into a substantive face-to-face discussion of the flag-burning case?

"No," said Brennan. "Contrary to belief, there's very little face-to-face debate. Our decisions are based on what we write, on the drafts we circulate to one another. What happens at the conferences is only a scratching of the surface. You really don't get into it until you have to write out your position, and then it changes back and forth as you read what the other justices have to say. Writing does a better job than if we were trying to decide a case just sitting around a table and arguing with one another. You're much more careful about what you're going to say if you write it down."

"You say the decisions are more careful," I said, "but it's still hard for me to understand how certain justices can carefully vote, for example, to execute the retarded or teenagers."

A case in point, *Joshua DeShaney* v. *Winnebago County Department of Social Services,* one of the most poignant in the recent history of the Court, concerned a child, Joshua DeShaney, who had been beaten so often and so brutally by his father that he became permanently retarded and will be institutionalized for life. A county social worker who knew the boy was being abused took no action, so the county never took the child into custody.

Accordingly, a majority of the Court ruled that the child and his mother had no claim for damages because the state had not inflicted the violence on the child—the father had—and so it was not responsible. Although one of its agents had had continuing knowledge of what was going on, the state had not placed the child under its protection.

In his indignant dissent, Brennan said it was eerie that the county social worker had chronicled in detail what was happening to the child; and, indeed, when she heard about the last and most devastating beating, she said, "I just knew the phone would ring someday and Joshua would be dead."

Yet six members of the Court had failed to see—Brennan stressed in his dissent—that "inaction can be every bit as abusive of power as action. . . . I cannot agree that our Constitution is indifferent to such indifference."

Only Thurgood Marshall and Harry Blackmun were as appalled as Brennan at the majority view. In his dissent, Blackmun—in a rare anguished cry from the heart in the history of the Court's opinions—wrote, "Poor Joshua!"

Brennan's customary optimism and his conviction that the Court will one day fully live up to the Constitution does sometimes waver. For instance, when he is confronted by the coldness of colleagues, as in the case of Joshua DeShaney.

But he keeps bounding back. "You'd be amazed at the mail I've gotten since my retirement," he said. "Holy Moses! All these people agreeing with me about the way the Court and the country should be going. It's been an eye opener for me."

As always, Brennan sees so much injustice in the land—while still believing that the Constitution can redress it when enough Americans really know the power and promise of that document.

He often refers to this passage from a 1986 speech he made to the American Bar Association's Section on Individual Rights and Responsibilities:

We do not yet have justice, equal and practical, for the poor, for the members of minority groups, for the criminally accused, for the displaced persons of the technological revolution, for alienated youth, for the urban masses, for the unrepresented consumer—for all, in short, who do not partake of the abundance of American life. . . . The goal of universal equality, freedom and prosperity is far from won and . . . ugly inequities continue to mar the face of our nation. We are surely nearer the beginning than the end of the struggle.

On days when he sees that end as being terribly far away, Brennan's spirits are invariably lifted by a passage in William Butler Yeats's play *Cathleen ni Hoolihan*. "It's about a dream," he said, "that although old, is never old." The dream is that no one anywhere will be denied his or her inherent dignity and rights; and in the play, that dream is personified by a figure called the Poor Old Woman.

As he has to visitors for more than 30 years, Brennan—in his soft, hoarse voice—read me the passage:

"Did you see an old woman going down the path?" asks Bridget.

"I did not," replies Patrick, who came into the house just after the old woman left it, "but I saw a young girl and she had the walk of a queen."

Brennan smiled. "We can't give up," he said. "We can't despair. We have to keep taking up the cudgels, and the first thing you know, by God, we'll abolish the death penalty and we'll make the Fourteenth Amendment come alive for everyone, so that there will be justice for all."

In this regard, Brennan has been vigorously advocating for years that law schools involve their students in clinics that deal with clients among the poor and those who are otherwise marginalized in this society. (The American Bar Association notes that 80 percent of Americans have no access to the legal help they need because they can't afford a lawyer.)

Brennan now sees more and more law schools changing in ways he approves. "The students are learning firsthand about how the law can actually affect people's lives," he said. "They learn not only from law books but from actual cases involving actual people. And that experience is going to lead to more improvement in the lives of many."

Eventually, perhaps, the words carved above the entrance of the Supreme Court—EQUAL JUSTICE UNDER LAW—may be more than rhetoric.

On the other hand, there are law students, I told Brennan, who out of decent motives—to combat racism and sexism, for example—have been working to establish speech codes on their campuses. The codes punish offensive speech and sometimes go as far as to lead to suspension or expulsion. Even some law school professors are supporting this kind of censorship.

I told him that at Stanford, student organizations, including the Asian Law Association, Black Law Students Association, Native American Law Students Association, the Asian American Students Association and the Jewish Law Students Association advocate these codes.

Brennan shook his head. "I'll be damned," he said.

I asked him what he would do about the speech codes proliferating at colleges around the country.

"I can tell you what I think they ought to do," he said. "They ought to just abolish all of them."

Unfortunately, if these speech-code cases reach the Supreme Court, he will not be there to say just that. But much of what Brennan has said will last—as future justices quote from opinions of his that will shape the course of constitutional debate for as long as there is a Constitution.

And the core of all William Brennan has said and done is his unyielding conviction that if freedom of expression is eroded, so, eventually, will be the rest of our liberties.

When I asked him if he had a favorite part of the Constitution, he replied, "The First Amendment, I expect. Its enforcement gives us this society. The other provisions of the Constitution merely embellish it."

The following tribute by Associate Justice of the United States Supreme Court Byron R. White originally appeared in The Yale Law Journal.

Tribute to the Honorable William J. Brennan, Jr.

Byron R. White

William J. Brennan, Jr., will surely be remembered as among the greatest Justices who have ever sat on the Supreme Court. And well he should be.

He took his seat on October 16, 1956 and sat continuously through thirty-four Terms until he retired in July of last year. Over these years he wrote 425 opinions for the Court, 220 concurring opinions, 492 full or partial dissents, and 16 separate opinions. He averaged four dissents per Term under Earl Warren, twenty under Warren Burger, and stayed busy at it under Chief Justice Rehnquist. Furthermore, few Associate Justices in history have authored the number of majority opinions that have so markedly changed the face of our fundamental law. A few examples will follow.

Brown v. Board of Education predated Bill Brennan, but he authored the unanimous opinion in *Green v. County School Board,* a decision that announced that freedom of choice by school children and their parents was not enough. Further measures had to be taken to eliminate segregation and its effects "root and branch," a phrase that has permanently entered the lexicon of equal protection jurisprudence. He also authored the opinion in *Keyes v. School District No. 1, Denver, Colorado,* which sent the *Brown/Green* commands to the North and West.

Bill Brennan was a major force in developing multilevel equal protection analysis. In *Frontiero v. Richardson* and *Craig v. Boren,* he set

27

down his firm, insightful views about how the equal protection clause should be applied in the context of gender discrimination. *Goldberg v. Kelly,* a decision and opinion of which Bill is quite justifiably proud, dealt with the procedures that were required to prevent arbitrary deprivations of entitlements. It is regarded to have created a new kind of property, and it subjected the bureaucracy to oversight under the due process clause.

Brother Brennan also wrote *Baker v. Carr,* which not only exemplified his determination to expand access to the courts by the powerless, but also paved the way for the reapportionment revolution. Chief Justice Warren at one time remarked that *Baker v. Carr* was as important as, if not more important than, any decision handed down during his regime. And the reapportionment line of cases added another phrase to the equal protection lexicon—one man/one vote.

Of course, it may be that Bill's best known opinion is *New York Times Co. v. Sullivan.* That decision went far towards constitutionalizing and limiting the manner and extent to which state libel laws could penalize oral or written expression injurious to the reputation of public officials. His opinion, among other things, announced that a public official could not recover for the publication of a defamatory falsehood without proving that it was published with " 'actual malice'—that is, with knowledge that it was false or with reckless disregard of whether it was false or not." Such a privilege to publish inadvertent defamation was essential to the proper functioning of a free press. The *Sullivan* case, not unexpectedly, spawned an entire line of decisions fleshing out the implications of that holding. It is worth noting that not all of these were satisfactory to Justice Brennan.

Brennan, Jr., also authored *Freedman v. Maryland,* a case that focused on the procedures that were necessary when the publication of certain kinds of expression was to be regulated or forbidden. The *Freedman* opinion also referred to the possible "chilling effect" of a particular regulation, a phrase now often encountered in constitutional discourse.

Bill Brennan was a principal architect in developing another concept used in adjudicating the validity of state legislative or administrative regulation of expression, the concept of overbreadth—that is, permitting a defendant who himself would have no First Amendment defense to escape liability or other sanctions by asserting the rights of others whose expression the law could not proscribe. Under the overbreadth analysis, until the state cures the regulation's unconstitutional overbreadth, the regulation may not be enforced against anyone.

These few cases only exemplify the many, many opinions that have come from the pen of Justice Brennan and that have contributed so much to movement in the constitutional and statutory law. The volume and quality of Justice Brennan's work leads one to wonder how and why this remarkable rise to eminence occurred. There are, however, some reasons that are beyond speculation.

Anyone who knows Bill Brennan would surely agree that he is as amiable as anyone can be. He is quiet and gentle, friendly and sociable, unfailingly polite, sensitive and sympathetic. He is interested in others, and those others realize it. And among other things, he is an excellent conversationalist, in large part because he is an acute observer of current events, but also because of his fine sense of humor. Being with Bill Brennan is always a pleasant personal experience.

The short of it is that he was an extremely enjoyable colleague, and I have no doubt that his personal warmth contributed a great deal to his effectiveness as a Justice, particularly when combined with his other admirable qualities. Bill is a very principled man with a highly developed sense of what is right and wrong, mete and proper. And he lives by his principles. He is honest, forthright, and courageous. He was dedicated to his work and worked hard and long, arriving earlier than most but always getting home for dinner. He is a personally disciplined person and followed a set routine. For the most part, he did his own certiorari work, and I suspect that if he missed reading a number of petitions every morning, it would have been worse to him than going without coffee.

Strength of character is often measured by how one deals with adversity. And all of us who watched Bill Brennan through those years when his first wife, Marjorie Leonard Brennan, struggled with and finally succumbed to cancer deeply admired the way he cared for his wife and still quietly and effectively carried out his work. And this is to say nothing of how he coped with and survived his own bout with cancer. It should also be said that Bill has three outstanding children, all very successful in their own right. The Brennans are a close family, very supportive of one another. It is plain enough that his family life played a major role in his great success as a Justice.

He is very bright and quick, has an Irish gift for language, and was obviously blessed with sufficiently good health to permit him to endure his rigorous schedule through the years. He took good care of himself. For years when he lived in Georgetown, he rose early and walked several miles before coming to the office at about 7:30 a.m. He later switched to a stationary bicycle, which, as Marjorie once told us, he rode to Newark and back every morning.

Neither should it be forgotten that prior to coming to Court, Bill had been practicing law for nine years, had been a colonel in the army for a substantial time, and had been a state court judge in his native New Jersey for seven years, for a year as a trial judge and then six years as an appellate judge, four of them on the New Jersey Supreme Court. He was thus a man of impressive experience when he arrived at the Supreme Court in 1956 and had little trouble getting up to speed.

When I arrived in 1962, it was evident that Bill's stature was already firmly established. For eighteen terms of Court, from 1962 until Potter Stewart retired, I sat beside Bill Brennan during oral arguments, and for years sat beside him in Conference. No one from such a vantage point could help being impressed with his intelligence and grasp of the material with which we work. And as the years wore on I was glad that someone with a better memory than mine could recall the Court's past practices and explain the internal common law of the Court.

Bill Brennan's view of the role of the judge in our federal system also had much to do with his rise. He was convinced that the judicial function was critical to a government of laws and that the judicial role was deliberately made part of the structure of government, with the intention that it be exercised not only with reason but with "passion." That quality he defined in his 1987 Cardozo lecture to the Association of the Bar of the City of New York as "the range of emotional and intuitive responses to a given set of facts or arguments, responses which often speed into our consciousness far ahead of the lumbering syllogisms of reason. . . . Sensitivity to one's intuitive and passionate responses, and awareness of the range of human experience, is therefore not only an inevitable but a desirable part of the judicial process, an aspect more to be nurtured than to be feared." For him the Constitution aimed at protecting the individual, including the powerless ones. Implementing this purpose lay at the heart of the judicial function, which he believed should be performed with the essential dignity and worth of each individual in the forefront of the judge's mind.

In interpreting the majestic, open-ended clauses of the Constitution, to be forever bound by the perhaps undiscoverable intent of the Framers was not for him. In his 1985 lecture at Georgetown University he made this unmistakably clear: "[T]he genius of the Constitution rests not in any static meaning it might have had in a world that is dead and gone, but in the adaptability of its great principles to cope with current problems and current needs.'' And the judge should proceed with ''a spar-kling vision of the supremacy of the human dignity of every individual.''

Bill Brennan at the same time was a thoroughly practical and realistic Justice. He was absolutely dedicated to the Court as an institution and realized that the Court should not overstep its legitimate role, but as I understood some of his many eloquent dissents in recent years, he thought that the majority in these cases had a far too narrow view of the Court's function in this modern world. He remained true to the vision of the Court that he had from the outset, a vision that kept him close to the cutting edge and produced such opinions as *New York Times Co. v. Sullivan* which, said one Court watcher, caused much dancing in the streets.

Bill Brennan was a friend and a mighty force. We miss him around the table and wish him well.

For twenty-three years Associate Justices Thurgood Mar-
shall and William Brennan worked closely together on the
Supreme Court in their passionate commitment to human dig-
nity and the civil rights of the less privileged. Here Marshall
speaks of the legal vision that animated his associate's work
on the bench. This tribute and the two that follow originally
appeared in Harvard Law Review.

A Tribute to Justice William J. Brennan, Jr.

Thurgood Marshall

The *Harvard Law Review* paid its first tribute to Justice William J.
Brennan, Jr., in its eightieth volume; the year was 1966. I had not yet
become one of his Brethren, and he had not yet sat for a third of the
years he would serve on the Court. But already he had made his mark:
"In the entire history of the Court," declared Chief Justice Earl Warren,
in his contribution to that tribute, "it would be difficult to name another
Justice who wrote more important opinions in his first ten years than
has [Justice Brennan]."

Nearly a quarter century has since passed, and the expectations en-
gendered by that first decade have been richly fulfilled. "[A]ge," as
Samuel Johnson observed, "will perform the promises of youth." For
thirty-four Terms, Justice Brennan's constitutional vision emboldened
the Supreme Court's work and enlightened its jurisprudence. It is hard
to fathom what his departure may mean for the Court, beyond this stark
truth: my friend and colleague Bill Brennan is irreplaceable. I welcome,
then, this chance to augment the *Review*'s tribute to a remarkable Justice
and an extraordinary man.

Many have said much about Justice Brennan's warmth toward colleagues, his legal acuity, his grasp of the Court's dynamics, and his

32

doctrinal innovations in countless areas of the law. All this, of course, is true and worth noting. Indeed, I would add to the list: he had, as well, a remarkable talent for crisply summarizing his view of a case during the Court's post-argument conferences. Invariably brief and trenchant, these summaries greatly contributed, I think, to Justice Brennan's influence.

But, important as these formidable skills were, they fail to reveal the essence of the man. To my mind, what so distinguished Justice Brennan was his faithfulness to a consistent legal vision of how the Constitution should be interpreted. That vision was based on an unwavering commitment to certain core principles, especially first amendment freedoms and basic principles of civil rights and civil liberties. Justice Brennan's commitment to these interpretive principles was never in doubt. It did not depend on the peculiarly compelling facts of a case; it was never outweighed by the lesser values that sometimes compete for a judge's allegiance. On this question of fidelity to principles, the late Chief Justice's summary of Justice Brennan's first ten years held true for the next twenty-four: "He . . . interprets the Bill of Rights as the heart and life blood of [the Constitution]. His belief in the dignity of human beings—all human beings—is unbounded. . . . These beliefs are apparent in the warp and woof of all his opinions."

Perhaps nowhere has that commitment to human dignity been more palpable than in Justice Brennan's belief—which I share—that the eighth amendment proscribes the death penalty as cruel and unusual punishment. One of his early analyses of capital punishment was a sixty-five-page dissent in *McGautha v. California,* a case in which juries had been given unbounded discretion to assign the death sentence. After canvassing the circumstances in which due process required states to exercise powers according to some procedure, Justice Brennan concluded that the death penalty required no less: "life itself is an interest of such transcendent importance that a decision to take a life may require procedural regularity far beyond a decision simply to set a sentence at one or another term of years."

That the *McGautha* dissent dealt only with procedure was unavoidable, for the eighth amendment issue had not been raised. But some would see a broader significance in that emphasis, concluding with Professor Post that Justice Brennan's "focus on process rather than power . . . pervade[d] his entire approach to constitutional law" and "deeply influenced both the Warren and the Burger Courts."

But, as Justice Brennan demonstrated the following year in *Furman v.*

Georgia, his concern with the death penalty was *not* just about process—it was above all about power. In *Furman,* he concluded that under the eighth amendment "death stands condemned as fatally offensive to human dignity." I alone shared that view, however, and it seems that the procedural analysis was indeed more persuasive. Ultimately, the Court did restrict jury discretion in capital cases and the manner in which death sentences could be imposed. I have no doubt that Justice Brennan's opinion in *McGautha* planted the seed for this change in doctrine. It is one of those Brennan dissents that, in time, came to command a majority.

Despite Justice Brennan's success in imposing procedural limitations on capital punishment—last year, there were "only" sixteen executions in the United States—he has held firm to the view that the eighth amendment bars all death sentences. Some may infer from our repeated dissents a stubborn adherence to a personal belief. But, as those who have read his writings on this subject know, Justice Brennan's conception of the eighth amendment springs from that application of basic constitutional principles that has marked all of his work. As he said in his Holmes lecture, delivered at Harvard just four years ago:

> Mutilations and tortures . . . would not, I submit, be saved from unconstitutionality by having the convicted person sufficiently anesthetized such that no physical pain were felt; rather, they are unconstitutional because they are inconsistent with the fundamental premise of the eighth amendment that "even the vilest criminal remains a human being possessed of common human dignity." . . . The calculated killing of a human being by the state involves, by its very nature, an absolute denial of the executed person's humanity and thus violates the command of the eighth amendment.

Justice Brennan's commitment to human dignity has prevailed in more hopeful contexts, such as the fourteenth amendment's guarantee of equal protection. Though *Brown v. Board of Education* promised a new era of educational opportunity for Afro-Americans, that promise, of course, soon foundered on the famous stagnating phrase, "with all deliberate speed." In a few specific instances such as the Little Rock case, the Court did rebuff Southern resistance to integration. But it was Justice Brennan's opinion more than a decade later in *Green v. County School Board* that probably did most to restore *Brown*ian motion to the fourteenth amendment. In that decision, which unanimously rejected a "freedom of choice" plan in Virginia, Justice Brennan concluded that "the burden on a school board today is to come forward with a plan that promises realistically to work, and promises realistically to work *now.*" *Green* was followed by Justice Brennan's decision in *Keyes v. School District No. 1,* in which the Court first found unconstitutional segregation in a Northern school district.

This commitment to eradicating dual school systems was matched by a recognition that other steps were needed to redress discrimination. Thus, Justice Brennan led the way in important cases upholding affirmative action—including the joint opinion in *Regents of the University of California v. Bakke,* signed by four of the five Justices who affirmed the right to consider race in university admissions. In that opinion, the theme of human dignity was again sounded: "we cannot . . . let color blindness become myopia which masks the reality that many 'created equal' have been treated within our lifetimes as inferior both by the law and by their fellow citizens." This awareness of the legacy of discrimination also informed Justice Brennan's opinions sustaining private programs of affirmative action against attack under title VII. And it was Justice Brennan's opinion in *Katzenbach v. Morgan,* a crucial voting rights case, that established broad boundaries for Congress' enforcement powers under the fourteenth amendment.

"Rights intended to protect all," Justice Murphy noted years ago, "must be extended to all." Justice Brennan recognized that the Court's work in strengthening equal protection doctrine had left women behind. It was his plurality opinion in *Frontiero v. Richardson* that, for the first time, explicitly tested the constitutionality of gender discrimination by something tougher than the "rational relationship" standard. Inveighing against "an attitude of 'romantic paternalism' which, in practical effect, put women, not on a pedestal, but in a cage," Justice Brennan concluded that classifications based on gender were inherently suspect and that the Air Force's payment of lower benefits to spouses of female military officers than to those of male officers violated equal protection. With his subsequent opinion in *Craig v. Boren,* the deferential "rationality" test for sex discrimination was interred for good.

Despite his fidelity to core beliefs, there was nothing of the aloof philosopher in Justice Brennan; he was, in Whitman's phrase, "no stander above men and women." Rather, Bill Brennan has always been known for his ability to work with colleagues. He, more than any other man I have known, combines a gifted understanding of the law with a rare appreciation of social relations. His canny ability to forge a majority was most apparent in the drafting process—as he pruned a paragraph here or recast a thought there to accommodate his colleagues' concerns.

Nonetheless, Justice Brennan never compromised on what was essential, and this meant that he was often in dissent—particularly in more recent years, as the Court retreated from positions it had once embraced. Although he did not pride himself on being a voice in the wilderness, neither did he falter in the dissenter's role. Indeed, he told an interviewer a few years ago, "I have always felt that a member of this Court is duty-bound to continue stating the constitutional principles that have governed his decisions, even if they are in dissent, against the day when they may no longer be in dissent."

Even on statutory issues, Justice Brennan was willing—within the limits of stare decisis—to dissent persistently if the issue was important. Nowhere is this better illustrated than in his opinions concerning habeas corpus—dissents prompted by the erosion of his majority opinion in *Fay v. Noia,* the high-water mark of the Great Writ.

Fay, of course, involved a collateral attack on a conviction obtained with a coerced confession. Writing for the Court, Justice Brennan found that there was power to review the conviction, derived from the historical role of habeas: "Its root principle is that in a civilized society, government must always be accountable to the judiciary for a man's imprisonment: if the imprisonment cannot be shown to conform with the fundamental requirements of the law, the individual is entitled to his immediate release." But a disturbing series of subsequent opinions—each occasioning a distressed dissent from Justice Brennan—has since curtailed the reach of the writ.

That restrictive process culminated last year, when the Court subjugated the writ to rules governing retroactivity: in *Teague v. Lane,* a majority declined even to examine a habeas claim of constitutional violation because, if accepted, the claim would create a "new" application of the sixth amendment from which (the Court decided) the petitioner should not benefit. In dissent, Justice Brennan reaffirmed the importance of the courts' power "to grant writs . . . whenever a person's liberty is unconstitutionally restrained" and lamented the majority's willingness to foreclose "opportunit[ies] to check constitutional violations and to further the evolution of our thinking in some areas of the law."

The dissent in *Teague* is emblematic of Justice Brennan's jurisprudence. It again reflects his concern about questions of process—though, in this instance, it is the process controlling vindication of rights rather than the process by which government reaches out against its citizens. In that respect, the *Teague* dissent echoes another line of landmark Brennan opinions, beginning with *Bivens v. Six Unknown Named Agents of the Federal Bureau of Narcotics,* which for the first time permitted actions for damages when federal authorities violate certain constitutional rights. "[U]nless such rights are to become merely precatory," Justice Brennan wrote, "[litigants] must be able to invoke the existing jurisdiction of the courts for the[ir] protection."

The *Teague* dissent is also notable for valuing the "evolution of our thinking." Notwithstanding Justice Brennan's commitment to core principles, those principles did not always lead him to the same conclusions. He believed that constitutional doctrine moves forward, "as litigants and judges develop a better understanding of the world in which we live," and this was reflected in his own views—for example, his application of the first amendment. During his initial Term on the Court, Justice Brennan wrote the majority opinion in *Roth v. United States,* the bench-mark obscenity case that upheld a bookseller's conviction. He reaffirmed, in that decision, the established view that " 'certain well-defined and narrowly limited classes of speech' " lay outside the first amendment's protection—including "material which deals with sex in a manner appealing to prurient interest" and " '[l]ibelous utterances.' " In time, however, he came to rethink both exceptions. The first to be revised was libel, which was placed in an altogether new light by Justice Brennan's historic opinion in *New York Times Co. v. Sullivan.* Recognizing that "erroneous statement . . . must be protected if the freedoms of expression are to be given the 'breathing space' that they 'need . . . to survive,' " Justice Brennan held for the Court that public officials must meet a higher standard of proof in winning damages from their detractors. Ten years later, he similarly reached a new understanding of obscenity doctrine, though he was unable to persuade a majority. In *Paris Adult Theater I v. Slaton,* he concluded that "the concept of 'obscenity' cannot be defined with sufficient specificity and clarity to provide fair notice to persons who create and distribute sexually oriented materials, [or] to prevent substantial erosion of protected speech."

Finally, no account of Justice Brennan's first amendment contributions could omit his decisions in the flag-burning cases. There, against a backdrop of politically charged national debate, Justice Brennan garnered a majority of the Court with his calm insistence on basic truths: a state may not "foster its own view of the flag by prohibiting expressive conduct relating to it," he wrote, for "[i]f there is a bedrock principle underlying the First Amendment, it is that the Government may not prohibit the expression of an idea simply because society finds the idea itself offensive or disagreeable.''

One cannot, in so few pages, do justice to this Justice's career; scores of important opinions remain unmentioned. Indeed, these include the ones thought most significant by Chief Justice Warren and by Justice Brennan himself: *Baker v. Carr* (preparing the way for one person, one vote by surmounting the ''political question'' barrier) and *Goldberg v. Kelly* (precluding the termination of welfare benefits without an evidentiary hearing). Nor are his important opinions confined to the core principles I have stressed, for Justice Brennan is a man of catholic interest and ecumenical insights. His decision, for example, in *Penn Central Transportation Co. v. New York City* for the first time accommodated historic preservation laws within the Constitution's restrictions on deprivation of property. And, in his last week on the Court, Justice Brennan brought his insight to bear on the controversy over the right to die, arguing in dissent that the due process clause includes ''a right to evaluate the potential benefit of [medical] treatment . . . and to make a personal decision whether to subject oneself to the intrusion.''

It is customary to close a tribute of this sort by borrowing praise from an ancient scribe. But it seems equally fitting to measure this honoree by his own words. In his Holmes lecture, Justice Brennan described the vision of law that has animated his work on the bench:

I am convinced that law can be a vital engine not merely of change but of . . . civilizing change. That is because law, when it merits the synonym justice, is based on reason and insight. . . . Sometimes, these insights appear pedestrian, such as when we recognize, for example, that a suitcase is more like a home than it is like a car. On occasion, these insights are momentous, such as when we finally understand that separate can never be equal. I believe that these steps, which are the building blocks of progress, are fashioned from a great deal more than the changing views of judges over time. I believe that problems are susceptible to rational solution if we work hard at making and understanding arguments that are based on reason and experience.

It was that credo that sustained Justice Brennan, both in his prevailing hours—when the Court accepted new insights into the Constitution's ideal of human dignity—and in times of dissent. The Court will do well if it can adhere to that credo and pursue that ideal in the years ahead. But regardless of whether future Justices succeed in those tasks, I think they will look back on the contribution of William J. Brennan, Jr., and say (as Hamlet said, awed by *his* father's spirit), "[He] was a man, take him for all in all; [we] shall not look upon his like again."

As labels such as "activist" or "liberal" or "conservative" fail with any real consistency to describe the opinions of the multidimensional Justice Brennan, the Honorable Abner J. Mikva suggests "Brennanist." He is a judge in the U.S. Court of Appeals for the District of Columbia Circuit.

A Tribute to Justice William J. Brennan, Jr.
Abner J. Mikva

The Supreme Court of the United States would appear to be a very egalitarian institution. Every member of the Court, from the Chief Justice down to the most junior Associate Justice, has a single vote. Since voting determines the result in every case, every motion for stay, every petition for certiorari, many assume that voting is the real power exercised by individual Justices. Indeed, many court-watchers identify, rank, and measure each Justice through a quantification process. They will count up the number of times that a Justice votes with the majority, the number of times that he or she aligns with one "bloc" or another (which in turn is derived from a quantitative analysis of voting patterns), and the number of times that he or she votes "for" or "against" some cause. Although this statistical process is necessarily somewhat arbitrary, it allows the publication of neat tables in law reviews and provides a basis for identifying a Justice as either "liberal" or "conservative," as a "strict constructionist" or a "Great Dissenter."

This unidimensional analysis does not explain the real difference that an individual Justice can make on the Court. John Marshall and Melville Fuller were both Chief Justices. Both probably voted with the majority, and could be identified with blocs and causes, with equal frequency. Yet the impact that each had on the Court and the country was totally different in kind, in quantity, and in quality.

If any Justice defies such simplistic efforts at description, it has to be William J. Brennan, Jr. Indeed, the statistical approach totally confuses his real role on the Court. It seems as though every news story describing his departure from the Court talked at length about his "activism" and "liberal" influence—both labels stemming from the number of times that he voted with the "liberal bloc." But how does one then explain Justice Brennan's enduring leadership, given the present Court's decidedly conservative makeup? Justice Brennan authored several important opinions for the Court last Term, including two first amendment decisions: *Rutan v. Republican Party,* invalidating a state patronage system, and *United States v. Eichman* invalidating the Flag Protection Act recently passed by Congress. And what explains his role in the previous Term when he authored more opinions than almost any other Justice, including such momentous cases as *Texas v. Johnson,* holding that flag burning is constitutionally protected expression? Simply put, utilizing statistical measures to describe Justice Brennan is about as meaningful as chronicling Babe Ruth's feats based on the number of times he came to bat.

If labels like "liberal" or "conservative" or "activist" have any usefulness at all, I would like to propose "Brennanist" as a new label, meaning one who influences colleagues beyond measure and builds coalitions at every level—personal and intellectual, on issues and on semantics, and most of all on the strength of his own integrity. Justice Brennan has, of course, had his critics throughout his long tenure on the Supreme Court. He has stepped on large toes over the last thirty-three years—including those of the Catholic Church, law-enforcement groups, and elected officials. Those critics have never suggested, however, that he proceeded from any but the purest of motives in reaching his decisions. Perhaps that is the unique combination of qualities that Justice Brennan brought to the Court: his absolute integrity, his great compassion, and the political skill to bring people together. Purists usually are not good politicians.

Quantifiers also miss the boat on Justice Brennan when they label the causes that he championed. It is true that he usually voted to uphold the constitutional protections afforded criminal defendants, and he has consistently opposed imposition of the death penalty, at least since *Furman v. Georgia.* But the major opinions in those areas, from *Miranda v. Arizona* and *Escobedo v. Illinois* to *Furman,* are not his. It is also true that Justice Brennan lined up on the pro-choice side of the abortion controversy and was roundly denounced by many of his co-religionists, but he did not author *Roe v. Wade* or any of its progeny. He also has been classified as protective of pornography and other first amendment "excesses," yet he struggled with the problems that pornography presents to a community and successfully carved out an exception pertaining to the young.

It is quite possible that the quantifiers would miss the areas where Justice Brennan's opinions have made the most difference. He continues to think that *New York Times Co. v. Sullivan,* announcing the actual malice standard for defamation claims brought by public officials, was his most important opinion, although some might quarrel and urge *Goldberg v. Kelly* as his most significant contribution. Indeed, one could hardly imagine first amendment or procedural due process jurisprudence without those cases. Trial and appellate judges may complain about the difficulties that the actual malice test presents in a libel case, but it provides the media one of their most important constitutional bulwarks in pursuing their calling vis-à-vis public persons. State and local officials similarly continue to complain about the burdens that *Goldberg v. Kelly* imposes on the administration of social programs. Although the Court has engaged in some retrenchment on the principle that benefits may not be denied or removed without some kind of hearing and process, it is difficult to imagine a jurisprudence that did not at least have to reckon with that precedent when reviewing the process.

Perhaps Justice Brennan's greatest contribution to our democratic system was his decision and opinion for the Court in *Baker v. Carr.* It is hard to recollect how our political landscape differed almost thirty years ago, when Justice Brennan stated that one person had one vote and that the Constitution required political boundaries to reflect that truth. There are still some die-hard critics of this example of Justice Brennan's "activism." They complain that the Constitution does not say anything about how redistricting is to be accomplished and that therefore judges should not be involved in the process. They look back with nostalgia at the more tranquil admonition of Justice Felix Frankfurter that judges should stay out of that "political thicket." It is certainly true that the judiciary has been subject to a great deal of fist-shaking and threats from the political branches of government because of its involvement. But still we cheer the revolution in Eastern Europe, which brought with it the very electoral reform that Justice Brennan prodded for in *Baker v. Carr.*

There are other items that the statisticians would in all likelihood miss. In *Penn Central Transportation Co. v. New York,* Justice Brennan reconciled the myriad Supreme Court cases that had interpreted and applied the takings clause of the fifth amendment. The standard he fashioned in that case has allowed municipalities to fashion useful zoning and landmark protection laws without triggering the takings clause. In *Burger King Corp. v. Rudzewicz,* he brought some order out of the chaos that has described judicial treatment of state efforts to obtain "long-arm" jurisdiction over foreign enterprises and persons. Justice Brennan's decision was so carefully tailored that Justice Stevens' concerns over unfairness have not materialized. The majority opinion is a good example of Justice Brennan's capacity to spoon flexibility into a doctrine to preserve "fair play and substantial justice."

Even some of Justice Brennan's better known opinions might escape the quantifiers, because the results have been so readily accepted that they no longer receive the adjectives "liberal" or "activist." Such landmarks as *Bivens v. Six Unknown Agents of the Federal Bureau of Narcotics* (recognizing a private cause of action for violations of the fourth amendment), *Monell v. Department of Social Services* (subjecting municipalities to liability for civil rights violations under section 1983), *Lemon v. Kurtzman* (announcing the tripartite establishment clause test), and *Frontiero v. Richardson* (suggesting that gender is a suspect classification) are all accepted parts of the judicial landscape. At the time of their authorship, the cases were much more controversial than they appear today.

Justice Brennan plied his Supreme Court trade for thirty-three years—through three Chief Justices, eight Presidents, and thousands upon thousands of petitions for the Court to hear a case. His mark is large, indelible, and worthy of frequent attention. Students of his opinions will marvel at the breadth of his interests, and biographers will marvel at his geniality and way with people; the bean-counters have already chronicled him as a "liberal activist" and won't let facts confuse them. But his impact on our jurisprudence is vastly greater than the sum of all those particulars. He has made a huge difference in the way cases have been resolved and the law has been formed. His greatest attribute of all was his unshakable belief that one could sit on the highest court, wrestle with the most complex and consequential issues, and still never forget that doing justice was the name of the game. Chief Justice Taney virtually apologized for the harsh result in *Dred Scott v. Sandford;* Justice Black expressed some regret over his decision in *Korematsu v. United States* upholding the wartime exclusion of Japanese-Americans; recent opinions in the criminal law field by judges at every level indicate reluctance to impose some of the draconian punishments they impose. Justice Brennan experienced no such difficulties in his long tenure on the Court. Law and justice went together in his way of thinking, and that fueled his immeasurable contribution to both.

Nina Totenberg, legal affairs correspondent for National Public Radio and a regular contributor to "The MacNeil/ Lehrer Newshour," here pays tribute to truly a "great man," a gentle soul, and a good friend.

A Tribute to Justice William J. Brennan, Jr.
Nina Totenberg

Some years ago I brought my sister Amy to meet Justice Brennan. He very generously spent considerable time with us, inquiring about her work as a lawyer and her life. She had just learned a day earlier that she was pregnant, and in his grandfatherly way, he rejoiced with her. Many months later I came by his chambers at the end of the Term to say good-bye for the summer.

"Nina," he asked, "that baby should be coming pretty soon, shouldn't it?"

"That baby," I replied, "was born two weeks ago."

"Oh my," said the Justice, a huge grin crossing his face, as he reached for a pen and paper. "Name?" he demanded. "Address?"

A few days later a letter arrived in Atlanta, addressed to the baby:

Dear Clara,

Welcome! Welcome! Welcome! It's a great world if you will make it so. Enjoy every minute of it.

Love,
William J. Brennan, Jr.

That letter, I think, is emblematic of Justice Brennan, of his wonderful warmth of spirit, his eternal optimism, his joy in living, and his firm belief that things will turn out well if one just tries to make it so.

45

Much has been and will be written about William Brennan the Justice and legal mind, and I will leave much of that to others more qualified than I am on that score. Suffice it to say that I have always been somewhat amused by the continuing debate over "judicial activism" versus "judicial restraint." Certainly Justice Brennan's last triumph on the Supreme Court—*Metro Broadcasting, Inc. v. FCC*—has been criticized as the ultimate in judicial activism, and yet Justice Brennan's opinion upholding affirmative action programs (some might even say quotas) in the awarding of broadcast licenses is based on deference to a specifically stated congressional mandate—the hallmark of judicial restraint. Conversely, Justice Brennan's admirers have repeatedly cited his devotion to the protection of individual liberties, but *Metro Broadcasting* is an opinion that defers to congressionally approved group classifications, not to individualism.

This debate will rage on for years, but, for the purposes of this tribute, I write about the persona of a great Justice. He is an improbable looking villain or inspirational leader—though his critics and admirers describe him that way. At 5' 6" tall, he has a mischievous Irish grin and a springy step reminiscent of Jimmy Cagney. He's Yankee Doodle Dandy dressed up in judicial robes.

Behind that open-hearted and twinkling exterior is a mind of enormous force and determination, a mind that by most accounts has been at the forefront of molding American jurisprudence over the last three-and-a-half decades. As two of his conservative critics put it in an article in the *National Review* several years ago: "an examination of Brennan's opinions, and his influence upon the opinions of his colleagues, suggests that there is no individual in this country, on or off the Court, who has had a more profound and sustained impact upon public policy in the United States" over the last quarter century.

One of the great fringe benefits of being a reporter is that every once in a while you get to have a real talk with someone who has properly and deservedly earned enormous stature. And on even rarer occasions that person becomes a friend. It's not an easy friendship because each of you must recognize that the other has a job to do that may well be at odds with yours. But I consider one of the luckiest days of my life to be the day in the early 1980s when Justice William J. Brennan, Jr., finally agreed to see me. I had tried for many years to talk to him without any success. I know now that for fifteen years his wife Marjorie's cancer tortured him, that he would rush home every afternoon to care for her, and that on some occasions he felt like giving up his seat on the Court altogether. Some who know him better than I say that some of his bitterest dissents were written when Marjorie was so terribly ill. All of this took its toll, and to the outside world, Justice Brennan appeared to withdraw more and more in the 1970s. After Marjorie's death, Justice Brennan plummeted, according to his family. But soon, he began to date his longtime secretary, Mary Fowler. Within months, he dictated a memo to the Court conference, informing the Brethren that he and Mary had gotten married and were on their honeymoon in Bermuda.

Suddenly, he was born again. And I slipped through the office door, eventually to do a long series of interviews.

In Washington, where cynicism is often justified, it is quite an amazing thing to learn more and more about a "great man" and to find that he really is great, that his beliefs are genuine, that his work is his life, that his soul is a gentle one, and that he has a rare gift of perception and a tolerance of others, even when their beliefs threaten his.

We will not see anyone like him again, in part because no one will come to the Court having witnessed and absorbed into his or her experience such a breadth of history as Justice Brennan has. He grew to maturity at a time of enormous political ferment in this country, a time when there was incredible poverty and repression, a time when children worked as laborers twelve and fourteen hours a day, a time when attempts at unionizing workers were put down with ruthless force, and Justice Brennan witnessed some of those struggles firsthand. Born in 1906 to Irish immigrant parents, he was the second of eight children. His father, a coal shoveler and oiler for furnaces, was a leader in the early labor movement. When the Newark police helped to bust a local trolley workers' strike, Justice Brennan's father helped put together a labor slate to run for city office. William Brennan, Sr., was elected to the city commission and was named director of public safety with jurisdiction over the city police and fire departments. The police were promptly put out of the business of union busting.

Justice Brennan's background in New Jersey politics enabled him, I suspect, to have a particularly acute perception of the pragmatic reality of gerrymandering and legislative malapportionment. The result: the now famous *Baker v. Carr*. He has remarked on occasion that it was his experience with intricate gerrymandering plans in New Jersey that enabled him to understand and penetrate the intricacies of the Voting Rights Act cases that came to the Court over the years. Anybody who has read *Gingles* knows what a herculean task it is to parse out these voting cases. But unlike most of us, Justice Brennan's understanding of legal issues transcends enormously his own experience. He has an uncanny ability to see issues, not just from the perspective of a white, male octogenarian, but also through the eyes of the black, the young, the alien, the handicapped, and the female. This past Term, in an opinion that virtually banned political patronage in low- and mid-level government jobs, he wrote about what it's like to have a government job, and you could have sworn upon reading it that he'd spent his whole life as a low-level bureaucrat.

Speaking for myself, I never can quite figure out how this man, born before women even had the vote, bred in a sexist environment, has become such an advocate for a constitutional interpretation that protects women. Any woman who has spent any time with the Justice can see that he treats women with a very special manner. He is an old-world gentleman, very definitely. And yet, when it comes to sex discrimination, well, he "gets it." In our lengthy interviews several years ago, I tried to get him to be a bit introspective about his views on women. Introspection is not his forte, and he would have none of it. Growing impatient, he began interrogating me. Here's the exchange:

> Brennan: Isn't gender discrimination very obvious discrimination? Isn't it?
> Totenberg: It is to me.
> Brennan (now irritated): No, isn't it!
> Totenberg: mmmmm. . . .
> Brennan: Now, the next question has to be, what are the justifications for it?
> Totenberg: Well, the justifications existed for a long time.
> Brennan (interrupting): Yes, but the justifications were all stereotypes. That women's place was in the home, that women's place was to bring up the children, while father became the breadwinner. Those are all stereotypes.
> Totenberg: Justice Brennan, you're eighty years old. You grew up in America at a time when those stereotypes were fact. How come you don't think that?
> Brennan: Why should I think that? If only I could get you to understand what I've said over and over and over and over again. Once you get here, and you have that fabulous document to apply, and that becomes your responsibility, things that you hadn't seen in the context of the restraints of the Bill of Rights suddenly become

apparent as the subject of those restraints, and my job is to see that these restraints are applied and enforced.

There have been times when discovering the true meaning of the Constitution has not been so easy for Justice Brennan, and one of his endearing qualities is the ability to admit it. Perhaps the most famous subject of his intellectual wrestling is obscenity. Over the years he engaged in valiant and, he now admits, fruitless efforts to define it. Indeed, he wrote his first opinion defining obscenity when he was on the New Jersey Supreme Court. "I tried and tried and tried and tried and waffled back and forth," he says. "And I finally gave up." But by the time Justice Brennan was ready to declare obscene material for adults generally protected, the Court had taken a different approach in *Miller v. California*. Still, one can't help but think that if it weren't for Justice Brennan's genuine revulsion at pornography, he wouldn't have tried so hard to define it and for so long.

The Justice does tell one hilarious story about obscenity cases, a story that dates back to his days as a student at Harvard Law School. His teacher, the great Zachariah Chaffee, used as a case study *Public Welfare Pictures Corp. v. Brennan*. The case involved a sex education movie called *The Naked Truth* and a license that had been sought to show the movie. The Newark Commissioner of Public Safety, William J. Brennan, Sr., had refused the license, and the courts had ordered him to grant it. Professor Chaffee used the case as a model for how to fight censorship. When the junior Brennan went home with this tale from the classroom, the senior Brennan hit the roof!

On a more serious note, I think that Justice Brennan's many opinions in the area of church-state relations were not, within his soul, always easy for him. From the moment of his confirmation hearings, when he was asked about his Catholicism and how it would affect his decisionmaking, he knew this would be an issue. And he always said that his duty as a Justice was to interpret the Constitution without regard to his own religious feelings. Justice Brennan is a religious man, a devout Catholic who attends mass every week. Yet, as we all know, he is the author of opinions erecting a high wall of separation between church and state, including decisions banning parochial school aid, and he has consistently joined the pro-choice *Roe v. Wade* majority. My sense is that this has not always been easy, that it has required a good deal of introspection, and some courage too, for there has been talk of movement inside the Church to deny him the sacraments.

In writing about Justice Brennan's impact on the Court, one must deal always with his reputation as a consensus builder, a molder of opinion, a playmaker. The Justice gets quite put out when asked about this, heatedly denying it. What he does do, I think, is accurately judge his colleagues and figure out what is doable.

The description he gave one of his law clerks in an interview in the *New York Times* some years ago, if you study it, is a pretty sensitive and shrewd description of garnering a five-Member Court majority:

> It really isn't very mysterious or complex, what we do . . . in these chambers. We debate the issues, the merits, and when it comes time to write, we discuss the various possible approaches. We ask about some of the approaches. Will this be rejected by Lewis Powell or Harry Blackmun? Will Thurgood agree with this? Has John Stevens written any cases which may suggest how he is thinking and about which we should be aware? What does Sandra think? You try to get, in advance of circulation, a sense of what will sell, what the others can accept. And you write it that way, and when it works out—and maybe you have suggestions that come in and perhaps you make substantial revisions—but when it works out and you have a Court, you are delighted.

Justice Brennan's critics and admirers both have painted him on occasion as some sort of a political Svengali on the Court, persuading others by his charm. He hates that notion, noting that he likes to communicate with other Justices by memo when discussing business. And I don't think it is his charm that wins cases. But it is a special kind of perceptiveness that sees the problems of a case and can translate them in a way that appeals to the critical Justice or Justices needed for a majority. In the flag-burning cases, for example, he emphasized that the burning of Old Glory was a political protest, not just a violent act, and thereby held the votes of conservative Justices Antonin Scalia and Anthony Kennedy. Now, maybe Justices Scalia and Kennedy would have stuck on that side of the issue no matter what, and maybe they saw it just as he did, but I suspect a good deal of Brennanesque thinking went into emphasizing the political nature of the protest, so as to avoid the result the Warren Court reached in, for instance, the draft card burning cases.

Justice Brennan would be the first to say he's lost Court majorities too. Court sources say he lost the Court majority in the *Patterson* civil rights case two Terms ago because he would not alter his views to get a fifth vote.

In Washington, where compromise is the name of the game and false faces are put forward as a way of life, Justice Brennan is special not only for his devotion to principle, but also for his utter lack of hypocrisy. He has written for decades about the need for a wide spectrum of ideas in government, and he seems not to care one whit about the ideological views of his law clerks. In an era when some of the conservative members of the Court seem to hire law clerks as if they were political aides, Justice Brennan continues to hire clerks as varied as University of Chicago conservatives and labor liberals. When the Reagan administration's Assistant Attorney General for Civil Rights, William Bradford Reynolds, called Justice Brennan an "extremist" and "a threat" to the nation, Justice Brennan replied blandly, "He's entitled to his first amendment rights." And when I asked the Justice about the reports I'd heard that his wife Mary thought some of his views to be off-the-wall, he said, this time with great affection, "She too is entitled to her first amendment rights."

Over the last decade, Justice Brennan's views have prevailed less and less frequently. He became known more and more for his dissents and said quite openly that he hoped they would one day become law. Those dissents could be biting, but in person he demonstrated, as always, a complete lack of malice or envy. When I visited him in his chambers this spring, he said quite matter-of-factly that time and changing Court majorities had passed him by. I tried to say something politic, but he shushed me, saying candidly, "Look, I had my way for twenty-five years, now it's their turn." As I left, he winked at me, again the optimist, warning me "not to count the old dog out yet." A few days later the Court handed down *Metro Broadcasting*.

On my last visit, I'd come to record a short interview, so that we could rerun the old ones, updated, and I of course asked him if he was going to retire. "ABSOLUTELY NOT!" he yelled at me, demanding to know if I was going to quit. When I said no, he said he saw no reason that he should either. I know he did not want to retire.

But he had always said that he would leave the Court if he feared he could no longer do the work. His first loyalty was to the Court as an institution. He, after all, was the Justice chosen by the Court to tell Justice William O. Douglas that Douglas was too ill to continue.

Justice Brennan said in our interviews in 1987 that he only hoped that if he became ill, he would "recognize it, and . . . just surrender."

In early summer, when he realized he'd had a stroke, he surrendered. He has taken senior status, plans to sit on circuit panels, to teach, and to write.

I expect I'll be writing about him again soon. The leprechaun of the Supreme Court may have retired, but he'll not be idle for long.

Justice of the New Jersey Supreme Court Daniel J. O'Hern clerked for Justice Brennan early in his tenure on the U.S. Supreme Court—the 1957 Term. Here he reflects on the temper of that time and the humanity of a judge who fulfilled in his lifetime the precepts of the Eighty-second Psalm. This piece and the one that follows first appeared in St. John's Law Review.

In Honor of William J. Brennan, Jr.
Daniel J. O'Hern

I am honored to have been asked to write a Foreword to your symposium issue celebrating the Bicentennial of the Bill of Rights. I am especially pleased that the issue is dedicated to retired Justice William J. Brennan, Jr., as an acknowledgment of his contributions to safeguarding and extending the basic freedoms set forth in the Bill of Rights. I am also pleased to join in the issue with a person as creative as Professor Charles L. Black, Jr., with his unique perception of the relationship between the civilizing influences of law and poetry.

I leave it to others to comment on the legal achievements of Justice Brennan. His substantive accomplishments are towering, and their detailed analysis will engage the best of legal minds for decades. I prefer to share with your readers some reflections on the personal qualities of Justice Brennan that so favorably struck me in the fortunate year that I spent with him as a clerk on the United States Supreme Court. His concern for the life of the Court and for the quality of its work was exhaustive and all-encompassing. Most significant to me was the intense quality of humanity that he brought to his work from the very beginning. That quality brings to mind the timeless message of the Eighty-second Psalm and Justice Brennan's fulfillment in his lifetime of that Psalm.

Let the weak and the orphans have justice.
Be fair to the wretched and destitute.
Rescue the weak and needy.
Save them from the clutches of the wicked.

The world has turned many times since that wonderful day when fate granted me the opportunity to become a clerk of Justice Brennan for the Supreme Court's October 1957 Term. It is so difficult now to recall the temper of that time, following shortly after the McCarthy era. The American public had a consuming curiosity about confidential advisors to their high officers of government. The Justices' law clerks came in for what was described as "some rather ill-tempered and ill-intentioned scrutiny." The law clerks were characterized as a "second team," as "ghostwriters," and, more insinuatingly, as "wielders of unorthodox influence." The charge was made that "the influence they exert comes from the political Left." How amusing all of this seems now! Actually, all that any of that band of law clerks ever achieved with Justice Brennan was lifelong friendship. To this day, he remembers not only the two of us who clerked for him, but each and every clerk for the Court during that Term. And so enduring is that personal relationship that we have from time to time visited with him as a group and renewed memories of that wonderful year.

I am sure that none of us had any sense at that time of the majestic influence that Justice Brennan was to have on the life of American law. Who could have foreseen that he would serve on the Court longer than all but a handful of Justices and help to bring about one of the most remarkable transformations in American law? One thing is certain: we were surely not the ones to bring about this transformation. For the truth of the matter is that law clerks have no such influence on men such as Justice Brennan—and today we may say women. His philosophy was as clear and fixed then as it is today. In *Speiser v. Randall* he set forth the principles from which he has never departed:

Where one party has at stake an interest of transcending value—as a criminal defendant his liberty . . . the procedures by which the facts of the case are determined assume an importance fully as great as the validity of the substantive rule of law to be applied. And the more important the rights at stake the more important must be the procedural safeguards surrounding those rights.

That philosophy had been clear as early as 1953 from his dissent in

State v. Tune in which he would have allowed a capital defendant to inspect before trial a copy of his own confession. In his characteristically plain way, he expressed the views that would carry him throughout his career:

It shocks my sense of justice that in these circumstances counsel for an accused facing a possible death sentence should be denied inspection of his confession which, were this a civil case, could not be denied.

[W]e ought not in criminal cases, where even life itself may be at stake, forswear in the absence of clearly established danger a tool so useful in guarding against the chance that a trial will be a lottery or mere game of wits and the result at the mercy of the mischiefs of surprise.

In the ordinary affairs of life we would be startled at the suggestion that we should not be entitled as a matter of course to a copy of something we signed.

[T]he majority['s] view [denying discovery] sets aside the presumption of innocence and is blind to the superlatively important public interest in the acquittal of the innocent.

The holding of this case gives the majority's protestation that "In this State our courts are always mindful of the rights of the accused" a hollow ring. The assurance seems doubly hollow in light of the emphasis upon formalism in this case while it has been our boast in all other causes that we have subordinated the procedural niceties to decisions on the merits.

These themes were repeated throughout Justice Brennan's career, the emphasis on the human aspect or individual justice of the case and a disdain for formalism.

The central theme and organizing principle of all of his years on the Court has been to fulfill the role of the judge as the impartial guardian that stands between the citizen and the state. He summarized this judicial concern for the individual in *Fay v. Noia,* a 1963 decision that extended the scope of the writ of habeas corpus. In speaking of the varied expressions of the writ of habeas corpus as a great constitutional privilege, he wrote: "Behind them may be discerned the unceasing contest between personal liberty and government oppression." He quoted Justice Holmes in stating that "Habeas Corpus cuts through all forms and goes to the very tissue of the structure." Again a desire to get away from formalities and get to the heart of the issue.

I have often pondered whence came Justice Brennan's sense of injustice. Did it spring, perhaps, from some inherited distrust for English authority? If so, it is consistent then with the great ideals of our society.

> The founders of our institutions, deeply distrustful of judges beholden to the Crown, sought to guarantee forever liberty under law. To preserve their freedoms, they created three branches of government, and vested executive, legislative, and judicial powers in these separate agencies to guarantee the independence of each.

In describing the need for such judicial independence, Justice Frankfurter recalled the words of John Adams in the First Constitution of Massachusetts:

> It is essential to the preservation of the rights of every individual, his life, liberty, property and character, that there be an impartial interpretation of the laws, and administration of justice. It is the right of every citizen to be tried by judges as free, impartial and independent as the lot of humanity will admit.

In every sense, Justice Brennan fulfilled this ideal of the judge who was as free, impartial, and independent as the lot of humanity will admit. Though he may now gain some surcease from his labor, is not the preservation of the Bill of Rights by an independent judiciary the enduring legacy of Justice Brennan's life on the Court? He has given us an ideal that each may follow. It could never have been said more eloquently than by his successor, Justice Souter, at his own confirmation hearings: "Justice Brennan is going to be remembered as one of the most fearlessly principled guardians of the American Constitution that it has ever had and ever will have." In doing so, Justice Brennan has allayed the fears of Professor Charles L. Black, Jr., who was quoted as saying:

> Law in latter days has gained much in realism, in hard-headedness, in disdain for orotundity and rhetorical glitter. This gain, like all

gains, comes with its built-in peril—in this case the deadly peril of the loss of the poetry of law. . . . The poetry of law is the motive for solving problems, the sacred stir toward justice, our priceless discontent at the remoteness of perfect law.

Justice Brennan has never lost that sacred stir toward justice; nor has he yielded to discontent at the remoteness of perfect law. Like the psalmist, he knows that this is an imperfect world and that judges, like poets, can only strive to give it meaning.

Peter Strauss, Betts Professor of Law at Columbia Univer-
sity, celebrates the qualities of a man and judge who never
failed to treat decisions in their human dimensions. Professor
Strauss clerked for Justice Brennan during the 1965 Term.

Justice Brennan

Peter L. Strauss

The editors of the *St. John's Law Review* have given me the boon of
a few pages in which to celebrate Justice Brennan with you. The problem for a former law clerk, for anyone who has known this man, is to
know where to begin, and how to keep the appreciation within manageable compass.

We often think of judges as calculating rationalists, the best of them
(like Holmes) people of piercing if sometimes rather sardonic intellect,
professionals whom we call upon to transcend personal engagement,
and professionals whom we celebrate for their powers of reason in
manipulating the somewhat disembodied doctrines of law. From this
perspective we measure their contributions to jurisprudence—the intellectual structures of law they have helped to build. William J. Brennan,
Jr., is a giant in these respects, as the editors' dedication to him of
these pages amply illustrates. He has indeed made an extraordinary
contribution to the safeguarding of fundamental human freedoms and
the Bill of Rights during his lengthy tenure on the Supreme Court.
During his extraordinary decades on the Court, and under his leadership,
the law moved closer to its ambition to be "no respecter of persons"
than it had ever been in our history—whether one measures that movement in terms of race, gender, political power or economic class. His
name is more closely associated with the development of our first
amendment liberties than any since Holmes and Brandeis—and those
Justices were generally in dissent.

Here, however, I want to stress more personal qualities of warmth and personal engagement. These qualities are ones that have always marked his face-to-face interactions with others. If you, dear reader, have not had the pleasure of a Brennan greeting embrace, you must simply imagine the glow, the interest in you, the drawing in, the utter lack of pretension or self-importance. Among his law clerks in chambers, he might as well make the coffee as you or his secretary would— whoever got there first; if your child was sick, he would work a little harder(!) to give you time to be with her. In discussion, all subjects were open, and candor was the rule. Children and spouses, once met, were enthusiastic subjects of later conversations; he expected to be as involved in your family as you were in his. No letter waited a day for a thoughtful and warm response.

The law clerk's relationship with a judge holds not a little peril for the judge. The whole idea is that the judge hasn't the time to do all that is needful, and takes on clerks to supply the extra effort. But then, the clerk has not the experience, the maturity in law, or ultimately the responsibility of decision; a clerk's misstep is likely to embarrass the judge much more than the clerk. Judges respond in various ways. Work assignments may be structured to emphasize the more routine or more readily double-checked of chamber's duties—evaluation of certiorari petitions, preparation for oral argument, secondary responsibilities in opinion-drafting. In working with law clerks, a judge may choose to emphasize his or her personal exposure to the clerk's errors, to point out errors or failings that—uncaught—would have served to embarrass. Radiating confidence, Justice Brennan took just the opposite tack: he could assess the certiorari petitions so much more quickly than we, and he certainly didn't want to waste our time in preparing him for arguments he could assess himself; why didn't we put our effort into the opinions he had asked us to help him draft? He reviewed that work with care, of course—a cartload of books went into chambers along with the draft, and much changed opinions often emerged—but the only words we heard were words of thanks and appreciation. You could review the changes for yourself to see where things hadn't been quite as he wanted; but silence and more changes than usual were the strongest criticisms his clerks were likely to hear.

One afternoon, I recall my co-clerk and I asking the Justice in the course of conversation what was the most troubling case he had ever sat on. The answer, which came easily enough, underscores the human qualities I am seeking to address, and how they reflected themselves in his judging. It was a case that had come before him early in his tenure on the New Jersey Supreme Court, in which he had cast the deciding vote. The judicial image here is not Holmes, but Solomon—wisdom not as reason alone, but as reason informed by passion.

Joe and Louise Lavigne had married in 1947, and gave birth to Diane in 1949, shortly before Joe's graduation from college. Family stresses led them to place Diane in foster care when she was seven months old, and they then virtually abandoned her. The agency returned Diane to the Lavignes when the foster parents became unavailable after seven months; two months later, still stressed, they agreed to release her for adoption (they testified that the agency refused to accept a foster care placement again). Diane was at this point sixteen months old. She was placed in an adoptive home at age one and a half, but the adoption had not yet become final when, eight months later, changing circumstances led the Lavignes to conclude that they now *could* care for their daughter, and they first asked and then sued to have Diane returned to them. The four judges of the lower New Jersey courts who heard the case before it came to the Supreme Court had all agreed that parents could seek to reclaim custody during the year that New Jersey law permitted an adoption agency to rescind a placement. They also found that the Lavignes had demonstrated themselves to be fit parents, with their stresses now behind them, so that their natural biological relationship with Diane should be permitted to prevail. As the state's one-year trial period itself suggested, they argued, Diane could be expected to adjust to the loss of her adoptive "parents" once she had been returned to her biological family—for which she might otherwise spend a lifetime in search.

What made the case hard for the Justice, he told us, was not so much the law as his own parenthood. His daughter was about Diane's age at the time; empathizing with both sets of parents (he harbored no doubts that the Lavignes deeply and genuinely repented their earlier decision), he saw terrible hurt on both adult sides of the controversy, and no clearly better resolution for Diane. What he recalled as ultimately shaping his judgment—and so deciding the case—was an interchange with the Lavignes' counsel refusing to recognize the mutuality of pain in the case. The argument was that within a year Diane would have forgotten her adoptive parents entirely; it would be as though they had never existed for her. "My daughter is about Diane's age; are you saying, counsel, that if she were to be placed with another family, within a year she would have forgotten me entirely?" As in that earlier, biblical exchange, counsel for one side had been led to put the case in terms that denied the inevitable tragedy of the outcome.

This insistence on treating decision in its human dimension was often evident during my term with the Justice—perhaps never more strongly so than in *Schmerber v. California,* a case that arose late in the Term and in which, again, the Justice cast the deciding vote. The question was whether a driver suspected of drunk driving had a fifth amendment privilege to refuse cooperation with a blood test on grounds that it might be incriminatory. The Justice eventually wrote a well-respected opinion holding that the fifth amendment privilege did not apply, but that the relevant constitutional constraint was the fourth amendment's protection against unreasonable searches and seizures. What stands out in memory is the difficulty he encountered in coming to this judgment. He was assigned the opinion, we understood, because it was evident in conference that he would be the fifth vote for whatever would be the result in the case. He wrestled for days, if not weeks, with which way that would be; at the center of that concern, I came to believe, was less the implication for doctrine than the readily imagined, human encounter between Mr. Schmerber and the forces of the state. As any who have read his opinions quickly understand, protecting the citizen from the state has been a major theme of his work; and the forcible extraction of blood—minor an operation as it is—involves a significant degree of constraint. Yet he also well understood that the stakes in human carnage were high; and here the manner in which the state couched its argument, stressing its own recognition of the demands of dignity, permitted him to find a route that kept that constraint within acceptable bounds.

Perhaps nowhere in the Justice's canon is this quality more apparent than in his decision for the Court in *Goldberg v. Kelly.* The case has been celebrated for giving impetus to the due process explosion and criticized for its lack of realism in addressing due process issues. For today, its important characteristic lies in its responsiveness to the terrible human facts revealed in the record before the Court. From the characteristics of these plaintiffs and their dealings with New York social service officials emerges an understanding of what procedures are called for to make those encounters meaningful for them. *Their* illiteracy, *their* disadvantage in dealings with officials, the suspicion in which *they* may be held, the desperation of *their* circumstances if even general relief is withheld, the humane premises of the programs under which they seek assistance—all contribute to the Court's striking result. One can believe, indeed I do, that a focus on individuals can be manipulated by counsel for effect, especially in programmatic litigation such as this was; that, correspondingly, such a focus can mislead, can produce results that, on the whole, are more costly than beneficial to the groups the decision purports to favor. Justice Black's dissent warns of consequences that appear to have been borne out, and by the time the Court revisits the issue in *Mathews v. Eldridge,* it is addressing due process issues in terms of systemic impact rather than the facts of this case. Nonetheless, the humaneness of this opinion, its insistence on the dignity of even the least among us, captures that side of the Justice I want here to celebrate.

History has taught us again and again the risks we take in looking to the judiciary and judicial modes of action for the determination of large issues of policy in competition with the people's representatives. For general rules, as Holmes remarked in another context, citizens' rights are best "protected in the only way that they can be in a complex society, by their power, immediate or remote, over those who make the rule." The judicial forte lies not in the creation of general policy, but in measuring the power of particular circumstances that arise in dispute. To measure that power with a yardstick that insists upon the worthiness of us all and that reaches toward the pain of personal encounter is the most difficult and the most praiseworthy. It would be so easy to take refuge behind the distance of "objectivity" and law's hard reason. It is this openness to humanity that, for me, marks Justice Brennan's most precious gift.

In 1965 Owen Fiss began his clerkship for Justice Brennan. In this piece he recalls the turbulent sixties, the challenges that faced the Warren Court, the decisions that defined it, and the faith that guided it. Owen Fiss is the Sterling Professor of Law at Yale University, and his article originally appeared in The Yale Law Journal.

A Life Lived Twice

Owen Fiss

Retirement celebrations are odd events. They are a mixture of joy and sadness, and that is emphatically true of those in honor of Justice Brennan.

Not since the retirement of Justice Holmes in the early 1930's has the nation been more generous in its tributes to a retiring justice. Justice Brennan served the Court for nearly thirty-four years and now, at a mere 84 (Holmes was 90), retires with a grandeur that is indeed stunning. In this, there is reason for joy because the Justice fully deserves all the accolades and honors that have been bestowed upon him. I rejoice in Brennan's glory and feel the pleasures of the moment, but I would be less than honest if I did not also acknowledge my sadness on this occasion, not just for the Justice who so loved his work, but even more for the law. His retirement imperils the achievements of the Warren Court in new and profound ways.

The Warren Court refers to that extraordinary phase of Supreme Court history that began in the mid-1950's, with *Brown* v. *Board of Education* and the appointments of Earl Warren (1954) and William J. Brennan, Jr. (1956), and which reached its apogee in the early 1960's, when Justice Frankfurter retired and the liberal wing of the Court achieved a solid majority. Aside from Warren and Brennan, that majority included Hugo Black, William O. Douglas, and Frankfurter's replacement, Arthur J. Goldberg, who served from 1962 until 1965 and then was replaced by Abe Fortas. In 1967, the group of five was strengthened when Thurgood Marshall replaced Tom Clark. Now and then, they picked up the vote of Potter Stewart or Byron White or even that of their most forceful critic, John Harlan, a conservative who often found himself encumbered by his commitment to stare decisis. Earl Warren retired from the chief justiceship in 1969, but the phase of Supreme Court history that bears his name continued into the early 1970's, probably until 1974. I clerked for Justice Brennan during the term of Court that began in October 1965 and ended the next summer.

Like everything else, law always has an antecedent. The roots of the jurisprudence of the Warren Court can be found in earlier periods, most especially in those decisions of the Supreme Court in the 1930's, when the Court gave important life to the principle guaranteeing freedom of speech, elevating the dissents of Holmes and Brandeis to majority status, and also began to intervene in criminal proceedings to assure a modicum of procedural fairness. But there was something distinctive and special about the Warren Court, almost a new beginning. *Brown* itself undertook the most challenging of all constitutional tasks, making good on the nation's promise of racial equality. Even more importantly, that case embodied both a conception of law and a set of commitments that evolved into a broad-based program of constitutional reform. The Court saw the Bill of Rights and the Civil War Amendments as the embodiment of our highest ideals and soon made them the standard for judging the established order.

In the 1950's, America was not a pretty sight. Jim Crow reigned supreme. Blacks were systematically disenfranchised and excluded from juries. State-fostered religious practices, like school prayers, were pervasive. Legislatures were grossly gerrymandered and malapportioned. McCarthyism stifled radical dissent, and the jurisdiction of the censor over matters considered obscene or libelous had no constitutional limits. The heavy hand of the law threatened those who publicly provided information and advice concerning contraceptives, thereby imperiling the most intimate of human relationships. The states virtually had a free hand in the administration of justice. Trials often proceeded without counsel or jury. Convictions were allowed to stand even though they turned on illegally seized evidence or on statements extracted from the accused under coercive circumstances. There were no rules limiting the imposition of the death penalty. These practices victimized the poor and disadvantaged, as did the welfare system, which was administered in an arbitrary and oppressive manner. The capacity of the poor to participate in civic activities was also limited by the imposition of poll taxes, court filing fees, and the like.

These were the challenges that the Warren Court took up and spoke to in a forceful manner. The result was a program of constitutional reform almost revolutionary in its aspiration and, now and then, in its achievements. Of course the Court did not act in a political or social vacuum. It drew on broad-based social formations like the civil rights and welfare rights movements. At critical junctures, the Court looked to the executive and legislative branches for support. The dual school system of Jim Crow could not have been dismantled without the troops in Little Rock, the Civil Rights Act of 1964, the interventions of the Department of Justice and HEW, the suits of the NAACP Legal Defense Fund, or the black citizens who dared to become plaintiffs or, even more, to break the color line or march on behalf of their rights. The sixties would not have been what they were without the involvement of all of these institutions and persons, and the world would have looked very different. Yet the truth of the matter is that it was the Warren Court that spurred the great changes to follow, and inspired and pro-tected those who sought to implement them.

A constitutional program so daring and so bold was, of course, the work of many minds. As is customary, we use the name of the chief justice to refer to this period of Supreme Court history, and in Warren's case that practice seems especially appropriate. Earl Warren was a man of great dignity and vision, in every respect a leader, who discharged his duties (even the most trivial, such as admitting new members to the bar) with a grace and cheerfulness that were remarkable. He presided in a way that filled the courtroom with a glow. Yet the substance of the Court's work, the revolution that it effectuated in our understanding of the Constitution, drew on the talents and ideas of all those who found themselves entrusted with the judicial power at that unusual moment of history.

Justice Brennan's contribution to the ensemble known as the Warren Court had many dimensions. He was devoted to the values we identify with the Warren Court—equality, procedural fairness, freedom of speech, and religious liberty—and he was prepared to act on them. More importantly, he was the justice primarily assigned the task of speaking for the Court. The overall design of the Court's position may have been the work of several minds, fully reflecting the contributions of such historic figures as Black, Douglas, and Warren, but it was Brennan who by and large formulated the principle, analyzed the precedents, and chose the words that transformed the idea into law. Like any master craftsman, he left his distinctive imprint on the finished product.

Warren and Brennan were invariably on the same side in the great constitutional cases of the day. They served together for thirteen terms and agreed in 89% of the more than 1400 cases they decided. Indeed, it is hard to think of a case of any import where they differed. As chief justice, Warren had the responsibility of assigning the task of speaking for the Court when his side prevailed. Sometimes, as in *Reynolds* v. *Sims* and *Miranda* v. *Arizona,* where he felt the need for the imprimatur of his office, or where the issue was especially close to his heart, Warren wrote the opinion. But generally he turned to Justice Brennan.

In part, this reflected the unusual personal tie that developed between the two. The Chief—as Justice Brennan always called him—visited Brennan's chambers frequently, and each visit was an important occasion for the chambers as a whole and for Justice Brennan in particular. One could see at a glance the admiration and affection that each felt for the other. The relationship between Earl Warren and William Brennan was one of the most extraordinary relationships between two colleagues that I have ever known; surely, it must be one of the most famous in the law.

But more than personal sentiment was involved. In turning to Brennan, Warren could be certain that the task of writing the opinion for the Court was in the hands of someone as thoroughly devoted as he was to the Court as an institution. An assignment is always an expression of trust, and Warren could depend on Brennan to formulate and express the Court's position—to declare the principle and attend to the details that constitute the law—in a way that would strengthen the Court in the eyes of both the public and the profession, and thus enhance its capacity to do its great work. Brennan was, in the highest and best sense of the word, a statesman: not a person who tempers principle with prudence, but rather someone who is capable of grasping a multiplicity of conflicting principles, some of which relate to the well-being of the institution and remind the judge that his duty is not just to speak the law, but also to see to it that it becomes an actuality—in the words of *Cooper* v. *Aaron,* to make sure that the law becomes "a living truth."

Brennan could be trusted to choose his words in a way that would minimize the disagreement among the justices, not only to avoid those silly squabbles that might interfere with the smooth functioning of a collegial institution, as the Court most certainly is, but also to produce a majority opinion and strengthen the force of what the Court had to say. Only five votes are needed for a decision to become law, but the stronger the majority and broader the consensus, the more plausible is its claim for authority. Brennan could also be trusted to respect the traditions of the bar and to pay homage to the principle of stare decisis. He always tried to build from within. Sometimes that was not possible, for the break with the past was just too great. Yet, even then, Brennan's inclination, once again rooted in a concern for the Court's authority, was to minimize the disruption, and to find, if at all possible, a narrow path through the precedents. Brennan also understood that reform as bold as the Court tried to effectuate required a coordination, not a separation, of powers, and that gratuitous confrontations with the other branches were to be avoided. In fact, as evident from Justice Brennan's opinion in *Katzenbach* v. *Morgan,* affirming a broad conception of congressional power under section 5 of the Fourteenth Amendment, every effort was made to invite the other branches of government to participate and collaborate in the program of constitutional reform inspired by the Court.

Aside from a proper regard for institutional needs, a successful opinion requires a mastery of legal craft, which Warren also found in Brennan. Justice Brennan was as much the lawyer as the statesman. Law is a blend of the theoretical and the technical, and though there were others as gifted as Brennan in the formulation of a theoretical principle, there was no one in the ruling coalition—certainly not before Fortas's appointment—who had either the patience or the ability to master the technical detail that is also the law. Everyone on the Court, law clerk and justice alike, admired Brennan's command of vast bodies of learning, ancient and modern. He knew the cases and the statutes, and how they interacted, and understood how the legal system worked and how it might be made to work better. Among the majority, he was the lawyer's judge.

Even Brennan's most theoretically ambitious opinions, like *New York Times* v. *Sullivan,* bear the lawyer's mark. In that case Justice Brennan spoke of the national commitment to a debate on public issues that is "uninhibited, robust, and wide-open," and he has been justly celebrated many times for reformulating the theory of freedom of speech associated with the work of Alexander Meiklejohn in a fresh and original way. Meiklejohn, then in his nineties, saw Brennan's opinion in *New York Times* v. *Sullivan* "as an occasion for dancing in the streets." Of even greater importance to the lawyers and judges among us (Mei-klejohn was a political theorist) was Brennan's analysis of the common law of libel and his deft reformulation of doctrine—the announcement of the "actual malice" requirement—in order to create a rule that, one, would be operational and, two, would effectuate a just accommodation of reputational interests and democratic values. *New York Times* v. *Sullivan* is a great decision, a fountainhead of freedom in our day, only because it is an exercise in political philosophy made law.

In 1968, Richard Nixon ran against the Warren Court, and in so doing, attacked Justice Brennan as much as anyone, perhaps more so, given the commanding role that Brennan played on that Court. But history soon took an odd turn: the Warren Court collapsed, but Brennan remained. Prior to the election of 1968, but clearly with a view as to its likely outcome, Earl Warren tendered his resignation to President Johnson in an effort to turn the leadership of the Court over to Johnson's confidant, Abe Fortas. The Senate, however, balked on the elevation of Fortas, and his nomination for the chief justiceship was soon withdrawn. Yet following the 1968 election, Nixon made good on Earl Warren's resignation and began his presidency with the appointment of Warren Burger as chief justice. In addition, Fortas was forced to resign from the Court, due to the disclosure of financial improprieties; and with the resignations of John Harlan and Hugo Black, President Nixon found himself able to make three other appointments during his first term in office. Over time, one of those appointments—Harry A. Blackmun—evolved into a justice whose view of the Constitution turned out to be similar to those who sat on the Warren Court. But the two other appointments—Lewis Powell and William Rehnquist—were of a different character. There were differences between the views of Powell and Rehnquist, but the views of both were at odds with the jurisprudence that reigned supreme during the sixties.

The final dissolution of the Warren Court occurred with the resignation of Douglas in 1975 and his replacement by John Paul Stevens. The balance of power had decisively shifted, and was then locked in place by two accidents of history: Jimmy Carter had no appointments to make, a distinction he shared with no other President in our history who completed a full term, while Ronald Reagan had three—Antonin Scalia (to fill the vacancy created by Burger's resignation), Sandra Day O'Connor (to replace Stewart), and Anthony Kennedy (to replace Powell). In 1986, at the same time he appointed Scalia, President Reagan elevated Rehnquist to the chief justiceship, but that change only conformed outward appearances to the inner reality. For much of the seventies and eighties it was Rehnquist who led the Court, building the necessary coalitions, setting the agenda, and formulating the methods of revision. Even during Burger's years, it was the Rehnquist Court.

These changes ushered in a new phase of Supreme Court history, and Justice Brennan found himself working in a wholly new environment. He could turn to Marshall and, to a considerable extent, Blackmun, for support, but from there on in the going was rough. No longer a dominant figure in the ruling coalition, Brennan became part of the opposition, pitted against a majority driven by a contrary vision of American law and life. The new majority believed that the doctrine of the Warren Court was mistaken and had to be limited, corrected, and perhaps even eradicated.

Brown, of course, was not overruled, but it has been drained of much of its generative power. Arresting the trajectory that was implicit in cases like *Green* v. *School Board of New Kent County, Swann* v. *Charlotte-Mecklenburg Board of Education,* and *Keyes* v. *School Dist. No. 1, Denver,* all ultimately rooted in *Brown,* the Court ruled that school systems that contain a large number of all-black and all-white schools are constitutionally acceptable. According to the new majority, *Brown* condemned not the inequality resulting from the actual separation of the races, but only the use of racial criteria as a method of assignment. As a result, the Court has allowed school boards to assign students to schools on the basis of neighborhoods, even where there is residential segregation: it also effectively insulated suburban communities—invariably white—from the reach of court orders trying to desegregate the inner-city schools. School boards remain obliged to correct for vestiges of past practices, such as racial gerrymandering, but the Rehnquist Court has shifted the emphasis and underscored the limited nature of the remedial obligation, both geographically and temporally.

Even outside of the school desegregation context, which might have been thought to be a category unto itself, the egalitarianism of the Warren Court has been curbed by new renderings of the provision that constituted that Court's nerve center—the equal protection clause. In cases like *Moose Lodge No. 107* v. *Irvis,* which upheld the award of a state liquor license to a club that openly discriminated on the basis of race, a sharp distinction was drawn between state and society, confining the ban on discrimination to state action narrowly understood. In addition, the Court ruled that in order to establish a denial of equal protection it is not enough to show that the state action especially disadvantages minorities; it must be shown that such an effect is intended by the state. In the mid-1970's, the Court also effectively removed the poor from the scope of the equal protection clause, leaving the war on poverty more vulnerable than ever to the vicissitudes of politics. In the same case, the Court declared that education was not a fundamental right, thereby bringing to a halt the process of enumerating rights that would warrant special solicitude under the equal protection clause. Even the commitment to strict numerical equality in the apportionment context has been diluted, as the Court became more and more tolerant of departures from the "one person, one vote" standard.

The Rehnquist Court also created new cracks in the wall between church and state by allowing the state to engage in practices, such as the maintenance of a creche, that earlier would have been unthinkable. In addition, the Court's commitment to maintaining public debate that is "uninhibited, robust, and wide-open" has been compromised during this period. Lacking the steely tolerance for political protest that characterized the Warren Court at its most determined moment, the Court under Rehnquist upheld laws that denied political activists the opportunity to reach the public at shopping centers or in front of certain government buildings, or through posting posters on utility poles, demonstrating in public parks, and picketing in residential neighborhoods. It also refused to create access to the networks for editorial advertisements sponsored by a group of businessmen criticizing the Vietnam War. On the other hand, a number of laws trying to limit political expenditures were struck down as violative of the First Amendment, even though these measures were conceived as means of preserving the vitality of democratic politics by preventing the wealthy from drowning out the voices of the less affluent in society. In these cases, and others, the new majority seemed to be confounding the protection of speech with the protection of property.

In the criminal context, the new majority lifted the ban on the application of the death penalty that had its roots in the sixties and that formally took effect in the early seventies. Since 1976 more than 140 persons convicted of crimes have been put to death, and Rehnquist, both as a judge and in discharge of his administrative responsibilities as head of the Judicial Conference of the United States, seems determined to institute a series of procedural reforms that would expedite and facilitate that process. Similarly, the Court has sought to shift the balance of advantage in the criminal process, relaxing some of the restrictions on the investigatory techniques of the police, most notably the rule excluding illegally seized evidence.

During the 1960's the Court had opened the doors of the federal trial courts for writs of habeas corpus and injunctions against state criminal proceedings. This was done to ensure that state criminal proceedings adhered to minimum standards of fairness and to make certain that these proceedings were not used for improper purposes, such as the harassment of political activists. During the 1970's and 1980's those doors were closed. *Fay* v. *Noia* and *Dombrowski* v. *Pfister,* opinions by Brennan that gave substance to the view that federal courts are the primary forum for the protection of federal rights, were emptied of all operative significance. A similar fate befell *Goldberg* v. *Kelly,* also written by Justice Brennan, which had extended the due process revolution of the sixties from the criminal to the civil domain. Today, government is allowed to act to the detriment of individuals, to inflict grievous suffering on them, for example, by denying disability benefits or terminating parental rights, without providing some of the most elementary forms of due process.

The law does not move slowly, but it does move unevenly, and during the last twenty years all has not been bleak, even for someone with Brennan's outlook. There have been a few bright moments. The most significant are *Roe* v. *Wade,* a 1973 decision creating a right to abortion, and *Regents of the University of California* v. *Bakke,* which, in effect, indicated that certain preferential treatment programs for minorities were permissible, a ruling later to be extended to women in *Johnson* v. *Transportation Agency.* No one should belittle those achievements, or any of the others that might come to mind, but they should not be taken as representative of the judicial era of which they are a part. *Roe* v. *Wade* and *Bakke* did not insert new premises into the law, but built on understandings of an earlier time. These cases were hard-fought victories that sharply divided the Court, and to this day survive by the narrowest of margins. At present, they define the outer limits of the law, barely tolerated, without any generative power of their own.

The danger to these decisions would have significantly increased if the campaign to place Robert Bork on the Court had been successful. As a law professor, as Solicitor General during the Nixon and Ford administrations, and as a federal appellate judge, Bork was a principal figure in the attack on the Warren Court and a relentless critic of *Roe* v. *Wade* and *Bakke* and the precedents upon which they were based. President Reagan's decision in 1987 to nominate him to the Supreme

Court forced the Senate to consider carefully the jurisprudence of both Bork and the traditions which he so criticized, and the result was a series of hearings that offered the country an extraordinary seminar on constitutional law. The importance of those hearings and the decision of the Senate to reject the nomination cannot be denied. It should be understood, however, that contrary to what some have maintained, Bork would not have been a transformative appointment; that transformation had already occurred a decade earlier and continues to this day.

Living through this period was not easy for Justice Brennan. It proved to be a test of sorts, and as such brought to the fore many of his strengths. Value commitments that were shared in the sixties became distinguishing features of the Justice in the seventies and eighties and, as a result, are now recognized as a source of his identity and also his greatness. In some instances, his understanding of the Constitution evolved over time. A striking example is the change in his position on obscenity. In 1973 he rejected the strategy that he had created in 1957 in *Roth* v. *United States* and refined throughout the sixties—of keeping censorship to a minimum by providing a narrow definition of that genre of speech that falls outside the ambit of First Amendment protection—and took up a position close to the absolutism of Black and Douglas. Brennan indicated that characterizing sexually explicit material as obscene was not a sufficient justification for restricting its availability to consenting adults.

For the most part, however, the seventies and eighties were for Brennan a period devoted primarily to defending the achievements of the Warren Court. At times that consisted of demanding that the Court take the inevitable next step, say, of extending the egalitarianism of *Brown* to issues of gender; most of the time, however, he had to confront the most blatant retrenchment. In this context the nation learned what his clerks knew first hand—namely, that the Justice is extraordinarily strong-minded—and when the day was done, he emerged as a national hero, a freedom fighter of sorts. On issues of detail Brennan is conciliatory, but when it comes to what he regards as matters of principle he is adamant and, in the best sense of the word, stubborn.

This stubbornness expressed itself in many ways, not the least of which was the profusion of dissents. One enterprising law clerk, more familiar with Lexis than I, calculated that over his career Justice Brennan wrote dissenting opinions in 2,347 cases, mostly during the 1970's and 1980's. Of those, 1,517 were in death penalty cases, and a great number of them were formulaic dissents from the denial of certiorari, jointly issued with Marshall. But even subtracting these, the number of dissenting opinions remains impressive—830. During the last term alone, the Justice wrote dissenting opinions in 23 cases. During the term I clerked, one of the halcyon days of the Warren Court, Brennan wrote a dissenting opinion in only one case, *United States* v. *Guest,* and it is not even clear whether that opinion would be regarded as a dissent. As commentators soon realized, though his opinion in that case was labeled a "dissent," it actually set forth a view of congressional authority which, when read in conjunction with Justice Clark's separate concurrence, had the support of a majority of five justices and which, along with *Katzenbach* v. *Morgan,* later was used to provide the constitutional foundation for the Civil Rights Act of 1968.

The escalation in the number of Justice Brennan's dissents during the Rehnquist years is indeed striking, all the more so because it is so much greater than the number of dissenting opinions written by the first Justice Harlan or Justice Holmes, both of whom are often referred to as the great dissenters. Over their careers, Harlan wrote 134 dissents and Holmes 81, but these numbers seem trivial when compared to the number of Brennan's dissents. It would be a mistake, however, to view Justice Brennan, even during this second phase of his career on the Court, as we view Holmes or the first Harlan, as another great dissenter or, as the enterprising clerk declared, the greatest dissenter.

As a matter of collegial style, both Harlan and Holmes were loners, and in addition, Holmes's philosophic outlook supremely suited him to the role of dissenter. Holmes viewed history, or even the action of his brethren, much as a spectator might. At times he was prepared to raise his voice in protest, as he did in *Lochner* v. *New York* and *Abrams* v. *United States,* but he did so with an indifference as to whether he persuaded his colleagues or managed to obtain their votes. Holmes spoke to the future, and as it turned out he was prophetic, but his basic intent was to speak his mind and let the chips fall wherever they might. Justice Brennan, on the other hand, never, but never, was a loner nor a spectator, but always was thoroughly engaged with his colleagues, passionately working to build a majority; in the 1950's and 1960's he did so to implement the revolution, in the 1970's and 1980's to stop the counterrevolution. The Brennan dissents of the 1970's and 1980's spoke not to the future, but to his colleagues. More often than not they read like majority opinions that just fell short of one or two votes. In one notable instance involving congressional power under the commerce clause, he soon managed to sway one of the previous majority to switch, thereby transforming the position he originally articulated in dissent into the law of the land.

Moreover, while the second phase of Brennan's career is marked by an extraordinary number of dissents, one should not be misled by the numbers. The dissents were not at the core of his mission. At the occasional law clerk dinners held during the 1970's and 1980's, he would wryly announce the tallies to the assembled. We would cheer the resistance offered by his dissents. But it was obvious that the Justice's true source of pleasure came in the cases in which he somehow—miraculously, I think—formed a majority that held the line. Rehnquist was usually on the other side, and because of his seniority, Brennan acted as a shadow chief justice and often assigned himself the task of speaking for the odd coalition that he pulled together. Justice Brennan's last term on the Court was marked by a large number of dissents, but of equal, even greater, significance is the fact that in two important cases—one involving flagburning, the other patronage—he was able to speak for the majority in support of freedom of speech. It was entirely fitting that on the last day of his last term on the Court, after almost thirty-four years of service, he announced an opinion for a majority of the Court upholding an FCC policy—born of another era—that favored minority interests in awarding broadcasting licenses. Later that afternoon, Justice Brennan received the prognosis from his doctor that led to his decision to retire.

Justice Brennan is a proud man, not in the least bit arrogant—indeed he is one of the most modest men I have ever known—but he is someone who takes a very special pride in his work. He is a fighter who likes to win, and as such, would be pained to see an earlier victory reversed, especially when, as in the line of cases that undid *Dombrowski,* the new majority, also trying to build from within, turned Brennan's doctrinal creations to another purpose. The fight in Brennan no doubt accounted for the sense of engagement that carried him through the seventies and eighties, and helps explain the unusual role he created for himself during that period. It was, however, dwarfed by an even more significant factor: his devotion to the institution.

In the Warren Court era, this devotion accounted for Brennan's role as Court spokesman and for the distinctive nature of his opinions. He took no pleasure in speaking alone, but always tried to speak through the Court and to mold judicial doctrine in a way that was fully sensitive to the needs of that institution. His first priority was to have the Court speak authoritatively and his second was to produce an opinion that would strengthen the effectiveness of the Court. He strove to avoid any gestures that would either dissolve or splinter the majority, infuriate those on the other side of the bench, or set into motion a political dynamic that would undermine the ability of the Court to achieve all that it might. During the second half of his tenure, these same sentiments shaped his strategy of resistance. Dissent was always a possibility, but his first priority was that the Court speak to the issue in an authoritative manner, because he continued to believe in the Court and that law mattered. He remained committed to working through the institution, not to propounding his views, speaking his mind, or otherwise indulging himself. Dissent was a reluctant last resort—almost an acknowledgment of failure.

In this way, Brennan served as the bridge between the Constitution that was and the Constitution that is. He was the mediating force in the negative dialectic between the Warren and Rehnquist Courts. I can assure you that there is no one left on the Court, not even Justice Marshall (for whom I also clerked), who can play that role in quite the way that Brennan did. At the hands of Rehnquist and those inclined to follow him, the Warren Court has suffered grievously, and today, without Brennan on the bench, the work of that institution stands more in jeopardy than ever. Some, like Scalia, appear determined to chart their own process of revision, but the danger they pose to the body of law associated with the Warren Court is every bit as great.

Of course, Justice Brennan has left us a written legacy. The pages of the United States Reports are filled with his opinions, both dissents and majority opinions. A few years back, still another of his law clerks surveyed the leading casebooks on constitutional law and reported that of all the so-called "principal" cases featured in those books, Justice Brennan had written more than any other justice in the entire history of the Supreme Court. These opinions define the field within which the present Court operates; for some they will act as constraints, for others a resource—and if the testimony of Brennan's replacement, David Souter, is to be believed, for some they might even act as an inspiration. But these opinions will not compensate for the loss of Brennan's vote, even less for his absence within the councils of the Court.

During the October 1965 Term, the conferences were held on Fridays. Later that day, or more commonly on Saturdays, when the Justice would regularly have lunch with his clerks, he would describe what transpired at conference, or at least what he thought we should know about the conference. Some sense of the inner workings of the Court was also conveyed during the dinners he had with his clerks during the late 1960's and early 1970's. At that time the law clerk dinners were an annual event and the number of former clerks small enough that we could sit around a table upstairs at the Occidental. Those were also the days—prior to the publication of *The Brethren*—when he could assume that law clerks could be trusted with a confidence. The Justice was not a man for gossip, or small talk about his colleagues (though his interest in the personal lives of his clerks was boundless—he treated us as members of his family). But he saw himself as a teacher, supplementing and enriching what we might have learned in the classroom, and he believed that understanding the dynamics among the justices was a crucial part of our education, especially if, as he hoped, we would go on to become teachers. He wanted us and our students to know how law was truly made.

His role in the deliberations was not the principal point of these conversations, but one could see in an instant how the personal qualities that drew us to the man—the quickness and clarity of his mind, the warmth of his personality, the energy that he brought to argument, his sensitivity to the views of others—were present in the Conference Room and, even more, accounted for much of what happened there. In conference, Justice Brennan always had more than one vote. Who could possibly resist him when he grabbed you by the elbow, or put his arm around your shoulder, and began, "Look, pal ..."?

For many, including myself, the Justice's retirement will only compound the sense of disaffection with the Court that now pervades the academy and large sections of the profession. For a previous generation, the Supreme Court was an institution of respect and admiration. Today the Court is seen as alien and hostile, less devoted to reaffirming and actualizing our national ideals than to protecting the established order, strengthening the hand of those who serve it and belittling those who might challenge it. It is this perception that contributed to the rise of the Critical Legal Studies movement and its many cognates during the late seventies and that gives this movement such widespread support in the academy today. Yet the same disaffection is shared by those who have more moderate or centrist commitments, those who still believe in the redemptive possibility of law.

This disaffection is rooted in the overall pattern of decisions over the last two decades. It is exacerbated, however, by the person of the Chief Justice who, despite his amiability, appears so determined in his mission that he is willing to disregard even the most elementary principles of the craft, and who managed, in his two confirmation proceedings, to cast doubt on his own integrity. In the first, he mischaracterized Justice Jackson's position in the deliberations leading to *Brown* in an effort to explain away a memorandum he wrote as a law clerk supporting *Plessy* v. *Ferguson*; in the second, he failed to explain adequately why he did not recuse himself in a case involving military surveillance of civilians during the Nixon administration in which, of course, he was an assistant attorney general.

The Warren Court had its critics, as was known to anyone who, like myself, studied at Harvard in the early sixties and witnessed Justice Brennan's anger—soon abated—at the leading faction of the Harvard professorate and a number of scholars associated with that school who denounced the Court in terms most emphatic. This anger expressed itself in many ways, one quite trivial: the Justice decided to end his practice of taking his clerks, as a matter of course, from his own law school. My fellow clerk was his first from Yale—the stronghold of support for what the Court was then trying to accomplish—and on the last day of my clerkship I received a poem written by a friend in the name of the Justice entitled "Ode to My Last Harvard Clerk." This too would pass. But even in those days it was understood that Harvard did not speak for the profession as a whole, and even less so for the young, who looked to the Court as an inspiration, the very reason to enter the profession. Today, the situation is completely different. The disaffection with the Court is not localized, but pervades the profession, and swells within those who are just now being initiated into it. For some, the Rehnquist Court speaks to their ideals, but for most it is a source of cynicism and doubt.

Under these circumstances it is often difficult to see or present the body of learning known as constitutional law as worthy of respect and admiration. It is also difficult to know how the Court might continue to play its historic function in the republic: how can it speak authoritatively and effectively to the issues that divide us if the bar feels so alienated from it? To some, this loss of authority might not seem so tragic, given the present course of decision. But I wonder whether such a view is inappropriately short-sighted, seeing only what is, without regard to what was and what might be. For all that it accomplished, and still might, there is reason to believe in the Court. Yet I recognize that it becomes more and more difficult to do so under the terms and conditions of the governing coalition.

In musing on this predicament, my mind often turns to the Justice, and I glance at the photograph that appears as the frontispiece of these Tributes. While the Justice represents many things for me, probably none is more important than his attachment to the Court as an institution. It is this attachment that unifies the two phases of his career and accounts for the unusual role that he created for himself during the last twenty years, as he saw so much that he created and so much that he believes in dismantled and destroyed. Justice Brennan served through these years in a cheerful and determined manner, always with an unqualified devotion to the Court. I wonder whether those, like myself, who wish to honor him and that extraordinary age of American law that he helped bring into being, might not look to him as an exemplar and an inspiration. He resisted, tenaciously, but kept the faith—why can't we?

William J. Maledon, now an attorney in Phoenix, Arizona, clerked for Justice Brennan during the 1972 Term. Chief Justice Warren had retired three years before, and the Court had entered a state of flux. Maledon considers the role Justice Brennan played on the Court, and the integrity he maintained, in the seventies. This piece originally appeared in Arizona State Law Journal.

Justice William J. Brennan, Jr.: A Personal Tribute

William J. Maledon

Most attorneys know William J. Brennan, Jr., only through his written opinions over his thirty-four years on the United States Supreme Court and his much less frequent speeches and published articles. I, on the other hand, had the extreme good fortune to serve as one of his law clerks during the Court's 1972 Term and, in the process, to work closely with him and observe his decision-making process. Since then, I have kept in touch with the Justice, often writing or visiting and always attending his triennial clerkship reunions. Justice Brennan is much more than his written opinions and his public statements. He is one of the most caring, friendly, and professionally committed persons I have ever known. What I learned from him went far beyond the law. His qualities as a person, not just his enormous capabilities as a Supreme Court Justice, make his retirement from the Court a loss for all of us.

At the start of the 1972 Term, the Court was in a state of flux, perhaps becoming more conservative and certainly becoming less predictable. Chief Justice Burger and Justice Blackmun by then had been on the Court for several years and were beginning to make their presence felt by distancing themselves from the approaches taken by their

predecessors (Earl Warren and Abe Fortas). Justices Powell and Rehnquist were each starting their first full Term on the Court, and it was
not clear yet how their presence (and the loss of Justices Black and
Harlan) would affect the Court. Justices Stewart and White were sea-
soned veterans, but it was often difficult to predict how they would
vote on a case and even more difficult to predict how they might be
influenced by the new members of the Court. And Justices Douglas,
Marshall, and Brennan, although ideologically aligned on most issues,
had very different styles and seemed to interact with the other Justices
in very different ways.

In my efforts to analyze the Court as I began my clerkship, I concluded from what I knew (or thought I knew) of the other Justices that
Justice Brennan would probably be in the minority in most important
cases, which would be a significant change from the position he had
been in during the Warren Court years and even during the first few
years (1969–71 Terms) of the Burger Court. I also concluded that Justice Brennan's new-found minority position on the Court might engender some frustration for him and might make him (and his chambers)
somewhat more isolated from the rest of the Court. This did not trouble
me; it simply made me wonder what my clerkship would be like. I
came to the job knowing that Justice Brennan had been, for more than
fifteen years, one of the most influential and respected members of the
Court—a Justice who was known for writing some of the Court's most
forward-thinking and most carefully reasoned opinions and who had a
reputation for being able to "put a Court together" even when divergent
views or a strong opposition seemed to make it impossible to do so.
But I wondered, as I started my clerkship, how Justice Brennan would
react to the changes at the Court and to what extent those changes
would affect both his ability to influence other members of the Court
and his resolve to do so.

The answers came quickly. I learned during the first few weeks of
my clerkship that Justice Brennan did not intend to concede anything
and that he would simply work harder (if that was possible) to make
his voice heard. He quickly perceived that some important cases on the
Court's docket would entail extensive debate and would probably divide
the Court. The abortion cases, the obscenity cases, the so-called "Northern" school desegregation cases, and the school financing cases, just to
name a few, were on the Court's docket for the 1972 Term. There also
were suggestions in the press that the new Court might seek to overrule
some of the important decisions of the Warren Court, particularly in the

areas of first amendment freedoms and criminal procedure. Rather than panic, however, Justice Brennan methodically addressed the issues, thoroughly prepared his arguments and counterarguments, listened and reacted to the positions of his colleagues, and built coalitions on individual cases by persuasively yet deferentially discussing the issues with other Justices. In the *Keyes* case, for example, Justice Brennan put together a majority in an important but controversial school desegregation case, even though Justice White had recused himself from the case and there seemed to be a strong likelihood that the remainder of the Court would be equally divided. Similarly, in *Frontiero* v. *Richardson*, Justice Brennan fashioned a plurality opinion (with Justice Stewart concurring in the judgment) declaring discrimination based on sex to be subject to the "strict scrutiny" test under the fourteenth amendment—a far-reaching decision that provided the basis for several subsequent Supreme Court cases (and numerous lower court cases) striking down sex-based classifications.

Justice Brennan's efforts and influence during the 1972 Term should not be measured, however, only by the cases that he authored for the Court that Term. He was substantially responsible for garnering a majority or for shaping the Court's opinions in a number of significant cases that Term in which he was not the principal author. He had a special influence and standing among other members of the Court, which seemed to be due not only to his renowned legal intellect and his ability to express himself, but also to his somewhat uncanny ability to sense the important issues in a case, to understand and acknowledge the positions of other Justices on an issue, and to build a consensus for his position when it seemed unlikely or even impossible that he could do so. He is, to say the least, a master tactician whose integrity and ability were never questioned and who had the respect of all of his colleagues, even those with whom he frequently disagreed.

That is not to say that Justice Brennan always got his way. On the contrary, he was frequently in the minority during the 1972 Term. Indeed, during that Term, Justice Brennan cast 122 dissenting votes—more than the total of his dissenting votes for the previous six Terms combined. Coupled with his dissenting votes that Term were at least twenty-seven major dissenting opinions, far more than the Justice had written in any of his sixteen previous Terms on the Court. Unquestionably, Justice Brennan's role on the Court changed significantly during the 1972 Term. He was now the spokesman and caretaker for ideological principles that had flourished during the Warren Court era but were now under attack by the newly constituted and generally more conservative Court.

Throughout it all, however, Justice Brennan held his ground, relentlessly championing the constitutional rights and freedoms of every person without regard for a person's socioeconomic standing or the unpopularity of a person's views. He viewed his work on the Court, I believe, as that of a public trustee appointed to protect and preserve the fundamental values upon which our system of government is based. He was determined not to betray that trust. When it was clear that he could not obtain a majority for his position, he would structure and write a dissenting or separate opinion that was designed to appeal to the conscience of the Court both then and in the future. Those dissenting or separate opinions—often prophetic as well as eloquent—were viewed by the Justice to be every bit as important as a majority opinion because they often tempered the views of the majority or served to remind the majority and lower courts of prior precedent and limiting legal principles.

It would be incorrect to leave you with the impression that my respect and admiration for Justice Brennan stem only from his enormous intellect, ability, and professional commitment. Perhaps more than anything else, Justice Brennan stood out in my mind during my year with him, and has continued to do so ever since, for his genuine warmth, openness, and friendliness with everyone who came in contact with him. Be it a stranger on the street, a law clerk, a security guard, or a member of Congress, Justice Brennan was and is always the same—friendly, engaging, and unassuming. Everyone he met, he treated with dignity and respect, always having time to exchange pleasantries and to offer a warm greeting. I never heard him utter a harsh word about anyone, even persons who criticized him or who said things about him that would cause rage in most people.

He would refer to a colleague as "Pal," he would cheerfully greet Court personnel by their first names or nicknames, he would refer to me and my two co-clerks as "his boys," and he affectionately referred to me as "Will." The zest and friendliness of Justice Brennan was then and continues to be now a veritable legend around the Court. And when I finished my clerkship with the Justice, I realized that I had learned from him much more than legal principles and lawyering skills; I also had learned from him how to be a better person. In my own dealings with people, I try to emulate his friendliness, respect, and courtesy for others. I try to follow his example of not reacting in anger when others are rude or spiteful toward me. I do not always succeed, but then few of us will ever become the person that Justice Brennan is.

As a Supreme Court Justice and as a man, Justice Brennan can be categorized, I believe, only in superlatives. During his tenure, he was probably the most influential member of the Court and was the architect or author of some of the Court's most important decisions of all time. For thirty-four years, Justice Brennan worked tirelessly and skillfully to ensure that every person in this country was afforded the full measure of the rights and freedoms to which he or she is entitled under the Constitution and federal laws. In his humble and unassuming way, he was the people's representative on the Court. His influence and accomplishments on the Court unquestionably will mark him as one of our greatest Supreme Court Justices. And whether we know it or not now, all of us will miss his presence on the Court.

Virginia A. Seitz considers her expectations when she began clerking for Justice Brennan in 1988, expectations that he, as her mentor, never failed to meet.

Recollections of Justice Brennan
Virginia A. Seitz

Every young lawyer who decides to clerk looks to his judge or her judge to be a mentor. We expect so much. We expect intellectual growth and development. We expect professional guidance. We expect everything from our judge. We expect help in answering the question: "What kind of a lawyer shall I be?" But we do not expect that the judge we clerk for will also help us answer the more important question: "What kind of person shall I be?"

Justice Brennan helped with all of those things by his example, his humanity, his humor, his humility. He showed me, like my parents had before him, what kind of a person we should aspire to be. And that is a gift beyond price.

In the mundane details of daily life in his chambers, Justice Brennan reveals substantial truths about himself. When I clerked for him, he was 81 years old and had been 30 years on the bench. By the time he arrived at the office each morning, 7:30 at the latest, he had already read the *New York Times* and the *Washington Post* and had ridden half an hour on his exercise bike. The hour and a half that followed he spent reviewing petitions for *certiorari* or briefs for the next sittings. At 9:00 o'clock, when his clerks straggled in, this man had already been working for four hours.

That was the time called "morning coffee" in his chambers where the business of the chambers was accomplished. The justice would pose particularly tricky questions from petitions for *certiorari*, or would dis-

84

cuss which way he was leaning in cases pending before the Court, and set his clerks one against the other and watch the fireworks. He would take a particularly outrageous position on some case and challenge you to talk him out of it. He would then, inevitably, at some point in the discussion say, "Didn't I write an opinion on that once?", turn around, pull a book off his shelf and open it to the exact page and the exact quote that answered precisely the legal issue being addressed at that time.

Equally inevitably, he would think of a story that would relate to one of the cases we were discussing. He would tell you about his first day at the Supreme Court when Earl Warren took him around to the lounge where all the justices were sitting. He walked in and Earl Warren tried to introduce him, but they were watching the World Series and said, "Shut up and sit down till the end of the inning."

Another great story he was fond of telling was when his former professor and colleague, Felix Frankfurter, rushed into his office after the first time Justice Brennan voted in Supreme Court cases and said, "You can't vote like that," and Brennan looked at him and said, "I can and did."

We all felt in those morning coffee sessions that we were in the presence of a great judge. But more importantly, with his unfailing warmth and affection and playfulness, we all knew we were in the presence of a wonderful and decent man.

We were not the only ones. He is the best-loved man in the building. The other justices recognize and appreciate his affability and charm. There was a famous clerk story on the clerk grapevine my year involving Justice Brennan. At a conference, the justices were discussing a case that had been argued that morning. One of the justices suggested that the result in the case was controlled by a case that had been decided in the 1960s. Another young justice erupted, "We can't follow that decision; its reasoning is spinach." The justices lapsed into an embarrassed silence, except for Justice Brennan, who laughed uproariously. "That's funny," he said to his colleague, slapping him on the back, "I wrote it." A somewhat embarrassed justice related this story to the clerks upon returning to chambers and said, "Thank God it was Justice Brennan; if it had been anyone else, I would have been in trouble for years."

It is not only the justices who feel Justice Brennan's warmth. The security detail at the Court is of a significant size, scattered in various parts of the building to assure that no one enters the justices' chambers.

As Justice Brennan makes his way through the hall, he greets all guards by name and asks about their families. He knows the name of everyone in the building. He stops to chat with the clerks and secretaries from all chambers. His warmth and interest in people knows no limits of rank. He is always most interested in whomever he is talking to at the moment.

A second example. While I was clerking for Justice Brennan, the father of my best friend died. My friend's mother came to stay with my friend, and I took them around the building to cheer her up. We met the justice in his chambers, and he recalled—I don't know how—that this was my friend whose father had died. He shooed my friend and me from the chambers and took her mother into his office. They emerged laughing a half an hour later. When I thanked him for his thoughtfulness, he laughed and told me that my friend's mother, who was a physicist, had been helping him with his upcoming speech about space law.

The man never ceases to amaze.

Finally, let me give you a backhanded compliment the justice once received. A tradition among law clerks at the Court is to take the other justices to lunch one at a time. When the very conservative law clerks of one very conservative justice took Justice Brennan to lunch, they considered him their arch-enemy. I asked one of them, upon his return, how it had gone. He paused, and then said a bit defensively, "Well, if everyone were as wonderful as Justice Brennan, his legal philosophy would work."

It seems to me that Justice Brennan is the embodiment of a successful person—not because he is a Supreme Court Justice, but because he is living a life entirely true to his own personal values. He is a living affirmation of the beauty, the value, and the joy of a life of service and integrity.

Now the supervising attorney of the Office of the Appellate Defender in New York City, E. Joshua Rosenkranz clerked for Justice Brennan during the 1987–88 Term. This reminiscence of the Justice—generous but not unrealistic in its praise, rich with admiration and humor—was originally published in Nova Law Review.

Dear Boss: A Law Clerk's Tribute to Justice Brennan

E. Joshua Rosenkranz

Dear Boss,

An unfamiliar voice on my answering machine was the first to tell me you retired. He claimed to be a booker from *Nightline* who wanted to ask a former law clerk some background questions about you. Bad joke, I thought. The next message, a commiserating friend bearing the same report, convinced me otherwise. Bad dream. Countless messages repeated the theme. Try as I might, I could not rouse myself. The harsh reality crept in: Bad news.

I did not return any of my numerous messages that day. As to Ted Koppel, he would understand that I would rather speak with his booker next time, when he bears good news. As to my friends and colleagues who offered empathy, I was grateful. But I doubted that they would understand how I felt, and I lacked the words and the energy to articulate it. It has taken me until now to assimilate the barrage of thoughts and emotions your retirement triggered. Even now I write with the disheartening caveat that my words could never do you justice. I pray only that they do not cross the line separating heartfelt homage from maudlin mush.

In the moments after I eased the telephone receiver into its cradle, I was puzzled not so much by your decision to retire as by my own profound sense of loss. I thought I had prepared myself for the news. At times, part of me even wished it would arrive already. After thirty-four years wedded to the Supreme Court—forty-one years to the bench—you deserve some time to yourself. And after seven years wedded to each other, Mary and you deserve some time together. So I would never begrudge you the rest you so richly deserve. Nevertheless, the news left me with a void. While I probably could not have articulated the loss precisely, I knew it was different from the loss that so many in the general public felt.

Like others, I worry about the future of the law. From any legal perspective, your retirement is a loss. The Court's liberal minority lost its anchor. The American people lost their most loyal and vocal advocate for equality, liberty, privacy, and justice. Every downtrodden individual in the country—the homeless, the needy, the victim of bigotry, the religiously oppressed, the political gadfly, the handicapped, the immigrant, the criminal defendant, the prisoner—lost a sympathetic ear. The Court lost whatever balance it had; you would no longer be there to defy all odds and whomp up an occasional astounding victory as if out of a top hat. Each of these losses is distressing.

As profound as these losses are, however, they are not the losses that I most lament. Perhaps that is because everyone else is so preoccupied with the survival of the Republic that my anxiety would be redundant. More likely, it is because I consider the hysteria exaggerated.

I share (or, more accurately, I inherited) your faith in the Court. I therefore have little fear that anyone could dismantle the jurisprudential fortress you built over a lifetime. You built it of durable stuff—compassion, justice, and eternal truths. The passage of time and the heat of debate have served only to temper it. The onslaught of eager new judicial personnel may fret your fortress's parapets, but will never penetrate its walls.

Nor am I among those who bemoan your retirement as if it squelched your dissenting voice. Even if you never utter another word of comment on the law (an unfathomable thought, indeed), your voice, immortalized in 140 volumes of United States Report, will continue to "soar with passion and ring with rhetoric." Like you, I am optimistic that your dissents of yesterday will become the next century's laws. You have penned much of the script that the Court will follow when it hands down edicts to my children.

So, you see, Boss, my confidence that the law and the Court will survive your departure is not so much a slight as it is a salute to the central role you have played.

Like everyone who has known you, I was saddened also by your acknowledgement that poor health forced you off the bench. It goes without saying that I feel your pain.

I confess that your submission opened up an emotion other than pure empathy, a feeling as disturbing as it was elusive. It seemed at first incongruous. Before I met you, I thought of you as a superhero—a warrior of boundless strength, undying commitment, limitless compassion, incisive intellect. You reinforced and deepened that impression with every contact we had. As infantile as it may seem (especially for one as irreverent as I), I was never willing to entertain the possibility that any harm could penetrate you. When you publicly acknowledged a weakness, I thought you would have to relinquish your superhero status.

That thought passed quickly though. You could still be my superhero without being superhuman. In fact, that made so much more sense. In the first place, you have always been more content to view yourself as a "flesh-and-blood human being[]" than as a "demigod[] to whom objective truth has been revealed." More importantly, it is your humanity, limitations and all, that makes you so worthy of admiration and emulation. Your personal victories are all the more awe inspiring when viewed in light of constraints you overcame to achieve them; the most extraordinary feat becomes unremarkable when the absence of obstacles preordains success. Similarly, I could never even aspire to emulate you without some sense that you and I suffer some of the same human constraints.

The sense of loss that struck me hardest and has lingered longest stems from something that none of the pundits or commentators, in all their hysteria, ever mentioned. Not that I can blame them for missing it. It derives from an experience they never had: Your retirement means the end of a line of Brennan law clerks.

I wonder whether you could ever fully appreciate how deeply you have touched each of us law clerks—109 in all. I trust that you could sense our love and admiration better than I am about to describe it.

I went to law school because I wanted to be Atticus Finch, Harper Lee's unflinchingly ethical and kindhearted lawyer who undertook the hopeless defense of a black laborer unjustly accused of raping a white woman. Law school taught me perhaps how to reason like a lawyer, but Atticus taught me what it means to be a lawyer.

When I joined your Chambers one year out of law school, you became my Atticus of the judiciary. I already knew how judges reason, but you taught me what it means to be a judge. Not until I saw you in action did I fully understand that the judge's final question in every case should be not, "is this logical?," but "is this right?" As you have so eloquently put it, "[s]ensitivity to one's intuitive and passionate responses, and awareness of the range of human experience, is . . . not only an inevitable but a desirable part of the judicial process, an aspect more to be nurtured than feared." You taught me that "the greatest threat to" liberties "is formal reason severed from the insights of passion." A judge "who operates on the basis of reason alone" can never adequately address "[w]hether the government treats its citizens with dignity," because such a judge cuts himself off "from the wellspring from which concepts such as dignity, decency, and fairness flow."

Your opinions are rife with illustrations of these principles. For me these principles come alive more in your approach to the death penalty than anywhere else. It should be no surprise to anyone that you were the first on the Court to argue that an execution is, under all circumstances, "cruel and unusual punishment." That proposition followed naturally from your conviction that everyone, "even the vilest criminal[,] remains a human being possessed of common human dignity," and that the state's "calculated killing of a human being" amounts to the most cynical "denial of the executed person's humanity."

You penned those words in 1972, fifteen years before my clerkship began. Yet the words, and the sentiments they carried, recurred more often during my year at the Court than anything else you wrote. Whenever a state has executed a human being, you have issued the same words, purporting to convey no more than the reaffirmation that you were "[a]dhering to [your] view." In the dark-eyed night, when most executions occurred, I often telephoned the Clerk's office to convey that you were filing "the standard dissent," as if there was something prosaic about it: Another death, another dissent.

There wasn't. The words remain the same, but each execution is a wrenching experience in your Chambers. Each execution sends another pang through your heart. Even though some find you "simply contrary, tiresome, or quixotic," you refuse to play any part in an injustice that so thoroughly hacks away at "common human dignity." Your repeated incantation in the face of majority will is your way of saying what Atticus captured in the precept, "before I can live with other folks I've got to live with myself. The one thing that doesn't abide by majority rule is a person's conscience." It is your own statement, "as an individual: 'here I draw the line.' "

You defend that line with the vigor and valor of a knight defending the king's palace. I learned this one day when I handed you a draft of a dissent from the Court's decision to deny a stay of execution. It was a particularly troublesome case. This indigent prisoner would not be facing execution if his court-appointed trial lawyer had been minimally competent. The last paragraph of my draft contained the most spirited attack that I had ever drafted. I said to you, "Boss, please focus closely on the last paragraph. I think it may cross the line." You took the draft with one hand and held my arm with the other and interrupted, "Josh, when it comes to state-sponsored death, there is no line."

We lost that one. The prisoner met his death on schedule at precisely 1:00 a.m. (midnight in Louisiana). At 1:45 a.m., I left my office. On my way home I gazed up at the inscription that capped the Court's towering columns: the facade of "Equal Justice Under Law."

The hypocrisy still burned in my mind the next morning, when I delivered the news to you. I asked you the same question Atticus's son asked after the jury of twelve white men returned a cowardly guilty verdict: "How could they do it, how could they?" Atticus's answer was: "I don't know, but they did it. They've done it before and they did it tonight and they'll do it again and when they do it—seems that only children weep."

Your response, eloquent in its silence, was at the same time disturbingly similar and comfortingly different. First, you held up five fingers, a gesture whose meaning we understood all too well: "Five justices have the power to do whatever they want. They've done it before and they did it last night and they'll do it again." Then you uncharacteristically turned away from me. As you did, I saw a tear in the corner of your eye. To this day, I am not sure why you tried to hide it from me. Didn't you realize that it meant everything to me to know that Atticus was partially wrong? Sometimes the children are not alone.

Remarkably, though, your tears are never bitter or prostrate. Through thick and thin, you retain your optimism that one day—and it will be "a great day for your country, [because] it will be a great day for our Constitution"—the Court will look back at the enormity of its mistake and adopt your view. That optimism, as much as your compassion and keen intellect have combined to make you a model judge.

As much as you taught me about being a judge, you taught me even more about being a human being.

My mind wanders to you often, more often these days than even when I first left those marble halls. The picture of you that usually comes to mind is not the picture one might expect. It is not the portrait that peers at me from the wall of my office, that robed figure who would look austere but for the sparkle in his eyes. It is not the image of you on the bench, listening intently to every twist of every argument, hanging on to every word of your colleagues' questions for the slightest hint of their inclination. It is not even the picture of you that I grew most accustomed to seeing: the Boss, dwarfed behind that enormous double desk that used to be Louis Brandeis', poring over an opinion.

The picture that comes to mind most often is this: You are talking to someone in the hallway or on the stairs—a guard, a gardener, a janitor. You pick up your previous conversation with him, and remember it as if he were your closest friend. You talk about him, and never about yourself. You use his name in every sentence. Or you call him, "Pal." You grasp onto his arm while talking, and you never let go as long as the conversation lasts. (We used to call it "taking the pulse." I would bet that each of your law clerks at some point dreamt up some inane topic to discuss with you, just to feel the assurance of your grip.) As you part, you reiterate how delighted you are to have seen him. And he believes that he has made your day just by talking to you. He feels that way not because you put on a good act, but because it is true.

That same tenderness permeates every one of your relationships, whether with friends, colleagues, family, or passing acquaintances. Your law clerks all felt it. I will never forget the first time I handed you a proposed draft of a dissent. I had spent weeks planning it, researching it, and writing it. In keeping with our routine, my three coclerks all tinkered with it before you laid eyes on it. You took the draft and exclaimed, "Oh, splendid, Josh. Thank you very, very much." To hear your tone, one would have thought I had just contributed profoundly to the law.

I am embarrassed to confess that, for a moment, you had me believing that was true. Just then something drew my eyes to the bookshelf to your left. The bottom three shelves were filled with those tired old books—probably 50 or so—with dusty red bindings. Each bore the same title: "The Opinions of Mr. Justice Brennan." The first one was dated 1956. As I turned to leave, my head still in the clouds, the absurdity hit me. You were thanking me, as if the opinion would never have been written but for me; as if the U.S. Reports would have had twenty-three blank pages under the caption, "BRENNAN, J., dissenting." You really meant it. But you had been authoring Supreme Court opinions without my help for six years longer than I had been alive.

Even so, no matter how many corrections you make, you return every draft, emblazoned with the word, "SPLENDID," followed by a battalion of exclamation points. (The running joke is, we can tell how much you really like a draft by counting the exclamation points. Any less than four is the Brennan equivalent of, "this sucks.")

Your gentleness and generosity to those around you is surpassed only by your graciousness. At the last clerk's reunion, one of my predecessors recounted a particularly telling illustration, with which we are all familiar. The only task, outside of our legal work, that you ever permitted us to perform for you was to prepare your coffee when we met with you each morning at 9:00 a.m. sharp. Like the Levites' offerings, it became a ritual that was passed down from one "Coffee Clerk" to the next. "Decaf, black, no sugar," was the formula. "Be sure it is very weak, like dishwater." Finally, "always check to see how much he drank, because he will never tell you if you've done it wrong."

There is a humorous, and equally telling, epilogue to this story. I was the designated Coffee Clerk among my generation of clerks. (The honor fell automatically to the only one of us who was unmarried and therefore had no claim of entitlement to be in bed at 7:30 a.m., when you arrived at the Court.) You polished off the cup on the first day. I congratulated myself heartily for mastering the technique, and painstakingly adhered to the same formula every morning for a year with equally satisfying results.

It was not until two years later that I learned the truth, Boss. The revelation came from your last Coffee Clerk. As she tells it, one morning the whole group went down to the cafeteria because the Chamber coffee machine was on the blink. She noticed you serving yourself undiluted decaf, and adding milk and sugar. Only through rigorous cross-examination did she extract your confession that this was how you have always preferred your coffee. As an avid coffee drinker, I am incredulous at the grace of a man who could tolerate years of drinking our tepid concoction just to avoid any possibility of embarrassing us.

All these reminiscences bring me back to a comment that a friend made not too long ago. It referred to the time you, Mary, and I went out to dinner in Georgetown. We were with close friends, so I abandoned the formality that I might have displayed in public, and called you, "Boss"—like we all did in Chambers—rather than "Justice." Months later, one of our dinner companions commented to me that the title sounded too informal, even disrespectful. I explained that he could not have been further from the truth: "Boss" is a term of endearment, a way of expressing both our love and our deep admiration for you. "Boss" evokes all those wonderful images of you—on the bench delivering opinions brimming with passion and dissents rife with optimism; behind your massive desk, scrawling, "Splendid," on a clerk's draft; listening patiently to an admiring acquaintance; advising and caring for your clerks. At least eleven other people in the building could be called "Justice," but no one else merits the title, "Boss."

Just after you resigned, *The New York Times* interviewed a would-be law clerk, who no longer had a Brennan clerkship to complete her legal education. Her closing thought was this: "His clerks called him 'Boss' and I don't think I ever will. I felt kind of sad that that would never happen." I suspect she could not have appreciated the full significance of her words.

I feel privileged to be among the group who will always call you "Boss." I lament the loss for all those would-be law clerks over the years who will not have the chance.

Part II

The Jurisprudence of Justice William J. Brennan, Jr.

Justice William J. Brennan, Jr., served on the U.S. Supreme Court from 1956 to 1990; few justices in our history have contributed as much to the development of constitutional law as has Brennan. Perhaps his three most important opinions for the Court were *New York Times* v. *Sullivan,* which established the modern law of freedom of speech and press; *Baker* v. *Carr,* which enabled the Court to require the reapportionment of state legislatures according to the principle of ''one man, one vote''; and *Goldberg* v. *Kelly,* which extended due process to protect an individual from being cut off government benefits without a hearing. All of these decisions were written in the 1960s during the era of Chief Justice Earl Warren. In those years, Brennan often found himself in the Court's center, rejecting the view of Justices Black and Douglas, which gave absolute protection to free speech, as well as that of Justices Frankfurter and Harlan, which typically rejected the individual's constitutional claim in favor of the state.

On the Supreme Court, Justice Brennan was able to forge majorities for positions he favored, even when it appeared there would not be four other votes for those positions. And when he found he could no longer support views he had once held, he corrected himself, as shown by his voting to reverse his 1957 *Roth* decision in which he held obscene speech was unprotected by the Constitution. Off the Court, in speeches and articles, he argued effectively for nurturing liberty that was under attack by antilibertarian forces in the executive branch and the Supreme Court:

> [T]here exists in modern America the necessity for protecting all of us from arbitrary action by governments more powerful and more pervasive than any in our ancestors' time. Only if the amendments are construed to preserve their fundamental policies will they ensure the maintenance of our constitutional structure of government for a free society.[1]

Whereas many justices who passionately believe in their vision of the Constitution are able to articulate those views forcefully only in individual dissenting or concurring opinions, Brennan was able to craft Court majorities, thereby ensuring that his views became the law of the Constitution rather than merely an opinion of an individual justice. Perhaps the most remarkable example of Brennan's consensus-building was the last opinion he wrote for the Court, *Metro Broadcasting, Inc., v. FCC*.[2] The case involved the constitutionality of an affirmative action program undertaken by the Federal Communications Commission. Such affirmative action plans had been disapproved by the Court the previous year in *Richmond* v. *J. A. Croson Co.* Brennan was able to distinguish the *Croson* case on the grounds it involved an affirmative action plan established by local government, while the FCC case involved affirmative action by the federal government, which was not subject to the same restrictions under the Constitution. That distinction persuaded Justices White and Stevens to switch their votes from *Croson* and join Brennan's opinion in *Metro Broadcasting*. Brennan recognized that the Supreme Court is a collegial institution. No matter how firm an individual justice is in the rightness of his or her beliefs, Brennan realized the shortsightedness of clinging stubbornly to one's views without accommodating, to the extent possible, the ideas of other justices. "After

---

1. Brennan, "State Constitutions and the Protection of Individual Rights," 90 *Harv. L. Rev.* 489, 495 (1977).
2. 497 U.S. 547 (1990).

all, collegiality *is* important; unanimity *does* have value; feelings *must* be respected.''[3]

The Supreme Court that Brennan joined in 1956 was hospitable to his views. As he himself observed, he wrote sixteen opinions that first year on the Court, not one of them a dissent, while in the 1984 Term he wrote fifty-six opinions, forty-two of which were dissents. He believed strongly in the value of dissent when that was necessary:

> [T]he obligation that all of us, as American citizens have, and that judges, as adjudicators, particularly feel, is to speak up when we are convinced that the fundamental law of our Constitution requires a given result. I cannot believe that this is a controversial statement. The right to dissent is one of the great and cherished freedoms that we enjoy by reason of the excellent accident of our American births. [4]

He believed that the force of reasoned argument expressed through his countless dissenting opinions would ultimately pervail, and this faith explains, perhaps, why he rarely despaired even though, during the 1970s and 1980s, his views were typically in the minority on the Court. Brennan routinely dissented from the Court's actions upholding obscenity convictions and death sentences, knowing his dissents would not cause the Court to change its mind. He took his inspiration from the dissent of the first Justice Harlan in *Plessy* v. *Ferguson,* in which the majority held that the separate but equal doctrine did not violate the Constitution. Harlan's dissent, wrote Brennan, ''is the quintessential voice crying in the wilderness.''

He stood alone; not a single other justice joined him.

> In his appeal to the future, he transcended, without slighting, mechanical legal analysis; he sought to announce fundamental constitutional truths as well. He spoke not only to his peers, but to his society, and, more important, across time to later generations. He was, in this

3. Brennan, "In Defense of Dissents," 37 *Hastings L.J.* 427, 429 (1986).
4. Id. at 438.

sense, a secular prophet, and we continue, long after *Plessy* and *Brown,* to benefit from his wisdom and courage. [5]

Brennan made an important contribution toward furthering the development of individual rights by recognizing and encouraging a trend in state courts to construe their constitutional provisions expansively. In an article he wrote in 1977, "State Constitutions and the Protection of Individual Rights,"[6] he wondered why state courts in the 1970s were emphasizing rights under their constitutions rather than the U.S. Constitution. He surmised that the reason for this development was that "these state courts discern, and disagree with, a trend in recent opinions of the U.S. Supreme Court to pull back from, or at least suspend for the time being" vigorous protection of individual rights under the U.S. Constitution. [7]

One of Brennan's major efforts on the Court was to bring disfavored minorities and the politically powerless into the mainstream of American life. He played a major part in the political empowerment of the cities and suburbs through his "one-man, one-vote" decisions. To achieve a similar result in the area of sex discrimination, he had to lose the battle to win the war. In 1973 he wrote an opinion in *Frontiero* v. *Richardson* for four members of the Court in which he said that women, like blacks, are deserving of the Constitution's most stringent protection when laws discriminate against them. Lacking a fifth vote to make a majority, he revisited the question in 1976 of how much scrutiny is to be given to laws that classify on the basis of sex, and this time, by lowering a notch the degree of scrutiny to which sex-based classifications are entitled, he got six votes for treating sex-based laws as deserving of "intermediate" scrutiny.[8]

During the 1980s, many governmental officials, both on and off the Court, argued for a more modest role for the Court and the Constitution. For example, Justice Antonin Scalia narrowly read the protections of the Bill of Rights and criticized Justice Brennan's willingness to strike down state laws on the grounds they interfered with a person's "liberty" interests protected by the due process clauses of the Fifth and Fourteenth amendments. For Scalia, unless history is clear that a partic-

---

5. Id. at 431–32.
6. 90 *Harv. L. Rev.* at 489.
7. Id. at 495.
8. *Craig* v. *Boren,* 429 U.S. 190 (1976).

ular state practice claimed to violate due process was disapproved by the framers of the Constitution and the amendments, the individual must turn to legislatures for protection, not Supreme Court justices.

In a spirited debate with Justice Scalia in the case of *Michael H.* v. *Gerald D.,* handed down one year prior to Justice Brennan's retirement, Brennan took issue with Scalia's narrow view of due process, which rejected a father's due process claim of parental rights over his illegitimate child.[9]

[Justice Scalia] ignores the kind of society in which our Constitution exists. We are not an assimilative, homogenous society, but a facilitative, pluralistic one, in which we must be willing to abide someone else's unfamiliar or even repellent practice because the same tolerant impulse protects our own idiosyncracies. In a community such as ours, "liberty" must include the freedom not to conform. [Justice Scalia] today squashes this freedom. . . . The document that he construes is unfamiliar to me. It is not the living charter that I have taken to be our Constitution; it is instead a stagnant, archaic hidebound document steeped in the prejudices and superstitions of a time long past. *This* Constitution does not recognize that times change. I cannot accept an interpretive method that does such violence to the charter that I am bound by oath to uphold.

Off the Court, Justice Brennan's views were often criticized by officials in the executive branch, particularly Attorney General Edwin Meese, who criticized judges such as Brennan for ignoring the framers' intent and substituting their own values for that of the Constitution's. To such critics, Brennan spoke out in public defense of his constitutional jurisprudence at a speech at Georgetown University School of Law:

There are those who find legitimacy in fidelity to what they call "the intentions of the framers." In its most doctrinaire incarnation, this view demands that Justices discern exactly what the framers thought about the question under consideration and simply follow that intention in resolving the case before them. It is a view that feigns self-

9. The question involved in the case was whether the father of a child born while the mother was married to, and living with, another man, had any rights of visitation under the Constitution.

effacing deference to the specific judgments of those who forged our original social compact. But in truth, it is little more than arrogance cloaked as humility. It is arrogant to pretend that from our vantage we can gauge accurately the intent of the framers on application of principle to specific, contemporary questions. Apart from the problematic nature of the sources, our distance of two centuries cannot but work as a prism refracting all we perceive.

One who attempts to describe Justice Brennan's jurisprudence would do well to follow the remarks Brennan made on the occasion of the centennial celebration of Justice Hugo Black: It is "his own opinions and writings that so clearly tell us his constitutional faith. It is in these interpretations, not in my or other approaches, that one discerns the extraordinary nature of this man."[10] And the words he used on the occasion of the retirement of another justice he greatly admired, William O. Douglas, apply equally well to the insights of William J. Brennan, Jr.: "[H]is truly great record epitomized the truth that great judges are also great teachers. No voice has more powerfully and lucidly articulated for all Americans the values we must protect and preserve for freedom to live."[11]

Constitutional Interpretation

The genius of the Constitution resides not in any static meaning that it had in a world that is dead and gone, but in its adaptability to interpretations of its great principles that cope with current problems and current needs.[12]

Justice Brennan firmly believed that the intent of the framers with respect to constitutional interpretation was for justices to make the Constitution relevant to present-day problems. The most pressing problem facing the modern Court, Brennan felt, was not the allocation of powers between the state and federal governments, which had been the Court's chief concern during the 1930s and before. Instead,

---

10. Brennan, "Remarks on the Occasion of the Justice Hugo L. Black Centennial," 38 *Ala. L. Rev.* 223 (1987).

11. Brennan, "Dedication to William O. Douglas," 55 *Wash. Law. Rev.* 283, 284 (1980).

12. Brennan, "Constitutional Adjudication," 40 *Notre Dame Law.* 559, 568 (1965).

"the chief subject of the cases coming to the Court has concerned the relationship of the individual with government—state and federal—that is, with the interpretation and application of the limitations upon governmental power embodied primarily in the Bill of Rights."[13] Brennan relished the challenge of refereeing disputes between the individual and the government. For him, the law was to be found by seeking "justice" rather than relying on "fine-spun technicalities and abstract rules."[14]

Because the constitutional text is often ambiguous, justices are required to interpret it. "The encounter with the constitutional text has been, in many senses," said Brennan, "my life's work."[15] Twenty years before he voiced his disagreement with Attorney General Meese and Justice Scalia over their belief that the Constitution could be interpreted by determining the "original intent" of the framers, Justice Brennan was developing a different philosophy of constitutional interpretation:

[W]e must keep in mind that while the words of the Constitution are binding, their application to specific problems is not often easy. For the Founding Fathers knew better than to pin down their descendants too closely. Enduring principles rather than petty details were what they sought to write down. Thus it is that the Constitution does not take the form of a litany of specifics. There are therefore very few cases where the constitutional answers are clear, all one way or all the other.[16]

Brennan understood the appeal of a jurisprudence of original intent that looked to historical practices to determine the meaning of the Constitution:

No doubt it is easier for judges to apply specific and simple legal rules than to struggle first to interpret and then to apply broadly worded principles to circumstances that perhaps were not contemplated when those principles were first articulated. Indeed, if it were possible to find answers to all constitutional questions by reference

---

13. Id. at 560.
14. Id. at 563.
15. Brennan, "The Constitution of the United States: Contemporary Ratification" (speech given at Georgetown University School of Law, October 12, 1985).
16. Supra note 20 at 265.

to historical practices, we would not need judges. Courts could be staffed by professional historians who could be instructed to compile a comprehensive master list of life in 1791. Cases could be decided based on whether a challenged practice or rule or procedure could be located on that great list. If the historians worked hard enough, they could "solve" constitutional law for now and for all time.[17]

However, he did not believe this was possible nor, even though easier, that it was the correct approach: "The framers surely understood that judging would not be easy or straightforward: No doubt that is why they took such great pains to ensure the independence of [federal] judges."[18]

It was not just the difficulty of determining the intent of the framers that caused Brennan to reject original intent as the sole legitimate way of interpreting the Constitution; he also believed that better results would be achieved by letting sitting justices determine the meaning of the Constitution in their times:

> The constant for Americans, for our ancestors, for ourselves, and we hope for future generations, is our commitment to the constitutional ideal of libertarian dignity protected through law . . . Justices yet to sit, like their predecessors, are destined to labor earnestly in that endeavor—we hope with wisdom—to reconcile the complex realities of their times with the principles which mark a free people.[19]

Critics of Brennan's approach claimed that it was result-oriented; Brennan responded that the original-intent doctrine was not value-neutral, since the consequence of applying that doctrine almost always guarantees that the constitutional right asserted by the individual would be rejected; only in the rare case can it be said that the framers specifically intended that a particular practice be banned, since most cases involve practices that were not even contemplated by the framers, such as wiretapping, banning birth control devices, etc.

It is in determining the meaning of due process that Brennan's ap-

---

17. Brennan, "Constitutional Adjudication and the Death Penalty: A View from the Court," 100 *Harv. L. Rev.* 313, 326 (1986) (the 1986 Oliver Wendell Holmes, Jr., Lecture, Harvard Law School, September 5, 1986).

18. Id.

19. Supra note 20 at 569.

proach was most at odds with the advocates of original intent. For Brennan, there can be no "static solution" to determine the meaning of due process.

> Each age must seek its own way to the unstable balance of those qualities that make us human, and must contend anew with the questions of power and accountability with which the Constitution is concerned. If we progress, it is only because we are sensitive to the complexity of these tasks and do not take refuge in the illusion of rational certainty.[20]

Although Brennan's critics claimed that his approach ignores the text of the Constitution and substitutes the subjective views of the individual justice, Brennan strongly believed that it was essential to have a written document:

> Without a textual anchor for their decisions, judges would have to rely on some theory of natural right, or some allegedly shared standard of the end and limits of government, to strike out invasive legislation. But an appeal to normative ideals that lack any mooring in the written law—or in common law that has so solid a foothold as to possess the same stature—would in societies like ours be suspect, because it would represent so profound an aberration from majoritarian principles. A judge armed only with pure reason could not stand against a scared or frenzied mob. Few would dare it, and those few who did would likely be swept aside.[21]

Furthermore, Brennan believed that a text was necessary to rein in the otherwise unbounded discretion of a judge, reminiscent of Judge Learned Hand's criticism of rule by a Court made up of Platonic Guardians.

Summing up his philosophy in a tribute to Justice Black, Brennan said: "You may, with good reason, believe that I espouse an evolutionary concept of the Constitution. It postulates that while a thing may not be within the letter of the Constitution, yet it may be within the Consti-

---

20. Brennan, "Reason, Passion, and the 'Progress of the Law,' " 10 *Cardozo L. Rev.* 3 (1988).

21. Brennan, "Why Have a Bill of Rights?" 9 *Oxford J. Legal Stud.* 425, 432 (1989).

tution and within the intention of the makers because within the spirit and purpose of the great Charter.''

In addition to opposing the doctrine of original intent, Brennan rejected the concept of federalism as defined by justices who used it to limit the power of federal courts to protect individual rights out of respect for the states. In the 1950s and '60s, Justices Frankfurter and Harlan consistently relied on this concept to argue that the Bill of Rights should not apply as rigorously to the states as to the federal government. For Brennan, federalism meant something else:

> [T]o deny the States the power to impair a fundamental constitutional right is not to increase federal power but to limit the power of both federal and state governments in favor of safeguarding the fundamental rights and liberties of the individual. This, I think, promote rather than undermines the basic policy of avoiding excess concentration of power in government, federal or state, which underlies our concepts of federalism.[22]

Critics of Brennan's constitutional philosophy often point out that the Court's decision to find a state law unconstitutional is profoundly undemocratic, since a majority of unelected, lifetime-appointed justices on the U.S. Supreme Court are invalidating the joint action of a democratically elected state legislature and governor. Therefore, such Supreme Court action should be undertaken with great restraint. Those critics are even more concerned when the Court is asked to intervene in the political process, such as reapportionment. In his dissent from Brennan's opinion in *Baker* v. *Carr,* the first case that held that state legislative reapportionment could be challenged in federal court, Justice Harlan sharply criticized the Court's willingness to intrude:

> Those observers of the Court who see it primarily as the last refuge for correction of all inequality or injustice, no matter what its nature or source, will no doubt applaud this decision and its break with the past. Those who consider that continuing national respect for the Court's authority depends in large measure upon its wise exercise of

---

22. Brennan, "Extension of the Bill of Rights to the States," 34 *J. Urb. L.* 11, 23–24 (1966).

self-restraint and discipline in constitutional adjudication, will view the decision with deep concern.[23]

Brennan defended the reapportionment decisions as necessary to bring about equal protection of the laws: "Our decisions in the reapportionment cases have enforced this guarantee and the result should be, not the return of a discredited judicial intrusion into the field of political judgment, but a more effective operation of the processes by which political judgments are reached."[24] In short, the Court's decisions actually enhanced, rather than cut back on, majority rule.

To those who believe that the Bill of Rights as a whole is counter-majoritarian and an affront to democracy, Brennan disagreed: "It is simply a reasonable form of collective self-restraint—one which even those who often find themselves in the majority on issues that most matter to them can unreservedly endorse. There is nothing unusual to have bounds on official action and have the judiciary responsible for determining their reach."[25]

As much as he advocated judicial involvement where the state threatened individual liberty and dignity, he strongly opposed judicial involvement when sought by the state or powerful private interests who had other ways of having their voices heard. Brennan's views were greatly influenced by the Supreme Court's actions in the early 1900s, much criticized in subsequent years, striking down state and federal economic legislation that attempted to strengthen rights of workers through minimum wage and maximum hours laws, set up social insurance programs, protect unionization, etc. Such actions led President Franklin D. Roosevelt to threaten to pack the Court with justices who would sustain such legislation. Brennan believed the Court should not return to those days when the Constitution was used to strike down such economic regulations: "Constitutional adjudication now leaves the States the widest latitude to deal with the dynamics of social and economic change in seeking to satisfy their needs and further their progress."[26] Rather, the Court should become actively involved only when

---

23. *Baker* v. *Carr,* 369 U.S. 186, 339–40 (1962) (dissenting opinion).
24. Brennan, "Some Aspects of Federalism," 39 *N.Y.U.L. Rev.* 945, 955 (1964) (address to Conference of Chief Justices, New York, August 7, 1964).
25. Brennan, "Why Have a Bill of Rights?," 9 *Oxford J. Legal Stud.* 425, 434 (1989).
26. 39 *N.Y.U. L. Rev.* 945 at 954.

individuals who are without clout in the legislatures seek the Court's assistance. Examples of such individuals, spelled out in the famous 1938 Supreme Court case *United States* v. *Carolene Prods. Co.,*[27] are members of "discrete" and "insular" minorities.

Thus when the Court used the contract clause of the Constitution to protect investors in governmental bonds by striking down legislation that attempted to modify the terms of those bonds, Brennan dissented. He observed that the modern Court had been giving the states wide latitude in regulating property rights under the various clauses of the Constitution concerned with private property—the taking and the due process clauses of the Fifth Amendment and the contract clause of the Constitution. Brennan believed that bondholders could protect themselves in the bond marketplace by refusing to deal with states that modified their contracts. As a sophisticated investor, the bondholder "is the paradigm of a litigant who is neither 'discrete' nor 'insular' in appealing for this Court's time or protection."[28] He ended his dissent with a reminder of what happened in the 1930s:

> [T]his Court should have learned long ago that the Constitution—be it through the contract or due process clause—can actively intrude into such economic and policy matters only if my brethren are pre- pared to bear enormous institutional and social costs. Because I con- sider the potential dangers of such judicial interference to be intolerable, I dissent. [29]

In 1976 the Court used the Tenth Amendment—the so-called state's rights amendment—to invalidate a federal law enacted pursuant to Con- gress's commerce power. The law, which regulated the wages and hours of state employees, was found to be unconstitutional because it inter- fered with the sovereign rights of the states and therefore inconsistent with federalism. Brennan again filed an angry dissent. "Judicial restraint in this area merely recognizes that the political branches of our govern- ment are structured to protect the interest of the states, as well as the nation as a whole, and that the states are fully able to protect their own

---

27. 304 U.S. 144, 144 n. 4 (1938).
28. *U.S. Trust Co.* v. New Jersey, 431 U.S. 1, 62 n. 18 (1977).
29. Id. at 62.

interests" in Congress.[30] Brennan could not resist pointing out that "my brethren frequently remand powerless individuals to the political process" by denying them access to court using various judicially created doctrines. Here, in contrast, the states,

> entities with perhaps the greatest representation in the political process, have lost a legislative battle, but when they enter the courts and repeat the arguments made in the political branches, the Court welcomes them with open arms, embraces their political cause, and overrides Congress's political decision.[31]

Perhaps it was the force of these two dissents that caused the Court to retreat from these positions in future years: the Tenth Amendment case was overruled in 1985, and the Court has largely ignored the contract clause case.

Brennan has criticized the Court when it has usurped what he viewed as Congress's prerogative to legislate. In one case, a negligence suit was brought against the company that built helicopters for the United States, by the father of a Marine helicopter pilot who drowned when he was unable to escape from a Marine helicopter he was flying that had crashed in the ocean. The majority of the Court created a defense of immunity for government contractors who negligently designed equipment for the government, rejecting Brennan's argument in dissent that Congress had refused to enact such a defense by statute.

> Were I a legislator, I would probably vote against any law absolving multibillion-dollar private enterprises from answering for their tragic mistakes. . . . Some of my colleagues here would evidently vote otherwise (as they have here), but that should not matter here. We are judges, not legislators, and the vote is not ours to make.[32]

The typical result of the application of the doctrines of original intent and federalism as described above is that the Court rejects the claims of individuals arguing for constitutional protection. One might have assumed that Brennan, who opposed those doctrines, would embrace a

---

30. *National League of Cities* v. *Usery*, 426 U.S. 833, 876 (1976).
31. 426 U.S. at 878–79 n. 14.
32. *Boyle* v. *United Technologies Corp.*, 487 U.S. 500, 531 (1988).

jurisprudence that gave complete protection to claims of constitutional right. Yet he never joined Justices Black and Douglas, who would give absolute protection to such constitutional claims as freedom of speech, without regard for the reasons why the state might validly have for suppressing speech. Brennan's position can be described as one that was weighted heavily in favor of the individual, but in those rare cir-cumstances where the state had compelling reasons for overriding the individual's constitutional rights, the state could prevail.

Although Brennan did not support the absolutist position, his tributes to Black and Douglas reveal that the degree of disagreement with their approach was slight compared to his feelings about original intent and the federalism of Harlan and Frankfurter. Said Brennan of Black, "I expect most would say we were quite different, although as often as not we agreed on result in the cases."[33] Black also recognized that despite their different approaches to constitutional interpretation, they were basically on the same side. For example, in the case of *New York Times* v. *Sullivan,* Brennan's majority opinion gave First Amendment protection for the first time to defamatory speech, but not the absolute protection that Black and Douglas argued for in their dissent. Brennan wrote that shortly after the *Times* case, Black sent him the following note: "You know, of course, that despite my position and what I wrote, I think that the *Times* case is bound to be a very long step toward preserving the right to communicate ideas."[34]

Because Black was so opposed to the judiciary's balancing of the interests of the individual versus the state on the grounds that the fram-ers already did that balancing, it has been argued that Black was a supporter of original intent. Brennan disagreed:

> [Black] wasn't an adherent of the doctrine of original intent currently being debated, at least he was not an adherent to that doctrine in its most doctrinaire incarnation which, as I understand it, would have the justices accept that the framers had sufficient specific constitutional intentions that today's court need only locate them and apply them [to today's problems].[35]

---

33. Brennan, "Remarks on the Occasion of the Justice Hugo L. Black Centennial," 38 *Ala. L. Rev.* 223, 226 (1987).
34. Id. at 233.
35. Id. at 224.

If he rejected absolutism, original intent, and his colleagues' brand of federalism, what general principles animated Brennan? Perhaps the best summary of Brennan's approach to constitutional interpretation can be found in his tribute to Earl Warren, with whom Brennan served for thirteen of the sixteen years Warren was chief justice:

> His concern with fairness was also the hallmark of his jurisprudence. People were his concern, especially ordinary people—the disadvantaged, the downtrodden, the poor, the friendless. . . . He strongly believed that individual human dignity was a primary value fostered and protected by the Constitution.[36]

Access to the Federal Courts

While serving on the Warren Court, Brennan wrote several important opinions that opened the federal courthouse doors to persons asserting constitutional claims. In the 1970s and '80s he wrote numerous dissents chiding the majority for refusing to hear such claims. Even though the issues—standing, habeas corpus, abstention, etc.—seem technical and dry, Brennan's dissents were as passionate as those that dealt with substantive constitutional law matters such as free speech, the death penalty, and the rights of criminal suspects. Brennan believed strongly in the obligation of the federal courts to hear the claims of those left outside the political mainstream. Article III of the Constitution requires that federal judges be appointed to their jobs for life with salaries that cannot be reduced, to make them independent of the political branches of government. Brennan wrote of additional reasons why the framers of the Constitution included these provisions:

> The independence from political forces that they guarantee helps to promote public confidence in judicial determinations. . . . The security that they provide to members of the Judicial Branch helps to attract well-qualified persons to the federal bench. . . . The guarantee of life tenure insulates the individual judge from improper influences not

---

36. Brennan, "Chief Justice Warren," 88 *Harv. L. Rev.* 1 (1974).

only by other branches but by colleagues as well, and thus promotes judicial individualism.[37]

The majority of his colleagues was more willing to let Congress give judicial business to non-Article III judges, prompting Brennan to dissent in a 1986 case:

Our Constitution unambiguously enunciates a fundamental princi- ple—that the judicial power of the United States be reposed in an independent judiciary. It is our obligation zealously to guard that independence so that our tripartite system of government remains strong and that individuals continue to be protected against decision- makers subject to majoritarian pressures.[38]

Court decisions that denied access to federal courts to persons seeking relief meant, to Brennan, that they would be relegated to decisionmakers without the independence and expertise of federal courts—for example, state courts or federal agencies—or, worse, be left without anyplace to go for redress. No justice in our history has argued more forcefully for the necessity of opening the federal courthouse doors to enforce effec- tively the promises of the Constitution.

Judicially Created Doctrines

Even though a law might be unconstitutional, it may not be able to be challenged in federal court. For example, the dissenters in *Baker* v. *Carr* believed that challenges to malapportioned state legislatures pres- ent "political questions" that are nonjusticiable—that is, questions that federal courts have no power to remedy. Any remedy must be sought elsewhere—in the state courts or state legislatures; or in Congress, which is the branch of the federal government the Constitution entrusts to enforce the guaranty clause, the provision of the Constitution guaran- teeing every state a republican form of government. Although Brennan agreed that the guaranty clause could not be the basis for a federal

---

37. *Northern Pipeline Constr. Co.* v. *Marathon Pipe Line Co.,* 458 U.S. 50, 60 n. 10 (1982).
38. *CFTC* v. *Schor,* 478 U.S. 833, 867 (1986).

court remedy in a reapportionment suit, he found that the equal protection clause could be the basis for such a suit.

Baker v. *Carr* is not only one of Brennan's most important opinions but it is probably the most important case ever decided on the meaning of a "political question."

> Prominent on the surface of any case held to involve a political question is found a textually demonstrable constitutional commitment of the issue to a coordinate political department; or a lack of judicially discoverable and manageable standards for resolving it; or the impossibility of deciding without an initial policy determination of a kind clearly for nonjudicial discretion; or the impossibility of a court's undertaking independent resolution without expressing lack of the respect due coordinate branches of government; or an unusual need for unquestioning adherence to a political decision already made; or the potentiality of embarrassment from multifarious pronouncements by various departments on one question.[39]

The fact, said Brennan, that the court was asked to decide a "political case" did not make it a "political question." He distinguished previous cases decided by the Court involving the political question doctrine as presenting disputes between branches of the federal government—that is, problems of separation of powers. *Baker,* however, involved federal courts and state legislatures and therefore raised no separation-of-powers problems. Further, noted Brennan, there are judicially manageable standards under the equal protection clause, standards lacking if the case were brought under the guaranty clause, which is why previous cases had treated guaranty clause cases as raising nonjusticiable political questions.

As in *Baker,* justices such as Brennan, who believed in broad access to federal courts to litigate federal constitutional clashes, frequently clashed with justices such as Frankfurter and Harlan, who believed that the Court's legitimacy was endangered unless the Court used great self-restraint in deciding constitutional questions. The result of a refusal to hear a case was not a finding on the merits of the constitutional question but rather that the federal court was not the place for the case to be heard. It is therefore a less controversial decision than finding for—or

---

39. *Baker* v. *Carr,* 369 U.S. 186, 217 (1962).

against—the constitutional claim, since the issue could be raised elsewhere, perhaps even in federal court at a more appropriate time. For
the litigant who is turned away from court, however, the effect of the
decision may well be the same as the loss of the claim on the merits.
Brennan recognized the effect of the denial of standing when he wrote,
"The drafters of the Bill of Rights surely intended that the particular
beneficiaries of their legacy should enjoy rights legally enforceable in
courts of law."[40]

Early in his career, there were indications that Brennan would favor
wide access to judicial resolution of disputes. While Brennan served on
the New Jersey Supreme Court, he was concerned with efficient judicial
administration and was a great admirer of that court's chief justice,
Arthur Vanderbilt, a pioneer in judicial administration. During his first
year on the U.S. Supreme Court, Brennan spoke to the St. Thomas More
Society, noting that More realized "that the spirit of justice requires a
prompt hearing and settlement of suits; otherwise injustice is perpetu-
ated and aggravated."[41] The Warren Court that Brennan joined was
friendly to those seeking to gain access to the federal courts, with no
better example than Brennan's decision in *Baker* v. *Carr*. But the
Court's frequent posting of a "Do Not Enter" sign on the door of the
federal courthouse in the 1970s and '80s prompted many spirited dissents from Brennan.

Although the source of the political question doctrine was separation
of powers, most of the doctrines the Court developed to keep cases out
of federal court stem from the wording of the Constitution's Article III,
which deals with the federal courts, including the Supreme Court. Article III states that the federal judicial power shall extend to "cases"
and "controversies." Those words suggest that federal courts can only
resolve issues in the context of an adversarial contest, with a plaintiff
who has a real injury, and a defendant against whom the court can
enter a remedy. Out of these requirements developed the following
doctrines: standing—the plaintiff must be actually injured; ripeness—
the issues must be ready for resolution now rather than at some later
time; mootness—the case must be alive during all stages of the litigation. From the outset of our constitutional history, it was held that

---

40. *Valley Forge College* v. *Americans United,* 454 U.S. 464, 494 (1982).
41. Brennan, "Thomas More—Saint and Judge," 4 *Catholic Lawyer* 162 (1958)
(address, annual meeting, St. Thomas More Society, May 23, 1957, Washington, D.C.).

federal courts may not issue "advisory opinions"; thus, the Supreme Court will not answer questions from Congress or the president concerning the constitutionality of proposed action.

Although there is no real dispute among the justices about the need for these doctrines in the abstract, in a particular case there is much disagreement whether the plaintiff is sufficiently injured, whether the issues are ripe enough, etc. And, in general, the lineup of the justices is predictable based on their judicial philosophy: Brennan typically wanted to hear the constitutional claims of individuals, while justices such as Harlan, Frankfurter, and Powell wanted less federal court intrusion. The majority opinions of the Court that denied access to the federal courts did not usually discuss the merits of the constitutional claims; the dissenters would often accuse the majority of hostility to those claims as the reason for the majority's action.

In *Baker* v. *Carr* in 1962, Brennan set forth what has proven to be the most common definition of standing: Has the party seeking relief "alleged such a personal stake in the outcome of the controversy as to assure that concrete adverseness which sharpens the presentation of issues upon which the court so largely depends for illumination of difficult constitutional questions?"[42] As long as there is injury in fact alleged in good faith, Brennan would find standing. He applied the same injury-in-fact test in cases challenging administrative action based on nonconstitutional grounds, disagreeing with the majority's additional standing requirements in such cases.[43]

Brennan was willing to grant standing to persons whose injuries were far removed from the typical cases of economic losses. For example, he dissented from the Court's refusal to grant standing to litigants who claimed the right to have the budget of the Central Intelligence Agency published pursuant to the Constitution's requirement of the publication of the receipt and expenditure "of all public money."[44] He also would grant standing to challenge members of Congress who hold positions in the Reserves in violation of Article I, Section 6, clause 2, the incompatability clause.[45] Injuries to the plaintiffs as taxpayers and voters were sufficient for Brennan to grant standing, although he did not join the

---

42. 369 U.S. at 204.
43. *Barlow* v. *Collins,* 397 U.S. 159, 172 (1971).
44. *United States* v. *Richardson,* 418 U.S. 166 (1974).
45. *Schlesinger* v. *Reservists to Stop the War,* 418 U.S. 208, 235 (1974).

dissents of Justices Marshall and Douglas, who would have granted standing based on injuries to the plaintiffs as citizens.

Perhaps the best example of Brennan's belief that the Court was manipulating the standing doctrine was the case of *Warth* v. *Seldin*,[46] wherein the majority refused to hear claims brought by a variety of plaintiffs asserting that local officials enacted a zoning ordinance and took other actions to exclude low- and moderate-income people and members of minority groups from the city. In his dissent, Brennan chided the majority:

> While the Court gives lip service to the principle, oft repeated in recent years, that "standing in no way depends on the merits of the plaintiff's contention that particular conduct is illegal," . . . in fact, the opinion, which tosses out of court almost every conceivable kind of plaintiff who could be injured by the activity claimed to be unconstitutional, can be explained only by an indefensible hostility to the claim on the merits.[47]

Although Brennan understood the Court's reluctance to become embroiled in the complex issues of exclusionary zoning, as well as the fact that the merits "could involve grave sociological and political ramifications . . . courts cannot refuse to hear a case on the merits merely because they would prefer not to."[48] Recounting various claims of individuals who are forced to live in a nearby central city, Brennan described the injuries to one moderate-income, minority individual: "[S]he is living in a seventh-floor apartment with exposed radiator pipes, no elevator, and no screens, and violence, theft, and sexual attacks are frequent."[49]

In addition to injury to an individual, standing requires that there be a connection between the injury and actions of the defendant. The majority believed that there was no showing that there were developers willing to build low-income housing at prices that plaintiffs could afford; therefore it was not the actions of the city that caused the harm. Brennan, however, feared that this was an impossible burden, since the

---

46. 422 U.S. 490 (1975).
47. Id. at 520.
48. Id.
49. 422 U.S. at 525 n. 4.

city officials, by their actions, had made it impossible for developers to offer such housing. "Today's decision will be read as revealing hostility to breaking down even unconstitutional zoning barriers that frustrate the deep human yearning of low-income and minority groups for decent housing they can afford in decent surroundings."[50]

For similar reasons, the Court refused to grant standing to parents of black schoolchildren who claimed that the Internal Revenue Service refused to deny the tax-exempt status of private schools that discriminated against blacks. The Court said that their claimed injury—lack of white schoolchildren attending public schools—could not be traced to the IRS, and therefore there was no standing. Brennan, in dissent, was most disturbed by

> [t]he indifference evidenced by the Court to the detrimental effects that racially segregated schools, supported by tax-exempt status from the federal government, have on the respondents' attempt to obtain an education in a racially integrated school system. I cannot join such indifference, and would give the respondents a chance to prove their case on the merits.[51]

In refusing to permit a suit on the basis of the First Amendment's establishment clause challenging a federal grant of property to a religiously affiliated college, the majority of the Court held that a federal taxpayer had no standing to bring such a suit.[52] It distinguished a famous Warren Court decision, *Flast* v. *Cohen*, which did grant standing to a federal taxpayer in similar circumstances. Acknowledging that standing is normally denied to federal taxpayers, Brennan, in dissent, noted that suits raising establishment clause claims are an exception to that rule, since one of the purposes of that clause was to stop the government from using tax money to fund religious institutions. He concluded in language typical of his dissents in these kinds of cases:

> Plainly hostile to the framers' understanding of the establishment clause, and *Flast*'s enforcement of that understanding, the Court vents that hostility under the guise of standing, "to slam the courthouse

---

50. Id. at 528–29.
51. *Allen* v. *Wright,* 468 U.S. 737, 783 (1984).
52. *Valley Forge College* v. *Americans United,* 454 U.S. 464 (1982).

door against plaintiffs who [as the framers intended] are entitled to full consideration of their [establishment clause] claims on the merits."[53]

Habeas Corpus

Perhaps the most controversial exercise of federal court authority over state court decisions involves federal habeas corpus. Federal habeas corpus is a procedure in which a state prisoner who has been convicted in state court and has exhausted all of the available state remedies, attacks his conviction in federal court. A single federal judge exercising habeas jurisdiction has the authority to release a state prisoner from custody on the grounds that the prisoner was convicted in violation of the Constitution, even when a state supreme court of seven judges has found that there has been no constitutional violation. While on the New Jersey Supreme Court, Brennan objected to such federal court intervention; as a member of the U.S. Supreme Court, he became a believer in the necessity of such federal court action. He spoke often to conferences of state judges, explaining why federal habeas was needed. On those occasions he advised the state judges that such intervention could be minimized if the state took more care in adjudicating claims of constitutional violations; he even outlined specific steps the state could take to avoid federal court intervention. In one case on the Court, he remanded a case to the state courts to avoid federal habeas:

The Court is not blind to the fact that the federal habeas corpus jurisdiction has been a source of irritation between the federal and state judiciaries. It has been suggested that this friction might be ameliorated if the states would look upon our decisions . . . as affording them an opportunity to provide state procedures . . . for a full airing of federal claims. [In a footnote, he cited one of his speeches discussed above.][54]

Although the Constitution states that the privilege of the writ of habeas

---

53. Id. at 513, quoting from his opinion in an earlier case, *Barlow* v. *Collins,* 397 U.S. 159, 178 (1970).
54. *Henry* v. *Mississippi,* 379 U.S. 443, 453 (1965).

corpus shall not be suspended, except in wartime, the habeas corpus decisions by the Supreme Court have been based on a federal statute. As Brennan noted, however, the history of the writ reveals "the unceasing contest between personal liberty and government oppression."[55]

> It is no accident that habeas corpus has time and again played a central role in national crises, wherein the claims of order and of liberty clash most acutely, not only in England in the seventeenth century, but also in America from our very beginnings, and today. Although in form the Great Writ is simply a mode of procedure, its history is inextricably intertwined with the growth of fundamental rights of personal liberty.[56]

Justice Brennan was the leader in interpreting the statute in a way that was protective of individuals seeking relief, while Justices Harlan, Powell, and Chief Justice Rehnquist stressed that Brennan's approach was harmful to state-federal relations. Unlike a federalism that would allow the states to administer their criminal justice system without interference from the federal judiciary, Brennan believed "[f]ederalism is a device for realizing the concepts of decency and fairness which are among the fundamental principles of liberty and justice lying at the base of our civil and political institutions."[57]

Unlike decisions based on the Constitution where the Court is acting alone in interpreting that document, in the habeas corpus area Brennan stressed that Congress has instructed the federal courts to hear the case of a state prisoner, and there is a presumption of federal jurisdiction. "Where Congress has granted individuals the right to a federal forum, we cannot deny that right simply because we disagree with Congress's determination that federal review is desirable."[58] Brennan agreed that the federal courts have considerable latitude "to shape the availability of the writ, [but] Congress did not issue this Court a mandate to sharpen its skills at ad hoc legislating."[59]

---

55. *Fay* v. *Noia,* 372 U.S. 391, 400–401 (1963).
56. Id.
57. Brennan, "Federal Habeas Corpus and State Prisoners: An Exercise in Federalism," 7 *Utah L. Rev.* 423, 442 (1963) (second annual William H. Leary Lecture, Salt Lake City, Utah, October 26, 1961).
58. *Murray* v. *Carrier,* 477 U.S. 478, 518 (1986).
59. Id.

Brennan's most important habeas decision, *Fay* v. *Noia*,[60] decided in 1963, involved a state prisoner, convicted on the basis of a coerced confession and sentenced to life in prison, who failed to follow proper state procedure and was therefore not permitted to raise his constitutional claim in the state proceeding. His codefendants, who properly objected to the coerced confessions, were set free by the state. The question was whether federal habeas was available to a person who did not raise properly his federal claim in state court.

Paradoxically, federal habeas was available at this time to a person whose federal claim was heard in state court but was rejected by this court. As he later noted, Brennan believed federal courts were more needed in cases like *Fay*, where the state courts refused to hear the constitutional claim, "for without habeas review no court will ever consider whether the petitioner's constitutional rights were violated."[61]

Interpreting the federal statute, Brennan held that as long as the defendant did not "deliberately bypass" the state procedure, federal habeas was available to him. The dissenters believed that the federal courts had no authority to, in effect, punish the state for requiring defendants to follow proper procedure. Brennan concluded his opinion with a ringing endorsement of federal habeas:

[N]o just and humane legal system can tolerate a result whereby [the codefendants] are at liberty because their confessions were found to have been coerced yet [defendant], whose confession was also coerced, remains in jail for life. For such anomalies, such affronts to the conscience of a civilized society, habeas corpus is predestined by its historical role in the struggle for personal liberty to be the ultimate remedy. If the states withhold effective remedy, the federal courts have the power and the duty to provide it. Habeas corpus is one of the precious heritages of Anglo-American civilization. We do no more today than confirm its continuing efficacy.

By the mid-1970s, a majority of the Court was cutting back on federal habeas, and Brennan found himself dissenting in a case that limited, although it did not overrule, *Fay* v. *Noia*. (Fay was overruled one year after Brennan retired from the Court, in the case of *Coleman* v. *Thomp-*

---

60. 372 U.S. 391 (1963).
61. *Murray* v. *Carrier*, 477 U.S. 478, 520 (1986).

son.[62]) In *Wainwright* v. *Sykes,*[63] the majority established a more difficult standard to obtain federal habeas relief for defendants whose counsel failed to follow proper procedure in raising their constitutional claims in state court. Although the failure in *Sykes* was a tactical decision by counsel, Brennan correctly anticipated that the case would be applied to inadvertent mistakes by counsel—the Court so held in a case ten years after *Sykes.*[64]

> Punishing a lawyer's unintentional errors by closing the federal court-house door to his client is both a senseless and misdirected method of deterring the slighting of state rules. It is senseless because un-planned and unintentional action of any kind generally is not subject to deterrence; and, to the extent that it is hoped that a threatened sanction addressed to the defense will induce greater care and caution on the part of trial lawyers, thereby forestalling negligent conduct or error, the potential loss of all valuable state remedies would be suffi-cient to this end. And it is a misdirected sanction because even if the penalization of incompetence or carelessness will encourage more thorough legal training and trial preparation, the habeas applicant, as opposed to his lawyer, hardly is the proper recipient of such a penalty.[65]

Brennan was particularly disturbed by visiting the sins of the lawyers on their clients in those cases where defendants were indigent and had no realistic choice of counsel:

> Indeed, if responsibility for error must be apportioned between the parties, it is the state, through its attorneys' admissions and certifica-tion policies, that is more fairly held to blame for the fact that practicing lawyers too often are ill prepared or ill equipped to act carefully and knowledgeably when faced with decisions governed by state procedural requirements.[66]

He concluded by stating that courts might have to "reconsider whether

---

62. 111 S. Ct. 2546 (1991).
63. 433 U.S. 72 (1976).
64. *Murray* v. *Carrier,* 477 U.S. 478 (1986).
65. *Sykes,* 433 U.S. at 113.
66. Id. at 114.

they can continue to indulge the comfortable fiction that all lawyers are skilled or even competent craftsmen in representing the fundamental rights of their clients."[67]

The Court also cut back on the scope of habeas where the defendant has raised and lost the constitutional claim in state court and seeks to relitigate it in federal court. The Supreme Court had long allowed this second bite at the apple, but in *Stone* v. *Powell*[68] it disallowed federal habeas when the state prisoner claimed a violation of the Fourth Amendment. In *Stone,* the defendant claimed that evidence had been admitted at trial that was the product of an unreasonable search and seizure; the Court held that as long as there had been the opportunity for a full and fair hearing in the state proceeding, federal habeas would not be permitted. The majority reasoned that state judges were just as competent to decide federal constitutional issues as federal judges and that Fourth Amendment claims did not involve fair trial issues but were merely concerned with deterring police misconduct. Brennan disagreed:

> Enforcement of *federal* constitutional rights that redress constitutional violations directed against the "guilty" is a particular function of *federal* habeas review, lest judges trying the "morally unworthy" be tempted not to execute the supreme law of the land. State judges popularly elected may have difficulty resisting popular pressures not experienced by federal judges given lifetime tenure designed to immunize them from such influences, and the federal habeas statutes reflect the congressional judgment that such detached federal review is a salutary safeguard against *any* detention of an individual "in violation of the Constitution or laws . . . of the United States."[69]

In his dissent, Brennan feared that in the future, constitutional rights other than the Fourth Amendment would also be precluded from federal habeas if there was an opportunity for a full and fair hearing in state court. Ten years later, in the case of *Kimmelman* v. *Morrison,*[70] he wrote for the majority in holding that habeas was available to a defendant seeking federal habeas that his Sixth Amendment right to effective

---

67. Id. at 118.
68. 428 U.S. 465 (1976).
69. *Stone* v. *Powell,* 428 U.S. 465, 525 (1976).
70. 477 U.S. 365 (1986).

assistance of counsel was violated. And Brennan's replacement, David Souter, wrote for the majority in 1993 that federal habeas is open to defendants claiming they were not given Miranda warnings, citing Brennan's opinion in *Kimmelman*.[71]

One year before Brennan's retirement, the Court imposed another substantial limitation on federal habeas, prompting Brennan to dissent: With rare exceptions, federal habeas petitioners may not raise and get the benefit of new constitutional rules to attack their convictions. Only defendants seeking direct review of their convictions can raise new constitutional claims. Although Brennan agreed that, in general, it is better for the Court to decide new constitutional claims on direct review from the state courts, he noted that sometimes habeas is the better method, sometimes the *only* method, for review. By waiting for direct review, time has elapsed and the unconstitutional practice continues— and lower federal courts who can only hear constitutional claims arising in state courts on habeas are precluded from developing the law. He believed that society has benefited in the past from hearing the kinds of cases the Court now refuses to hear:

> And although a favorable decision for a petitioner might not extend to another prisoner whose identical claim has become final, it is at least arguably better that the wrong done to one person be righted than that none of the injuries inflicted on those whose convictions have become final be redressed, despite the inequality in treatment.[72]

The Court extended its holding to habeas cases in which defendants seek to challenge the death penalty imposed through unconstitutional sentencing procedures, prompting Brennan to dissent:

> This extension means that a person may be killed although he or she has a sound constitutional claim that would have barred his or her execution had this Court only announced the constitutional rule before his or her conviction and sentence became final. It is intolerable that the difference between life and death should turn on such a fortuity of timing, and beyond my comprehension that a majority of this Court will so blithely allow a state to take a human life though

---

71. *Withrow* v. *Williams*, 113 S. Ct. 1745 (1993).
72. *Teague* v. *Lane*, 489 U.S. 288, 339 (1989).

the method by which sentence was determined violates our Constitution.[73]

Abstention

One of the reasons the majority of the Court cut back on the scope of federal habeas corpus was for reasons of comity—that is, respect by federal courts for state courts and state procedures. Comity has played a major part in the development of the doctrine of abstention, another device by which federal courts refuse to hear a claim despite the fact that it appears to be within their jurisdiction. In abstention cases, litigants who seek relief in federal court are told to go to state court—for example, when their federal claim is a defense to a state criminal prosecution. Brennan noted that withholding habeas corpus relief is a form of abstention with one important difference: In abstention outside the habeas context "federal jurisdiction has been withheld partly because of ongoing proceedings or the possibility of future proceedings in the state courts; in the habeas context, the state proceedings have already taken place and the petitioner's federal claim has not been considered on the merits."[74] He therefore believed that abstaining in the habeas context was even more suspect than other types of abstention, since the defendant is prevented from ever raising the federal constitutional claim.

Justice Brennan was the leader on the Court for narrowing the scope of abstention, observing "the virtually unflagging obligation of the federal courts to exercise the jurisdiction given them."[75] Justice Brennan wrote that "[a]bstention from the exercise of federal jurisdiction is the exception, not the rule,"[76] and is limited to three general categories where there are good reasons to let the case be heard in state court with the possibility of returning to federal court if the federal issue has not been litigated. And even in those instances where abstention is normally appropriate, Brennan wrote that federal courts could enjoin

---

73. *Penry* v. *Lynaugh,* 492 U.S. 302, 341 (1989).
74. *Murray* v. *Carrier,* 477 U.S. 478, 518 n. 1 (1986).
75. *Colorado River Water Conservation Dist.* v. *United States,* 424 U.S. 800, 817 (1976).
76. *Colorado River Water Conservation Dist.* v. *United States,* 424 U.S. 800, 813 (1976).

state proceedings and decide the federal issue if the state was acting in bad faith and to harass the individual.[77]

Suing the States

The Eleventh Amendment prohibits a federal suit by a citizen of one state against another state. A suit by a citizen against his or her own state in federal court has been barred by the ancient doctrine of "sovereign immunity"—that is, the king cannot be sued without his consent. It is not surprising that Brennan advocated a narrow scope for sovereign immunity, "born of systems of divine right that the framers abhorred."[78]

> [N]one can gainsay that a state may grievously hurt one of its citizens. Our expanding concepts of public morality are thus offended when a state may escape legal redress for its wrongs. . . . Our constitutional commitment, recited in the Preamble, is to "establish Justice."[79]

The majority of the Court, complained Brennan in dissent, "has aggressively expanded" the states' immunity in federal court.

> If this doctrine were required to enhance the liberty of our people in accordance with the Constitution's protections, I could accept it. If the doctrine were required by the structure of the federal system created by the framers, I could accept it. Yet the current doctrine intrudes on the ideal of liberty under law by protecting the States from the consequences of their illegal conduct.[80]

Congressional Protection of Individual Rights

Justice Brennan's efforts to protect the dignity and liberty of individuals were not limited to decisions interpreting the Constitution. As already discussed, he interpreted the habeas corpus statute in a way sympathetic to habeas petitioners. Similarly, he wrote opinions giving

---

77. *Dombrowski* v. *Pfister,* 380 U.S. 479 (1965).
78. *Employees* v. *Missouri Public Health Dep't.,* 411 U.S. 279, 323 (1973).
79. Id.
80. Id.

Congress broad powers to enforce the provisions of the civil rights amendments. He also wrote many important opinions sympathetically reading federal civil rights laws in behalf of persons whose constitutional rights were violated.

Expanding Constitutional Rights

Although Brennan's opinions protecting individual rights are usually ones in which a law is *invalidated* as unconstitutional, he wrote several important opinions *upholding* congressional action expanding individual rights. Congress was given the power in the three civil rights amendments—the Thirteenth, Fourteenth, and Fifteenth amendments—"to enforce" the amendments "by appropriate legislation." Although cases decided by the Supreme Court soon after the civil rights amendments were passed held that Congress had no more power than the Supreme Court, the majority in a 1965 case rejected that narrow interpretation. In that case, Brennan wrote that pursuant to the Fourteenth Amendment's Enforcement Provision, Section 5, Congress could make it a crime for private individuals to conspire to deprive persons from using state facilities on the basis of race, even though the amendment itself is not violated by such acts of private individuals.[81]

Brennan continued to uphold Congress's power under Section 5, to add to the substantive protection of the amendments, beyond what the Supreme Court had held was protected. Brennan's opinion in *Katzenbach* v. *Morgan*[82] held that Congress could prohibit the state from requiring English literacy as a condition for voting in elections, even though requiring literacy tests had been previously held by the Court not to violate the Constitution. To prevent Congress from going the other direction and cutting back on Supreme Court decisions that protect individuals, Brennan said, "Congress's power under Section 5 is limited to adopting measures to enforce the guarantees of the amendment; Section 5 grants Congress no power to restrict, abrogate, or dilute these guarantees."[83]

Justices who were concerned with federal intrusion into state matters, such as Harlan and Rehnquist, objected to Brennan's willingness to

---

81. *United States* v. *Guest,* 383 U.S. 745, 782–83 (1966).
82. 384 U.S. 641 (1966).
83. 384 U.S. at 651 n. 10.

expand Congress's power. Among other objections, these justices believed that the Court was, in effect, giving Congress the power to interpret finally the meaning of the Constitution, although ever since the 1803 case of *Marbury* v. *Madison* it had been the Court's job to say what the Constitution meant.

Sympathetic Interpretation of Civil Rights Laws

The most common way for redressing violations of constitutional rights by state or local officials is for the person injured to bring suit under the Federal Civil Rights Act, 42 U.S.C., Section 1983. Prior to 1978, liability under Section 1983 extended only to the offending officials, not to the city or municipal department who employed the official. As a result, even if the injured party prevailed in the lawsuit, no money would be recovered in the event the official was judgmentproof and uninsured. Writing the opinion for the Court in the case of *Monell* v. *New York City Dept. of Social Services,*[84] Justice Brennan overruled the earlier Supreme Court case that held that cities could not be sued under Section 1983. Brennan examined the legislative history surrounding the congressional enactment of the precursor to Section 1983 in 1871 and concluded that Congress "intended to give a broad remedy for violations of federally protected civil rights."[85] He also defined the scope of municipal liability, rejecting the argument that recovery is permitted merely because an official injures the plaintiff: rather,

> it is when execution of a government's policy or custom, whether made by its lawmakers or by those whose edicts or acts may fairly be said to represent official policy, inflicts the injury that the government as an entity is responsible under Section 1983.[86]

In a decision two years later, Brennan wrote that cities cannot defend on the grounds that they are immune from liability if the officials acted with a good faith, though mistaken, belief that their actions were constitutional. Even though the officials have such a qualified immunity, Brennan refused to extend that immunity to cities and municipal depart-

---

84. 436 U.S. 658 (1978).
85. Id. at 685.
86. Id. at 694.

ments. As he had written in a previous case involving Section 1983, government is "the social organ to which all in our society look for the promotion of liberty, justice, fair and equal treatment, and setting of worthy norms and goals for social conduct."[87]

> A damages remedy against the offending party is a vital component of any scheme for vindicating cherished constitutional guarantees, and the importance of assuring its efficacy is only accentuated when the wrongdoer is the institution that has been established to protect the very rights it has transgressed.[88]

Since the officials are immune, immunizing the government as well would leave the wronged party without a remedy: "The injustice of such a result should not be tolerated."[89]

While Section 1983 is the primary federal law for vindicating constitutional rights, Title VII of the Civil Rights Act of 1964 is the major federal statute for remedying discrimination in employment. Justice Brennan authored the first opinion for the Court upholding voluntary affirmative action plans entered into between union and management.[90] Although the text of Title VII seemed to prohibit the use of race, whether the motive was, on the one hand, to discriminate against minorities, or, on the other, to help minorities because of past discrimination, Brennan wrote that a literal reading of the law must give way to the spirit of the law, which permitted voluntary affirmative action plans. How could it be, felt Brennan, that Congress, so concerned about discrimination against blacks, would want to deny voluntary plans aimed at redressing traditional patterns of segregation?

Remedies Against Federal Officials Under the Constitution

One of Justice Brennan's most original contributions to the development of remedies for constitutional violations involved suits against federal officials directly under the Constitution. Under his 1971 decision

---

87. *Adickes* v. *Kress & Co.,* 398 U.S. 144, 190 (1970).
88. *Owen* v. *City of Independence,* 445 U.S. 622, 651.
89. Id.
90. *United Steelworkers* v. *Weber,* 4434 U.S. 193 (1979).

in *Bivens* v. *Six Unknown Fed. Narcotics Agents,*[91] individuals whose constitutional rights were violated could recover against the offending officers for damages only if there was a federal or state statute authorizing such suits. Although Congress had provided such a remedy against state and local officials under Section 1983, there was no such congressional statute against federal officials. In *Bivens,* an individual claimed that federal agents violated his rights by entering his apartment without a warrant or probable cause and arresting him, all in violation of the Fourth Amendment, prohibiting unreasonable searches and seizures. Brennan held that such claims could be brought directly under the Fourth Amendment, without a federal statute, even though the amendment "does not in so many words provide for its enforcement by an award of money damages for the consequences of its violation."[92] In dissent, Justice Black argued that it is up to Congress to determine whether to create judicial remedies for such wrongs, while Justice Blackmun was concerned about the "avalanche of new federal cases" the decision would bring.

After *Bivens,* Brennan authored two more decisions implying damage remedies from the Constitution: A person claiming she was discriminated against in employment by a congressman because of her sex may sue under the Fifth Amendment for violation of the due process clause;[93] and a prisoner claiming federal prison officials administered cruel and unusual punishment has a claim directly under the Eighth Amendment.[94] In the latter case he summarized *Bivens* as broadly establishing the rule "that the victims of a constitutional violation by a federal agent have a right to recover damages against the official in federal court despite the absence of any statute conferring such a right."[95] The exceptions he developed were twofold: If there were "special factors counseling hesitation" in developing a right, or if Congress had specifically provided a substitute, equally effective remedy.[96]

The Court has not been willing in recent years to imply remedies for other constitutional violations by federal officials, finding that the two exceptions apply. Brennan dissented in the most recent case, *Schweiker*

---

91. 403. U.S. 388 (1971).
92. Id. at 387.
93. *Davis* v. *Passman,* 442 U.S. 228 (1979).
94. *Carlson* v. *Green,* 446 U.S. 14 (1980).
95. Id. at 18.
96. Id.

v. *Chilicky,*[97] a case applying the exceptions to a claimed violation of due process. The Court's recent decisions indicate it is adopting the views of the dissenters in *Bivens* rather than Brennan's approach in that case.

Governmental Takings of Private Property

[N]or shall private property be taken for public use without just compensation.[98]

Although Justice Brennan is commonly thought of as being interested only in those constitutional issues that restrict government from infringing rights of liberty rather than property, his decisions involving the Fifth Amendment's takings clause are probably the most important of any justice ever to have served on the Court. That clause provides that the government may not take private property for public use without just compensation. Traditionally that meant that the government had to pay the landowner for the fair market value for property taken in a condemnation proceeding. The more recent cases, however, have involved different governmental actions, such as zoning. If a local zoning commission zoned an individual's land that resulted in a prohibition of development intended by the individual, was that a taking entitling the person to compensation? In 1981 Brennan wrote an opinion for two other justices that would provide such compensation for "inverse" condemnation:

Police power regulations such as zoning ordinances and other land-use restrictions can destroy the use and enjoyment of property in order to promote the public good just as effectively as formal condemnation or physical invasion of property.[99]

In a 1987 case, a majority of the Court adopted his reasoning and required compensation in inverse condemnation cases.

---

97. 487 U.S. 412 (1988).
98. U.S. Constitution, Amendment V.
99. *San Diego Gas & Elec. Co.* v. *San Diego,* 450, U.S. 621, 652 (1981).

Probably the most difficult issue for the Court in this area has been to determine when a government action is considered a "regulation" not requiring just compensation and when it is a "taking" that would require such compensation. If every governmental action affecting private property is a taking, that would dissuade government from enacting health, environmental, safety, and other regulations; on the other hand, if every action is merely a regulation, private property would be unprotected. Justice Brennan wrote the most important modern opinion for the Court in *Penn Central Transp. Co.* v. *New York City,*[100] involving a challenge to New York City's historic landmarks law as applied to the owner of Grand Central Terminal, who was denied permission to build a multistory office building above the terminal. Recognizing the importance of land-use controls to government for aesthetic and other purposes on the one hand, Brennan was also sensitive to the potential for singling out individuals to bear the brunt of such laws without just compensation. In upholding the law as a noncompensable regulation, Brennan noted that the government had good reasons to restrict the use and the owner could still develop the terminal site as well as adjacent parcels. The result was to permit historic preservation while, at the same time, serving notice to cities that the Court would be looking over their shoulders if they went too far in restricting rights of property.

The balance that Brennan would strike in the takings area was weighted in favor of upholding governmental action as a regulation: "I believe that states should be afforded considerable latitude in regulating private development, without fear that their regulatory efforts will often be found to constitute a taking."[101] In recent years, the majority of the Court was striking the balance in the other direction—for example, striking down land-use restrictions on development of coastal areas in *Nollan* v. *California Coastal Comm'n.*[102] Brennan decried this development as one interfering with government's ability to balance private development with the public's interest, accusing the Court of "substituting its own narrow view of how this balance should be struck. Its reasoning is hardly suited to the complex reality of natural resource protection in the twentieth century."[103]

---

100. 438 U.S. 104 (1978).
101. *Nollan* v. *California Coastal Comm'n.*, 483 U.S. 825 (1987).
102. Id. at 864, n. 14.
103. Id. at 864.

Due Process

[N]or shall any state deprive a person of life, liberty, or property, without due process of law.[104]

With the possible exception of the constitutionality of affirmative action plans, no constitutional issue faced by the Court in the past thirty years has been as controversial as determining what kinds of interests are protected from state restriction under the due process clauses of the Fifth and Fourteenth amendments. Indeed, throughout our history, the Court's due process decisions have been its most divisive, both on and off the Court: The 1857 *Dred Scott* case, the first substantive due process decision, held that a federal law prohibiting slavery in the territories interfered with a slaveowner's constitutionally protected property interest in his slave; the 1905 case of *Lockner* v. *New York* held that a state law setting maximum hours of work violated the rights of workers and their employers to enter into contracts; and the 1973 case of *Roe* v. *Wade* held that a state law interfering with a woman's right to have an abortion violated her fundamental right to privacy protected by due process.

The *Lockner* line of cases in which the Court protected economic rights has been rejected by the Court for more than fifty years, but since the 1965 case of *Griswold* v. *Connecticut*, the Court has, to varying degrees, protected certain rights of personal liberty, particularly rights concerning procreation. In *Griswold,* the Court invalidated a state law prohibiting married couples from using birth control devices on the grounds it interfered with the right to privacy derived from several provisions of the Bill of Rights. Justice Douglas's majority opinion explicitly declined to rely on due process, but three other opinions that found the law unconstitutional relied on due process or the Ninth Amendment.

In dissent, Justice Black would uphold the law, since it did not violate any specific provision of the Constitution; he criticized the use of due process as it boils down to "subjective considerations of natural justice," not interpreting the Constitution. A few years later, in another dissent, Black worried that the due process clause liberally interpreted "could easily swallow up all other parts of the Constitution" and that

---

104. U.S. Constitution, Amendment XIV, Section 1.

it would make the Constitution mean "what the judges say it is at a given moment, not what the founders wrote into the document." For Black, a Constitution "must have written standards that mean something definite and have an explicit content."[105]

In recent Senate confirmation hearings of nominees for the Supreme Court, a nominee's views of due process have become the most important issue to many senators. A major reason for Judge Robert Bork's failure to win Senate confirmation was his disagreement with the Court's willingness to use substantive due process to protect fundamental personal rights. Bork's views were quite similar to that of Justice Black, whose most biting dissents were from Court decisions upholding due process claims. In most areas of constitutional law, Black and Brennan were in agreement on the result of a case, if not its reasoning, but in interpreting the meaning of due process, Black and Brennan were often on opposite sides.

What divides the justices—and the senators—is determining the meaning of the words "liberty" and "property." In his 1968 opinion for the Court in *Goldberg* v. *Kelly*[106] Brennan broadly defined the latter term and held that a person receiving welfare benefits has a statutory entitlement to those benefits, which cannot be cut off without a hearing. "It may be realistic today to regard welfare entitlements as more like 'property' than a 'gratuity.' Much of the existing wealth in this country takes the form of rights that do not fall within traditional common-law concepts of property."[107] Since the individual was seeking a hearing prior to the agency cutting off benefits, cases such as *Goldberg* are called "procedural" due process cases. Cases such as *Griswold,* which involve legislative rather than administrative agency action, are referred to as "substantive" due process cases and have generated greater controversy. To the extent that the issue is whether the individual has an interest protected by due process, however, it matters little whether the case involves substantive or procedural due process. Thus Justice Black's concerns in *Griswold* were echoed in his dissent in *Goldberg*:

[I]t is obvious that today's result does not depend on the language of the Constitution itself or the principles of other decisions, but

---

105. *Goldberg* v. *Kelly*, 397 U.S. 254, 277 (1968).
106. Id.
107. Id. at 263 n. 8.

solely on the collective judgment of the majority as to what would be a fair and humane procedure in this case.[108]

A generation earlier, the major due process issue dividing the Court was the meaning of due process in the area of state criminal procedure. Justice Black took the view that Fourteenth Amendment due process meant that the states were bound by the criminal procedure provisions of the Bill of Rights—the Fourth, Fifth, Sixth, and Eighth amendments. Justices Frankfurter and Harlan, however, argued that the states were not so restricted and that only those state procedures that were "fundamentally unfair" violated due process. Justice Brennan took a middle position: He believed that the important provisions of the criminal procedure amendments bound the states and thus disagreed with Frankfurter and Harlan, but believed that due process did more than just incorporate provisions of the Bill of Rights; thus Brennan was in conflict with Black. That disagreement came to a head in the case of *In re Winship,*[109] where Brennan, for the Court, held that when a juvenile is charged with an act that would constitute a crime if committed by an adult, the state must prove its case beyond a reasonable doubt to comport with due process. Since there is no specific provision in the Bill of Rights that establishes that standard of proof, however, Black dissented, criticizing the Court for substituting its view of what is fair for that of the popularly elected legislators, which determined that less proof was sufficient for juvenile offenders:

> [T]he right of self-government that our Constitution preserves is just as important as any of the specific individual freedoms preserved in the Bill of Rights. The liberty of government by the people, in my opinion, should never be denied by this Court except when the decision of the people, as stated in laws passed by their chosen representatives, conflicts with the express or necessarily implied commands of our Constitution.[110]

In cases decided soon after *Goldberg,* the Court held that many other nontraditional property and liberty interests were protected by due process,

---

108. Id. at 276.
109. 397 U.S. 358 (1970).
110. Id. at 385.

including drivers' licenses, attendance at public school, and repossession of goods bought on credit. But in *Paul* v. *Davis*, the majority refused to find that a person's interest in his reputation was a protected liberty or property interest, suggesting that an interest is "property" or "liberty" only if recognized by state law or one of the specific provisions of the Bill of Rights. Brennan decried the narrowness of the Court's holding in his dissent:

> I have always thought that one of this Court's most important roles is to provide a formidable bulwark against governmental violation of the constitutional safeguards securing in our free society the legitimate expectations of every person to innate human dignity and sense of worth.[111]

Shortly after *Paul,* the Court held that discharge of a public employee for insubordination implicates no liberty interest and therefore the employee is not entitled to a hearing as a matter of due process. The majority was concerned that federal courts would be turned into a forum for litigating "incorrect or ill-advised personal decisions."[112] Brennan responded in dissent:

> [T]he federal courts *are* the appropriate forum for ensuring that the constitutional mandates of due process are followed by those agencies of government making personnel decisions that pervasively influence the lives of those affected thereby.[113]

The case that best sets forth the costs and benefits of substantive due process is *Moore* v. *East Cleveland.*[114] In that case, a city prohibited all but nuclear families from living in the same home. In his opinion for three members of the Court, Justice Powell acknowledged how treacherous substantive due process had been for the Court, but despite the risks, it could not be abandoned. Far from being a doctrine without limits, substantive due process was informed by looking to history, basic values, and tradition. In his concurrence, Justice Brennan noted that restricting living

---

111. 424 U.S. 693, 734–35 (1976).
112. *Bishop* v. *Wood*, 426 U.S. 341, 350 (1976).
113. Id. at 354.
114. 431 U.S. 494 (1978).

arrangements to nuclear families was nothing more than a preference for the living patterns in "white suburbia," while extended families were common to immigrant populations and blacks. In prohibiting extended families, the city "has chosen a device that deeply intrudes into family associational rights that historically have been central, and today remain central, to a large proportion of our population."[115]

The debate that occurred between Justices Scalia and Brennan the year before the latter's retirement on the relationship between history and due process has been introduced above. In *Michael H.* v. *Gerald D.*,[116] Justice Scalia would define a protected liberty interest as a tradition found in American history. Brennan believed that this limitation was a response to concerns expressed by critics of due process, such as Justice Black, that due process is nothing more than judges' preferences substituted for that of democratically elected legislators. Brennan would not discount the importance of tradition but objected to Scalia's insistence that only those interests "specifically protected" by historical practices are liberty interests. For Brennan, the question is whether the interest asserted—in this case, the specific parent-child relationship of the biological father to his daughter—is "close enough to the interests that we already have protected to be deemed an aspect of 'liberty' as well."[117] Scalia would ignore Supreme Court decisions handed down since the enactment of the Bill of Rights and the Fourteenth Amendment and look to the specific practices in the states at the time of these enactments. Brennan, in contrast, would look to those precedents and take into consideration societal changes to give meaning to "liberty." In *Michael H.*, only Chief Justice Rehnquist agreed with Scalia's strict historical approach to determine the meaning of liberty.

A similar debate between Brennan and Scalia took place in the case of *Burnham* v. *Superior Court of Cal*,[118] decided in 1990, Brennan's last year on the Court. For more than a hundred years, the Court has handed down decisions interpreting due process in the context of personal jurisdiction of state courts over nonresident defendants. In *Burnham*, all of the justices agreed that a state court could take jurisdiction over such a defendant who was voluntarily present in the state, but there was no majority opinion. Justice Scalia's opinion, joined by three

---

115. Id. at 510.
116. 491 U.S. 110 (1989).
117. 491 U.S. at 142.
118. 495 U.S. 604 (1990).

other justices, reasoned that since a defendant's presence had always been a sufficient basis for jurisdiction, therefore it met due process because of its historical pedigree. Brennan, joined by three others, though agreeing that history was important, argued it cannot be the *only* factor; even old rules of jurisdiction "must satisfy contemporary notions of due process."[119]

Scalia attacked Brennan's test as one that leaves it up to each justice's subjective assessment of what is fair and just, but Brennan countered that there were several factors for the Court to consider, including the burden on the defendant, the state's interest, and the plaintiff's interest in obtaining relief, an analysis that is not "dependent on personal whim" [and] "well within our competence to employ."[120] Brennan attacked Scalia's approach on several grounds: It is not at all certain that transient jurisdiction had always been recognized as a basis for jurisdiction; a traditional rule can, over time, become unreasonable; and, despite Scalia's assertion that states would change an old rule that had become unreasonable, Brennan believed there was little incentive for a state to make it harder for its resident plaintiffs to sue nonresident defendants.

In his last year on the Court, Brennan once again found himself in dissent in a due process case, this time concerning the issue of the "right to die." In *Cruzan* v. *Director, Mo. Health Dept.*,[121] the majority held that, assuming a competent person has the liberty interest not to be kept alive by artificial nutrition and hydration, a state may insist that an incompetent person be kept alive by such means unless the person has expressed her wish to be disconnected by "clear and convincing" evidence. No such showing had been made in this case, and therefore the state could prevent the parents of the incompetent person from cutting off life support. Brennan dissented, arguing that the Court was not giving enough weight to the incompetent's fundamental interest in being free from unwanted medical treatment, based on deeply rooted history and tradition. On the other side, Justice Scalia concurred in the judgment, but believed due process had no role to play in these right-to-die cases. In words reminiscent of Justice Harlan's dissent in *Baker* v. *Carr,* Scalia said, "This Court need not, and has no authority to,

---

119. Id. at 630.
120. Id. at 635 n. 7.
121. 497 U.S. 261 (1990).

inject itself into every field of human activity where irrationality and oppression may theoretically occur, and if it tries to do so it will destroy itself.[122]

Perhaps Brennan's most important contribution to the developing law of privacy was his 1972 opinion for the Court in *Eisenstadt* v. *Baird*.[123] The case involved a state law that prohibited the distribution of contraceptives to unmarried persons. *Griswold* was a case involving married persons. Since the law involved discrimination between married and unmarried persons, it was decided on the basis of equal protection rather than due process, but Brennan's opinion striking down the law contained language that laid the groundwork for the next Term's abortion decision, *Roe* v. *Wade*, by focusing on the right of the individual with respect to procreative choices.

> If under *Griswold* the distribution of contraceptives to married persons cannot be prohibited, a ban on distribution to unmarried persons would be equally impermissible. It is true that in *Griswold* the right of privacy in question inhered in the marital relationship. Yet the marital couple is not an independent entity with a mind and heart of its own, but an association of two individuals each with a separate intellectual and emotional makeup. If the right of privacy means anything, it is the right of the *individual,* married or single, to be free from unwarranted governmental intrusion into matters so fundamentally affecting a person as the decision whether to bear or beget a child.[124]

In 1977 Brennan struck down a state law that restricted distribution of contraceptives to all persons, married and unmarried alike, unless distributed by a licensed pharmacist. He rejected the state's attempt to uphold the law by distinguishing *Griswold,* which banned contraceptive use, and *Eisenstadt,* which discriminated against the unmarried. In *Carey* v. *Population Servs. Int'l.,*[125] Brennan stated that *Griswold* and later decisions such as *Eisenstadt* could not be read so narrowly; instead, they stand for the proposition that ''the Constitution protects individual

---

122. 497 U.S. at 300–301.
123. 405 U.S. 438 (1972).
124. 405 U.S. at 453.
125. 431 U.S. 678 (1977).

decisions in matters of childbearing from unjustified intrusion by the state."[126] Only if the state had a compelling state interest could the prohibition of distribution of nonmedical contraceptives to adults except through licensed pharmacists be sustained, and there was no such compelling interest.

A provision in the law involved in the *Carey* case prohibited the distribution of nonprescription contraceptives to persons less than sixteen years of age, unless distributed by a physician. Writing for three other justices in this part of the opinion, Brennan noted that the constitutional rights of minors had been a "vexing" one for the Court; previous decisions indicated that minors did possess some constitutional rights. "[T]he right of privacy in connection with decisions affecting procreation extends to minors as well as to adults."[127] Instead of requiring the state to come up with a compelling state interest, which was the test for the restriction on adults, Brennan adopted a less rigorous but still burdensome test for the state: It must show there was a "significant" state interest in the limits on access to contraceptives for minors. Brennan was reluctant to find that discouraging minors' sexual activity by drastically restricting distribution of contraceptives was the reason for the law; in any case, there was no evidence that such restriction discouraged sexual activity, and the law was held unconstitutional. As is typical in these due process cases since *Griswold,* the dissents were particularly biting. Justice Rehnquist observed that if the framers "could have lived to know that their efforts had enshrined in the Constitution the right of commercial vendors of contraceptives to peddle them to unmarried minors," it is "not difficult to imagine their reaction."[128]

In 1988, twenty years after his opinion in *Goldberg,* Justice Brennan gave a speech that set forth in detail his philosophy of due process, echoing many of his concerns that had surfaced in his judicial opinions. "Due process asks whether government has treated someone fairly, whether individual dignity has been honored, whether the worth of an individual has been acknowledged."[129] He noted that merely because government officials have operated according to standard rules, there is

---

126. Id. at 687.
127. 431 U.S. at 693.
128. 431 U.S. at 717.
129. Brennan, "Reason, Passion, and the 'Progress of the Law,' " 10 *Cardozo L. Rev.* 3, 16) (Forty-second annual Benjamin N. Cardozo Lecture, New York, September 17, 1987).

no guarantee that due process has been met. "They must plumb their conduct more deeply, seeking answers in the more complex equations of human nature and experience." Judges who determine the meaning of due process have a difficult job.

> [They must] be sensitive to the balance of reason and passion that mark a given age, and the ways in which that balance leaves its mark on the everyday exchanges between government and citizen. To do so, we must draw on our own experience as inhabitants of that age, and our own sense of the uneven fabric of social life. We cannot delude ourselves that the Constitution takes the form of a theorem whose axioms need more logical deduction.[130]

Whereas the concerns of the American colonists were about arbitrary action by the king and Parliament that could be resolved by regularized procedures, today's bureaucratic state presents different problems: "The greatest threat to due process principles is formal reason severed from the insights of passion."[131] The problem today is not unpredictability and whim, as in the eighteenth century; rather, "modern citizens fear that routine government procedures may translate their personal stories into an alien standard language."[132]

Brennan used *Goldberg* as an example of a case that takes account of reason and passion. It was not, as some believe, just a case seeking to make the welfare system more rational, although rationality is desirable; more than that, "the decision can be seen as an expression of the importance of passion in governmental conduct, in the sense of attention to the concrete human realities at stake."[133] Although the state procedures for hearings after benefits were terminated were rational, due process was violated because the system "lacked that dimension of passion, of empathy, necessary for a full understanding of the human beings affected by those procedures."[134]

A judge or administrator who uses reason alone "is cut off from the wellspring from which concepts such as dignity, decency, and fairness flow."

---

130. Id.
131. Id. at 17.
132. Id. at 19.
133. Id at 20.
134. Id.

In *Goldberg,* the application of standard rules to all recipients was simply blind to the brute fact of dependence. A government insensitive to such a reality cannot be said to treat individuals with the respect that due process demands—not because its officials do not reason, but because they cannot understand.[135]

Equal Protection

[N]or deny to any person within its jurisdiction the equal protection of the laws.[136]

A common refrain in Brennan's speeches was his great concern about the have-nots in our society:

Society's overriding concern today is with providing freedom and equality of rights and opportunities, in a realistic and not merely formal sense, to all the people of this nation. Society is concerned with securing justice, equal and practical, to the poor, the members of minority groups, to the criminally accused, to the displaced persons of the technological revolution, to the alienated youth, to the urban masses, and to the unrepresented consumers—to all, in short, who do not yet partake of the abundance of American life.[137]

It is therefore not surprising to find that Brennan, as Supreme Court justice, tried to redress those inequalities at every opportunity in his judicial opinions, where he pushed to expand the reach of the equal protection clause. Indeed, he was criticized by President Reagan's assistant attorney general for civil rights, William Bradford Reynolds, for espousing a "radical egalitarian jurisprudence."[138] In Brennan's early years on the Court, his efforts were quite successful—*Baker* v. *Carr*

---

135. Id. at 22.
136. U.S. Constitution, Amendment XIV, Section 1.
137. Brennan, "Are Citizens Justified in Being Suspicious of the Law and Legal System?," 43 *Univ. of Miami L. Rev.* 981 (1989) (fourth annual Robert B. Cole Lecture Series, University of Miami Law School, January 27, 1989).
138. Address at University of Missouri-Columbia School of Law (September 12, 1986).

led to cases holding that equal protection requires one person, one vote, in state elections; and a state's refusal to provide welfare benefits to persons newly arriving from other states was struck down in Brennan's opinion in *Shapiro* v. *Thompson.* Perhaps his most important contribution to equal protection jurisprudence occurred after the Warren Court era was over: Brennan got the Court to adopt a rigorous test for dealing with legislation that discriminated on the basis of sex. But by the end of his career on the Court, it was clear that his dream of the Constitution as a source of ensuring equality for the powerless was not shared by a majority of his colleagues.

As discussed below, legislative classifications will be held constitutional unless there is discrimination against a protected class, such as a racial minority. In the field of social and economic legislation, probably as a reaction against the kind of interference the Court engaged in during the *Lockner* era, it is virtually impossible to challenge successfully a law on equal protection grounds. In such cases, equal protection analysis consists of merely going through the motions of applying the "rational basis test." Brennan argued, without success, that such extreme deference to the legislature was wrong. He would examine with care even economic legislation to ensure that the classifications used were rational.

In *U.S. R.R. Retirement Bd.* v. *Fritz,*[139] federal legislation denied railroad workers who retired before 1974 certain retirement benefits that were given workers who retired after 1974. The majority upheld the law, without examining the legislative history of the law, which showed that Congress had been told by both labor and management witnesses that no such discrimination would occur. Brennan, noting that others had commented on "Congress's unfortunate tendency to pass railroad retirement legislation drafted by labor and management representatives without adequate scrutiny," suspected "that Congress may have been misled."[140] In such circumstances, Brennan believed that the Court had the responsibility to look after those whose interests were ignored by everyone else, even though former railroad workers could not be considered a historically disfavored minority triggering stricter scrutiny.

139. 449 U.S. 166 (1980).
140. Id. at 193.

Fundamental Rights

In cases such as *Shapiro* v. *Thompson,* Brennan developed a new type of equal protection analysis: Infringement on certain "fundamental rights"—in *Shapiro,* the right to travel—was found to violate equal protection. Previously, equal protection cases were solely concerned with discrimination on the basis of certain classifications within a statute, such as race. Race classifications were considered "suspect" and could be used only if there was a "compelling state interest," an almost impossible burden for the state to meet. *Shapiro* held that penalizing the exercise of the fundamental right of interstate movement likewise triggered the compelling state interest test. In addition, Brennan's opinion indicated that the law violated equal protection because it denied welfare aid "upon which may depend the ability of the families to obtain the very means to subsist—food, shelter, and other necessities of life."[141]

In dissent, Harlan objected to this new use of equal protection:

[W]hen a statute affects only matters not mentioned in the [Constitution] and is not arbitrary or irrational, I must reiterate that I know nothing which entitles this Court to pick out particular human activities, characterize them as "fundamental," and give them added protection under an unusually stringent equal protection test.[142]

In language reminiscent of his dissent from Brennan's opinion in *Baker* v. *Carr,* Harlan showed his concern for the impact of the Court's decision on the other branches of government, state and federal:

[The decision] reflects to an unusual degree the current notion that the Court possesses a peculiar wisdom all its own whose capacity to lead this nation out of its present troubles is contained only by the limits of judicial ingenuity in contriving new constitutional principles to meet each problem as it arises. For anyone who, like myself, believes that it is an essential function of this Court to maintain the constitutional divisions between state and federal authority and

---

141. 394 U.S. 618, 627 (1969).
142. Id. at 677.

among the three branches of the federal government, today's decision is a step in the wrong direction.[143]

Harlan's worry that the Court would protect an ever-increasing number of "fundamental rights" under equal protection proved unnecessary; the Burger Court rejected the implications of cases such as *Shapiro* and *Goldberg* that necessities of life were fundamental rights. Most importantly, in the 1973 case of *San Antonio School Dist.* v. *Rodriguez,*[144] which challenged inequality of school financing within a state, the Court held that education was not a fundamental right triggering stringent equal protection review: A right is fundamental only if it is "explicitly or implicitly guaranteed by the Constitution."[145] With one exception, no more fundamental rights have been found by the Court to merit heightened equal protection scrutiny. That exception was Brennan's decision *Plyer* v. *Doe,*[146] in which the total denial of a free public education to children of illegal aliens was found to violate equal protection because of its discrimination against a semisuspect class—children of illegal aliens—and the infringement on a quasi-fundamental right by totally denying any education to the children. Expressing concerns similar to Justice Harlan's in *Shapiro,* Chief Justice Burger said in dissent that the solution to the problem of aliens "is to defer to the political processes, unpalatable as that may be to some."[147]

Just as the Burger Court refused to intervene in the area of welfare and other necessities such as food and shelter, so it found no constitutional restrictions on the state refusing to pay for poor women to have abortions, even though it paid for childbirth. The majority of the Court found that refusal to fund did not impinge on a fundamental privacy right because, unlike prohibitions and regulations of abortion, there was no restriction imposed by the state. Brennan's dissent, reminiscent of *Carolene Products* concerns, noted that the legislation affected only the poor, "that segment of our society which, because of its position of political powerlessness, is least able to defend its privacy rights from

---

143. Id. at 677.
144. 411 U.S. 1 (1973).
145. Id. at 1.
146. 457 U.S. 202 (1982).
147. 457 U.S. at 254.

the encroachments of state-mandated morality. The instant legislation thus calls for more exacting judicial review than in most other cases."[148]

Sex Discrimination

Until the Burger Court era, laws that discriminated on the basis of sex did not violate equal protection. The first time the Court invalidated such a law was in 1971, finding irrational a statute that automatically preferred a man over a woman equally qualified to serve as administrator of an estate, *Reed* v. *Reed.*[149] In 1973 Brennan wrote an opinion joined by only three other justices that, for the first time, stated that such laws should not be analyzed under the rational basis test, the normal equal protection standard that was used in the *Reed* case. Instead, such a law is to be reviewed by the Court the same way as a law that discriminates on the basis of the other suspect classifications— race, alienage, or national origin. Such laws are subject to strict scrutiny and cannot survive unless there is a compelling state interest and the discrimination is necessary to achieve that interest. Brennan wrote that sex-based classifications share with the other suspect classes several characteristics: a history of sex discrimination that "was rationalized by an attitude of 'romantic paternalism' which, in practical effect, put women, not on a pedestal, but in a cage."[150] Additionally, women suffer from discrimination in schools, jobs, and the political arena. Sex, like race, is a characteristic that is immutable, bearing no relationship to ability. Finally, noted Brennan, Congress in passing the 1964 Civil Rights Act, prohibiting sex discrimination in employment, thereby concluded that such treatment is arbitrary.

The Court finally agreed on the appropriate standard of review in the 1976 case of *Craig* v. *Boren,*[151] in an opinion written by Brennan. For the first time the Court adopted an intermediate level test for equal protection, much more stringent than the rational basis test but not as stringent as the strict scrutiny test advocated by Brennan in the 1973 case. Brennan articulated the test as follows: "[C]lassifications by gen-

---

148. *Harris* v. *McRae,* 448 U.S. 297, 332 (1980).
149. 404 U.S. 71 (1971).
150. *Frontiero* v. *Richardson,* 411 U.S. 677, 684 (1973).
151. 429 U.S. 190 (1976).

der must serve important government objectives and must be substantially related to achievement of those objectives."[152] *Craig* involved a law that discriminated against men—women could buy 3.2 percent beer at age eighteen, while men had to be twenty-one. Thus the intermediate level test is used whenever the government classifies on the basis of sex. Since *Craig,* the test has been used outside the area of sex discrimination—in *Plyer* v. *Doe,* a children of illegal aliens case, and in *Carey* v. *Population Services,* striking down limitations under due process on minors' access to contraceptives.

One of the few times Brennan and Douglas took opposing sides involved a case decided prior to *Craig* in which tax benefits were given widows but not widowers. Viewing the tax statute as compensating for past discrimination against women, Douglas upheld it under the rational basis test; Brennan dissented, viewing the law as one that furthered the stereotype that women but not men needed special treatment from government, as opposed to poor persons regardless of sex. Both before and after *Craig,* Brennan wrote several opinions for the Court striking down laws that were claimed to compensate women for past discrimination. For example, in invalidating a state law under which husbands but not wives may be ordered to pay alimony after a divorce, Brennan observed that such legislative classifications "carry the inherent risk of reinforcing stereotypes about the 'proper place' of women and their need for special protection."[153]

The one case in which Brennan was willing to allow the state to take sex into account, *Johnson* v. *Transportation Agency,*[154] was an employment discrimination case brought under Title VII of the Civil Rights Act of 1964, in which a state agency preferred a woman applicant over a marginally more qualified male. Brennan permitted sex to be considered as a factor, since the job involved—road dispatcher—was one from which women had been traditionally underrepresented. The case was decided under a federal statute, not the Constitution, but the opinion suggested that this type of affirmative action plan is the kind that Brennan would find satisfied equal protection under intermediate scrutiny.

---

152. Id. at 197.
153. *Orr* v. *Orr,* 440 U.S. 268, 283 (1979).
154. 480 U.S. 616 (1987).

Race Discrimination

The decision that changed the Court's thirteen-year approach to remedying school segregation since *Brown* v. *Board of Education* was Brennan's opinion in *Green* v. *County School.*[155] In *Green,* the school board
argued that its adoption of a freedom of choice plan whereby students
could choose which school to attend was not unconstitutional, even
though no white student had chosen to go to the black schools and 85
percent of the white school was white. Although *Brown* permitted
school boards to desegregate "with all deliberate speed," the Court
was losing patience by the time of *Green.* School boards have "the
affirmative duty to take whatever steps might be necessary to convert
to a unitary system in which racial discrimination would be eliminated
root and branch."[156] Clearly, the "deliberate" from "all deliberate
speed" was now removed: "The burden on a school board today is to
come forward with a plan that promises realistically to work, and promises realistically to work now."[157] Years later, Rehnquist criticized
Green as a "drastic expansion" of *Brown,* by changing the constitutional obligation from one of ending segregation by law to focusing on
achieving racial mixing in the schools.

Rehnquist's dissent criticizing *Green* came in the first case addressing
segregation in a northern school setting, another Brennan opinion. In
Keyes v. *School Dist. No. 1,*[158] involving the Denver school district,
Brennan held that intentional discrimination by school district officials
resulted in the same liability as if there were state laws mandating
segregation, as in the southern school context. Further, the same remedies that apply to southern school districts apply to those in the north,
including busing.

Affirmative Action

The most controversial issue for the Court since the 1970s, with the
possible exception of abortion, has been affirmative action. In affirmative action cases, programs designed to favor minorities are challenged

---

155. 391 U.S. 430 (1968).
156. Id. at 437, 438.
157. Id. at 439.
158. 413 U.S. 189 (1973).

by whites—or, as in the *Johnson* case, men—as violating their rights to equal protection. Is the Constitution, in the words of Justice Harlan dissenting in *Plessy* v. *Ferguson* in 1896, "color-blind, and neither knows nor tolerates classes among citizens"?[159] Or can the government, which for so long intentionally discriminated against blacks and other racial minorities, make up for that mistreatment by attempting to create a level playing field? Most of the justices have been divided into two camps, one side believing that any use of race, either "benign" or hostile, should be treated with strict scrutiny, the other believing that there is a clear difference between the two types of legislation and that affirmative action programs can pass constitutional muster.

Although Brennan was a supporter of affirmative action programs, he was aware of their dangers. His first opinion discussing such programs, *UJO* v. *Carey*,[160] involved creation of voting districts on the basis of race to ensure the election of blacks to comply with the federal Voting Rights Act. The creation of the new electoral districts separated the Hasidic Jewish community into several districts, resulting in the loss of Hasidic representatives. Although agreeing that the redistricting was permissible to comply with the Voting Rights Act, Brennan was troubled by the use of race on the following grounds: First, it may not be easy to detect if the use of race is benign or hostile to minorities. Second, the use of race:

> may serve to stimulate our society's latent race consciousness, suggesting the utility and propriety of basing decisions on a factor that ideally bears no relationship to an individual's worth or needs . . . and may act to stigmatize its recipient groups [and may] imply to some the recipients' inferiority and especial need for protection.[161]

Third, "even a benign policy of assignment by race is viewed as unjust by many in our society, especially by those individuals who are adversely affected by a given classification."[162] He noted that the burden is often borne by politically powerless whites, such as the Hasidim in this *UJO*.

---

159. 163 U.S. 537, 559 (1896).
160. 430 U.S. 144 (1977).
161. Id. at 173, 174.
162. Id. at 174.

The year after *UJO,* the Court decided the most famous of the affirmative action cases, *Regents of Univ. of California* v. *Bakke.*[163] There was no majority opinion of the Court: Brennan jointly authored an opinion with three other justices. Joint opinions are very unusual occurrences; normally, one justice writes an opinion, and the others merely sign on in agreement. The result of the case was that the medical school's affirmative action plan to admit minorities was struck down and the white applicant was ordered to be admitted. The joint opinion dissented from the invalidation of the plan on the grounds that there had been past societal discrimination against minorities that justified the medical school's reservation of sixteen slots for minorities out of a class of one hundred.

The joint opinion began by noting that our founding principles—"all men are created equal"—were not applied to blacks, either during slavery, the days of "separate but equal," or even during the days after *Brown,* when school boards delayed desegregation. The claim that the law must be color-blind was more a description of aspiration rather than reality, and therefore we cannot "let color-blindness become myopia which masks the reality that many 'created equal' have been treated within our lifetimes as inferior both by the law and by their fellow citizens."[164] Noting that human equality is associated with the proposition that differences in color should not be relevant to how persons should be treated, the opinion pointed out that, nonetheless, the Court had never adopted Justice Harlan's color-blind theory that racial classifications are always invalid. The real question is whether such classifications should be treated as suspect, as they would if the legislature used them to discriminate against minorities, triggering strict scrutiny by the Court and almost certain invalidation of the plan.

The joint opinion first dismissed the claim that whites, as a class, deserve the heightened scrutiny reserved to the powerless groups in society; it then said that the medical school's use of race was not irrelevant, nor was it to stigmatize whites by signifying inferiority or racial hatred. But having decided that strict scrutiny was inappropriate, the opinion rejected the claim that the rational basis test should be used; instead, it opted for the intermediate level of review, first set forth in Brennan's opinion in *Craig* v. *Boren.* Echoing Brennan's opinion in

---

163. 438 U.S. 265 (1978).
164. 438 U.S. at 327.

UJO, it reasoned that the use of race had the potential of stigmatizing its recipients, was an immutable characteristic outside the individual's control and unrelated to merit or achievement, and might disadvantage discrete and insular whites, such as the Hasidim in *UJO.*

During the eleven-year interval between *Bakke* and *Richmond* v. *J. A. Croson & Co.*[165] in 1989, a majority of the Court could not agree on the level of scrutiny to be used in affirmative action race cases. In *Croson,* a case invalidating the city of Richmond's affirmative action plan to increase the number of minority businesses engaged in city construction projects, six justices agreed that such programs should be treated with strict scrutiny, with Brennan joining a dissent. To many observers of the Court, *Croson* signaled the end to affirmative action programs. Yet, on the final day of the 1989 Term, Brennan's last, he authored the opinion for a majority in *Metro Broadcasting* v. *FCC,*[166] which held that affirmative action plans established by the federal government should be subject to the intermediate level scrutiny advocated in his *Bakke* joint opinion. *Croson* was distinguished as involving a state program, whereas more deference is owed to Congress when it uses benign racial classifications. The FCC's plan made it easier for minorities to be awarded new broadcast licenses and to purchase certain existing stations. The plan was challenged by nonminority broadcasters. Brennan wrote that the governmental interest, to increase diversity of broadcast viewpoint, was an important one, and that the FCC's plan favoring minority broadcasting was substantially related to that interest. The dissenters, who believed *Croson* was controlling, would use strict scrutiny for all racial classifications and would find the plan unconstitutional.

The First Amendment

The Religion Clauses

Congress shall make no law respecting an establishment of religion, or prohibiting the free exercise thereof.[167]

---

165. 488 U.S. 469 (1989).
166. 497 U.S. 547 (1990).
167. U.S. Constitution, Amendment I.

Under his interpretation of the establishment clause, Justice Brennan strongly opposed government attempts to support religion. He wrote opinions for the Court finding unconstitutional payment by the state to public school teachers to teach parochial school students in their schools after regular classes,[168] and he invalidated a similar program funded by the federal government for low-income students in parochial schools.[169] He also consistently found violative of the establishment clause state sponsorship of religious activities such as prayer in public schools. At the same time, he interpreted the free exercise clause to require government to take steps to accommodate the religious practices of individuals. The majority of justices currently on the Supreme Court read the establishment clause not to require such strict separation, while reading the free exercise clause as not requiring the degree of accommodation of religious practices that Brennan did.

Establishment Clause

Brennan's concurring opinion in the 1963 case of *Abington School Dist.* v. *Schempp,*[170] which held Bible reading in the public schools to be unconstitutional, is characteristic of his approach to constitutional interpretation. Because the topic of Bible reading in the schools was so controversial, he felt obligated to set forth his reasoning in great detail— seventy-four pages—inviting critics and supporters alike to respond.

Acknowledging that the immediate concern of the framers was to prevent Congress from setting up an official federal church, and that Madison and Jefferson might have permitted the religious exercises at issue, Brennan nonetheless did not find history dispositive: The historical record is ambiguous; the framers gave no consideration to the particular issue, since the schools in the eighteenth century were largely sectarian, not public; the religious diversity of the United States today is much greater than it was in 1791; and public schools must serve this diverse community. If the public schools were permitted to conduct such religious exercises, it would be inconsistent with their public function: "the training of American citizens in an atmosphere free of parochial, divisive, or separatist influences of any sort—an atmosphere in

---

168. *Grand Rapids School Dist.* v. *Ball,* 473 U.S. 373 (1985).
169. *Aguilar* v. *Felton,* 473 U.S. 402 (1985).
170. 374 U.S. 203 (1963).

which children may assimilate a heritage common to all American groups and religions. . . . This is a heritage neither theistic nor atheistic, but simply civic and patriotic.''[171] In finding that the Bible reading violated the establishment clause, Brennan rejected the arguments based on a reading of constitutional text and history that the clause applies only to the federal government, not the states: That reading "underestimates the role of the establishment clause as a coguarantor, with the free exercise clause, of religious liberty. The framers did not entrust the liberty of religious beliefs to either clause alone.''[172]

In an important part of his opinion, Brennan distinguished the establishment clause from the free exercise clause with respect to the relevance of the fact that children who did not want to participate in the Bible readings could be excused from attendance. The excusal provision, he felt, was irrelevant to the establishment clause, which was violated once the activities were found to be essentially religious exercises undertaken for religious aims regardless of possible coercion. For a free exercise violation, however, there must be some element of coercion present, which he found present despite the excusal provision, since young schoolchildren would be subject to peer pressure to conform—they would stay in the room while the Bible was being read to avoid being singled out and teased by others. In dissent, Justice Stewart found that there could be no establishment clause violation without coercion, a position taken by several members of the current Supreme Court who require coercion for violation of either clause.

In *Schempp,* Brennan stressed that not all cooperation between religion and government violates the establishment clause: There is a violation only when the government activity raises "those dangers—as much to church as to state—which the framers feared would subvert religious liberty and the strength of a system of secular government.''[173] It is not government hostility but government neutrality that the clause requires. To make the point specifically, he then listed several activities he said would not violate the establishment clause, including provision of military chaplains, teaching about the Bible in the public schools, and the use of "In God We Trust" on currency. When a challenge was made twenty years later to invocational prayers in legislative bodies, one of

---

171. Id. at 242.
172. Id. at 256.
173. Id. at 295.

the activities he said was constitutional in *Schempp,* he dissented from the Court's approval of such prayers and said: "After much reflection, I have come to the conclusion that I was wrong then and that the Court is wrong today. I now believe that the practice of official invocational prayer . . . is unconstitutional."[174]

The reasons Brennan changed his mind were several: First, he once believed that legislators, since they are adults, are free from peer pressure, unlike the students in *Schempp,* who might fear their fellow students' reactions if they sought to be excused from prayer. He now believed that legislators might be unwilling to oppose the prayers for fear of what their constituents might think. Second, he rejected the majority's reasoning that the "unique history" of the establishment clause—the fact that the First Congress, which approved that clause in the First Amendment, simultaneously authorized paid chaplains for its proceedings—was determinative of the constitutionality of legislative prayers. Unlike the majority, Brennan was unwilling to assume that authorizing chaplains meant that Congress was carefully considering its actions were constitutional: "Legislators, influenced by the passions and exigencies of the moment, the pressure of constituents and colleagues, and the press of business, do not always pass sober constitutional judgment on every piece of legislation they enact."[175] Further, in determining the meaning of a constitutional amendment, it is not enough to look at Congress's intent: The intent of the ratifiers—that is, the state legislatures—must also be consulted.

Finally and most important, expressing once again his fervent belief in the proper method of constitutional interpretation, he said: "To be truly faithful to the framers, 'our use of the history of their time must limit itself to broad purposes, not specific practices.' "[176]

> [T]he members of the First Congress should be treated, not as sacred figures whose every action must be emulated, but as the authors of a document meant to last for the ages. Indeed, a proper respect for the framers themselves forbids us to give so static and lifeless a meaning to their work. To my mind, the Court's focus here on a

174. *Marsh* v. *Chambers,* 463 U.S. 783, 796 (1983).
175. Id. at 814.
176. Id. at 816.

narrow piece of history is, in a fundamental sense, a betrayal of the lessons of history.[177]

Probably the most frequent establishment clause challenge in recent years has been to government-sponsored religious displays during the Christmas holidays. Brennan dissented from the Court's 1984 opinion permitting a city to display its crèche in a public park, believing that each part of the three-part test developed by the Court in establishment clause cases was violated: The purpose for the display was religious; it had the primary effect of placing the city's approval behind specific religious beliefs; and it results in entanglement of government and religions, since other groups will press for their religious symbols in future displays. Once again, the majority relied on the history of such displays, but Brennan responded that such practices did not occur until well after the establishment clause was adopted and therefore does not have the historical pedigree of legislative prayers. Concluded Brennan, the Court has taken "a coercive, though perhaps small, step toward establishing the sectarian preferences of the majority at the expense of the minority, accomplished by placing public facilities and funds in support of the religious symbolism and theological tidings that the crèche conveys."[178]

In *Edwards* v. *Aguillard*,[179] Brennan wrote the Court's opinion invalidating a state law that forbids the teaching of evolution in public schools unless creationism is also taught. He noted that the Court has been vigilant in ensuring compliance with the establishment clause in elementary and secondary schools because

[f]amilies entrust public schools with the education of their children, but condition their trust on the understanding that the classroom will not purposely be used to advance religious views that may conflict with the private beliefs of the student and his or her family. Students in such institutions are impressionable and their attendance is involuntary.... The state exerts great authority and coercive power through mandatory attendance requirements, and because of the stu-

---

177. Id. at 817.
178. *Lynch* v. *Donnelly,* 465 U.S. 668, 725–26 (1984).
179. 482 U.S. 578 (1987).

dents' emulation of teachers as role models and the children's susceptibility to peer pressure.[180]

He found that the first part of the three-part test was violated: It was
not to advance academic freedom, as was argued by the state, but rather
to endorse a religious viewpoint, similar to Arkansas' purpose in enacting a statute that forbade the teaching of evolution in the famous
Epperson case in 1968:

> These same historical and contemporaneous antagonisms between
> the teachings of certain religious denominations and the teaching of
> evolution are present in this case. The preeminent purpose of the
> Louisiana legislature was clearly to advance the religious viewpoint
> that a supernatural being created humankind.[181]

In the 1983 case upholding invocational prayers at legislative sessions, *Marsh* v. *Chambers,* the Court did not use the three-part *Lemon*
test, developed in the 1971 case, *Lemon* v. *Kurtzman.*[182] Brennan objected to the Court's failure to use that test—had it been used, he
believed, the prayers would have been found to violate the establishment
clause. Since the *Marsh* decision, several members of the Court have
urged the abandonment of the *Lemon* approach. Justice Scalia has been
particularly insistent that *Lemon* should be rejected. Brennan defended
the test as being protective of establishment clause interests, but he has
also been an advocate of other methods of analysis that are available
to justices in the future who are dissatisfied with *Lemon.* Brennan's
preferred approach was set forth in his concurrent opinion in *Schempp:*

> What the Framers meant to foreclose, and what our decisions under
> the establishment clause have forbidden, are those involvements of
> religious with secular institutions which (a) serve the essentially reli-
> gious activities of religious institutions; (b) employ the organs of
> government for essentially religious purposes; or (c) use essentially

---

180. Id. at 584.
181. 482 U.S. at 591.
182. 403 U.S. 602 (1971).

religious means to serve governmental ends, where secular means would suffice.[183]

He also wrote a decision for a majority of the Court that used a strict scrutiny-compelling state interest test, the same methodology used in equal protection and substantive due process cases. In that case, *Larson* v. *Valente*,[184] a state preferred established religions over newer ones, prompting Brennan to write: "The clearest command of the establishment clause is that one religious denomination cannot be officially preferred over another."[185] In the crèche case discussed above, where the Court did use *Lemon,* Brennan thought it was a watered-down version of that test and reminded the Court that the strict scrutiny test of *Larson* was available.

Free Exercise

Early in his tenure on the Court, Brennan was a strong proponent of government accommodation of an individual's religious practices. In 1961 he dissented from Chief Justice Warren's majority opinion upholding Sunday closing laws that had the effect of putting Orthodox Jewish merchants, whose Sabbath was Saturday, at a disadvantage with their competitors whose Sabbath was Sunday. "Put[ting] an individual to a choice between his business and his religion," said Brennan, is prohibited by the free exercise clause.[186] Although the burden on religion was indirect since it did not compel a person to affirm a repugnant belief or prohibit a religious practice, Brennan felt the effect on individuals was similar and therefore the state had to exempt them unless there was compelling state interest, which he believed was lacking.

Two years later, in the case of *Sherbert* v. *Verner,* Brennan wrote an opinion for a unanimous Court on a related issue: whether a state, under the free exercise clause, could deny unemployment compensation benefits to a person who was fired because she would not work on

---

183. 374 U.S. at 294, 295.
184. 456 U.S. 228 (1982).
185. Id. at 244.
186. *Braunfeld* v. *Brown,* 366 U.S. 599, 611 (1961).

Saturday, her Sabbath Day. He first found the denial of benefits pressured her to give up her Sabbath:

> The ruling forces her to choose between following the precepts of her religion and forfeiting benefits, on the one hand, and abandoning one of the precepts of her religion in order to accept work, on the other hand. Governmental imposition of such a choice puts the same kind of a burden upon the free exercise of religion as would a fine imposed against appellant for her Saturday worship.[187]

He distinguished the Sunday closing laws as involving a strong state interest in having one uniform day of rest for all workers. Adopting the strict scrutiny test for free exercise claims, Brennan found no such compelling state interest present and required the state to provide the benefits. Brennan emphasized that the Court's holding did not result in establishing a religion by requiring the state to provide benefits to Sabbatarians: The decision "reflects nothing more than the governmental obligation of neutrality in the face of religious differences, and does not represent that involvement of religious with secular institutions which it is the object of the establishment clause to forestall."[188]

Just as Brennan fought to keep alive the *Lemon* three-part test as the standard of review in establishment clause cases, so he tried to keep the compelling state interest test of *Sherbert* alive in free exercise cases. The majority refused to apply that test in three cases between 1986 and 1988, prompting Brennan to file strong dissents in cases involving free exercise claims by prisoners seeking to practice their religion; by Native Americans objecting to the federal government using public land in ways incompatible with their religion; and by a member of the military.

In the military case, involving the Air Force's absolute prohibition of service personnel wearing a hat indoors, even a yarmulke worn by an Orthodox Jew for religious purposes, the majority rejected the strict scrutiny test because the case arose in the context of the military, whose regulations are traditionally given great deference. In dissent, Brennan would continue to use the strict scrutiny test even in assessing military regulations but noted that even under a lesser degree of scrutiny, the

---

187. *Sherbert* v. *Verner,* 374 U.S. 398, 404 (1963).
188. 374 U.S. at 409.

absolute rule should not survive. The Air Force feared that allowing an exception for an admittedly unobtrusive yarmulke meant they would have to allow a turban to a Sikh, a saffron robe to a Yogi, and dreadlocks to a Rastafarian. Brennan responded that those cases might be different from yarmulkes and that current Air Force regulations that allow religious items that are not visible tend to favor mainstream Christians. For Brennan, "the Constitution requires the selection of criteria that permit the greatest possible number of persons to practice their faiths freely."[189]

Brennan's concluding paragraphs revealed how central was the free exercise clause to his vision of the Constitution:

> Our constitutional commitment to religious freedom and to acceptance of religious pluralism is one of our greatest achievements. . . . Almost two hundred years after the First Amendment was drafted, tolerance and respect for all religions still set us apart from most other countries and draws to our shores refugees from religious persecution from around the world.
>
> [I]nstitutions dominated by a majority are inevitably, if inadvertently, insensitive to the needs and values of minorities when these needs and values differ from those of the majority. The military, with its strong ethic of conformity and unquestioning obedience, may be particularly impervious to minority needs and values.
>
> The Court and the military services have presented patriotic Orthodox Jews with a painful dilemma—the choice between fulfilling a religious obligation and serving their country. Should the draft be reinstated, compulsion will replace choice. Although the pain the services inflict on Orthodox Jewish servicemen is clearly the result of insensitivity rather than design, it is unworthy of our military because it is unnecessary.[190]

Although the compelling state interest test of *Sherbert* was reaffirmed in the context of unemployment compensation claims by the Court in 1981 and again, in an opinion by Brennan, in 1987, the Court in a 1990 case, *Employment Division* v. *Smith*,[191] refused to apply that test, noting that it had been applied only in the unemployment compensation

---

189. *Goldman* v. *Weinberger,* 475 U.S. 503, 521 (1986).
190. Id. at 523, 524.
191. 494 U.S. 872 (1990).

area. Instead the Court concluded that "generally applicable, religion-neutral laws that have the effect of burdening a particular religious practice need not be justified by a compelling governmental interest."[192] Brennan joined three other justices who would have maintained the strict scrutiny test.

Freedom of Expression

Congress shall make no law . . . abridging the freedom of speech, or of the press, or the right of the people peaceably to assemble.[193]

One of the reasons Brennan was so protective of free speech was that his life's work as a judge was a never-ending exercise of that right. In a speech he gave in 1985, "In Defense of Dissents,"[194] he stressed the importance of expressing one's convictions: "We are a free and vital people because we not only allow, we encourage debate, and because we do not shut down communication as soon as a decision is reached."[195] He believed that the judge whose reasoning in a judicial opinion came closest to the truth would eventually prevail, on the Supreme Court and with the public:

As law-abiders, we accept the conclusions of our decision-making bodies as binding, but we also know that our right to continue to challenge the wisdom of that result may be accepted by those who disagree with us. So we debate and discuss and contest and always we argue. If we are right, we generally prevail. The process enriches all of us, and it is available to, and employed by, individuals and groups representing all viewpoints and perspectives.[196]

---

192. 494 U.S. at 886 n. 3. (Congress, by law, has restored the *Sherbert* test in free exercise cases through the Religious Freedom Restoration Act of 1993, 103 P.L. 141, 107 Stat. 1488.)

193. U.S. Constitution, Amendment I.

194. 37 *Hastings L.J.* 427 (1986).

195. Id. at 437.

196. Id.

Just as his opinions in the area of free speech typically defended the rights of nonestablishment speakers, so he defended the right of judges to dissent from their colleagues:

[T]he obligation that all of us, as American citizens have, and that judges, as adjudicators, particularly feel, is to speak up when we are convinced that the fundamental law of our Constitution requires a given result. I cannot believe that this is a controversial statement. The right to dissent is one of the great and cherished freedoms that we enjoy by reason of the excellent accident of our American births.[197]

Freedom of Speech

Defamation

Brennan's majority opinion in *The New York Times* v. *Sullivan*[198] is perhaps the most important free speech opinion ever written. The case involved the question of the extent to which the First Amendment limited the power of states to award damages to public officials who claimed they were libeled by critics of their conduct in office. Brennan stressed the importance of the First Amendment in a free society; its purpose is "to assure unfettered interchange of ideas for the bringing about of political and social changes desired by the people."[199] He made the connection between free speech and politics even more direct in an opinion he wrote the next year: "[S]peech concerning public affairs is more than self-expression; it is the essence of self-government."[200] Not just "abstract discussion" is protected but also "vigorous advocacy."[201] Noting that those who wrote the First Amendment wanted open discussion free from government suppression, Brennan concluded his sum-

197. Id. at 438.
198. 376 U.S. 256 (1964).
199. 376 U.S. at 269, quoting his opinion in *Roth* v. *United States,* 354 U.S. 476, 484 (1989).
200. *Garrison* v. *Louisiana,* 379 U.S. 64, 74–75 (1964).
201. 376 U.S. at 269, quoting his opinion in *NAACP* v. *Button,* 371 U.S. 415, 429 (1963).

mary of the purposes of the First Amendment with one of the most famous statements ever made about freedom of expression:

> Thus we consider this case against the background of a profound national commitment to the principle that debate on public issues should be uninhibited, robust, and wide open, and that it may well include vehement, caustic, and sometimes unpleasantly sharp attacks on government and public officials.[202]

The Court had never decided the constitutionality of the Sedition Act of 1798, which made it a crime to defame the United States government, the Congress, or the president. In concluding that the Sedition Act, which punished seditious libel, did violate the First Amendment, Brennan made it clear that the First Amendment did more than limit government's ability to censor speech before it was uttered; it also limited the ability of government to punish speech critical of government after it was made.

The New York Times case involved a libel suit brought by a public official for damages arising from a newspaper advertisement containing some false factual statements about the official. The official argued that the First Amendment does not protect false statements, since previous cases had said that libelous utterances are not protected speech, but Brennan wrote that there must be some constitutional protection in the context of criticism of public officials: "Erroneous statement is inevitable in free debate, and . . . it must be protected if the freedoms of expression are to have the 'breathing space' that they 'need . . . to survive.' "[203] The standard that Brennan crafted to accommodate free speech on the one hand and protection of an official's reputation on the other has been used by the Court in defamation cases ever since:

> The constitutional guarantees require, we think, a federal rule that prohibits a public official from recovering damages for a defamatory falsehood relating to his official conduct unless he proves that the statement was made with "actual malice"—that is, with knowledge

---

202. 376 U.S. at 270.
203. 376 U.S. at 271–72, quoting Brennan's opinion in *NAACP* v. *Button*.

that it was false or with reckless disregard of whether it was false or not.[204]

Although Brennan's opinion is viewed as being quite protective of free speech interests, three concurring justices believed he did not go far enough: Critics of public officials' conduct in office should be absolutely protected for their statements, even for statements made knowing they were false. The concurring justices felt that Brennan's approach would lead to a balancing away of the First Amendment. There were indications that Brennan would not give absolute protection to First Amendment interests in a speech he gave shortly before *The New York Times* case: "Does freedom of the press give anyone a right to print that someone else is a Communist or a criminal when he knows this is not true? Even the staunchest exponents of freedom of the press would agree that it is proper for government to provide the injured person some remedy against the publisher of such a damaging falsehood."[205] And in a speech given a few months after *The New York Times* case, he implicitly defended his less absolute approach: "[W]hen we speak of criticism as the lifeblood of an open society, we think particularly of comment based on knowledge, not ignorance; on fact, not misrepresentation; on respect, not fear; on confidence, not suspicion. Criticism which is falsely premised, hostile, erosive, and destructive hardly serves noble ends."[206]

In his opinion for the Court that applied the standard of *The New York Times* case in a criminal libel case the next Term, he explained why the intentional or reckless false statement was not protected:

The use of calculated falsehood, however, would put a different cast on the constitutional question. Although honest utterance, even if inaccurate, may further the fruitful exercise of the right of free speech, it does not follow that the lie, knowingly and deliberately published about a public official, should enjoy a like immunity. At the time the First Amendment was adopted, as today, there were

---

204. Id. at 279–80.
205. Brennan, "Ordered Liberty: The Beginning Lawyer's Challenge," 42 *Michigan State B.J.* 13, 15 (1964).
206. Brennan, "Some Aspects of Federalism," 39 *N.Y.U.L. Rev.* 945, 951 (1964).

those unscrupulous enough and skillful enough to use the deliberate or reckless falsehood as an effective political tool to unseat the public servant or even topple an administration. . . . That speech is used as a tool for political ends does not automatically bring it under the protective mantle of the Constitution. For the use of the known lie as a tool is at once at odds with the premises of democratic government and with the orderly manner in which economic, social, or political change is to be effected.[207]

Many of the cases after The New York Times case dealt with the extension beyond "public officials" to "public figures" and private individuals who are involved in a newsworthy event. In a 1967 case, Brennan was successful in applying the standard of The New York Times case to suits brought by private individuals involved in matters of public interest. He warned that if the press were not protected, "[w]e create a grave risk of serious impairment of the indispensable service of a free press in a free society if we saddle the press with the impossible burden of verifying to a certainty the facts associated in news articles with a person's name, picture, or portrait."[208] He argued against a mere negligence standard for false reporting because, as he said in a later case, that would force the press to engage in self-censorship "by instituting less frequent and more costly reporting at a higher level of accuracy."[209] For those of his colleagues who were more concerned about an individual's privacy and reputation, he admitted that "the press has, on occasion, grossly abused the freedom it is given by the Constitution. All must deplore such excesses. In an ideal world, the responsibility of the press would match the freedom and public trust given it. But from the earliest days of our history, this free society, dependent as it is for its survival upon a vigorous free press, has tolerated some abuse."[210] Brennan's view ultimately did not prevail, when the Court in the 1975 case of Gertz v. Welch[211] adopted a negligence standard rather than The New York Times standard when private individuals involved in matters of public interest claimed they were defamed; the Court reasoned that

207. Garrison v. Louisiana, 379 U.S. 64, 75 (1964).
208. Time, Inc., v. Hill, 385 U.S. 374, 389 (1967).
209. Gertz v. Welch, 418 U.S. 323, 366 (1974).
210. Rosenbloom v. Metromedia, 403 U.S. 29, 51 (1971).
211. 418 U.S. 323 (1974).

private individuals, unlike public figures or officials, do not thrust themselves in the public limelight and therefore should not assume the risk of rough treatment by the press.

Brennan was also unsuccessful in getting the Court to put constitutional restrictions on speech far removed from *The New York Times*'s case concern with political speech: false credit reporting on a private individual. In a 1985 case[212] he argued in dissent that punitive damages could not be awarded for such reporting without meeting the *The New York Times* case malice standard. Thus Brennan's position on the Court in defamation cases moved from the center, when he wrote *The New York Times* case majority opinion, to one of dissenting from the Court's frequent rejection of First Amendment protections for speakers and the press.

Obscenity

Just as Brennan was the leader on the Court in the development of the application of the First Amendment to defamation, so was he the justice who has been most responsible for developments in the law of obscenity and its relation to the First Amendment. It was his 1957 opinion in *Roth* v. *United States*[213] in which the Court first squarely held that obscenity is not protected by the First Amendment. "[I]mplicit in the history of the First Amendment is the rejection of obscenity as utterly without redeeming social importance."[214] *Roth* defined obscenity in the following way: "whether to the average person, applying contemporary community standards, the dominant theme of the material taken as a whole appeals to prurient interest."[215] Justice Douglas, joined by Justice Black, dissenting, would give full protection to obscenity; without proof that it causes misconduct, it should be as protected as any other speech.

Despite *Roth*'s apparent restrictive reading of the First Amendment, the opinion, in other ways was speech-protective:

[S]ex and obscenity are not synonymous. . . . The portrayal of sex, e.g., in art, literature, and scientific works, is not itself sufficient

---

212. *Dun & Bradstreet* v. *Greenmoss Builders,* 472 U.S. 749 (1985).
213. 354 U.S. 476 (1957).
214. 354 U.S. at 484.
215. Id. at 489.

reason to deny material the constitutional protection of freedom of speech and press. Sex, a great and mysterious motive force in human life, has indisputably been a subject of absorbing interest in mankind through the ages; it is one of the vital problems of human interest and public concern. . . .

It is therefore vital that the standards for judging obscenity safeguard the protection of freedom of speech and press for material which does not treat sex in a manner appealing to prurient interest.[216]

As with their differing approaches to whether obscenity could be punished, Brennan differed from Douglas and Black with respect to whether censorship boards could stop obscene films from being shown in the first place: While Douglas and Black would ban any censorship scheme, Brennan approved the concept of such boards but wrote that "[a]ny system of prior restraints of expression comes to this Court bearing a heavy presumption against its constitutional validity."[217] And in the most important movie censorship case, *Freedman* v. *Maryland*,[218] Brennan set up very rigid requirements before a censorship system could be approved as constitutional.

In the *Roth* decision and in many opinions he wrote after that case, Brennan tried to walk a tightrope between those who would give absolute protection to obscenity and others who wanted to broaden *Roth*'s definition of obscenity. In response to the absolutists, he argued that the *Roth* definition was not too vague for publishers to understand what they were forbidden to publish. Justice Stewart once described the difficulty of describing in words what was obscene by admitting that his test for obscenity was, "I know it when I see it."[219] Brennan resisted attempts to make it easier to prove obscenity by opposing efforts to define community standards at the local community rather than the national community[220] and by permitting conviction even if a book was not "utterly" worthless.[221] He also defended as a worthy effort the Court's policy of obscenity convictions by reading books or viewing

216. Id. at 487–88.
217. *Bantam Books* v. *Sullivan,* 372 U.S. 58, 70 (1963).
218. 380 U.S. 51 (1965).
219. *Jacobellis* v. *Ohio,* 378 U.S. 184, 197.
220. Id. at 195.
221. *Memoirs* v. *Massachusetts,* 383 U.S. 413, 419 (1966).

movies, although Justice Douglas countered: "If despite the Constitution ... this nation is to embark on the dangerous road of censorship ... this Court is about the most inappropriate Supreme Board of Censors that could be found."[222]

In 1973 Brennan in effect conceded that Douglas was right at least as to obscene material read or viewed by consenting adults.[223] In that year, a five-justice majority rewrote the *Roth* standards in an attempt to clarify the definition of obscenity; Brennan wrote a dissent for three other justices, urging the Court to abandon its efforts begun sixteen years earlier in *Roth*.[224] His opinion was not a ringing endorsement of the value of obscene speech but expressed other concerns. He characterized the Court's experience dealing with obscenity as demanding more time than any other First Amendment issue, generating disharmony of views and remaining resistant to stable and manageable standards. Brennan's reasons for abandoning his efforts to control obscenity included the difficulty in separating protected speech from unprotected obscenity; an inability to get a majority of the justices to agree on a test after *Roth;* the Court's practice of summarily reversing obscenity convictions without giving guidance to courts or publishers by written opinions; and the problem of vagueness, which, Brennan now believed, after years of experience, was inherent in obscenity cases.

It was the problem of vagueness that most troubled him: Vague standards were unfair to defendants who lacked notice of what they could and could not write, chilled protected speech of persons who might censor their writing to avoid prosecution, and burdened the courts that had to try obscenity cases without clear standards. "[T]he effort to suppress obscenity is predicated on unprovable, although strongly held, assumptions about human behavior, morality, sex, and religion. The

---

222. *Kingsley Int'l: Pictures Corp.* v. *Regents,* 360 U.S. 684, 690 (1959).

223. He concurred in a 1982 case upholding a state law that criminalized the sale of child pornography, *New York* v. *Ferber,* 458 U.S. 747, but dissented in a case that could result in criminalizing "pictures of topless bathers at a Mediterranean beach, of teenagers in revealing dresses, and even of toddlers romping unclothed," *Osborne* v. *Ohio,* 495 U.S. 103, 131 (1990).

224. The new test changed *Roth* in two ways: First, a work need no longer be "utterly" without redeeming social value; instead, it is enough if it lacks "serious" value; second, the "community standards" under which obscenity is to be determined need not be the national community. *Miller* v. *California,* 413 U.S. 15 (1973). There were five cases handed down at the same time, all decided by five-to-four votes. Brennan's most important dissent was in *Paris Adult Theatre* v. *Slaton,* 413 U.S. 49 (1973).

existence of these assumptions cannot validate a statute that substantially undermines the guarantees of the First Amendment.''[225] Douglas appreciated Brennan's conversion: ''I applaud the effort of my Brother Brennan to forsake the low road which the Court has followed in this field.''[226]

In *FCC* v. *Pacifica Foundation*,[227] the FCC ban on the broadcast of George Carlin's ''Filthy Words'' monologue at certain times of the day was upheld by the Court: The government's interests, which were found to outweigh the First Amendment rights of the speaker and willing listeners, were to protect the privacy of the home from those who did not want to hear the monologue and to keep children from being exposed to the words. In dissent, Brennan noted that the privacy of the homeowner could be protected by the offended individual turning off the radio, and that parents, not government, have the right to decide what their children should hear: ''As surprising as it may be to individual members of this Court, some parents may actually find Mr. Carlin's unabashed attitude toward the seven 'dirty words' healthy.'' He observed that the Court's rationale could result in banning from the air works by Shakespeare, Joyce, Hemingway; political speeches such as the Nixon tapes; and many portions of the Bible.[228]

But Brennan was not only disturbed by what he saw as an assault on the First Amendment; he also criticized the Court for its

> inability to appreciate that in our land of cultural pluralism, there are many who think, act, and talk differently from the members of this Court, and who do not share their fragile sensibilities. It is only an acute ethnocentric myopia that enables the Court to approve the censorship of communications solely because of the words they contain.[229]

Like the substantive due process case in which a city tried to keep out nonnuclear families through the zoning power, he saw the FCC's ruling and the Court's approval of it as ''another of the dominant culture's inevitable efforts to force those groups who do not share its mores to

---

225. 413 U.S. at 109–10.
226. 413 U.S. at 72.
227. 438 U.S. 726 (1978).
228. 438 U.S. at 771.
229. Id. at 775.

conform to its way of thinking, acting, and speaking.''[230] If similar attempts are made to keep rap songs off the air in the 1990s, Brennan's *Pacifica* dissent will be cited by those who believe they are protected speech.

Brennan also objected to another method for restricting nonobscene speech: the use of zoning ordinances to keep adult movie theaters out of residential areas although other theaters or businesses are permitted. In *Renton* v. *Playtime Theatres,*[231] the majority upheld such laws on the grounds that they are not aimed at the content of speech but at the secondary effects adult movies have on the social decay of neighborhoods. Brennan found the ordinance to discriminate on the basis of content and believed that the ''secondary effects'' test can result in masking what is really an attempt to suppress speech on the basis of content. The *Renton* analysis, he feared in a later case, may be expanded beyond the secondary effects of pornographic films to permit regulation of political speech because of such secondary effects as congestion, visual clutter, or security.[232]

Discrimination on the Basis of Content

Paralleling his equal-protection opinions dealing with laws that discriminate against powerless minorities are his free-speech opinions that dealt with laws discriminating on the basis of the content of expression. For example, he held unconstitutional a state law that banned all residential picketing except in the case of the picketing at a place of employment involved in a labor dispute.[233] Even though Brennan agreed that residential privacy was an important value, the First Amendment prohibits the state from preferring one type of message—labor picketing, in this case—over all others. When the government discriminates on the basis of viewpoint—for example, permitting an incumbent teachers' union, but not the rival union, to have access to teachers' mailboxes and the interschool mail system—Brennan argued that such censorship was prohibited whether the mail system was considered a public or a nonpublic forum.[234]

---

230. Id. at 777.
231. 475 U.S. 41 (1986).
232. *Boos* v. *Barry,* 485 U.S. 312 (1988).
233. *Carey* v. *Brown,* 447 U.S. 455 (1980).
234. *Perry Educ. Assn.* v. *Perry Local Educators' Ass'n.,* 460 U.S. 37 (1983).

Even where the government's restrictions were not ostensibly based on content, Brennan was concerned that censorship may have motivated the government's action. In *City Council* v. *Taxpayers for Vincent,*[235] the city of Los Angeles banned the posting of signs on public property. The majority of the Court upheld the ordinance, finding the city's interest in eliminating visual clutter to be substantial. Although recognizing the city's interest in aesthetics, Brennan believed that the First Amendment interests were given short shrift. Banning signs on city property would work to the disadvantage of persons running for office who wanted to reach a wide audience with little cost—the alternatives of posting signs on private property or distributing handbills would not be adequate. Where aesthetic concerns are asserted, Brennan had come up with a test in an earlier case in which the city of San Diego banned commercial billboards. Before upholding such a ban based on aesthetics, "a court must be convinced that the city is seriously and comprehensively addressing aesthetic concerns with respect to its environment."[236] The reason for his stringent test, which has not been adopted by the majority of the Court, is his fear that "[t]he asserted interest in aesthetics may be only a facade for content-based suppression."[237] Neither San Diego nor Los Angeles could satisfy that stringent test in Brennan's view.

Perhaps Brennan's most famous opinions illustrating his concern with government favoring certain ideas over others were the two flag-burning cases decided late in his career. In *Texas* v. *Johnson,*[238] involving the burning of the flag as a political protest, the state punished desecration of the flag to preserve the flag as a symbol of nationhood and national unity. "If there is a bedrock principle underlying the First Amendment, it is that the government may not prohibit the expression of an idea simply because society finds the idea itself offensive or disagreeable."[239] It does not matter that the expressive activity comes in the form of nonverbal conduct rather than speech, for "the government may not prohibit expression simply because it disagrees with its message," regardless "of the particular mode in which one chooses to express an

---

235. 466 U.S. 789 (1984).
236. *Metromedia, Inc.,* v. *City of San Diego,* 453 U.S. 490, 531 (1981).
237. *City Council* v. *Taxpayers for Vincent,* 466 U.S. 789, 822 (1984).
238. 491 U.S. 397 (1989).
239. Id. at 414.

idea.''[240] Although he recognized the special place the flag holds in our society, ''[t]he way to preserve [its] special role is not to punish those who feel differently about these matters. It is to persuade them that they are wrong.''[241]

In 1990, the year after *Johnson,* Brennan overthrew the federal law criminalizing the conduct of anyone who "knowingly mutilates, defaces, physically defiles, burns, maintains on the floor or ground, or tramples upon" a flag of the United States. In *United States* v. *Eichman,*[242] Brennan found that the federal law suffered from the same defect as the Texas law: suppression of expression out of concern for its likely communicative impact. Although he acknowledged that flag desecration was quite offensive to some, that was true of much expression that the Court had protected in other First Amendment cases. The principles for which the flag stands are strengthened by permitting the conduct: "Punishing desecration of the flag dilutes the very freedom that make this emblem so revered, and worth revering."[243]

Restrictions on Speech in Certain Places

The Supreme Court has permitted government to impose different levels of restrictions on speech depending on where the speech takes place. In so-called public forums, such as sidewalks and parks, speech is less able to be restricted than in nonpublic forums, such as libraries and prisons. Typically, Brennan dissented from the Court's willingness to allow government to restrict speech in both public and nontraditional forums. For example, he believed, contrary to the majority, that the absolute ban on picketing in front of homes in a residential neighborhood was too broad, *Frisby* v. *Schultz.*[244] Although the town had a substantial interest in the privacy of persons in their homes, residential streets are public forums, and the state's interest in limiting coercive and intrusive residential picketing could be achieved by a narrower ordinance than one that banned all picketing. In a similar dissent, Brennan rejected the argument that a city's interest in the privacy of transit riders from having to view political advertising justified the ban of such

---

240. Id. at 416.
241. Id. at 419.
242. 496 U.S. 310 (1990).
243. Id. at 319.
244. 487 U.S. 474 (1988).

advertising while accepting commercial and public service advertising. Once a public forum is established, the city cannot favor "bland commercialism and noncontroversial public service messages" over more controversial political speech.[245] Although the city argued that censorship was for a benign purpose—keeping offensive messages from transit riders—Brennan argued, "Surely that minor inconvenience is a small price to pay for the continued preservation of so precious a liberty as free speech."[246]

In *Greer* v. *Spock*,[247] a majority upheld military regulations denying access to persons who wanted to distribute leaflets and hold a political rally on base streets and parking lots that were open to civilians. The majority stressed the military's need to train soldiers to fight; in dissent, Brennan said that readiness to fight does not require excluding such persons "unless, of course, the battlefields are the streets and parking lots, or the war is one of ideologies and not men."[248] Just as he argued for the rights of persons in the military to exercise religious freedom in *Goldman* v. *Weinberger,* so he believed that freedom of expression "does not evaporate with the mere intonation of interests such as national defense, military necessity, or domestic security."[249] Brennan argued for a more flexible approach than offered by a public forum rationale; otherwise, once a forum is determined to be nonpublic, government could suppress speech even if the speech were compatible with the activities occurring at the location. Thus he would permit distribution of leaflets and political rallies in areas on the base open to civilians, noting the benefits of exposing members of the military "to the moderating influence of other ideas,"[250] rejecting the majority's view that opening up military bases to such activities would destroy the neutrality of the armed forces.

Where expressive activities take place in a public forum, such as a state fairgrounds, Brennan would place a heavy burden on the state to restrict those activities. While the majority of the Court upheld a prohibition of free literature distribution on the fairgrounds other than at assigned booths, Brennan believed there were alternative ways of the

---

245. *Lehman* v. *City of Shaker Heights,* 418 U.S. 298, 315 (1974).
246. Id. at 320–21.
247. 424 U.S. 828 (1976).
248. Id. at 852.
249. Id. at 852.
250. Id. at 869.

state achieving its purpose in avoiding crowd congestion, and therefore the ban was unconstitutional.[251] Contrary to the majority's view that a personal mailbox is not a public forum, Brennan believed that it was a place that was appropriate for expressive activities and was therefore a public forum: "The mails from the early days of the Republic have played a crucial role in communication."[252]

Brennan dissented from the Court's approval of the Federal Communication Commission's permitting broadcast licensees to refuse absolutely to air paid advertisements on public issues while accepting commercial advertisements. Noting that access to the airwaves was limited, Brennan would have required broadcasters to accept at least some public issue advertising:

> [A]s the system now operates, any person wishing to market a particular brand of beer, soap, toothpaste, or deodorant has direct, personal, and instantaneous access to the electronic media. . . . Yet a similar individual seeking to discuss war, peace, pollution, or the suffering of the poor is denied this right to speak.[253]

While the Court has held that streets and parks are forums appropriate for First Amendment activities, Brennan felt that this should be even more so for the broadcast media, since they "are dedicated *specifically* to communication."[254] He recognized that broadcasters have an interest in not being forced by the government to broadcast messages they did not want to air, but noted that the First Amendment interests in at least some access to paid advertisements by those who wanted to speak outweighed the broadcasters' opposing interests. Brennan believed that the public schools were places where First Amendment rights should be nourished, rejecting the argument that schoolchildren needed to be protected from ideas that were unfit for them. In *Board of Education* v. *Pico*,[255] a school board ordered the removal of certain books from high school and junior high school libraries that it felt were "anti-American, anti-Christian, anti-Semitic, and just plain filthy." Brennan wrote for a plurality of the Court that the First Amendment did limit the

251. *Heffron* v. *Int'l. Soc. for Krishna Consciousness,* 452 U.S. 640 (1981).
252. *U.S. Postal Service* v. *Council of Greenburgh,* 453 U.S. 114, 138 (1981).
253. *CBS* v. *Democratic National Committee,* 412 U.S. 94, 200 (1973).
254. Id. at 195.
255. 457 U.S. 853 (1982).

school board's actions—just as adult citizens have the right of access to ideas in order to exercise their rights of free speech and press, "such access prepares students for active and effective participation in the pluralistic, often contentious society in which they will soon be adult members."[256] He concluded: "[L]ocal school boards may not remove books from school library shelves simply because they dislike the ideas contained in those books."[257]

When the Court upheld a high school principal's censorship of a school-sponsored newspaper in the case of *Hazelwood School Dist. v. Kuhlmeier,*[258] Brennan filed a strongly worded dissent. Although Brennan would permit the censorship of articles that disrupt classwork or invade the rights of the others, the articles in *Hazelwood*—involving teenage pregnancy and divorce—were censored merely because the principle found them "inappropriate, personal, sensitive, and unsuitable." Just as the public must tolerate speech it dislikes, so "public educators must accommodate some student expression even if it offends them or offers views or values that contradict those the school wishes to inculcate."[259] Brennan was disturbed by the effect of the principal's action on the student journalists whose work was censored:

[U]nthinking contempt for individual rights is intolerable from any state official. It is particularly insidious from one to whom the public entrusts the task of inculcating in its youth an appreciation for the cherished democratic liberties that our Construction guarantees.[260]

And he was also disturbed that the Court's opinion sent exactly the wrong message to high school students who thought they were exercising protected freedoms in writing the newspaper articles: "The young men and women of Hazelwood East expected a civics lesson, but not the one the Court teaches them today."[261]

---

256. Id. at 868.
257. Id. at 872.
258. 484 U.S. 260 (1988).
259. Id. at 280.
260. Id. at 290.
261. Id. at 291.

Freedom of Association

The First Amendment does not explicitly protect freedom of association but, as Brennan wrote, "the Court has recognized a right to associate for the purpose of engaging in those activities protected by the First Amendment—speech, assembly, petition for the redress of grievances, and the exercise of religion."[262] He noted that the specific rights of the First Amendment could not be effective against state interference unless individuals could form groups and that the Court has long recognized as implicit in the individual rights under that amendment "a corresponding right to associate with others in pursuit of a wide variety of political, social, economic, educational, religious, and cultural ends."[263]

One of the most important freedom of association cases was Brennan's opinion for the Court in *NAACP* v. *Button*,[264] in which Virginia attempted to stop the NAACP's practice of referring desegregation cases to specified lawyers on the grounds of improper solicitation of legal business. Brennan observed that the NAACP's purposes were to achieve "the lawful objectives of equality of treatment by all government, federal, state, and local" for all blacks and was thus "a form of political expression." Since the legislative branches were not hospitable to the NAACP's goals, "litigation may well be the sole practicable avenue open to a minority to petition for redress of grievances."[265] Although it was not a traditional political party, the NAACP, through its litigation, served an important purpose. For black Americans, "association for litigation may be the most effective form of political association."[266] In one of the first cases requiring the state to show a compelling interest in order to uphold the infringement of First Amendment rights, Brennan found that the state did not meet that test and therefore invalidated the restriction as it applied to the NAACP's activities.

In contrast to the *Button* case, Brennan upheld a state's antidiscrimination law as applied to the associational rights of the male members of the U.S. Jaycees. In *Roberts* v. *United States Jaycees*,[267] Brennan held that Minnesota did have compelling interest in prohibiting the U.S.

---

262. *Roberts* v. *U.S. Jaycees*, 468 U.S. 609, 618 (1984).
263. Id. at 622.
264. 371 U.S. 415 (1963).
265. Id. at 429–30.
266. Id. at 431.
267. 468 U.S. 609 (1984).

Jaycees from excluding women from membership and that Minnesota advanced those interests "through the least restrictive means of achieving its ends."[268] Admitting women, said Brennan, did not have a serious burden on expressive activities of male members nor affect the philosophies or ideologies of its members.

Rights of Governmental Employees

The Supreme Court has been closely divided on the scope of First Amendment rights of governmental employees, with Justice Brennan pushing for expanded rights. As employer, the government does have interests in regulating the speech of its employees in ways that it could not regulate the speech of citizens in general. In *Keyishian* v. *Board of Regents*,[269] with four justices dissenting, Brennan invalidated provisions of a state law aimed at ridding "subversives" from college classrooms. The law required the removal of university faculty and staff for "treasonable or seditious" utterances or acts. Disturbed by the breadth and vagueness of the law, Brennan noted that carrying Communist books might subject a professor to dismissal. To ensure that they were in compliance with the law, faculty members might shy away from controversial topics. "Our nation is deeply committed to safeguarding academic freedom, which is of transcendent value to all of us and not merely to the teachers concerned. That freedom is therefore a special concern of the First Amendment, which does not tolerate laws that cast a pall of orthodoxy over the classroom."[270]

In contrast to the majority's upholding the dismissal of an assistant district attorney who circulated a questionnaire to her coworkers concerning the operation of the office, on the grounds that there were no issues of public concern, Brennan believed the employee's actions were protected by the First Amendment:

The Court's decision today inevitably will deter public employees from making critical statements about the manner in which government agencies are operated for fear that doing so will provoke their

---

268. Id. at 626.
269. 385 U.S. 589 (1967).
270. Id. at 603.

dismissal. As a result, the public will be deprived of valuable information with which to evaluate the performance of elected officials.[271]

Brennan was the author of important opinions holding that the First Amendment was violated when decisions concerning governmental employees' dismissal, promotion, transfer, recall after layoff, or hiring were based on the fact that the employees belonged to a political party different from that of the incumbent. Brennan believed that patronage infringes on freedom of belief and association, as well as harming the electoral process by favoring the incumbent party.

[P]ublic employees hold their jobs on the condition that they provide, in some acceptable manner, support for the favored political party. The threat of dismissal for failure to provide that support unquestionably inhibits protected belief and association, and dismissal for failure to provide support only penalizes its exercise. The belief and association which government may not ordain directly are achieved by indirection.[272]

Since First Amendment rights are at stake, the government must meet a heavy burden to sustain such practices, and Brennan was unconvinced that wholesale firings resulted in an efficient workforce. Nor was it necessary to fire nonpolicy-making employees to achieve the goal of loyalty to the new administration. "Limiting patronage dismissals to policymaking positions is sufficient to achieve this governmental end."[273] Finally, he rejected the argument that patronage dismissals are necessary to preserve the democratic process. "The process functions as well without the practice, perhaps even better, for patronage dismissals clearly also retard that process. Patronage can result in the entrenchment of one or a few parties to the exclusion of others."[274] Brennan noted that historically, patronage dismissals had been practiced by United States presidents, but that history could not validate an unconstitutional practice. In contrast, Justice Scalia would uphold patronage

---

271. *Connick* v. *Myers,* 461 U.S. 138, 170 (1983).
272. *Elrod* v. *Burns,* 427 U.S. 347, 359 (1976).
273. Id. at 367.
274. Id. at 369.

decisions because of the historical record: "[W]hen a practice not expressly prohibited by the text of the Bill of Rights bears the endorsement of a long tradition of open, widespread, and unchallenged use that dates back to the beginning of the Republic, we have no proper basis for striking it down."[275]

Freedom of the Press

Justice Brennan was a strong advocate of a free press "not for the benefit of the press so much as for the benefit of all of us. A broadly defined freedom of the press assures the maintenance of our political system and an open society."[276] Unlike other areas of the First Amendment, where he was willing to use a balancing test, prior restraints on the press, as occurred in the Pentagon Papers case, when the United States sought a court injunction to block publication of a government document in the hands of the press, were absolutely prohibited, with rare exceptions:

[O]nly governmental allegation and proof that publication must inevitably, directly, and immediately cause the occurrence of an event kindred to imperiling the safety of a transport already at sea can support even the issuance of an interim restraining order.[277]

Thus he did not join the majority in an opinion striking down a gag order issued by a state court enjoining the press from reporting on a murder trial because the majority opinion left open the possibility that such a gag order could be upheld in some circumstances. For Brennan, other methods to enforce the fair trial rights of criminal defendants guaranteed by the Sixth Amendment must be utilized:

[J]udges have at their disposal a broad spectrum of devices for ensuring that fundamental fairness is accorded the accused without necessitating so drastic an incursion on the equally fundamental and salutary

---

275. *Rutan* v. *Republican Party of Illinois,* 497 U.S. 62, 95 (1990).
276. *Time, Inc.,* v. *Hill,* 385 U.S. 374, 389 (1967).
277. *New York Times Co.* v. *United States,* 403 U.S. 713, 726–27 (1971).

constitutional mandate that discussion of public affairs in a free society cannot depend on the preliminary grace of judicial censors.[278]

Brennan encouraged cooperative efforts between the organized bar and the press but would not permit judges, on their own, from requiring the press not to publish:

> [T]he press may be arrogant, tyrannical, abusive, and sensationalist, just as it may be incisive, probing, and informative. But at least in the context of prior restraints on publication, the decision of what, when, and how to publish is for editors, not judges.[279]

Aside from the question of publishing information in its possession, cases arose in which the press sought access to information, typically criminal cases, where judges, at the request of the defendant and prosecution, closed the proceedings. Brennan believed that the First Amendment gave the public a right of access, independent of the defendant's right to a public trial guaranteed by the Sixth Amendment. Not every claim of access to information will be upheld; courts must see if historically there has been access to the information and whether access serves important goals. Brennan found special reasons for opening up criminal proceedings to the public:

> Open trials assure the public that procedural rights are respected, and that justice is afforded equally. Closed trials breed suspicion of prejudice and arbitrariness, which in turn spawns disrespect for law. Public access is essential, therefore, if trial adjudication is to achieve the objective of maintaining public confidence in the administration of justice.[280]

The First Amendment right of access was violated when a state law made it mandatory to close its proceedings to the public when a minor victim of a sex offense testified in a criminal trial. In applying a balancing test, Brennan found that a case-by-case approach to closing the

---

278. *Nebraska Press Ass'n.* v. *Stuart,* 427 U.S. 539, 572–73 (1976).
279. Id. at 613.
280. *Richmond Newspapers, Inc.,* v. *Virginia,* 448 U.S. 555, 595 (1980).

proceedings to protect the minor would have been as effective with less harm to First Amendment interests.[281]

Yet Brennan was willing to criticize the press for overreacting to Supreme Court decisions with which Brennan himself disagreed: "The press can and must assist the Court in mustering proper legal conclusions from the accumulated experience of the nation. But the press can be of assistance only if bitterness does not cloud its vision, nor self-righteousness its judgment."[282]

Rights of Persons Accused of Crime

One of Justice Brennan's favorite quotations was a statement by a great state supreme court justice, Walter Schaefer of Illinois: "The quality of a nation's civilization can be largely measured by the methods it uses in the enforcement of its criminal law."[283] Although Brennan was well aware that law abiding members of society were impatient with U.S. Supreme Court decisions interpreting the Constitution in ways that let persons accused of crime go free when the police violate their rights, he defended and explained the reasons for the Court's decisions:

> Too many of us seem to have forgotten the true office of the constitutional procedural safeguards against police tactics such as these. We have forgotten that these safeguards, while they do indeed make harder the conviction of an accused, were not provided for that purpose—the framers of the Constitution weren't "soft on criminals." These safeguards are checks upon government—to guarantee that government shall remain the servant and not the master of us all.[284]

As he put it more succinctly, dissenting in a case where the prosecutor intentionally violated the rights of the defendants yet the majority upheld the conviction: "Convictions are important, but they should not

---

281. *Globe Newspaper Co.* v. *Superior Court,* 457 U.S. 596 (1982).

282. Id. at 182.

283. Schaefer, "Justice, Federalism, and State Criminal Procedure," 70 *Harv. L. Rev.* 1, 26 (1956).

284. Brennan, "The Criminal Prosecution: Sporting Event or Quest for Truth?," 1963 *Wash. U. Law Q.* 279, 280.

be protected by any cost."[285] Brennan pointed out the dangers of allowing the police and prosecution to run roughshod over the rights extended to the accused: "We must remember that society's interest is equally that the innocent shall not suffer and not alone that the guilty shall not escape."[286]

Brennan was critical of lawyers who would not defend persons accused of crime, believing their refusal contributes to society's anger at constitutional protections of the accused:

> A first office of a lawyer in our society is to protect individual rights, especially those secured to people accused of trespassing society's laws. American lawyers cannot be mere private practitioners of the law. They have a public responsibility to maintain a system of government by law. That phrase—"government by law"—is no empty platitude. It is the essence of a free society. No nation possesses a code better designed to assure the civilized and decent administration of justice which is a free society's hallmark. But that code will provide only paper protection if our people are more concerned with prosecutions that are overturned than with fundamental principles that are upheld. Because it is only in upholding fundamental principles, even at the expense of freeing some not-very-nice people, that the protections for nice people are maintained.[287]

The importance Brennan attached to the Court's criminal procedure decisions was revealed when he answered a question first posed to Chief Justice Earl Warren after his retirement: "What decision during your tenure would have the greatest consequence for all Americans?" Warren's answer was *Baker* v. *Carr,* giving each American an equal vote. In contrast, Brennan answered, after twenty years service on the Court:

> I feel at least as good a case can be made that the series of decisions binding the states to almost all of the restraints of the Bill of Rights

---

285. *United States* v. *Hasting,* 461 U.S. 499, 527 (1983).

286. Brennan, "The Criminal Prosecution: Sporting Event or Quest for Truth?," at 291.

287. Brennan, "Law and Psychiatry Must Join in Defending Mentally Ill Criminals," 49 *ABAJ* 239 (1963).

will be even more significant in preserving and furthering the ideals we have fashioned for our society.[288]

Although in his later years on the Court he was most often in dissent from the majority's upholding various police practices as constitutional, in his first decade on the Court, Brennan upheld state claims over the dissents of other justices. For example, in 1959 he wrote an opinion holding that the double jeopardy clause does not prohibit the United States from prosecuting defendants for the same acts that led to their convictions in state court.[289] Justices Black, Warren, and Douglas dissented. In 1966 Justice Brennan wrote an opinion, over three dissents, permitting the taking of blood from an individual suspected of driving while intoxicated, even though the subject objected to the taking in the absence of counsel.[290] And two years later he joined Chief Justice Warren's famous opinion in *Terry* v. *Ohio*[291] upholding the practice of "stop and frisk," rejecting Justice Douglas's dissent, which noted that there was no probable cause or a warrant that Douglas believed was required by the Fourth Amendment.

Fourth Amendment

The right of the people to be secure in their persons, houses, papers, and effects, against unreasonable searches and seizures, shall not be violated, and no warrants shall issue, but upon probable cause, supported by oath or affirmation, and particularly describing the place to be searched, and the persons or things to be seized.[292]

Exclusionary Rule

Aside from the death penalty, the criminal procedure issue that has generated the most controversy on the Court in the past two decades

---

288. Brennan, "State Constitutions and the Protection of Individual Rights," 90 *Harv. L. Rev.* 489, 493 (1977).
289. *Abbate* v. *United States,* 359 U.S. 229 (1959).
290. *Schmerber* v. *California,* 384 U.S. 757 (1966).
291. 392 U.S. 1 (1968).
292. U.S. Constitution, Amendment IV.

has been the Fourth Amendment's exclusionary rule. Since 1914 the exclusionary rule has been applied in federal criminal cases to exclude from the trial evidence of a crime obtained by the government in violation of the Fourth Amendment. Since 1961 that same rule has applied to state criminal trials. Justice Brennan played an important part in developing the exclusionary rule—for example, by writing the most important decision concerning what type of evidence is to be excluded once the police have violated the Fourth Amendment. In *Wong Sun* v. *United States*[293] he applied the rule to exclude verbal evidence, finding no reasons to distinguish between physical and verbal evidence obtained in an unconstitutional manner.

Beginning in the 1970s, the Court began cutting back on the scope of the rule, most importantly in two 1984 cases, *United States* v. *Leon*[294] and *Massachusetts* v. *Sheppard.*[295] In those cases, Justice White wrote for the majority that evidence seized in violation of the Fourth Amendment was nonetheless admissible if the police reasonably relied on search warrants issued by a neutral judge. Justice White's opinions stated that the exclusionary rule was not part of the Fourth Amendment but was a remedy created by the courts solely to deter police violations of the amendment. Whether to apply the rule in a given case depended on a cost-benefit analysis.

Justice Brennan dissented, stating that the rule was part of the Fourth Amendment and that *admission* of the evidence in court was as much a violation as its initial *seizure.* Brennan understood the pressures on the Court to do something about crime, but that same pressure has existed since the amendment was added to the Constitution in 1791: "The task of combating crime and convicting the guilty will in every era seem of such critical and pressing concern that we may be lured by the temptations of expediency into forsaking our commitment to protecting individual liberty and privacy."[296] Moreover, said Brennan, it is not the exclusionary rule but the Fourth Amendment itself that requires the government to forgo some incriminating evidence—that is, the police may not seize evidence unless they have a warrant and probable cause: "This restriction of official power means that some incriminating evidence inevitably will go undetected if the government obeys

---

293. 371 U.S. 471 (1963).
294. 468 U.S. 897 (1984).
295. 468 U.S. 981 (1984).
296. *Leon,* 468 U.S. at 929–30.

these constitutional restraints. It is the loss of that evidence that is the 'price' our society pays for enjoying the freedom and privacy safe-guarded by the Fourth Amendment.''[297] Instead of government officials seeking solutions to crime control through costly and difficult measures,

> the relaxation of Fourth Amendment standards seems a tempting, costless means of meeting the public's demand for better law enforce-ment. In the long run, however, we as a society pay a heavy price for such expediency, because . . . the rights guaranteed in the Fourth Amendment ''are not mere second-class rights but belong in the catalog of indispensable freedoms'' [quoting from an opinion by Justice Jackson].[298]

Although Justice Brennan worried that the exclusionary rule would be completely abrogated by the Court, he was sometimes able to muster a bare majority to keep it alive, as in an opinion he wrote during his last Term on the Court. In *James* v. *Illinois*,[299] he explained why the cost-benefit analysis of *Leon* was weighted in favor of creating addi-tional exceptions to the exclusionary rule:

> The cost to the truth-seeking process of evidentiary exclusion invariably is perceived more tangibly in discrete prosecutions than is the protec-tion of privacy values through deterrence of future police misconduct. When defining the precise scope of the exclusionary rule, however, we must focus on systematic effects of proposed exceptions to ensure that individual liberty from arbitrary or oppressive police conduct does not succumb to the inexorable pressure to introduce all incrimi-nating evidence, no matter how obtained, in each and every crimi-nal case.[300]

More often, however, Brennan found himself dissenting from the evisceration of the exclusionary rule, in both Fourth and Fifth Amend-ment cases. What most troubled him was the willingness of the judicial branch to be a partner to illegal police action by admitting unconstitu-

---

297. Id. at 941.
298. Id. at 959–60.
299. 493 U.S. 307 (1990).
300. Id. at 319–20.

tionally obtained evidence: ''[I]t is monstrous that courts should aid or abet the law-breaking police officer.''[301] The approach used by the majority to admit illegally obtained evidence seemed to Brennan to be inconsistent with the Court's role as protector of constitutional rights:

> [T]he efficacy of the Bill of Rights as the bulwark of our national liberty depends precisely upon public appreciation of the special character of constitutional prescriptions. The Court is charged with the responsibility to enforce constitutional guarantees; decisions such as today's patently disregard that obligation.[302]

Expectation of Privacy

In the 1967 case of *Katz* v. *United States*,[303] the Court held that the Fourth Amendment was more concerned with protection of personal privacy than with protection of property. Thus, what a person ''seeks to preserve as private, even in an area accessible to the public, may be constitutionally protected.''[304] *Katz* held, for the first time, that eavesdropping by law enforcement agents on a person's conversation from a public phone booth violates the Fourth Amendment unless a search warrant is first obtained. *Katz* adopted Brennan's suggestion made in a dissent four years earlier, in the case of *Lopez* v. *United States*,[305] that electronic surveillance should be covered by the Fourth Amendment, even though the framers did not anticipate the development of such devices. The United States in the *Lopez* case argued that if electronic surveillance were regulated by the Fourth Amendment, other police techniques that involve more serious deception might be outlawed. Brennan responded:

> [T]here is a qualitative difference between electronic surveillance, whether the agents conceal the devices on their persons or in walls or under beds, and conventional police stratagems such as eaves-

---

301. *Harris* v. *New York,* 401 U.S. 222, 232, (1971).
302. *United States* v. *Havens,* 446 U.S. 620, 634 (1980).
303. 389 U.S. 347 (1967).
304. Id. at 351.
305. 373 U.S. 427 (1963).

dropping and disguise. The latter do not so seriously intrude upon the right of privacy. The risk of being overheard by an eavesdropper or betrayed by an informer or deceived as to the identity of one with whom one deals is probably inherent in the conditions of human society. It is the kind of risk we necessarily assume whenever we speak. But as soon as electronic surveillance comes into play, the risk changes crucially. There is no security from that kind of eavesdropping, no way of mitigating the risk, and so not even a residuum of true privacy.[306]

Although *Katz* adopted part of Brennan's views in *Lopez*—electronic eavesdropping by police on conversations are now covered by the Fourth Amendment—later cases rejected his additional suggestion that electronic recording of face-to face conversations between a secret agent and the defendant should also be covered.[307] To him, the need for scrutinizing all such electronic surveillance in a free society was obvious, for it "makes the police omniscient; and police omniscience is one of the most effective tools of tyranny.[308]

Most commentators assumed that *Katz*'s focus on personal privacy meant the Court would be sympathetic to expanding Fourth Amendment protections to a variety of activities. In fact, in succeeding decades, *Katz* did not prove to be very protective of privacy interests, much to Brennan's dismay. For example, the Court upheld as reasonable a warrantless police search of opaque, sealed trash bags placed on the curb outside the defendant's house, since uninvited persons could open the containers. In dissent, Brennan said:

Scrutiny of another's trash is contrary to commonly accepted notions of civilized behavior. I suspect, therefore, that members of our society will be shocked to learn that the Court, the ultimate guarantor of liberty, deems unreasonable our expectation that the aspects of our private lives that are concealed safely in a trash bag will not become public.[309]

---

306. Id. at 465–66.
307. *United States* v. *White,* 401 U.S. 745 (1971).
308. *Lopez,* 373 U.S. at 466.
309. *California* v. *Greenwood,* 486 U.S. 35, 46–47 (1988).

Brennan's vision of American society "is more dedicated to individual liberty and more sensitive to intrusions on the sanctity of the home."[310] than the Court's. He carefully set forth the privacy interests sacrificed by the Court's holding:

> A single bag of trash testifies eloquently to the eating, reading, and recreational habits of the person who produced it. A search of trash, like a search of the bedroom, can relate intimate details about sexual practices, health, and personal hygiene. Like rifling through desk drawers or interviewing phone calls, rummaging through trash can divulge the target's financial and professional status, political affiliations and inclinations, private thoughts, personal relationships, and romantic interests.[311]

His disapproval of the Court's abandonment of *Katz* was never more evident than in his dissent from the Court's upholding the warrantless observation of a greenhouse in a residential backyard by a police officer four hundred feet above the ground in a helicopter. After quoting a passage from George Orwell's book *Nineteen Eighty-four,* where a helicopter police patrol was snooping in to people's windows, Brennan concluded his opinion, "Who can read this passage without a shudder, and without the instinctive reaction that it depicts life in some country other than ours?"[312]

Probable Cause and Warrants

Justice Brennan was critical of the trend in the Burger Court and the Rehnquist Court to water down, or ignore altogether, the Fourth Amendment's requirements of warrants and probable cause prior to searches or arrests. In the most important probable-cause case in recent years, *Illinois* v. *Gates,*[313] Justice Rehnquist found there was probable cause to uphold a search pursuant to a warrant that was based on information from an anonymous informant. Rejecting earlier Court precedents because they were "overly technical," the majority adopted what

---

310. Id. at 56.
311. Id. at 50.
312. *Florida* v. *Riley,* 488 U.S. 445, 467 (1989).
313. 462 U.S. 213 (1983).

it considered to be a "practical," "nontechnical," and "common-sense" approach to determine probable cause. Objecting to this dilution of what constitutes probable cause, Brennan, in dissent, found that such words were no more than "code words for an overly permissive attitude toward police practices in derogation of the rights secured by the Fourth Amendment. Everyone shares the Court's concern over the horrors of drug trafficking, but under our Constitution only measures consistent with the Fourth Amendment may be employed by government to cure this evil."[314]

Although, as noted above, Brennan voted with the majority in *Terry* v. *Ohio,* which permitted a "stop and frisk" for weapons on something less than probable cause—"reasonable suspicion"—he consistently opposed making additional exceptions to the probable-cause standard. He resisted requests to expand police action based on reasonable suspicion by substituting for probable cause a balancing test that would weigh the intrusiveness of the police action with the seriousness of the crime. As he wrote for the majority in a 1979 case:

> Hostility to seizures based on mere suspicion was a prime motivation for the adoption of the Fourth Amendment. . . . The familiar threshold standard of probable cause for Fourth Amendment seizures reflects the benefit of extensive experience accommodating the factors relevant to the "reasonableness" requirement of the Fourth Amendment, and provides the relative simplicity and clarity necessary to the implementation of a workable rule. . . . [T]he protections intended by the framers could all too easily disappear in the consideration and balancing of the multifarious circumstances presented by different cases, especially when that balancing may be done in the first instance by police officers. . . . [With a few exceptions], the requisite "balancing" has been performed in centuries of precedent and is embodied in the principle that seizures are "reasonable" only if supported by probable cause.[315]

More often than not, the Court was willing to engage in ad hoc balancing and approve the use of "reasonable suspicion," as in *New*

---

314. Id at 290.
315. *Dunaway* v. *New York,* 442 U.S. 200, 213–14 (1979).

Jersey v. *TLO*[316] Although Brennan agreed that search warrants would be impractical to conduct searches of students in schools, he objected to the Court's willingness to do away with the probable-cause requirement and, once again, adopt a balancing test that sacrifices the liberty of individuals.

> In my view, the presence of the word "unreasonable" in the text of the Fourth Amendment does not grant a shifting majority of this Court the authority to answer all Fourth Amendment questions by consulting its momentary vision of the social good. Full-scale searches unaccompanied by probable cause violate the Fourth Amendment. I do not pretend that our traditional Fourth Amendment doctrine automatically answers all of the difficult legal questions that occasionally arise. I do contend that this Court has an obligation to provide some coherent framework to resolve such questions on the basis of more than a conclusory recitation of the results of a "balancing" test. The Fourth Amendment itself supplies that framework. . . .[317]

Occasionally something more than probable cause is needed to make a search reasonable—for example, operating on a person to retrieve evidence. In *Winston* v. *Lee*[318] Brennan authored an opinion that held that because the state did not have a compelling reason for giving the defendant a general anesthetic to remove a bullet—there was plenty of other evidence to connect him to the crime—the search was not reasonable.

Fifth Amendment Privilege Against Self-Incrimination

> No person . . . shall be compelled in any criminal case to be a witness against himself. . . .[319]

Probably the best-known criminal procedure case of all time is *Miranda* v. *Arizona*[320] written by Chief Justice Warren in 1966, requiring the police to give four warnings prior to questioning suspects who are

---

316. 469 U.S. 325 (1985).
317. Id. at 370.
318. 470 U.S. 753 (1985).
319. U.S. Constitution, Amendment V.
320. 384 U.S. 436 (1966).

in custody. *Miranda* relied to a significant extent on a decision by Justice Brennan written two years earlier, in *Malloy* v. *Hogan*,[321] involving the refusal to answer questions in a judicially supervised investigation of gambling. In that case the Court held for the first time that the Fifth Amendment privilege against self-incrimination, applicable to the federal government since 1791, when the amendment was added to the Constitution, now applies to the states as well. Further, *Malloy* made it clear for the first time that in determining the admissibility of confessions in criminal prosecutions, state or federal, the source of law is the Fifth Amendment's privilege against self-incrimination. Prior to *Malloy*, defendants who claimed their confessions were coerced relied on the due process clause, under which it was more difficult for defendants to exclude their confessions. In *Miranda* Chief Justice Warren was able to rely on *Malloy* to extend the privilege to confessions obtained by the police.

As was true in so many other areas of constitutional law, Brennan's position with the majority in the 1960s in cases such as *Malloy* and *Miranda* changed to that of dissenter in the 1970s and 1980s. As the Court cut back on *Miranda*, Brennan often gave advice to counsel on where to turn. For example, in a case that he believed cut back on *Miranda* by permitting further questioning after the defendant invoked his right to remain silent, Brennan said:

> In light of today's erosion of *Miranda* standards as a matter of federal constitutional law, it is appropriate to observe that no state is precluded by the decision from adhering to higher standards under state law. Each state has power to impose higher standards governing police practices under state law than is required by the Federal Constitution. . . . Understandably, state courts and legislatures are, as matters of state law, increasingly according protections once provided as federal rights but now increasingly depreciated by decisions of this Court.[322]

As the years went by, his criticism of the Court became sharper, as in a 1984 case that admitted a second confession preceded by warnings but after the initial confession had been obtained in violation of *Miranda*.

---

321. 378 U.S. 1 (1964).
322. *Michigan* v. *Mosley*, 423 U.S. 96, 120–21 (1975).

It is but the latest of the escalating number of decisions that are making this tribunal increasingly irrelevant in the protection of individual rights and that are requiring other tribunals to shoulder the burden.[323]

Sixth Amendment Right to Counsel

In all criminal prosecutions, the accused shall enjoy the right . . . to have the assistance of counsel for his defense.[324]

For Justice Brennan, the right to the assistance of counsel was "indispensable to the fair administration of our adversarial system of criminal justice" as it "safeguards the other rights deemed essential for the fair prosecution of a criminal proceeding."[325] He voted with the majority in both the famous *Gideon*[326] case in 1963, which held that indigent defendants are entitled to counsel paid for by the state at their felony trials, as well as in the *Argersinger*[327] case, which required counsel's appointment when defendants are sentenced to prison for minor offenses. He dissented from the Court's refusal to extend that right to persons who could be sentenced to imprisonment but are, in fact, only fined.[328]

Brennan's most important contribution to the developing Sixth Amendment law of the right to counsel paid for by the state was not the right to counsel at trial but the right at pretrial proceedings. In *United States* v. *Wade,* one of three important decisions he authored in 1967[329] involving the right to counsel at a lineup, Brennan noted that the wording of the Sixth Amendment "encompasses counsel's assistance whenever necessary to assure a meaningful 'defense.' " Providing counsel only at trial is insufficient because the accused can be confronted by the prosecution "at pretrial proceedings where the results might well settle the accused's fate and reduce the trial itself to a mere formality."

---

323. *Oregon* v. *Elstad,* 470 U.S. 298, 363 (1985).
324. U.S. Constitution, Amendment VI.
325. *Maine* v. *Moulton,* 474 U.S. 159, 168–69 (1985).
326. *Gideon* v. *Wainwright,* 372 U.S. 335 (1963).
327. *Arsinger* v. *Hamlin,* 407 U.S. 25 (1972).
328. *Scott* v. *Illinois,* 440 U.S. 367 (1979).
329. *United States* v. *Wade,* 388 U.S. 218 (1967); *Gilbert* v. *California,* 388 U.S. 263 (1967); *Stovall* v. *Denno,* 388 U.S. 293 (1967).

Brennan wrote that the realities of modern criminal prosecution have resulted in decisions that "have construed the Sixth Amendment guarantee to apply to 'critical' stages of the proceedings."[330] Counsel is needed at a lineup, said Brennan, to be able later to effectively cross-examine the witness who identified the defendant at the lineup; counsel must be notified of the lineup and be present, unless defendant validly waives his right. *Wade* was relied on when Brennan wrote that counsel must be provided indigents at preliminary hearings to determine whether there is sufficient evidence to present the case to the grand jury.[331] When the Court refused to extend the right to counsel at pretrial proceedings where the government displays photographs to a witness who identifies the defendant, Brennan dissented, accusing the majority of taking "another step toward the complete evisceration of the fundamental constitutional principles established by the Court" in the three 1967 cases.[332]

Brennan believed that the Sixth Amendment was violated when the state uses secret agents, such as informants or codefendants, to obtain information from the defendant after the prosecution has begun, unless defense counsel is present. As he explained in a much-quoted passage in the case of *Maine* v. *Moulton.*[333]

> The Sixth Amendment guarantees the accused, at least after the initiation of formal charges, the right to rely on counsel as a "medium" between him and the State. . . . [T]his guarantee includes the State's affirmative obligation not to act in a manner that circumvents the protections accorded the accused by invoking this right. . . . Accordingly, the Sixth Amendment is violated when the state obtains incriminating statements by knowingly circumventing the accused's right to have counsel present in a confrontation between the accused and a state agent.[334]

Brennan often disagreed with the majority on the meaning of "assistance of counsel." When the Court upheld a state law permitting counsel for indigent defendants not to argue all nonfrivolous issues on appeal, Brennan dissented, believing defendant had the personal right to make that decision. "The role of the defense lawyer should be above

---

330. *Wade,* 388 U.S. at 224–25.
331. *Coleman* v. *Alabama,* 399 U.S. 1 91970).
332. *United States* v. *Ash,* 413 U.S. 300, 326 (1973).
333. 474 U.S. 159 (1985).
334. Id. at 176.

all to function as the instrument and defender of the client's autonomy and dignity in all phases of the criminal process."[335] He also dissented from the Court's upholding a state law requiring an appointed defense counsel who wants to withdraw from the case to write down the reasons why the issue lacks merit. Unlike the majority, Brennan believed the rule harms defendants, since counsel is not acting as an advocate for the defendant; instead, "the indigent criminal appellant is truly alone."[336] And in a case where the majority upheld a state court's refusal to permit a defense witness to testify because the defendant's lawyer failed to comply with court rules requiring the listing of defense witnesses, Brennan's dissent once again addressed the proper relationship between counsel and defendant:

> Deities may be able to visit the sins of the father on the son, but I cannot agree that courts should be permitted to visit the sins of the lawyer on the innocent client.[337]

Eighth Amendment

Excessive bail shall not be required, nor excessive fines imposed, nor cruel and unusual punishments inflicted.[338]

Of all the areas of law that Brennan dealt with during his years on the Court, it was his death penalty opinions that brought together his core jurisprudential concerns: the limits of constitutional history in interpreting the Constitution; the obligation of courts, rather than legislatures, to interpret the Constitution; and the ability of judges to derive principles from the Constitution to apply to modern problems.

As he did in a few other areas of constitutional law, Brennan made it a practice to file a dissenting opinion every time the Court refused to review where a defendant sought to have his death sentence reversed. Although he recognized that some might view this practice as quixotic

---

335. *Jones* v. *Barnes,* 463 U.S. 745, 763 (1983).
336. *McCoy* v. *Court of Appeals of Wisconsin,* 486 U.S. 429, 455 (1988).
337. *Taylor* v. *Illinois,* 484 U.S. 400, 433 (1988).
338. U.S. Constitution, Amendment VIII.

or worse, he explained his reasons for filing these seemingly useless dissents:

[W]hen a Justice perceives an interpretation of the text to have departed so far from its essential meaning that justice is bound, by a larger constitutional duty to the community, to expose the departure and point toward a different path.

[T]this type of dissent constitutes a statement by the judge as an individual: "Here I draw the line."[339]

Brennan's most important death penalty opinion was his concurrence in the 1972 case of *Furman* v. *Georgia,*[340] the first Supreme Court case to invalidate the death penalty. All nine justices wrote opinions in the five-to-four case, but it was clear that two justices, Stewart and White, who voted to overturn the state laws before the Court, would not invalidate future statutes that were drafted in such a way as to avoid the problem of uncontrolled jury discretion in imposing the death penalty. Indeed, four years later, in the case of *Gregg* v. *Georgia,* the Court upheld death penalty statutes drafted along the lines suggested by White and Stewart. In *Furman,* Justice Brennan first set forth principles for applying the cruel and unusual punishments clause and then found the death penalty unconstitutional under all circumstances.

He believed that the purpose of the clause was to ban the infliction "of uncivilized and inhuman punishments," that any state punishment "must treat its members with respect for their intrinsic worth as human beings." In short, it must "comport with human dignity."[341] He then found several principles that courts should use to analyze particular punishments. Most importantly, a punishment must not be degrading to human dignity. To determine whether a punishment is degrading, one must look to several factors, including the pain associated with the punishment, both mental and physical; the extreme severity of the punishment; and finally, the enormity of the punishment. The reason for the banning of such punishments as the rack and the thumbscrew

---

339. Brennan, "In Defense of Dissents," 38 *Hastings L.J.* 427, 437 (1986).
340. 408 U.S. 238, 257 (1972).
341. Id. at 270.

is that they treat members of the human race as nonhumans, as objects to be toyed with and discarded. They are thus inconsistent with the fundamental premise of the clause that even the vilest criminal remains a human being possessed of common human dignity.[342]

A second principle is that a punishment must not be arbitrary, implicit in the word "unusual." Brennan believed that extremely severe punishments would not often be used, and therefore the Court must be alert to the arbitrary infliction of such punishments. Third, a severe punishment must not be unacceptable to contemporary society; to determine what society thinks, objective factors must be found. The fact that statutes permit the death penalty is not as reliable an indicator as whether the punishment is actually used. The final principle is that the punishment must not be excessive—that is, unnecessary. "The infliction of a severe punishment by the state cannot comport with human dignity when it is nothing more than the pointless infliction of suffering."[343] If a punishment is disproportionate to the crime or serves no penal purpose, it will be deemed excessive.

Applying these principles, Brennan found the death penalty unconstitutional. "Death is today an unusually severe punishment, unusual in its pain, in its finality, and in its enormity."[344] He noted that it is the only existing punishment that involves the conscious infliction of physical pain. It is a total denial of a person's humanity. Brennan would have invalidated the death penalty solely on a finding that "the deliberate extinguishment of human life by the state is uniquely degrading to human dignity,"[345] but the fact that it has been accepted in the United States for so many years led him to consider the second principle, that a severe punishment must not be arbitrarily inflicted. He noted the relative infrequency of prisoners actually being put to death—no more than 50 people a year out of 200 million—thus making the punishment rare, "little more than a lottery system." Nor was there any evidence that the persons executed were the worst criminals.

He then turned to the third principle, noting that the death penalty has been almost totally rejected by contemporary society. The debate,

---

342. Id. at 237–38.
343. Id. at 279.
344. Id. at 287.
345. Id. at 291.

said Brennan, has been essentially about the morality of the death penalty. The methods of execution have become more humane over time, the number of crimes for which death has been inflicted has drastically decreased, and some states have abolished entirely or greatly restricted the punishment. Brennan believed this trend to cut back on the use of the death penalty is evidence of a deep-seated reluctance to impose death and, at the least, "I must conclude that contemporary society views this punishment with substantial doubt."[346]

Finally, he considered whether the penalty of death is excessive. The state's first argument was that the death penalty stops the prisoner from committing further crimes, but Brennan observed that isolation and life imprisonment could do the same. Next, the state argued that death is a greater deterrent to murder than long imprisonment, but Brennan was unconvinced, since executions are so rare. Finally, it was argued that the death penalty protects society by fostering respect for law and discouraging vigilante justice; Brennan did not believe that the rare imposition of death had those beneficial effects. Moreover, he believed the use of death as a punishment actually lowered respect for life and brutalized society's values. The final justification for the death penalty was retribution—that is, criminals should die because they deserve it. But the actual practice of refusing to put people to death although the death penalty is available indicates society believes imprisonment serves the purpose of retribution as effectively as death. "As the history of the punishment of death in this country shows, our society wishes to prevent crime; we have no desire to kill criminals simply to get even with them."[347]

Brennan's inability to convince a majority of his colleagues of the unconstitutionality of the death penalty was perhaps his greatest regret during his thirty-four years on the Court. He accused the dissenters in *Furman* of failing to make and respond to arguments. "They failed to explore what values underlie their feelings and what values the Eighth Amendment was intended to serve."[348] And yet he did not lose hope in the process of constitutional decisionmaking:

I believe that a majority of the Supreme Court will one day accept that when the state punishes with death, it denies the humanity and

346. Id. at 300.
347. Id. at 305.
348. Holmes lecture at 330.

dignity of the victim and transgresses the prohibition against cruel and unusual punishment. That day will be a great day for our country, for it will be a great day for our Constitution.[349]

After Brennan's retirement, Justice Blackmun, who voted to uphold the death penalty in *Furman,* now believes "that the death penalty, as currently administered, is unconstitutional."[350] Like Brennan, he believed that the majority of the Court would one day come around to that view: "I may not live to see that day, but I have faith that eventually it will arrive."[351]

Brennan was troubled by the fact that race played so important a part in determining which defendants were sentenced to death. In *McCleskey* v. *Kemp,*[352] Brennan noted that a study of the death penalty in Georgia showed that "blacks who kill whites are sentenced to death at nearly *twenty-two times* the rate of blacks who kill blacks, and more than *seven times* the rate of whites who kill blacks,"[353] Because there was no proof that the jury that sentenced McCleskey to death did so because he was black and his victim was white, the majority rejected his claim that his sentence was unconstitutional.

Brennan's dissent echoed many of his opinions on the duty of the Court when faced with unpopular claims:

Those whom we would banish from society or from the human community itself often speak in too faint a voice to be heard above society's demand for punishment. It is the particular role of courts to hear these voices, for the Constitution declares that the majoritarian chorus may not alone dictate the conditions of social life. The Court thus fulfills rather than disrupts, the scheme of separation of powers by closely scrutinizing the imposition of the death penalty, for no decision of a society is more deserving of "sober second thought."[354]

---

349. Brennan, "Constitutional Adjudication and the Death Penalty: A View from the Court," 100 *Harv. L. Rev.* 313 (1986).

350. *Callins* v. *Collins,* 114 S. Ct. 1127, 1138 (1994) (Dissenting from denial of certiorari).

351. Id.

352. 481 U.S. 279 (1987).

353. Id. at 327.

354. Id. at 343, quoting Stone, "The Common Law in the United States," 50 *Harv. L. Rev.* 4, 25 (1936).

Brennan reminded the majority that it had been only relatively recently that the Court had used the Constitution to protect black Americans, and this case is a reminder that "we remain imprisoned by the past as long as we deny its influence in the present."

> It is tempting to pretend that minorities on death row share a fate in no way connected to our own, that our treatment of them sounds no echoes beyond the chambers in which they die. Such an illusion is ultimately corrosive, for the reverberations of injustice are not so easily confined. . . . [T]he way in which we choose those who will die reveals the depth of moral commitment among the living.[355]

Even though the majority rejected McCleskey's claim as a matter of constitutional law, the decision will not stop people from recognizing that race plays so important a part in who lives and who dies:

> The Court's decision today will not change what attorneys in Georgia tell other Warren McCleskeys about their chances of execution. Nothing will soften the harsh message they must convey, nor alter the prospect that race undoubtedly will continue to be a topic of discussion. McCleskey's evidence will not have obtained judicial acceptance, but that will not affect what is said on death row. However many criticisms of today's decision may be rendered, these painful conversations will serve as the most eloquent dissents of all.[356]

Conclusion

While he served on the Court, William Brennan was the country's most eloquent spokesman for a living Constitution. He believed that the Constitution's most important task was to enhance the dignity and freedom of each individual by curtailing government invasions of personal liberty. In his many speeches delivered to lawyers, judges, or law students, he constantly challenged the audience to champion the causes

---

355. Id. at 344.
356. Id. at 344–45.

he so passionately believed in: Lawyers in private practice should represent indigent persons and unpopular causes; law students should get involved in *pro bono* activities; state judges should use their state constitutions to protect those whom the Supreme Court was no longer protecting under the U.S. Constitution. Judges and lawyers, in his view, played a central role in society: "[O]ur profession dares never to forget that integrity and efficiency of the judicial process is the first essential in democratic society. The confidence of the people in the administration of justice is a prime requisite for free representative government."[357]

He believed strongly in the role of lawyers to bring about change:

> Lawyers must bring real morality into the legal consciousness. Moral arguments backed by the hard facts about discrimination and deprivation are still the most potent force in the world, whether in the courtroom, in the legislatures, or in the cities.[358]

From Brennan's judicial opinions, one might get the impression that he was solely concerned with individual rights, not responsibilities. Since the Constitution and most of its amendments are concerned with rights of individuals, not their duties, the focus of his judicial opinions on rights is understandable. His speeches, however, present a different picture:

> Just as important, if less often appreciated, is the way that liberty rests on individual and private responsibility. We say a great deal about the *"rights"* aspect of civil rights and liberties, but that's only half a loaf—we must stress also the equally important *responsibilities* of the citizen by which those rights are preserved. The job of making a democracy work is not an easy one. . . . Our nation simply cannot

---

357. Brennan, "Thomas More—Saint and Judge," 4 *Catholic Lawyer* 162, 166 (1958) (address, annual meeting, St. Thomas More Society, May 23, 1957, Washington, D.C.).

358. Brennan "Are Citizens Justified in Being Suspicious of the Law and Legal System?," 43 *Univ. of Miami L. Rev.* 981, 986 (1989) (fourth annual Robert B. Cole Lecture, January 27, 1989, University of Miami Law School).

function unless everyone does his part, beyond what the law absolutely requires that he do or not do.[359]

Warmth and compassion characterized not only his work as a jurist but also his interpersonal relationships. When Justice Souter, his replacement, awaited their meeting upon Souter's confirmation, he anticipated a friendly handshake; he was not prepared for the bear hug with which Brennan congratulated him. And Brennan believed the human touch was essential to judging. For him, two qualities were required for a judge. The first, reason, was necessary but not sufficient. The second quality, passion, he defined as "the range of emotional and intuitive responses to a given set of facts or arguments, responses which often speed into our consciousness far ahead of the lumbering syllogisms of reason." Put another way, these responses are "of the heart rather than the head."[360]

Justice Brennan had great faith in the U.S. Supreme Court as an institution vital to the success of the nation. He was fond of quoting Alexis de Tocqueville's observation about the role of the Supreme Court in the United States: "Scarcely any political question arises in the United States which is not resolved, sooner or later, into a judicial question."[361] Brennan realized that the controversial issues decided by the Court would inevitably be divisive among citizens and that, as the author of many controversial decisions, he would be subject to sharp criticism. Still, he argued, "But the freedom to disagree is the hallmark of a free society and better extremes of protest than the deadly order where there can be none at all."[362] He believed that the framers were wise to leave the resolution of these difficult issues up to the Supreme Court, for "our history has been that many a controversy that elsewhere is settled by the conquest of arms, is, eventually anyhow, settled by force of reason."[363]

---

359. Brennan, "Ordered Liberty: The Beginning Lawyer's Challenge," 42 *Mich. State Bar J.* 13, 15 (1963).

360. Brennan, "Reason, Passion, and the 'Progress of the Law,' " 10 *Cardozo L. Rev.* 3 (1988) (Forty-second annual Benjamin N. Cardozo Lecture, Association of the Bar of the City of New York, September 17, 1987).

361. 1 Tocqueville, *Democracy in America* 280 (Knopf ed., 1948).

362. Brennan, "State Court Decisions and the Supreme Court," 31 *Pa. B.A.Q.* 393, 394 (1960) (speech to Pennsylvania Bar Association, Pittsburgh, Pennsylvania, February 3, 1960).

363. Id. at 407.

Brennan believed that the Constitution had influence not just in this country but also abroad:

> As Americans we adapt our institutions to the ever-changing conditions of national and international life, those ideals of human dignity—liberty and justice for all individuals—will continue to inspire and guide us because they form the core of our Constitution. The Constitution with its Bill of Rights thus has a bright future, as well as a glorious past, for its spirit inheres in the aspirations not only of all Americans, but of all the people throughout the world who yearn for dignity and freedom.[364]

With the exception of Justice Stevens, and perhaps Ginsburg, the current Supreme Court is composed of justices who do not share Justice Brennan's vision that the Constitution is a living charter for expansively protecting individuals in a rapidly changing world. Until recently it was assumed by most Court commentators that it was only a matter of time before the libertarian decisions of the Warren Court would be overruled. However, the jointly written opinion by Justices Souter, O'Connor, and Kennedy in the 1992 abortion case *Planned Parenthood of Southeastern Pennsylvania* v. *Casey* indicates that those decisions will be retained, not because the authors of the joint opinion would have agreed with the Warren Court decisions in the first instance but because they believe that it is generally inappropriate to overrule earlier decisions merely because newly appointed justices disagree with them. This respect for the Court's precedents will ensure that many of Brennan's decisions written during the Warren Court era will not only survive but also, with the appointment of justices who share Brennan's vision, may actually thrive in the years to come.

In his judicial and nonjudicial writings, Justice Brennan was a passionate defender of civil rights and civil liberties whose influence will be felt by individuals, government officials, and courts both in this

---

364. Brennan, "The Worldwide Influence of the United States Constitution as a Charter of Human Rights," 15 *Nova L.J.* 1 (1991).

country and in emerging democracies throughout the world. History will judge him to be worthy of comparison to our greatest Supreme Court justices—John Marshall, Louis Brandeis, and Oliver Wendell Holmes, Jr.

Part III

The Opinions of
Justice William J. Brennan, Jr.

GOLDBERG, COMMISSIONER OF SOCIAL SERVICES OF THE CITY OF NEW YORK v. KELLY ET AL.

Argued October 13, 1969—Decided March 23, 1970

Appellees are New York City residents receiving financial aid under the federally assisted Aid to Families with Dependent Children program or under New York State's general Home Relief program who allege that officials administering these programs terminated, or were about to terminate, such aid without prior notice and hearing, thereby denying them due process of law. The District Court held that only a pre-termination evidentiary hearing would satisfy the constitutional command, and rejected the argument of the welfare officials that the combination of the existing post-termination "fair hearing" and informal pre-termination review was sufficient. *Held:*

1. Welfare benefits are a matter of statutory entitlement for persons qualified to receive them and procedural due process is applicable to their termination.

2. The interest of the eligible recipient in the uninterrupted receipt of public assistance, which provides him with essential food, clothing, housing, and medical care, coupled with the State's interest that his payments not be erroneously terminated, clearly outweighs the State's competing concern to prevent any increase in its fiscal and administrative burdens.

3. A pre-termination evidentiary hearing is necessary to provide the welfare recipient with procedural due process.

(a) Such hearing need not take the form of a judicial or quasi-judicial trial, but the recipient must be provided with timely and adequate notice detailing the reasons for termination, and an effective opportunity to defend by confronting adverse witnesses and by presenting his own arguments and evidence orally before the decisionmaker.

(b) Counsel need not be furnished at the pre-termination hearing, but the recipient must be allowed to retain an attorney if he so desires.

(c) The decisionmaker need not file a full opinion or make formal findings of fact or conclusions of law but should state the reasons for his determination and indicate the evidence he relied on.

(d) The decisionmaker must be impartial, and although prior involvement in some aspects of a case will not necessarily bar a welfare official from acting as decisionmaker, he should not have participated in making the determination under review.

Affirmed.

Mr. Justice Brennan delivered the opinion of the Court.

The question for decision is whether a State that terminates public

205

assistance payments to a particular recipient without affording him the opportunity for an evidentiary hearing prior to termination denies the recipient procedural due process in violation of the Due Process Clause of the Fourteenth Amendment.

This action was brought in the District Court for the Southern District of New York by residents of New York City receiving financial aid under the federally assisted program of Aid to Families with Dependent Children (AFDC) or under New York State's general Home Relief program. Their complaint alleged that the New York State and New York City officials administering these programs terminated, or were about to terminate, such aid without prior notice and hearing, thereby denying them due process of law. At the time the suits were filed there was no requirement of prior notice or hearing of any kind before termination of financial aid. However, the State and city adopted procedures for notice and hearing after the suits were brought, and the plaintiffs, appellees here, then challenged the constitutional adequacy of those procedures.

The State Commissioner of Social Services amended the State Department of Social Services' Official Regulations to require that local social services officials proposing to discontinue or suspend a recipient's financial aid do so according to a procedure that conforms to either subdivision (a) or subdivision (b) of § 351.26 of the regulations as amended. The City of New York elected to promulgate a local procedure according to subdivision (b). That subdivision, so far as here pertinent, provides that the local procedure must include the giving of notice to the recipient of the reasons for a proposed discontinuance or suspension at least seven days prior to its effective date, with notice also that upon request the recipient may have the proposal reviewed by a local welfare official holding a position superior to that of the supervisor who approved the proposed discontinuance or suspension, and, further, that the recipient may submit, for purposes of the review, a written statement to demonstrate why his grant should not be discontinued or suspended. The decision by the reviewing official whether to discontinue or suspend aid must be made expeditiously, with written notice of the decision to the recipient. The section further expressly provides that "[a]ssistance shall not be discontinued or suspended prior to the date such notice of decision is sent to the recipient and his representative, if any, or prior to the proposed effective date of discontinuance or suspension, whichever occurs later."

Pursuant to subdivision (b), the New York City Department of Social

Services promulgated Procedure No. 68-18. A caseworker who has doubts about the recipient's continued eligibility must first discuss them with the recipient. If the caseworker concludes that the recipient is no longer eligible, he recommends termination of aid to a unit supervisor. If the latter concurs, he sends the recipient a letter stating the reasons for proposing to terminate aid and notifying him that within seven days he may request that a higher official review the record, and may support the request with a written statement prepared personally or with the aid of an attorney or other person. If the reviewing official affirms the determination of ineligibility, aid is stopped immediately and the recipient is informed by letter of the reasons for the action. Appellees' challenge to this procedure emphasizes the absence of any provisions for the personal appearance of the recipient before the reviewing official, for oral presentation of evidence, and for confrontation and cross-examination of adverse witnesses. However, the letter does inform the recipient that he may request a post-termination "fair hearing." This is a proceeding before an independent state hearing officer at which the recipient may appear personally, offer oral evidence, confront and cross-examine the witnesses against him, and have a record made of the hearing. If the recipient prevails at the "fair hearing" he is paid all funds erroneously withheld. HEW Handbook, pt. IV, §§ 6200–6500. A recipient whose aid is not restored by a "fair hearing" decision may have judicial review. N. Y. Civil Practice Law and Rules, Art. 78 (1963). The recipient is so notified, 18 NYCRR § 84.16.

I

The constitutional issue to be decided, therefore, is the narrow one whether the Due Process Clause requires that the recipient be afforded an evidentiary hearing *before* the termination of benefits. The District Court held that only a pre-termination evidentiary hearing would satisfy the constitutional command, and rejected the argument of the state and city officials that the combination of the post-termination "fair hearing" with the informal pre-termination review disposed of all due process claims. The court said: "While post-termination review is relevant, there is one overpowering fact which controls here. By hypothesis, a welfare recipient is destitute, without funds or assets. . . . Suffice it to say that to cut off a welfare recipient in the face of . . . 'brutal need' without a prior hearing of some sort is unconscionable, unless overwhelming considerations justify it." *Kelly* v. *Wyman* (1968). The court rejected the argument that the need to protect the public's tax revenues supplied the requisite "overwhelming consideration." "Against the justified desire to protect public funds must be weighed the individual's overpowering need in this unique situation not to be wrongfully deprived of assistance. . . . While the problem of additional expense must be kept in mind, it does not justify denying a hearing meeting the ordinary standards of due process. Under all the circumstances, we hold that due process requires an adequate hearing before termination of welfare benefits, and the fact that there is a later constitutionally fair proceeding does not alter the result." Although state officials were party defendants in the action, only the Commissioner of Social Services of the City of New York appealed. We noted probable jurisdiction (1969), to decide important issues that have been the subject of disagreement in principle between the three-judge court in the present case and that convened in *Wheeler* v. *Montgomery,* also decided today. We affirm.

Appellant does not contend that procedural due process is not applicable to the termination of welfare benefits. Such benefits are a matter of statutory entitlement for persons qualified to receive them. Their termination involves state action that adjudicates important rights. The constitutional challenge cannot be answered by an argument that public assistance benefits are "a 'privilege' and not a 'right.' " *Shapiro* v. *Thompson* (1969). Relevant constitutional restraints apply as much to the withdrawal of public assistance benefits as to disqualification for unemployment compensation, *Sherbert* v. *Verner,* (1963); or to denial of a tax exemption, *Speiser* v. *Randall* (1958); or to discharge from public employment, *Slochower* v. *Board of Higher Education* (1956). The extent to which procedural due process must be afforded the recipient is influenced by the extent to which he may be "condemned to suffer grievous loss," *Joint Anti-Fascist Refugee Committee* v. *McGrath* (1951) (Frankfurter, J., concurring), and depends upon whether the recipient's interest in avoiding that loss outweighs the governmental interest in summary adjudication. Accordingly, as we said in *Cafeteria & Restaurant Workers Union* v. *McElroy* (1961), "consideration of what procedures due process may require under any given set of circumstances must begin with a determination of the precise nature of the government function involved as well as of the private interest that has been affected by governmental action." See also *Hannah* v. *Larche* (1960).

It is true, of course, that some governmental benefits may be administratively terminated without affording the recipient a pre-termination evidentiary hearing. But we agree with the District Court that when welfare is discontinued, only a pre-termination evidentiary hearing provides the recipient with procedural due process. Cf. *Sniadach* v. *Family Finance Corp.* (1969). For qualified recipients welfare provides the means to obtain essential food, clothing, housing, and medical care. Cf. *Nash* v. *Florida Industrial Commission* (1967). Thus the crucial factor in this context—a factor not present in the case of the blacklisted government contractor, the discharged government employee, the taxpayer denied a tax exemption, or virtually anyone else whose governmental entitlements are ended—is that termination of aid pending resolution of a controversy over eligibility may deprive an *eligible* recipient of the very means by which to live while he waits. Since he lacks independent resources, his situation becomes immediately desperate. His need to concentrate upon finding the means for daily subsistence, in turn, adversely affects his ability to seek redress from the welfare bureaucracy.

Moreover, important governmental interests are promoted by affording recipients a pre-termination evidentiary hearing. From its founding the Nation's basic commitment has been to foster the dignity and well-being of all persons within its borders. We have come to recognize that forces not within the control of the poor contribute to their poverty. This perception, against the background of our traditions, has significantly influenced the development of the contemporary public assistance system. Welfare, by meeting the basic demands of subsistence, can help bring within the reach of the poor the same opportunities that are available to others to participate meaningfully in the life of the community. At the same time, welfare guards against the societal malaise that may flow from a widespread sense of unjustified frustration and insecurity. Public assistance, then, is not mere charity, but a means to "promote the general Welfare, and secure the blessings of Liberty to ourselves and our Posterity." The same governmental interests that counsel the provision of welfare, counsel as well its uninterrupted provision to those eligible to receive it; pre-termination evidentiary hearings are indispensable to that end.

Appellant does not challenge the force of these considerations but argues that they are outweighed by countervailing governmental interests in conserving fiscal and administrative resources. These interests, the argument goes, justify the delay of any evidentiary hearing until after discontinuance of the grants. Summary adjudication protects the public fisc by stopping payments promptly upon discovery of reason to believe that a recipient is no longer eligible. Since most terminations are accepted without challenge, summary adjudication also conserves both the fisc and administrative time and energy by reducing the number of evidentiary hearings actually held.

We agree with the District Court, however, that these governmental interests are not overriding in the welfare context. The requirment of a prior hearing doubtless involves some greater expense, and the benefits paid to ineligible recipients pending decision at the hearing probably cannot be recouped, since these recipients are likely to be judgment-proof. But the State is not without weapons to minimize these increased costs. Much of the drain on fiscal and administrative resources can be reduced by developing procedures for prompt pre-termination hearings and by skillful use of personnel and facilities. Indeed, the very provision for a post-termination evidentiary hearing in New York's Home Relief program is itself cogent evidence that the State recognizes the primacy of the pubic interest in correct eligibility determinations and therefore in the provision of procedural safeguards. Thus, the interest of the eligible recipient in uninterrupted receipt of public assistance, coupled with the State's interest that his payments not be erroneously terminated, clearly outweighs the State's competing concern to prevent any increase in its fiscal and administrative burdens. As the District Court correctly concluded, "[t]he stakes are simply too high for the welfare recipient, and the possibility for honest error or irritable misjudgment too great, to allow termination of aid without giving the recipient a chance, if he so desires, to be fully informed of the case against him so that he may contest its basis and produce evidence in rebuttal."

II

We also agree with the District Court, however, that the pre-termination hearing need not take the form of a judicial or quasi-judicial trial. We bear in mind that the statutory "fair hearing" will provide the recipient with a full administrative review. Accordingly, the pre-termination hearing has one function only: to produce an initial determination of the validity of the welfare department's grounds for discontinuance of payments in order to protect a recipient against an erroneous termination of his benefits. Cf. *Sniadach* v. *Family Finance Corp.* (1969) (HARLAN, J., concurring). Thus, a complete record and a comprehensive opinion, which would serve primarily to facilitate judicial review and to guide future decisions, need not be provided at the pre-termination stage. We recognize, too, that both welfare authorities and recipients have an interest in relatively speedy resolution of questions of eligibility, that they are used to dealing with one another informally, and that some welfare departments have very burdensome caseloads. These considerations justify the limitation of the pre-termination hearing to minimum procedural safeguards, adapted to the particular characteristics of welfare recipients, and to the limited nature of the controversies to be resolved. We wish to add that we, no less than the dissenters, recognize the importance of not imposing upon the States or the Federal Government in this developing field of law any procedural requirements beyond those demanded by rudimentary due process.

"The fundamental requisite of due process of law is the opportunity to be heard." *Grannis* v. *Ordean* (1914). The hearing must be "at a meaningful time and in a meaningful manner." *Armstrong* v. *Manzo* (1965). In the present context these principles require that a recipient have timely and adequate notice detailing the reasons for a proposed termination, and an effective opportunity to defend by confronting any adverse witnesses and by presenting his own arguments and evidence orally. These rights are important in cases such as those before us, where recipients have challenged proposed terminations as resting on incorrect or misleading factual premises or on misapplication of rules or policies to the facts of particular cases.

We are not prepared to say that the seven-day notice currently provided by New York City is constitutionally insufficient *per se,* although there may be cases where fairness would require that a longer time be given. Nor do we see any constitutional deficiency in the content or form of the notice. New York employs both a letter and a personal conference with a caseworker to inform a recipient of the precise questions raised about his continued eligibility. Evidently the recipient is told the legal and factual bases for the Department's doubts. This combination is probably the most effective method of communicating with recipients.

The city's procedures presently do not permit recipients to appear personally with or without counsel before the official who finally determines continued eligibility. Thus a recipient is not permitted to present evidence to that official orally, or to confront or cross-examine adverse witnesses. These omissions are fatal to the constitutional adequacy of the procedures.

The opportunity to be heard must be tailored to the capacities and circumstances of those who are to be heard. It is not enough that a welfare recipient may present his position to the decisionmaker in writing or secondhand through his caseworker. Written submissions are an unrealistic option for most recipients, who lack the education attainment necessary to write effectively and who cannot obtain professional assistance. Moreover, written submissions do not afford the flexibility of oral presentations; they do not permit the recipient to mold his argument to the issues the decisionmaker appears to regard as important. Particularly where credibility and veracity are at issue, as they must be in many termination proceedings, written submissions are a wholly unsatisfactory basis for decision. The secondhand presentation to the decisionmaker by the caseworker has its own deficiencies; since the caseworker usually gathers the facts upon which the charge of ineligibility rests, the presentation of the recipient's side of the controversy cannot safely be left to him. Therefore a recipient must be allowed to state his position orally. Informal procedures will suffice; in this context due process does not require a particular order of proof or mode of offering evidence.

In almost every setting where important decisions turn on questions of fact, due process requires an opportunity to confront and cross-examine adverse witnesses. *E. g., ICC* v. *Louisville & N. R. Co.* (1913); *Willner* v. *Committee on Character & Fitness* (1963). What we said in *Green* v. *McElroy* (1959) is particularly pertinent here:

Certain principles have remained relatively immutable in our jurisprudence. One of these is that where governmental action seriously injures an individual, and the reasonableness of the action depends on fact findings, the evidence used to prove the Government's case must be disclosed to the individual so that he has an opportunity to show that it is untrue. While this is important in the case of documentary evidence, it is even more important where the evidence consists of the testimony of individuals whose memory might be faulty or who, in fact, might be perjurers or persons motivated by malice, vindictiveness, intolerance, prejudice, or jealousy. We have formalized these protections in the requirements of confrontation and cross-examination. They have ancient roots. They find expression in the Sixth Amendment. . . . This Court has been zealous to protect these rights from erosion. It has spoken out not only in criminal cases, . . . but also in all types of cases where administrative . . . actions were under scrutiny.

Welfare recipients must therefore be given an opportunity to confront and cross-examine the witnesses relied on by the department.

"The right to be heard would be, in many cases, of little avail if it did not comprehend the right to be heard by counsel." *Powell* v. *Alabama* (1932). We do not say that counsel must be provided at the pretermination hearing, but only that the recipient must be allowed to retain an attorney if he so desires. Counsel can help delineate the issues, present the factual contentions in an orderly manner, conduct cross-examination, and generally safeguard the interests of the recipient. We do not anticipate that this assistance will unduly prolong or otherwise encumber the hearing. Evidently HEW has reached the same conclusion.

Finally, the decisionmaker's conclusion as to a recipient's eligibility must rest solely on the legal rules and evidence adduced at the hearing. *Ohio Bell Bell. Tel. Co.* v. *PUC* (1937). To demonstrate compliance with this elementary requirement, the decision maker should state the reasons for his determination and indicate the evidence he relied on, cf. *Wichita R. & Light Co.* v. *PUC* (1922), though his statement need not amount to a full opinion or even formal findings of fact and conclusions of law. And, of course, an impartial decisionmaker is essential. Cf. *In re Murchison* (1955). We agree with the District Court that prior involvement in some aspects of a case will not necessarily bar a welfare official from acting as a decisionmaker. He should not, however, have participated in making the determination under review.

Affirmed.

EISENSTADT, SHERIFF *v.* BAIRD

Argued November 17–18, 1971—Decided March 22, 1972

Appellee attacks his conviction of violating Massachusetts law for giving a woman a contraceptive foam at the close of his lecture to students on contraception. That law makes it a felony for anyone to give away a drug, medicine, instrument, or article for the prevention of conception except in the case of (1) a registered physician administering or prescribing it for a married person or (2) an active registered pharmacist furnishing it to a married person presenting a registered physician's prescription. The District Court dismissed appellee's petition for a writ of habeas corpus. The Court of Appeals vacated the dismissal, holding that the statute is a prohibition on contraception *per se* and conflicts "with fundamental human rights" under *Griswold* v. *Connecticut.* Appellant, *inter alia,* argues that appellee lacks standing to assert the rights of unmarried persons denied access to contraceptives because he was neither an authorized distributor under the statute nor a single person unable to obtain contraceptives. *Held:*

1. If, as the Court of Appeals held, the statute under which appellee was convicted is not a health measure, appellee may not be prevented, because he was not an authorized distributor, from attacking the statute in its alleged discriminatory application to potential distributees. Appellee, furthermore, has standing to assert the rights of unmarried persons denied access to contraceptives because their ability to obtain them will be materially impaired by enforcement of the statute. Cf. *Griswold, supra; Barrows* v. *Jackson.*

2. By providing dissimilar treatment for married and unmarried persons who are similarly situated, the statute violates the Equal Protection Clause of the Fourteenth Amendment.

(a) The deterrence of fornication, a 90-day misdemeanor under Massachusetts law, cannot reasonably be regarded as the purpose of the statute, since the statute is riddled with exceptions making contraceptives freely available for use in premarital sexual relations and its scope and penalty structure are inconsistent with that purpose.

(b) Similarly, the protection of public health through the regulation of the distribution of potentially harmful articles cannot reasonably be regarded as the purpose of the law, since, if health were the rationale, the statute would be both discriminatory and overbroad, and federal and state laws already regulate the distribution of drugs unsafe for use except under the supervision of a license physician.

(c) Nor can the statute be sustained simply as a prohibition on contraception *per se,* for whatever the rights of the individual to access to contraceptives may be, the rights must be the same for the unmarried and the married alike. If under *Griswold, supra,* the distribution of contraceptives to married persons cannot be prohibited, a ban on distribution to unmarried persons would be equally impermissible, since the constitutionally protected right of privacy inheres in the individual, not the marital couple. If, on the other hand, *Griswold* is no bar to a prohibition on the distribution of contraceptives, a prohibition limited to unmarried persons would be underinclusive and invidiously discriminatory.

Affirmed.

BRENNAN, J., delivered the opinion of the Court, in which DOUGLAS, STWEART, and MARSHALL, J.J., joined.

MR. JUSTICE BRENNAN delivered the opinion of the Court.

Appellee William Baird was convicted at a bench trial in the Massachusetts superior Court under Massachusetts General Laws Ann., c. 272,

§ 21, first, for exhibiting contraceptive articles in the course of delivering a lecture on contraception to a group of students at Boston University and, second, for giving a young woman a package of Emko vaginal foam at the close of his address. The Massachusetts Supreme Judicial Court unanimously set aside the conviction for exhibiting contraceptives on the ground that it violated Baird's First Amendment rights, but by a four-to-three vote sustained the conviction for giving away the foam. *Commonwealth* v. *Baird* (1969). Baird subsequently filed a petition for a federal writ of habeas corpus, which the District Court dismissed (1970). On appeal, however, the Court of Appeals for the First Circuit vacated the dismissal and remanded the action with directions to grant the writ discharging Baird (1970). This appeal by the Sheriff of Suffolk County, Massachusetts, followed, and we noted probable jurisdiction (1971). We affirm.

Massachusetts General Laws Ann., c. 272, § 21, under which Baird was convicted, provides a maximum five-year term of imprisonment for "whoever ... gives away ... any drug, medicine, instrument or article whatever for the prevention of conception," except as authorized in § 21A. Under § 21A, "[a] registered physician may administer to or prescribe for any married person drugs or articles intended for the prevention of pregnancy or conception. [And a] registered pharmacist actually engaged in the business of pharmacy may furnish such drugs or articles to any married person presenting a prescription from a registered physician." As interpreted by the State Supreme Judicial Court, these provisions make it a felony for anyone, other than a registered physician or pharmacist acting in accordance with the terms of § 21A, to dispense any article with the intention that it be used for the prevention of conception. The statutory scheme distinguishes among three distinct classes of distributees—*first,* married persons may obtain contraceptives to prevent pregnancy, but only from doctors or druggists on prescription; *second,* single persons may not obtain contraceptives from anyone to prevent pregnancy; and, *third,* married or single persons may obtain contraceptives from anyone to prevent, not pregnancy, but the spread of disease. This construction of state law is, of course, binding on us. *E.g. Groppi* v. *Wisconsin* (1971).

The legislative purposes that the statute is meant to serve are not altogether clear. In *Commonwealth* v. *Baird, supra,* the Supreme Judicial Court noted only the State's interest in protecting the health of its citizens: "[T]he prohibition in § 21," the court declared, "is directly related to" the State's goal of "preventing the distribution of articles designed to prevent conception which may have undesirable, if not dangerous, physical consequences.'' In a subsequent decision, *Sturgis* v. *Attorney General* (1970), the court, however, found .''a second and more compelling ground for upholding the statute—namely, to protect morals through regulating the private sexual lives of single persons.'' The Court of Appeals, for reasons that will appear, did not consider the promotion of health or the protection of morals through the deterrence of fornication to be the legislative aim. Instead, the court concluded that the statutory goal was to limit contraception in and of itself—a purpose that the court held conflicted ''with fundamental human rights'' under *Griswold* v. *Connecticut,* (1965), where this Court struck down Connecticut's prohibition against the use of contraceptives as an unconstitutional infringement of the right of marital privacy.

We agree that the goals of deterring premarital sex and regulating the distribution of potentially harmful articles cannot reasonably be regarded as legislative aims of §§ 21 and 21A. And we hold that the statute, viewed as a prohibition on contraception *per se,* violates the rights of single persons under the Equal Protection Clause of the Fourteenth Amendment.

I

We address at the outset appellant's contention that Baird does not have standing to assert the rights of unmarried persons denied access to contraceptives because he was neither an authorized distributor under § 21A nor a single person unable to obtain contraceptives. There can be no question, of course, that Baird has sufficient interest in challenging the statute's validity to satisfy the ''case or controversy'' requirement of Article III of the Constitution. Appellant's argument, however, is that this case is governed by the Court's self-imposed rules of restraint, *first,* that ''one to whom application of a statute is constitutional will not be heard to attack the statute on the ground that impliedly it might also be taken as applying to other persons or other situations in which its application might be unconstitutional,'' *United States* v. *Raines* (1960), and, *second,* the ''closely related corollary that a litigant may only assert his own constitutional rights or immunities.'' Here, appellant contends that Baird's conviction rests on the restriction in § 21A on permissible distributors and that that restriction serves a valid health interest independent of the limitation on authorized distributees. Appellant urges, therefore, that Baird's action in giving away the foam fell squarely within the conduct that the legislature meant and had power to prohibit and that Baird should not be allowed to attack the statute in its application to potential recipients. In any event, appellant concludes, since Baird was not himself a single person denied access to contraceptives, he should not be heard to assert their rights. We cannot agree.

The Court of Appeals held that the statute under which Baird was convicted is not a health measure. If that view is correct, we do not see how Baird may be prevented, because he was neither a doctor nor a druggist, from attacking the statute in its alleged discriminatory application to potential distributees. We think, too, that our self-imposed rule against the assertion of third-party rights must be relaxed in this case just as in *Griswold* v. *Connecticut, supra.* There the Executive Director of the Planned Parenthood League of Connecticut and a licensed physician who had prescribed contraceptives for married persons and been convicted as accessories to the crime of using contraceptives were held to have standing to raise the constitutional rights of the patients with whom they had a professional relationship. Appellant here argues that the absence of a professional or aiding-and-abetting relationship distinguishes this case from *Griswold.* Yet, as the Court's discussion of prior authority in *Griswold* indicates, the doctor-patient and accessory-principal relationships are not the only circumstances in which one person has been found to have standing to assert the rights of another. Indeed, in *Barrows* v. *Jackson* (1953), a seller of land was entitled to defend against an action for damages for breach of a racially restrictive covenant on the ground that enforcement of the covenant violated the equal protection rights of prospective non-Caucasian purchasers. The relationship there between the defendant and those whose rights he sought to assert was not simply the fortuitous connection between a vendor and potential vendees, but the relationship between one who acted to protect the rights of a minority and the minority itself. And so here the relationship between Baird and those whose rights he seeks to assert is not simply that between a distributor and potential distributees, but that between an advocate of the rights of persons to obtain contraceptives and those desirous of doing so. The very point of Baird's giving away the vaginal foam was to challenge the Massachusetts statute that limited access to contraceptives.

In any event, more important than the nature of the relationship between the litigant and those whose rights he seeks to assert is the impact of the litigation on the third-party interests. In *Griswold,* the Court stated: "The rights of husband and wife, pressed here, are likely to be diluted or adversely affected unless those rights are considered in a suit involving those who have this kind of confidential relation to them." A similar situation obtains here. Enforcement of the Massachusetts statute will materially impair the ability of single persons to obtain contraceptives. In fact, the case for according standing to assert third-party rights is stronger in this regard here than in *Griswold* because unmarried persons denied access to contraceptives in Massachusetts, unlike the users of contraceptives in Connecticut, are not themselves subject to prosecution and, to that extent, are denied a forum in which to assert their own rights. Cf. *NAACP* v. *Alabama* (1958). The Massachusetts statute, unlike the Connecticut law considered in *Griswold,* prohibits, not use, but distribution.

For the foregoing reasons we hold that Baird, who is now in a position, and plainly has an adequate incentive, to assert the rights of unmarried persons denied access to contraceptives, has standing to do so. We turn to the merits.

II

The basic principles governing application of the Equal Protection Clause of the Fourteenth Amendment are familiar. As THE CHIEF JUSTICE only recently explained in *Reed* v. *Reed* (1971):

> In applying that clause, this Court has consistently recognized that the Fourteenth Amendment does not deny to States the power to treat different classes of persons in different ways. *Barbier* v. *Connolly* (1885). The Equal Protection Clause of that amendment does, however, deny to States the power to legislate that different treatment be accorded to persons placed by a statute into different classes on the basis of criteria wholly unrelated to the objective of that statute. A classification "must be reasonable, not arbitrary, and must rest upon some ground of difference having a fair and substantial relation to the object of the legislation, so that all persons similarly circumstanced shall be treated alike." *Royster Guano Co.* v. *Virginia* (1920)

The question for our determination in this case is whether there is some ground of difference that rationally explains the different treatment accorded married and unmarried persons under Massachusetts General Laws Ann., c. 272, §§ 21 and 21A. For the reasons that follow, we conclude that no such ground exists.

First. Section 21 stems from Mass. Stat. 1879, c. 159, § 1, which prohibited, without exception, distribution of articles intended to be used as contraceptives. In *Commonwealth* v. *Allison* (1917), the Massachusetts Supreme Judicial Court explained that the law's "plain purpose is to protect purity, to preserve chastity, to encourage continence and self restraint, to defend the sanctity of the home, and thus to engender in the State and nation a virile and virtuous race of men and women." Although the State clearly abandoned that purpose with the enactment of § 21A, at least insofar as the illicit sexual activities of married persons are concerned, the court reiterated in *Sturgis* v. *Attorney General,* that the object of the legislation is to discourage premarital sexual intercourse. Conceding that the State could, consistently with the Equal Protection Clause, regard the problems of extramarital and premarital sexual relations as "[e]vils . . . of different dimensions and proportions, requiring different remedies," *Williamson* v. *Lee Optical Co.* (1955), we cannot agree that the deterrence of premarital sex may reasonably be regarded as the purpose of the Massachusetts law.

It would be plainly unreasonable to assume that Massachusetts has prescribed pregnancy and the birth of an unwanted child as punishment for fornication, which is a misdemeanor under Massachusetts General Laws Ann., c. 272, § 18. Aside from the scheme of values that assumption would attribute to the State, it is abundantly clear that the effect of the ban on distribution of contraceptives to unmarried persons has at best a marginal relation to the proffered objective. What Mr. Justice Goldberg said in *Griswold* v. *Connecticut* (concurring opinion), concerning the effect of Connecticut's prohibition on the use of contraceptives in discouraging extramarital sexual relations, is equally applicable here. "The rationality of this justification is dubious, particularly in light of the admitted widespread availability to all persons in the State of Connecticut, unmarried as well as married, of birth-control devices for the prevention of disease, as distinguished from the prevention of conception." Like Connecticut's laws, §§ 21 and 21A do not at all regulate the distribution of contraceptives when they are to be used to prevent, not pregnancy, but the spread of disease. *Commonwealth* v. *Corbett* (1940), cited with approval in *Commonwealth* v. *Baird.* Nor, in making contraceptives available to married persons without regard to their intended use, does Massachusetts attempt to deter married persons from engaging in illicit sexual relations with unmarried persons. Even on the assumption that the fear of pregnancy operates as a deterrent to fornication, the Massachusetts statute is thus so riddled with exceptions that deterrence of premarital sex cannot reasonably be regarded as its aim.

Moreover, §§ 21 and 21A on their face have a dubious relation to the State's criminal prohibition on fornication. As the Court of Appeals explained, "Fornication is a misdemeanor [in Massachusetts], entailing a thirty dollar fine, or three months in jail. Massachusetts General Laws Ann. c. 272 § 18. Violation of the present statute is a felony, punishable by five years in prison. We find it hard to believe that the legislature adopted a statute carrying a five-year penalty for its possible, obviously by no means fully effective, deterrence of the commission of a ninety-day misdemeanor." Even conceding the legislature a full measure of discretion in fashioning means to prevent fornication, and recognizing that the State may seek to deter prohibited conduct by punishing more severely those who facilitate than those who actually engage in its commission, we, like the court of Appeals, cannot believe that in this instance Massachusetts has chosen to expose the aider and abetter who simply *gives away* a contraceptive to *20* times the *90-day* sentence of the offender himself. The very terms of the State's criminal statutes, coupled with the *de minimis* effect of §§ 21 and 21A in deterring fornication, thus compel the conclusion that such deterrence cannot reasonably be taken as the purpose of the ban on distribution of contraceptives to unmarried persons.

Second. Section 21A was added to the Massachusetts General Laws by Stat. 1966, c. 265, § 1. The Supreme Judicial Court in *Commonwealth* v. *Baird,* held that the purpose of the amendment was to serve the health needs of the community by regulating the distribution of potentially harmful articles. It is plain that Massachusetts had no such purpose in mind before the enactment of § 21A. As the Court of Appeals remarked, "Consistent with the fact that the statute was contained in a chapter dealing with 'Crimes Against Chastity, Morality, Decency and Good Order,' it was cast only in terms of morals. A physician was forbidden to prescribe contraceptives even when needed for the protection of health. *Commonwealth* v. *Gardner*. Nor did the Court of Appeals "believe that the legislature [in enacting § 21A] suddenly reversed its field and developed an interest in health. Rather, it merely made what it thought to be the precise accommodation necessary to escape the *Griswold* ruling."

Again, we must agree with the Court of Appeals. If health were the rationale of § 21A, the statute would be both discriminatory and overbroad. Dissenting in *Commonwealth* v. *Baird,* Justices Whittemore and Cutter stated that they saw "in § 21 and § 21A, read together, no public health purpose. If there is need to have a physician prescribe (and a pharmacist dispense) contraceptives, that need is as great for unmarried persons as for married persons." The Court of Appeals added: "If the prohibition [on distribution to unmarried persons] . . . is to be taken to mean that the same physician who can prescribe for married patients does not have sufficient skill to protect the health of patients who lack a marriage certificate, or who may be currently divorced, it is illogical to the point of irrationality." Furthermore, we must join the Court of Appeals in noting that not all contraceptives are potentially dangerous. As a result, if the Massachusetts statute were a health measure, it would not only invidiously discriminate against the unmarried, but also be overbroad with respect to the married, a fact that the Supreme Judicial Court itself seems to have conceded in *Sturgis* v. *Attorney General,* where it noted that "it may well be that certain contraceptive medication and devices constitute no hazard to health, in which event it could be argued that the statute swept too broadly in its prohibition." "In this posture," as the Court of Appeals concluded, "it is impossible to think of the statute as intended as a health measure for the unmarried, and it is almost as difficult to think of it as so intended even as to the married."

But if further proof that the Massachusetts statute is not a health measure is necessary, the argument of Justice Spiegel, who also dissented in *Commonwealth* v. *Baird,* is conclusive: "It is at best a strained conception to say that the Legislature intended to prevent the distribution of articles 'which may have undesirable, if not dangerous, physical consequences.' If that was the Legislature's goal, § 21 is not required" in view of the federal and state laws *already* regulating the distribution of harmful drugs. We conclude, accordingly, that, despite the statute's superficial earmarks as a health measure, health, on the face of the statute, may no more reasonably be regarded as its purpose than the deterrence of premarital sexual relations.

Third. If the Massachusetts statute cannot be upheld as a deterrent to fornication or as a health measure, may it, nevertheless, be sustained simply as a prohibition on contraception? The Court of Appeals analysis "led inevitably to the conclusion that, so far as morals are concerned, it is contraceptives per se that are considered immoral—to the extent that *Griswold* will permit such a declaration.'' The Court of Appeals went on to hold:

> To say that contraceptives are immoral as such, and are to be forbidden to unmarried persons who will nevertheless persist in having intercourse, means that such persons must risk for themselves an unwanted pregnancy, for the child, illegitimacy, and for society, a possible obligation of support. Such a view of morality is not only the very mirror image of sensible legislation; we consider that it conflicts with fundamental human rights. In the absence of demonstrated harm, we hold it is beyond the competency of the state.

We need not and do not, however, decide that important question in this case because, whatever the rights of the individual to access to contraceptives may be, the rights must be the same for the unmarried and the married alike.

If under *Griswold* the distribution of contraceptives to married persons cannot be prohibited, a ban on distribution to unmarried persons would be equally impermissible. It is true that in *Griswold* the right of privacy in question inhered in the marital relationship. Yet the marital couple is not an independent entity with a mind and heart of its own, but an association of two individuals each with a separate intellectual and emotional makeup. If the right of privacy means anything, it is the right of the *individual,* married or single, to be free from unwarranted governmental intrusion into matters so fundamentally affecting a person as the decision whether to bear or beget a child. See *Stanley* v. *Georgia* (1969). See also *Skinner* v. *Oklahoma* (1942); *Jacobson* v. *Massachusetts* (1905).

On the other hand, if *Griswold* is no bar to a prohibition on the distribution of contraceptives, the State could not, consistently with the Equal Protection Clause, outlaw distribution to unmarried but not to married persons. In each case the evil, as perceived by the State, would be identical, and the underinclusion would be invidious. Mr. Justice Jackson, concurring in *Railway Express Agency* v. *New York* (1949), made the point:

> The framers of the Constitution knew, and we should not forget today, that there is no more effective practical guaranty against arbitrary and unreasonable government than to require that the principles of law which officials would impose upon a minority must be im-

posed generally. Conversely, nothing opens the door to arbitrary action so effectively as to allow those officials to pick and choose only a few to whom they will apply legislation and thus to escape the political retribution that might be visited upon them if larger numbers were affected. Courts can take no better measure to assure that laws will be just than to require that laws be equal in operation.

Although Mr. Justice Jackson's comments had reference to administrative regulations, the principle he affirmed has equal application to the legislation here. We hold that by providing dissimilar treatment for married and unmarried persons who are similarly situated, Massachusetts General Laws Ann., c. 272 §§ 21 and 21A, violate the Equal Protection Clause. The judgment of the Court of Appeals is

Affirmed.

CRAIG ET AL. *v.* BOREN, GOVERNOR OF OKLAHOMA, ET AL.

APPEAL FROM THE UNITED STATES DISTRICT COURT FOR THE WESTERN DISTRICT OF OKLAHOMA

Argued October 5, 1976—Decided December 20, 1976

Appellant Craig, a male then between 18 and 21 years old, and appellant Whitener, a licensed vendor of 3.2% beer, brought this action for declaratory and injunctive relief, claiming that an Oklahoma statutory scheme prohibiting the sale of "nonintoxicating" 3.2% beer to males under the age of 21 and to females under the age of 18 constituted a gender-based discrimination that denied to males 18–20 years of age the equal protection of the laws. Recognizing that *Reed* v. *Reed* and later cases establish that classification by gender must substantially further important governmental objectives, a three-judge District Court held that appellees' statistical evidence regarding young males' drunk-driving arrests and traffic injuries demonstrated that the gender-based discrimination was substantially related to the achievement of traffic safety on Oklahoma roads. *Held:*

1. Since only declaratory and injunctive relief against enforcement of the gender-based differential was sought, the controversy has been mooted as to Craig, who became 21 after this Court had noted probable jurisdiction. See, *e. g., DeFunis* v. *Odegaard.*

2. Whitener has standing to make the equal protection challenge.

(a) No prudential objective thought to be served by limitations of *jus tertii* standing can be furthered here, where the lower court already has entertained the constitutional challenge and the parties have sought resolution of the constitutional issue.

(b) Whitener in any event independently has established third-party standing. She suffers "injury in fact" since the challenged statutory provisions are addressed to vendors like her, who either must obey the statutory provisions and incur economic injury or disobey the statute and suffer sanctions. In such circumstances, vendors may resist efforts to restrict their operations by advocating the rights of third parties seeking access to their market. See, *e. g., Eisenstadt* v. *Baird.*

3. Oklahoma's gender-based differential constitutes an invidious discrimination against males 18–20 years of age in violation of the Equal Protection Clause. Appellees' statistics (the most relevant of which show only that .18% of females and 2% of males in the 18–20-year-old age group were arrested for driving while under the influence of liquor) do not warrant the conclusion that sex represents an accurate proxy for the regulation of drinking and driving.

4. The operation of the Twenty-first Amendment does not alter the application of equal protection standards that otherwise govern this case. The Court has never recognized that application of that Amendment can defeat an otherwise established claim under the Equal Protection Clause, the principles of which cannot be rendered inapplicable here by reliance upon statistically measured but loose-fitting generalities concerning the drinking tendencies of groups. Reversed.

BRENNAN, J., delivered the opinion of the Court, in which WHITE, MARSHALL, POWELL, and STEVENS, J., and in all but Part II–D of which BLACKMUN, J., joined. POWELL, J., and STEVENS, J., filed concurring opinions. BLACKMUN, J., filed a statement concurring in part, STEWART, J., filed an opinion concurring in the judgment, BURGER, C. J., and REHNQUIST, J., filed dissenting opinions.

MR. JUSTICE BRENNAN delivered the opinion of the Court.

The interaction of two sections of an Oklahoma statute, Okla. Stat., Tit. 37, §§ 241 and 245 (1958 and Supp. 1976), prohibits the sale of "nonintoxicating" 3.2% beer to males under the age of 21 and to females under the age of 18. The question to be decided is whether such a gender-based differential constitutes a denial to males 18–20 years of age of the equal protection of the laws in violation of the Fourteenth Amendment.

This action was brought in the District Court for the Western District of Oklahoma on December 20, 1972, by appellant Craig, a male then between 18 and 21 years of age, and by appellant Whitener, a licensed vendor of 3.2% beer. The complaint sought declaratory and injunctive relief against enforcement of the gender-based differential on the ground that it constituted invidious discrimination against males 18–20 years of age. A three-judge court convened under 28 U. S. C. §§ 2281 sustained the constitutionality of the statutory differential and dismissed the action (1975). We noted probable jurisdiction of appellants' appeal (1976). We reverse.

I

We first address a preliminary question of standing. Appellant Craig attained the age of 21 after we noted probable jurisdiction. Therefore, since only declaratory and injunctive relief against enforcement of the gender-based differential is sought, the controversy has been rendered moot as to Craig. See, e. g., *DeFunis* v. *Odegaard* (1974). The question thus arises whether appellant Whitener, the licensed vendor of 3.2% beer, who has a live controversy against enforcement of the statute, may rely upon the equal protection objections of males 18–20 years of age to establish her claim of constitutionality of the age-sex differential. We conclude that she may.

Initially, it should be noted that, despite having had the opportunity to do so, appellees never raised before the District Court any objection to Whitener's reliance upon the claimed unequal treatment of 18–20-year-old males as the premise of her equal protection challenge to Oklahoma's 3.2% beer law. Indeed, at oral argument Oklahoma acknowledged that appellees always "presumed" that the vendor, subject to sanctions and loss of license for violation of the statute, was a proper party in interest to object to the enforcement of the sex-based regulatory provision. While such a concession certainly would not be controlling upon the reach of this Court's constitutional authority to exercise jurisdiction under Art. III, see, e. g., *Sierra Club* v. *Morton* (1972); our decisions have settled that limitations on a litigant's assertion of *jus tertii* are not constitutionally mandated, but rather stem from a salutary "rule of self-restraint" designed to minimize unwarranted intervention into controversies where the applicable constitutional questions are ill-defined and speculative. See, e. g., *Barrows* v. *Jackson* (1953). These prudential objectives, thought to be enhanced by restrictions on third-party stand-

ing, cannot be furthered here, where the lower court already has entertained the relevant constitutional challenge and the parties have
sought—or at least have never resisted—an authoritative constitutional
determination. In such circumstances, a decision by us to forgo consideration of the constitutional merits in order to await the initiation of a
new challenge to the statute by injured third parties would be impermissibly to foster repetitive and time-consuming litigation under the guise
of caution and prudence. Moreover; insofar as the applicable constitutional questions have been and continue to be presented vigorously and
"cogently," *Holden* v. *Hardy* (1898), the denial of *jus tertii* standing
in deference to a direct class suit can serve no functional purpose. Our
Brother BLACKMUN's comment is pertinent; "[I]t may be that a class
could be assembled, whose fluid membership always included some
[males] with live claims. But if the assertion of the right is to be
'representative' to such an extent anyway, there seems little loss in
terms of effective advocacy from allowing its assertion by" the present
jus tertii champion. *Singleton* v. *Wulff.*

In any event, we conclude that appellant Whitener has established
independently her claim to assert *jus tertii* standing. The operation of
§§ 241 and 245 plainly has inflicted "injury in fact" upon appellant
sufficient to guarantee her "concrete adverseness," *Baker* v. *Carr*
(1962), and to satisfy the constitutionally based standing requirements
imposed by Art. III. The legal duties created by the statutory sections
under challenge are addressed directly to vendors such as appellant. She
is obliged either to heed the statutory discrimination, thereby incurring
a direct economic injury through the constriction of her buyers' market,
or to disobey the statutory command and suffer, in the words of Oklahoma's Assistant Attorney General, "sanctions and perhaps loss of license." This Court repeatedly has recognized that such injuries establish
the threshold requirements of a "case or controversy" mandated by
Art. III. See, *e. g., Singleton* v. *Wulff* (doctors who receive payments
for their abortion services are "classically adverse" to government as
payer); *Sullivan* v. *Little Hunting Park* (1969).

As a vendor with standing to challenge the lawfulness of §§ 241 and
245, appellant Whitener is entitled to assert those concomitant rights of
third parties that would be "diluted or adversely affected" should her
constitutional challenge fail and the statutes remain in force. *Griswold*
v. *Connecticut.* Otherwise, the threatened imposition of governmental
sanctions might deter appellant Whitener and other similarly situated
vendors from selling 3.2% beer to young males, thereby ensuring that

"enforcement of the challenger restriction against the [vendor] would result indirectly in the violation of third parties' rights." *Warth* v. *Seldin* (1975). Accordingly, vendors and those in like positions have been uniformly permitted to resist efforts at restricting their operations by acting as advocates of the rights of third parties who seek access to their market or function. See, *e. g., Eisenstadt* v. *Baird* (1972).

Indeed, the *jus tertii* question raised here is answered by our disposition of a like argument in *Eisenstadt* v. *Baird.* There, as here, a state statute imposed legal duties and disabilities upon the claimant, who was convicted of distributing a package of contraceptive foam to a third party. Since the statute was directed at Baird and penalized his conduct, the Court did not hesitate—again as here—to conclude that the "case or controversy" requirement of Art. III was satisfied. In considering Baird's constitutional objections, the Court fully recognized his standing to defend the privacy interests of third parties. Deemed crucial to the decision to permit *jus tertii* standing was the recognition of "the impact of the litigation on the third-party interests." Just as the defeat of Baird's suit and the "[e]nforcement of the Massachusetts statute will materially impair the ability of single persons to obtain contraceptives," so too the failure of Whitener to prevail in this suit and the continued enforcement of §§ 241 and 245 will "materially impair the ability of" males 18–20 years of age to purchase 3.2% beer despite their classification by an overt gender-based criterion. Similarly, just as the Massachusetts law in *Eisenstadt* "prohibit[ed], not use, but distribution," and consequently the least awkward challenger was one in Baird's position who was subject to that proscription, the law challenged here explicitly regulates the sale rather than use of 3.2% beer, thus leaving a vendor as the obvious claimant.

We therefore hold that Whitener has standing to raise relevant equal protection challenges to Oklahoma's gender-based law. We now consider those arguments.

II

A

Before 1972, Oklahoma defined the commencement of civil majority at age 18 for females and age 21 for males. Okla. Stat., Tit. 15, § 13. In contrast, females were held criminally responsible as adults at age 18 and males at age 16. Okla. Stat., Tit. 10, § 1101 (a). After the Court of Appeals for the Tenth Circuit held in 1972, on the authority of *Reed* v. *Reed* (1971), that the age distinction was unconstitutional for purposes of establishing criminal responsibility as adults, *Lamb* v. *Brown*, the Oklahoma Legislature fixed age 18 as applicable to both males and females. Okla. Stat., Tit. 10, § 1101 (a). In 1972, 18 also was established as the age of majority for males and females in civil matters, Okla. Stat. Tit. 15, § 13, except that §§ 241 and 245 of the 3.2% beer statute were simultaneously codified to create an exception to the gender-free rule.

Analysis may appropriately begin with the reminder that *Reed* emphasized that statutory classifications that distinguish between males and females are "subject to scrutiny under the Equal Protection Clause." To withstand constitutional challenge, previous cases establish that classifications by gender must serve important governmental objectives and must be substantially related to achievement of those objectives. Thus, in *Reed*, the objectives of "reducing the workload on probate courts," and "avoiding intrafamily controversy," were deemed of insufficient importance to sustain use of an overt gender criterion in the appointment of administrators of intestate decedents' estates. Decisions following *Reed* similarly have rejected administrative ease and convenience as sufficiently important objectives to justify gender-based classifications. See, *e. g., Stanley* v. *Illinois* (1972). And only two Terms ago, *Stanton* v. *Stanton*, (1975), expressly stating that *Reed* v. *Reed* was "controlling," held that *Reed* required invalidation of a Utah differential age-of-majority statute, notwithstanding the statute's coincidence with and furtherance of the State's purpose of fostering "old notions" of role typing and preparing boys for their expected performance in the economic and political worlds.

Reed v. *Reed* has also provided the underpinning for decisions that have invalidated statutes employing gender as an inaccurate proxy for other, more germane bases of classification. Hence, "archaic and overbroad" generalizations, *Schlesinger* v. *Ballard*, concerning the financial position of servicewomen, *Frontiero* v. *Richardson*, and working women, *Weinberger* v. *Wiesenfeld* (1975), could not justify use of a gender line in determining eligibility for certain governmental entitlements. Similarly, increasingly outdated misconceptions concerning the role of females in the home rather than in the "marketplace and world of ideas" were rejected as loose-fitting characterizations incapable of supporting state statutory schemes that were premised upon their accuracy. *Stanton* v. *Stanton*. In light of the weak congruence between gender and the characteristic or trait that gender purported to represent, it was necessary that the legislatures choose either to realign their substantive laws in a gender-neutral fashion, or to adopt procedures for identifying those instances where the sex-centered generalization actually comported with fact. See, *e. g., Stanley* v. *Illinois.*

In this case, too, *"Reed,* we feel, is controlling . . . ," *Stanton* v. *Stanton.* We turn then to the question whether, under *Reed,* the difference between males and females with respect to the purchase of 3.2% beer warrants the differential in age drawn by the Oklahoma statute. We conclude that it does not.

B

The District Court recognized that *Reed* v. *Reed* was controlling. In applying the teachings of that case, the court found the requisite important governmental objective in the traffic-safety goal proffered by the Oklahoma Attorney General. It then concluded that the satistics introduced by the appellees established that the gender-based distinction was substantially related to achievement of that goal.

C

We accept for purposes of discussion the District Court's identification of the objective underlying §§ 241 and 245 as the enhancement of traffic safety. Clearly, the protection of public health and safety represents an important function of state and local governments. However, appellees' statistics in our view cannot support the conclusion that the gender-based distinction closely serves to achieve that objective and therefore the distinction cannot under *Reed* withstand equal protection challenge.

The appellees introduced a variety of statistical surveys. First, an analysis of arrest statistics for 1973 demonstrated that 18–20-year-old male arrests for "driving under the influence" and "drunkenness" substantially exceeded female arrests for that same age period. Similarly, youths aged 17–21 were found to be overrepresented among those killed or injured in traffic accidents, with males again numerically exceeding females in this regard. Third, a random roadside survey in Oklahoma City revealed that young males were more inclined to drive and drink beer than were their female counterparts. Fourth, Federal Bureau of Investigation nationwide statistics exhibited a notable increase in arrests for "driving under the influence." Finally, statistical evidence gathered in other jurisdictions, particularly Minnesota and Michigan, was offered to corroborate Oklahoma's experience by indicating the pervasiveness of youthful participation in motor vehicle accidents following the imbibing of alcohol. Conceding that "the case is not free from doubt," the District Court nonetheless concluded that this statistical showing substantiated "a rational basis for the legislative judgment underlying the challenged classification."

Even were this statistical evidence accepted as accurate, it nevertheless offers only a weak answer to the equal protection question presented here. The most focused and relevant of the statistical surveys, arrests of 18–20-year-olds for alcohol-related driving offenses, exemplifies the ultimate unpersuasiveness of this evidentiary record. Viewed in terms of the correlation between sex and the actual activity that Oklahoma seeks to regulate—driving while under the influence of alcohol—the statistics broadly establish that .18% of females and 2% of males in that age group were arrested for that offense. While such a disparity is not trivial in a statistical sense, it hardly can form the basis for employment of a gender line as a classifying device. Certainly if maleness is to serve as a proxy for drinking and driving, a correlation of 2% must be considered an unduly tenuous "fit." Indeed, prior cases have consistently rejected the use of sex as a decisionmaking factor even though the statutes in question certainly rested on far more predictive empirical relationships than this.

Moreover, the statistics exhibit a variety of other shortcomings that seriously impugn their value to equal protection analysis. Setting aside the obvious methodological problems, the surveys do not adequately justify the salient features of Oklahoma's gender-based traffic-safety law. None purports to measure the use and dangerousness of 3.2% beer as opposed to alcohol generally, a detail that is of particular importance since, in light of its low alcohol level, Oklahoma apparently considers the 3.2% beverage to be "nonintoxicating." Okla. Stat., Tit. 37, § 163.1 (1958); see *State ex rel. Springer* v. *Bliss* (1947). Moreover, many of the studies, while graphically documenting the unfortunate increase in driving while under the influence of alcohol, make no effort to relate their findings to age-sex differentials as involved here. Indeed, the only survey that explicitly centered its attention upon young drivers and their use of beer—albeit apparently not of the diluted 3.2% variety—reached results that hardly can be viewed as impressive in justifying either a gender or age classification.

There is no reason to belabor this line of analysis. It is unrealistic to expect either members of the judiciary or state officials to be well versed in the rigors of experimental or statistical technique. But this merely illustrates that proving broad sociological propositions by statistics is a dubious business, and one that inevitably is in tension with the normative philosophy that underlies the Equal Protection Clause. Suffice to say that the showing offered by the appellees does not satisfy us that sex represents a legitimate, accurate proxy for the regulation of drinking and driving. In fact, when it is further recognized that Oklahoma's statute prohibits only the selling of 3.2% beer to young males and not their drinking the beverage once acquired (even after purchase by their 18–20-year-old female companions), the relationship between gender and traffic safety becomes far too tenuous to satisfy *Reed*'s requirement that the gender-based difference be substantially related to achievement of the statutory objective.

We hold, therefore, that under *Reed,* Oklahoma's 3.2% beer statute invidiously discriminates against males 18–20 years of age.

D

Appellees argue, however, that §§ 241 and 245 enforce state policies concerning the sale and distribution of alcohol and by force of the Twenty-first Amendment should therefore be held to withstand the equal protection challenge. The District Court's response to this contention is unclear. The court assumed that the Twenty-first Amendment "strengthened" the State's police powers with respect to alcohol regulation, but then said that "the standards of review that [the Equal Protection Clause] mandates are not relaxed." Our view is, and we hold, that the Twenty-first Amendment does not save the invidious gender-based discrimination from invalidation as a denial of equal protection of the laws in violation of the Fourteenth Amendment.

The history of state regulation of alcoholic beverages dates from long before adoption of the Eighteenth Amendment. In the *License Cases* (1847), the Court recognized a broad authority in state governments to regulate the trade of alcoholic beverages within their borders free from implied restrictions under the Commerce Clause. Later in the century, however, *Leisy* v. *Hardin* (1890), undercut the theoretical underpinnings of the *License Cases.* This led Congress, acting pursuant to its powers under the Commerce Clause, to reinvigorate the State's regulatory role through the passage of the Wilson and Webb-Kenyon Acts. See, *e. g.,* *Clark Distilling Co.* v. *Western Maryland R. Co.* (1917) (upholding

Webb-Kenyon Act). With passage of the Eighteenth Amendment, the uneasy tension between the Commerce Clause and state police power temporarily subsided.

The Twenty-first Amendment repealed the Eighteenth Amendment in 1933. The wording of § 2 of the Twenty-first Amendment closely follows the Webb-Kenyon and Wilson Acts, expressing the framers' clear intention of constitutionalizing the Commerce Clause framework established under those statutes. This Court's decisions since have confirmed that the Amendment primarily created an exception to the normal operation of the Commerce Clause. See, *e.g., Hostetter* v. *Idlewild Bon Voyage Liquor Corp.* (1964). Even here, however, the Twenty-first Amendment does not *pro tanto* repeal the Commerce Clause, but merely requires that each provision "be considered in the light of the other, and in the context of the issues and interests at stake in any concrete case." *Hostetter* v. *Idlewild Bon Voyage Liquor Corp.*

Once passing beyond consideration of the Commerce Clause, the relevance of the Twenty-first Amendment to other constitutional provisions becomes increasingly doubtful. As one commentator has remarked: "Neither the text nor the history of the Twenty-first Amendment suggests that it qualifies individual rights protected by the Bill of Rights and the Fourteenth Amendment where the sale or use of liquor is concerned." P. Brest, Processes of Constitutional Decisionmaking, Cases and Materials, 258 (1975). Any departures from this historical view have been limited and sporadic. Two States successfully relied upon the Twenty-first Amendment to respond to challenges of major liquor importers to state authority to regulate the importation and manufacture of alcoholic beverages on Commerce Clause and Fourteenth Amendment grounds. See *Mahoney* v. *Joseph Triner Corp.* (1938). In fact, however, the arguments in both cases centered upon importation of intoxicants, a regulatory area where the State's authority under the Twenty-first Amendment is transparently clear, *Hostetter* v. *Idlewild Bon Voyage Liquor Corp.,* and touched upon purely economic matters that traditionally merit only the mildest review under the Fourteenth Amendment, see, *e.g., Joseph E. Seagram & Sons* v. *Hostetter* (1966) (rejecting Fourteenth Amendment objections to state liquor laws on the strength of *Ferguson* v. *Skrupa* (1963). Cases involving individual rights protected by the Due Process Clause have been treated in sharp contrast. For example, when an individual objected to the mandatory "posting" of her name in retail liquor establishments and her characterization as an "excessive drink[er]," the Twenty-first Amendment was held not to qualify the scope of her due process rights. *Wisconsin* v. *Constantineau* (1971).

It is true that *California* v. *LaRue* (1972) relied upon the Twenty-first Amendment to "strengthen" the State's authority to regulate live entertainment at establishments licensed to dispense liquor, at least when the performances "partake more of gross sexuality than of communication." Nevertheless, the Court has never recognized sufficient "strength" in the Amendment to defeat an otherwise established claim of invidious discrimination in violation of the Equal Protection Clause. Rather, *Moose Lodge No. 107* v. *Irvis* (1972), establishes that state liquor regulatory schemes cannot work invidious discriminations that violate the Equal Protection Clause.

Following this approach, both federal and state courts uniformly have declared the constitutionality of gender lines that restrain the activities of customers of state-regulated liquor establishments irrespective of the operation of the Twenty-first Amendment. See *e.g., White* v. *Fleming.* Even when state officials have posited sociological or empirical justifications for these gender-based differentiations, the courts have struck down discriminations aimed at an entire class under the guise of alcohol regulation. In fact, social science studies that have uncovered quantifiable differences in drinking tendencies dividing along both racial and ethnic liens strongly suggest the need for application of the Equal Protection Clause in preventing discriminatory treatment that almost certainly would be perceived as invidious. In sum, the principles embodied in the Equal Protection Clause are not to be rendered inapplicable by statistically measured but loose-fitting generalities concerning the drinking tendencies of aggregate groups. We thus hold that the operation of the Twenty-first Amendment does not alter the application of equal protection standards that otherwise govern this case.

We conclude that the gender-based differential contained in Okla. Stat., Tit. 37, § 245 constitutes a denial of the equal protection of the laws to males aged 18–20 and reverse the judgment of the District Court.

It is so ordered.

GREEN et al. *v.* COUNTY SCHOOL BOARD OF NEW KENT COUNTY et al.

Argued April 3, 1968—Decided May 27, 1968.

Respondent School Board maintains two schools, one on the east side and one on the west side of New Kent County, Virginia. About one-half of the county's population are Negroes, who reside throughout the county since there is no residential segregation. Although this Court held in *Brown* v. *Board of Education (Brown I),* that Virginia's constitutional and statutory provisions requiring racial segregation in schools were unconstitutional, the Board continued segregated operation of the schools, presumably pursuant to Virginia statutes enacted to resist that decision. In 1965, after this suit for injunctive relief against maintenance of allegedly segregated schools was filed, the Board, in order to remain eligible for federal financial aid, adopted a "freedom-of-choice" plan for desegregating the schools. The plan permits students, except those entering the first and eighth grades, to choose annually between the schools; those not choosing are assigned to the school previously attended; first and eighth graders must affirmatively choose a school. The District Court approved the plan, as amended, and the Court of Appeals approved the "freedom-of-choice" provisions although it remanded for a more specific and comprehensive order concerning teachers. During the plan's three years of operation no white student has chosen to attend the all-Negro school, and although 115 Negro pupils enrolled in the formerly all-white school, 85% of the Negro students in the system still attend the all-Negro school. *Held:*

1. In 1955 this Court, in *Brown* v. *Board of Education (Brown II),* ordered school boards operating dual school systems, part "white" and part "Negro," to "effectuate a transition to a racially nondiscriminatory school system," and it is in light of that command that the effectiveness of the "freedom-of-choice" plan to achieve that end is to be measured.

2. The burden is on a school board to provide a plan that promises realistically to work *now,* and a plan that at this late date fails to provide meaningful assurance of prompt and effective disestablishment of a dual system is intolerable.

3. A district court's obligation is to assess the effectiveness of the plan in light of the facts at hand and any alternatives which may be feasible and more promising, and to retain jurisdiction until it is clear that state-imposed segregation has been completely removed.

4. Where a "freedom-of-choice" plan offers real promise of achieving a unitary, nonracial system there might be no objection to allowing it to prove itself in operation, but where there are reasonably available other ways, such as zoning, promising speedier and more effective conversion to a unitary school system, "freedom of choice" is not acceptable.

5. The New Kent "freedom-of-choice" plan is not acceptable; it has not dismantled the dual system, but has operated simply to burden students and their parents with a responsibility which *Brown II* placed squarely on the School Board.   Vacated in part and remanded.

MR. JUSTICE BRENNAN delivered the opinion of the Court.
The question for decision is whether, under all the circumstances

here, respondent School Board's adoption of a "freedom-of-choice" plan which allows a pupil to choose his own public school constitutes adequate compliance with the Board's responsibility "to achieve a system of determining admission to the public schools on a nonracial basis. . . ." *Brown* v. *Board of Education (Brown II)*.

Petitioners brought this action in March 1965 seeking injunctive relief against respondent's continued maintenance of an alleged racially segregated school system. New Kent County is a rural county in Eastern Virginia. About one-half of its population of some 4,500 are Negroes. There is no residential segregation in the county; persons of both races reside throughout. The school system has only two schools, the New Kent school on the east side of the county and the George W. Watkins school on the west side. In a memorandum filed May 17, 1966, the District Court found that the "school system serves approximately 1,300 pupils, of which 740 are Negro and 550 are White. The School Board operates one white combined elementary and high school [New Kent], and one Negro combined elementary and high school [George W. Watkins]. There are no attendance zones. Each school serves the entire county." The record indicates that 21 school buses—11 serving the Watkins school and 10 serving the New Kent school—travel overlapping routes throughout the county to transport pupils to and from the two schools.

The segregated system was initially established and maintained under the compulsion of Virginia constitutional and statutory provisions mandating racial segregation in public education, Va. Const., Art. IX, § 140 (1902); These provisions were held to violate the Federal Constitution in *Davis* v. *County School Board of Prince Edward County,* decided with *Brown* v. *Board of Education, (Brown I)*. The respondent School Board continued the segregated operation of the system after the *Brown* decisions, presumably on the authority of several statutes enacted by Virginia in resistance to those decisions. Some of these statutes were held to be unconstitutional on their face or as applied. One statute, the Pupil Placement Act, Va. Code § 22–232.1 *et seq.* (1964), not repealed until 1966, divested local boards of authority to assign children to particular schools and placed that authority in a State Pupil Placement Board. Under that Act children were each year automatically reassigned to the school previously attended unless upon their application the State Board assigned them to another school; students seeking enrollment for the first time were also assigned at the discretion of the State Board. To September 1964, no Negro pupil had applied for admission to the

New Kent school under this statute and no white pupil had applied for admission to the Watkins school.

The School Board initially sought dismissal of this suit on the ground that petitioners had failed to apply to the State Board for assignment to New Kent school. However on August 2, 1965, five months after the suit was brought, respondent School Board, in order to remain eligible for federal financial aid, adopted a "freedom-of-choice" plan for desegregating the schools. Under that plan, each pupil, except those entering the first and eighth grades, may annually choose between the New Kent and Watkins schools and pupils not making a choice are assigned to the school previously attended; first and eighth grade pupils must affirmatively choose a school. After the plan was filed the District Court denied petitioners' prayer for an injunction and granted respondent leave to submit an amendment to the plan with respect to employment and assignment of teachers and staff on a racially nondiscriminatory basis. The amendment was duly filed and on June 28, 1966, the District Court approved the "freedom-of-choice" plan as so amended. The Court of Appeals for the Fourth Circuit, *en banc* affirmed the District Court's approval of the "freedom-of-choice" provisions of the plan but remanded the case to the District Court for entry of an order regarding faculty "which is much more specific and more comprehensive" and which would incorporate in addition to a "minimal, objective time table" some of the faculty provisions of the decree entered by the Court of Appeals for the Fifth Circuit in *United States* v. *Jefferson County Board of Education* (1967). Judges Sobeloff and Winter concurred with the remand on the teacher issue but otherwise disagreed, expressing the view "that the District Court should be directed . . . also to set up procedures for periodically evaluating the effectiveness of the [Board's] 'freedom of choice' [plan] in the elimination of other features of a segregated school system." *Bowman* v. *County School Board of Charles City County*. We granted certiorari.

The pattern of separate "white" and "Negro" schools in the New Kent County school system established under compulsion of state laws is precisely the pattern of segregation to which *Brown I* and *Brown II* were particularly addressed, and which *Brown I* declared unconstitutionally denied Negro school children equal protection of the laws. Racial identification of the system's schools was complete, extending not just to the composition of student bodies at the two schools but to every facet of school operations—faculty, staff, transportation, extracurricular activities and facilities. In short, the State, acting through the local school board and school officials, organized and operated a dual system, part "white" and part "Negro."

It was such dual systems that 14 years ago *Brown I* held unconstitutional and a year later *Brown II* held must be abolished; school boards operating such school systems were *required* by *Brown II* "to effectuate a transition to a racially nondiscriminatory school system." It is of course true that for the time immediately after *Brown II* the concern was with making an initial break in a long-established pattern of excluding Negro children from schools attended by white children. The principal focus was on obtaining for those Negro children courageous enough to break with tradition a place in the "white" schools. See, *e. g., Cooper* v. *Aaron.* Under *Brown II* that immediate goal was only the first step, however. The transition to a unitary, nonracial system of public education was and is the ultimate end to be brought about; it was because of the "complexities arising from the transition to a system of public education freed of racial discrimination" that we provided for "all deliberate speed" in the implementation of the principles of *Brown I.* Thus we recognized the task would necessarily involve solution of "varied local school problems." In referring to the "personal interest of the plaintiffs in admission to public schools as soon as practicable on a nondiscriminatory basis," we also noted that "[t]o effectuate this interest may call for elimination of a variety of obstacles in making the transition. . . ." Yet we emphasized that the constitutional rights of Negro children required school officials to bear the burden of establishing that additional time to carry out the ruling in an effective manner "is necessary in the public interest and is consistent with good faith compliance at the earliest practicable date." We charged the district courts in their review of particular situations to

> consider problems related to administration, arising from the physical condition of the school plant, the school transportation system, personnel, revision of school districts and attendance areas into compact units to achieve a system of determining admission to the public schools on a nonracial basis, and revision of local laws and regulations which may be necessary in solving the foregoing problems. They will also consider the adequacy of any plans the defendants may propose to meet these problems and to effectuate a transition to a racially nondiscriminatory school system.

It is against this background that 13 years after *Brown II* commanded the abolition of dual systems we must measure the effectiveness of respondent School Board's "freedom-of-choice" plan to achieve that end. The School Board contends that it has fully discharged its obligation by adopting a plan by which every student, regardless of race, may "freely" choose the school he will attend. The Board attempts to cast the issue in its broadest form by arguing that its "freedom-of-choice" plan may be faulted only by reading the Fourteenth Amendment as universally requiring "compulsory integration," a reading it insists the wording of the Amendment will not support. But that argument ignores the thrust of *Brown II*. In the light of the command of that case, what is involved here is the question whether the Board has achieved the "racially nondiscriminatory school system" *Brown II* held must be effectuated in order to remedy the established unconstitutional deficiencies of its segregated system. In the context of the state-imposed segregated pattern of long standing, the fact that in 1965 the Board opened the doors of the former "white" school to Negro children and of the "Negro" school to white children merely begins, not ends, our inquiry whether the Board has taken steps adequate to abolish its dual, segregated system. *Brown II* was a call for the dismantling of well-entrenched dual systems tempered by an awareness that complex and multifaceted problems would arise which would require time and flexibility for a successful resolution. School boards such as the respondent then operating state-compelled dual systems were nevertheless clearly charged with the affirmative duty to take whatever steps might be necessary to convert to a unitary system in which racial discrimination would be eliminated root and branch. See *Cooper* v. *Aaron*. The constitutional rights of Negro school children articulated in *Brown I* permit no less than this; and it was to this end that *Brown II* commanded school boards to bend their efforts.

In determining whether respondent School Board met that command by adopting its "freedom-of-choice" plan, it is relevant that this first step did not come until some 11 years after *Brown I* was decided and 10 years after *Brown II* directed the making of a "prompt and reasonable start." This deliberate perpetuation of the unconstitutional dual system can only have compounded the harm of such a system. Such delays are no longer tolerable, for "the governing constitutional principles no longer bear the imprint of newly enunciated doctrine." *Watson* v. *City of Memphis*. Moreover, a plan that at this late date fails to provide meaningful assurance of prompt and effective disestablishment of a dual system is also intolerable. "The time for mere 'deliberate speed' has run out," *Griffin* v. *County School Board,* "the context in which we must interpret and apply this language [of *Brown II*] to plans for desegregation has been significantly altered." *Goss* v. *Board of Education.* The burden on a school board today is to come forward with a plan that promises realistically to work, and promises realistically to work *now*.

The obligation of the district courts, as it always has been, is to assess the effectiveness of a proposed plan in achieving desegregation. There is no universal answer to complex problems of desegregation; there is obviously no one plan that will do the job in every case. The matter must be assessed in light of the circumstances present and the options available in each instance. It is incumbent upon the school board to establish that its proposed plan promises meaningful and immediate progress toward disestablishing state-imposed segregation. It is incumbent upon the district court to weigh that claim in light of the facts at hand and in light of any alternatives which may be shown as feasible and more promising in their effectiveness. Where the court finds the board to be acting in good faith and the proposed plan to have real prospects for dismantling the state-imposed dual system "at the earliest practicable date," then the plan may be said to provide effective relief. Of course, the availability to the board of other more promising courses of action may indicate a lack of good faith; and at the least it places a heavy burden upon the board to explain its preference for an apparently less effective method. Moreover, whatever plan is adopted will require evaluation in practice, and the court should retain jurisdiction until it is clear that state-imposed segregation has been completely removed.

We do not hold that "freedom of choice" can have no place in such a plan. We do not hold that a "freedom-of-choice" plan might of itself be unconstitutional, although that argument has been urged upon us. Rather, all we decide today is that in desegregating a dual system a plan utilizing "freedom of choice" is not an end in itself. As Judge Sobeloff has put it,

"Freedom of choice" is not a sacred talisman; it is only a means to a constitutionally required end—the abolition of the system of segregation and its effects. If the means prove effective, it is acceptable, but if it fails to undo segregation, other means must be used to achieve this end. The school officials have the continuing duty to take whatever action may be necessary to create a "unitary, nonracial system." [*Bowman* v. *County School Board* (C. A. 4th Cir. 1967) (concurring opinion)].

Accord, *Kemp* v. *Beasley* (C. A. 8th Cir. 1968). Although the general experience under "freedom of choice" to date has been such as to indicate its ineffectiveness as a tool of desegregation, there may well be instances in which it can serve as an effective device. Where it offers real promise of aiding a desegregation program to effectuate conversion of a state-imposed dual system to a unitary, nonracial system there might be no objection to allowing such a device to prove itself in operation. On the other hand, if there are reasonably available other ways, such for illustration as zoning, promising speedier and more effective conversion to a unitary, nonracial school system, "freedom of choice" must be held unacceptable.

The New Kent School Board's "freedom-of-choice" plan cannot be accepted as a sufficient step to "effectuate a transition" to a unitary system. In three years of operation not a single white child has chosen to attend Watkins school and, although 115 Negro children enrolled in New Kent school in 1967 (up from 35 in 1965 and 111 in 1966) 85% of the Negro children in the system still attend the all-Negro Watkins school. In other words, the school system remains a dual system. Rather than further the dismantling of the dual system, the plan has operated simply to burden children and their parents with a responsibility which *Brown II* placed squarely on the School Board. The Board must be required to formulate a new plan and, in light of other courses which appear open to the Board, such as zoning, fashion steps which promise realistically to convert promptly to a system without a "white" school and a "Negro" school, but just schools.

The judgment of the Court of Appeals is vacated insofar as it affirmed the District Court and the case is remanded to the District Court for further proceedings consistent with this opinion.

It is so ordered.

UNITED JEWISH ORGANIZATIONS OF
WILLIAMSBURGH, INC., ET AL. *v.* CAREY, GOVERNOR
OF NEW YORK, ET AL.

Argued October 6, 1976—Decided March 1, 1977

After New York State had submitted for the approval of the Attorney General
its 1972 reapportionment statute with respect to Kings County and two other
counties which were subject to §§ 4 and 5 of the Voting Rights Act of
1965, he concluded that as to certain districts in Kings County the State
had not met its burden under § 5 of demonstrating that the redistricting had
neither the purpose nor the effect of abridging the right to vote by reason
of race or color. In May 1974 the State submitted to the Attorney General
a revision of those portions of the 1972 plan to which he had objected,
including provisions for elections to the state senate and assembly from
Kings County. The 1974 plan did not change the number of districts with
nonwhite majorities but did change the size of the nonwhite majorities in
most of those districts. To attain a nonwhite majority of 65%, which it was
felt would be acceptable to the Attorney General for the assembly district
in which the Hasidic Jewish community was located (which had been 61%
nonwhite under the 1972 plan), a portion of the white population, including
part of the Hasidic community, was reassigned to an adjoining district, and
that community was also split between two senatorial districts though it had
been within one such district under the 1972 plan. Petitioners, on behalf of
the Hasidic community, brought this suit for injunctive and declaratory relief, alleging that the 1974 plan violated their rights under the Fourteenth and
Fifteenth Amendments. Petitioners contended that the plan "would dilute the
value of [their] franchise by halving its effectiveness," solely for the purpose
of achieving a racial quota, and that they were assigned to electoral districts
solely on the basis of race. Upon motions by the Attorney General (who
had advised the State that he did not object to the 1974 plan) and an
intervenor, the District Court dismissed the complaint, holding that petitioners enjoyed no constitutional right in reapportionment to separate community
recognition as Hasidic Jews; that the redistricting did not disenfranchise
them; and that racial considerations were permissible to correct past discrimination. The Court of Appeals affirmed. Noting that the 1974 plan left
approximately 70% of the Kings County senate and assembly districts with
white majorities and that only 65% of the county was white, the court held
that the plan would not underrepresent the white population. The court,
relying on *Allen* v. *State Board of Elections,* concluded that a State could
use racial considerations in an effort to secure the approval of the Attorney
General under the Voting Rights Act, reasoning that the Act contemplated

that he and the state legislature would have "to think in racial terms";
because the Act "necessarily deals with race or color, corrective action
under it must do the same. *Held:* The judgment is affirmed.

MR. JUSTICE WHITE, joined by MR. JUSTICE BRENNAN, MR. JUSTICE BLACK-
MUN, and MR. JUSTICE STEVENS, concluded that the use of racial criteria by
the State of New York in its 1974 plan in attempting to comply with § 5
of the Act and to secure the approval of the Attorney General did not violate
the Fourteenth or Fifteenth Amendment.

(a) Under § 5, new or revised reapportionment plans are among those
voting procedures, standards, or practices that may not be adopted by a
State covered by the Act without a ruling by the Attorney General or the
specified court that the plan does not have a racially discriminatory purpose
or effect. *Allen* v. *State Board of Elections.*

(b) Compliance with the Act in reapportionment cases will often necessitate the use of racial considerations in drawing district lines, and the Constitution does not prevent a State subject to the Act from deliberately creating
or preserving black majorities in particular districts in order to ensure that
its reapportionment plan complies with § 5. *Beer* v. *United States.*

(c) Permissible use of racial criteria is not confined to eliminating the
effects of past discriminatory districting or apportionment.

(d) A reapportionment cannot violate the Fourteenth or Fifteenth Amendment merely because a State uses specific numerical quotas in establishing
a certain number of black majority districts.

(e) Petitioners have not shown or offered to prove that minority voting
strength was increased under the 1974 plan in comparison with the 1966
apportionment and thus have not shown that New York did more than the
Attorney General was authorized to require it to do under the nonretrogres-
sion principle of *Beer* v. *United States, supra,* a principle that this Court
has accepted as constitutionally valid.

MR. JUSTICE WHITE, joined by MR. JUSTICE STEVENS AND MR. JUSTICE RE-
HNQUIST, concluded that, wholly aside from New York's obligations under
the Act to preserve minority voting strength in Kings County, the Constitution permits the State to draw lines deliberately in such a way that the
percentage of districts with a nonwhite majority roughly approximates the
percentage of nonwhites in the county. Though in individual districts where
nonwhite majorities were increased to about 65% it became more likely that
nonwhite candidates would be elected, as long as Kings County whites, as
a group, were provided with fair representation, there was no cognizable
discrimination against whites. See *Gaffney* v. *Cummings.*

MR. JUSTICE STEWARD, joined by MR. JUSTICE POWELL, concluded that,
having failed to show that the 1974 plan had either the purpose or effect
of discriminating against them because of their race, petitioners, who erroneously contend that racial awareness in legislative reapportionment is uncon-

stitutional *per se*, have offered no basis for affording them the constitutional relief that they seek.

WHITE, J., announced the Court's judgment, and delivered an opinion in which STEVENS, J., joined; in all but Part IV of which BRENNAN and BLACKMUN, JJ., joined; and in Parts I and IV of which REHNQUIST, J., joined. BRENNAN, J., filed an opinion concurring in part.

MR. JUSTICE BRENNAN, concurring in part.

I join Parts I, II, and III of Mr. JUSTICE WHITE's opinion. Part II effectively demonstrates that prior cases firmly establish the Attorney General's expansive authority to oversee legislative redistricting under § 5 of the Voting Rights Act. See, *e. g., Georgia* v. *United States (1973).* Part III establishes to my satisfaction that as a method of securing compliance with the Voting Rights Act, the 65% rule applied to Brooklyn in this instance was not arbitrarily or casually selected. Yet, because this case carries us further down the road of race-centered remedial devices than we have heretofore traveled—with the serious questions of fairness that attend such matters—I offer this further explanation of my position.

The one starkly clear fact of this case is that an overt racial number was employed to effect petitioners' assignment to voting districts. In brief, following the Attorney General's refusal to certify the 1972 reapportionment under his § 5 powers, unnamed Justice Department officials made known that satisfaction of the Voting Rights Act in Brooklyn would necessitate creation by the state legislature of 10 state assembly and senate districts with threshold nonwhite populations of 65%. Prompted by the necessity of preventing interference with the upcoming 1974 election, state officials complied. Thus, the Justice Department's unofficial instruction to state officials effectively resulted in an explicit process of assignment to voting districts pursuant to race. The result of this process was a countywide pattern of districting closely approximating proportional representation. While it is true that this demographic outcome did not "underrepresent the white population" throughout the county, indeed, the very definition of proportional representation precludes either underrepresentation or overrepresentation—these particular petitioners filed suit to complain that *they* have been subjected to a process of classification on the basis of race that adversely altered *their* status.

If we were presented here with a classification of voters motivated by racial animus, *City of Richmond* v. *United States* (1975) or with a classification that effectively downgraded minority participation in the franchise, *Georgia* v. *United States,* we promptly would characterize the resort to race as "suspect" and prohibit its use. Under such circumstances, the tainted apportionment process would not necessarily be saved by its proportional outcome, for the segregation of voters into "separate but equal" blocs still might well have the intent or effect of diluting the voting power of minority voters. See, *e.g., City of Richmond* v. *United States.* It follows, therefore, that if the racial redistricting involved here, imposed with the avowed intention of clustering together 10 viable nonwhite majorities at the expense of preexisting white groupings, is not similarly to be prohibited, the distinctiveness that avoids this prohibition must arise from either or both of two considerations: the permissibility of affording preferential treatment to disadvantage nonwhites generally, or the particularized application of the Voting Rights Act in this instance.

The first and broader of the two plausible distinctions rests upon the general propriety of so-called benign discrimination: The challenged race assignment may be permissible because it is cast in a remedial context with respect to a disadvantaged class rather than in a setting that aims to demean or insult any racial group. Even in the absence of the Voting Rights Act, this preferential policy plausibly could find expression in a state decision to overcome nonwhite disadvantages in voter registration or turnout through redefinition of electoral districts— perhaps, as here, through the application of a numerical rule—in order to achieve a proportional distribution of voting power. Such a decision, in my view, raises particularly sensitive issues of doctrine and policy. Unlike Part IV of MR. JUSTICE WWHITE's opinion, I am wholly content to leave this thorny question until another day, for I am convinced that the existence of the Voting Rights Act makes such a decision unnecessary and alone suffices to support an affirmance of the judgment before us.

I begin with the settled principle that not every remedial use of race is forbidden. For example, we have authorized and even required race-conscious remedies in a variety of corrective settings. See, *e g., Swann* v. *Charlotte-Mecklenburg Bd. of Education* (1971). Once it is established that circumstances exist where race may be taken into account in fashioning affirmative policies, we must identify those circumstances, and, further, determine how substantial a reliance may be placed upon race. If resort to the 65% rule involved here is not to be sanctioned, that must be because the benign use of such a binding numerical criterion (under the Voting Rights Act) generates problems of constitutional dimension that are not relevant to other, previously tolerated race-conscious remedies. As a focus for consideration of what these problems might or might not be, it is instructive to consider some of the objections frequently raised to the use of overt preferential race-assignment practices.

First, a purportedly preferential race assignment may in fact disguise a policy that perpetuates disadvantageous treatment of the plan's supposed beneficiaries. Accordingly, courts might face considerable difficulty in ascertaining whether a given race classification truly furthers benign rather than illicit objectives. An effort to achieve proportional representation, for example, might be aimed at aiding a group's participation in the political processes by guaranteeing safe political offices, or, on the other hand, might be a "contrivance to segregate" the group, *Wright* v. *Rockefeller,* thereby frustrating its potentially successful efforts at coalition building across racial lines. Compare, *e. g.,* the positions of the black plaintiffs in *Wright,* with the black intervenors. Indeed, even the present case is not entirely free of complaints that the remedial redistricting in Brooklyn is not truly benign. Puerto Rican groups, for example, who have been joined with black groups to establish the "nonwhite" category, protested to the Attorney General that their political strength under the 1974 reapportionment actually is weaker than under the invalidated 1972 districting. App. 295. A black group similarly complained of the loss of a "safe" seat because of the inadequacy of the 65% target figure. These particular objections, as the Attorney General argued in his memorandum endorsing the 1974 reapportionment, may be ill-advised and unpersuasive. Nevertheless, they illustrate the risk that what is presented as an instance of benign race assignment in fact may prove to be otherwise. This concern, of course, does not undercut the theoretical legitimacy or usefulness of preferential policies. At the minimum, however, it does suggest the need for careful consideration of the operation of any racial device, even one cloaked in preferential garb. And if judicial detection of truly benign policies proves impossible or excessively crude, that alone might warrant invalidating any race-drawn line.

Second, even in the pursuit of remedial objectives, an explicit policy of assignment by race may serve to stimulate our society's latent race consciousness, suggesting the utility and propriety of basing decisions on a factor that ideally bears no relationship to an individual's worth or needs. Furthermore, even preferential treatment may act to stigmatize its recipient groups, for although intended to correct systemic or institutional inequities, such a policy may imply to some the recipients' inferiority and especial need for protection. Again, these matters would not necessarily speak against the wisdom or permissibility of selective, benign racial classifications. But they demonstrate that the considerations that historically led us to treat race as a constitutionally "suspect" method of classifying individuals are not entirely vitiated in a preferential context.

Third, especially when interpreting the broad principles embraced by the Equal Protection Clause, we cannot well ignore the social reality that even a benign policy of assignment by race is viewed as unjust by many in our society, especially by those individuals who are adversely affected by a given classification. This impression of injustice may be heightened by the natural consequence of our governing processes that the most "discrete and insular" of whites often will be called upon to bear the immediate, direct costs of benign discrimination. Perhaps not surprisingly, there are indications that this case affords an example of just such decisionmaking in operation. For example, the respondent-intervenors take pains to emphasize that the mandated 65% rule could have been attained through redistricting strategies that did not slice the Hasidic community in half. State authorities, however, chose to localize the burdens of race reassignment upon the petitioners rather than to redistribute a more varied and diffused range of whites into predominatly nonwhite districts. I am in no position to determine the accuracy of this appraisal, but the impression of unfairness is magnified when a coherent group like the Hasidim disproportionately bears the adverse consequences of a race-assignment policy.

In my view, if and when a decisionmaker embarks on a policy of benign racial sorting, he must weigh the concerns that I have discussed against the need for effective social policies promoting racial justice in a society beset by deep-rooted racial inequities. But I believe that Congress here adequately struck that balance in enacting the carefully conceived remedial scheme embodied in the Voting Rights Act. However the court ultimately decides the constitutional legitimacy of "reverse discrimination" pure and simple, I am convinced that the application of the Voting Rights Act substantially minimizes the objections to preferential treatment, and legitimates the use of even overt, numerical racial devices in electoral redistricting.

The participation of the Attorney General, for example, largely relieves the judiciary of the need to grapple with the difficulties of distinguishing benign from malign discrimination. Under § 5 of the Act, the

Attorney General in effect is constituted champion of the interests of minority voters, and accompanying implementing regulations ensure the availability of materials and submissions necessary to discern the true effect of a proposed reapportionment plan. This initial right of review, coupled with the fact-finding competence of the Justice Department, substantially reduces the likelihood that a complicated reapportionment plan that silently furthers malign racial policies would escape detection by appropriate officials. As a practical matter, therefore, I am prepared to accord considerable deference to the judgment of the Attorney General that a particular districting scheme complies with the remedial objectives furthered by the Voting Rights Act.

Similarly, the history of the Voting Rights Act provides reassurance that, in the face of the potential for reinvigorating racial partisanship, the congressional decision to authorize the use of race-oriented remedies in this context was the product of substantial and careful deliberations. Enacted following "voluminous legislative" consideration, *South Carolina* v. *Katzenbach* (1966), the Voting Rights Act represents an unequivocal and well-defined congressional consensus on the national need for "sterner and more elaborate measures," *ibid.,* to secure the promise of the Fourteenth and Fifteenth Amendments with respect to exercise of the franchise. Insofar as the drawing of district lines is a process that intrinsically involves numerical calculations, and insofar as state officials charged with the task of defining electoral constituencies are unlikely simply to close their eyes to considerations such as race and national origin, the resort to a numerical racial criterion as a method of achieving compliance with the aims of the Voting Rights Act is, in my view, consistent with that consensus. Whatever may be the indirect and undesirable countereducational costs of employing such far-reaching racial devices, Congress had to confront these considerations before opting for an activist race-conscious remedial role supervised by federal officials. The "insidious and pervasive" evil of voting rights violations, and the "specially informed legislative competence" in this area, *Katzenbach* v. *Morgan* (1966), argue in support of the legitimacy of the federal decision to permit a broad range of race-conscious remedial techniques, including, as here, outright assignment by race.

This leaves, of course, the objection expressed by a variety of participants in this litigation: that this reapportionment worked the injustice of localizing the direct burdens of racial assignment upon a morally undifferentiated group of whites, and, indeed, a group that plausibly is peculiarly vulnerable to such injustice. This argument has both normative and emotional appeal, but for a variety of reasons I am convinced that the Voting Rights Act drains it of vitality.

First, it is important to recall that the Attorney General's oversight focuses upon jurisdictions whose prior practices exhibited the purpose or effect of infringing the right to vote on account of race, thereby triggering § 4 of the Act, 42 U. S. C. § 1973b (1970 ed. and Supp. V). This direct nexus to localities with a history of discriminatory practices or effects enhances the legitimacy of the Attorney General's remedial authority over individuals within those communities who benefited (as whites) from those earlier discriminatory voting patterns. Moreover, the obvious remedial nature of the Act and its enactment by an elected Congress that hardly can be viewed as dominated by nonwhite representatives belie the possibility that the decisionmaker intended a racial insult or injury to those whites who are adversely affected by the operation of the Act's provisions. Finally, petitioners have not been deprived of their right to vote, a consideration that minimizes the detrimental impact of the remedial racial policies governing the § 5 reapportionment. True, petitioners are denied the opportunity to vote as a group in accordance with the earlier districting configuration, but they do not press any legal claim to a group voice as Hasidim. Brief for Petitioners 6 n. 6. In terms of their voting interests, then, the burden that they claim to suffer must be attributable solely to their relegation to increased nonwhite-dominated districts. Yet, to the extent that white and nonwhite interests and sentiments are polarized in Brooklyn, the petitioners still are indirectly "protected" by the remaining white assembly and senate districts within the county, carefully preserved in accordance with the white proportion of the total county population. While these considerations obviously do not satisfy petitioners, I am persuaded that they reinforce the legitimacy of this remedy.

Since I find nothing in the first three parts of Mr. JUSTICE WHITE's opinion that is inconsistent with the views expressed herein, I join those parts.

EDWARDS, GOVERNOR OF LOUISIANA, ET AL. *v.* AGUILLARD ET AL.

APPEAL FROM THE UNITED STATES COURT OF APPEALS FOR THE FIFTH CIRCUIT

Argued December 10, 1986—Decided June 19, 1987

Louisiana's "Creationism Act" forbids the teaching of the theory of evolution in public elementary and secondary schools unless accompanied by instruction in the theory of "creation science." The Act does not require the teaching of either theory unless the other is taught. It defines the theories as "the scientific evidences." Appellees, who include Louisiana parents, teachers, and religious leaders, challenged the Act's constitutionality in Federal District Court, seeking an injunction and declaratory relief. The District Court granted summary judgment to appellees, holding that the Act violated the Establishment Clause of the First Amendment. The Court of Appeals affirmed.

Held:

1. The Act is facially invalid as violative of the Establishment Clause of the First Amendment, because it lacks a clear secular purpose.

(a) The Act does not further its stated secular purpose of "protecting academic freedom." It does not enhance the freedom of teachers to teach what they choose and fails to further the goal of "teaching all of the evidence." Forbidding the teaching of evolution when creation science is not also taught undermines the provision of a comprehensive scientific education. Moreover, requiring the teaching of creation science with evolution does not give school teachers a flexibility that they did not already possess to supplant the present science curriculum with the presentation of theories, besides evolution, about the origin of life. Furthermore, the contention that the Act furthers a "basic concept of fairness" by requiring the teaching of all of the evidence on the subject is without merit. Indeed, the Act evinces a discriminatory preference for the teaching of creation science and against the teaching of evolution by requiring that curriculum guides be developed and resource services supplied for teaching creationism but not for teaching evolution, by limiting membership on the resource services panel to "creation scientists," and by forbidding school boards to discriminate against anyone who "chooses to be a creation-scientist" or to teach creation science, while failing to protect those who choose to teach other theories or who refuse to teach creation science. A law intended to maximize the comprehensiveness and effectiveness of science instruction would encourage the teaching of all scientific theories about human origins. Instead, this Act has the distinctly different purpose of discrediting evolution by counterbalancing its teaching at every turn with the teaching of creationism.

(b) The act impermissibly endorses religion by advancing the religious belief that a supernatural being created humankind. The legislative history demonstrates that the term "creation science," as contemplated by the state legislature, embraces this religious teaching. The Act's primary purpose was to change the public school science curriculum to provide persuasive advantage to a particular religious doctrine that rejects the factual basis of evolution in its entirety. Thus, the Act is designed *either* to promote the theory of creation science that embodies a particular religious tenet *or* to prohibit the teaching of a scientific theory disfavored by certain religious sects. In either case, the Act violates the First Amendment.

2. The District Court did not err in granting summary judgment upon a finding that appellants had failed to raise a genuine issue of material fact. Appellants relied on the "uncontroverted" affidavits of scientists, theologians, and an education administrator defining creation science as "origin through abrupt appearance in complex form" and alleging that such a viewpoint constitutes a true scientific theory. The District Court, in its discretion, properly concluded that the postenactment testimony of these experts concerning the possible technical meanings of the Act's terms would not illuminate the contemporaneous purpose of the state legislature when it passed the Act. None of the persons making the affidavits produced by appellants participated in or contributed to the enactment of the law.

Affirmed.

BRENNAN, J., delivered the opinion of the Court, in which MARSHALL, BLACKMUN, POWELL, and STEVENS, JJ., joined, and in all but Part II of which O'CONNOR, J., joined. POWELL, J., filed a concurring opinion, in which O'CONNOR, J., joined. WHITE, J., filed an opinion concurring in the judgment. SCALLA, J., filed a dissenting opinion, in which REHNQUIST, C. J., joined.

JUSTICE BRENNAN delivered the opinion of the Court.

The question for decision is whether Louisiana's "Balanced Treatment for Creation-Science and Evolution-Science in Public School Instruction" Act (Creationism Act), La. Rev. Stat. Ann. §§ 17:286.1–17:286.7, is facially invalid as violative of the Establishment Clause of the First Amendment.

I

The Creationism Act forbids the teaching of the theory of evolution in public schools unless accompanied by instruction in "creation science." § 17:286.4A. No school is required to teach evolution or creation science. If either is taught, however, the other must also be taught. *Ibid.* The theories of evolution and creation science are statutorily defined as "the scientific evidences for [creation or evolution] and inferences from those scientific evidences." §§ 17.286.3(2) and (3).

Appellees, who include parents of children attending Louisiana public schools, Louisiana teachers, and religious leaders, challenged the constitutionality of the act in District Court, seeking an injunction and declaratory relief. Appellants, Louisiana officials charged with implementing the Act, defended on the ground that the purpose of the Act is to protect a legitimate secular interest, namely, academic freedom. Appellees attacked the Act as facially invalid because it violated the Establishment Clause and made a motion for summary judgment. The District Court granted the motion. The court held that there can be no valid secular reason for prohibiting the teaching of evolution, a theory historically opposed by some religious denominations. The court further concluded that "the teaching of 'creation-science' and 'creationism,' as contemplated by the statute, involves teaching 'tailored to the principles' of a particular religious sect or group of sects." The District Court therefore held that the Creationism Act violated the Establishment Clause either because it prohibited the teaching of evolution or because it required the teaching of creation science with the purpose of advancing a particular religious doctrine.

The Court of Appeals affirmed. The court observed that the statute's avowed purpose of protecting academic freedom was inconsistent with requiring, upon risk of sanction, the teaching of creation science whenever evolution is taught. The court found that the Louisiana Legislature's actual intent was "to discredit evolution by counterbalancing its teaching at every turn with the teaching of creationism, a religious belief." Because the Creationism Act was thus a law furthering a particular religious belief, the Court of Appeals held that the Act violated the Establishment Clause. A suggestion for rehearing en banc was denied over a dissent. We noted probable jurisdiction, and now affirm.

II

The Establishment Clause forbids the enactment of any law "respecting an establishment of religion." The Court has applied a three-pronged test to determine whether legislation comports with the Establishment Clause. First, the legislature must have adopted the law with a secular purpose. Second, the statute's principal or primary effect must be one that neither advances nor inhibits religion. Third, the statute must not result in an excessive entanglement of government with religion. *Lemon* v. *Kurtzman.* State action violates the Establishment Clause if it fails to satisfy any of these prongs.

In this case, the Court must determine whether the Establishment Clause was violated in the special context of the public elementary and secondary school system. States and local school boards are generally afforded considerable discretion in operating public schools. See *Bethel School Dist. No. 403* v. *Fraser.* "At the same time . . . we have necessarily recognized that the discretion of the States and local school boards in matters of education must be exercised in a manner that comports with the transcendent imperatives of the First Amendment." *Board of Education, Island Trees Union Free School Dist. No. 26* v. *Pico.*

The Court has been particularly vigilant in monitoring compliance with the Establishment Clause in elementary and secondary schools. Families entrust public schools with the education of their children, but condition their trust on the understanding that the classroom will not purposely be used to advance religious views that may conflict with the private beliefs of the student and his or her family. Students in such institutions are impressionable and their attendance is involuntary. See, *e. g. Grand Rapids School Dist.* v. *Ball.* The State exerts great authority and coercive power through mandatory attendance requirements, and because of the students' emulation of teachers as role models and the children's susceptibility to peer pressure. See *Bethel School Dist. No. 403* v. *Fraser.* Furthermore, "[t]he public school is at once the symbol of our democracy and the most pervasive means for promoting our common destiny. In no activity of the State is it more vital to keep out divisive forces than in its schools. . . ." *Illinois ex rel. McCollum* v. *Board of Education.*

Consequently, the Court has been required often to invalidate statutes which advance religion in public elementary and secondary schools. See, *e. g., Grand Rapids School Dist.* v. *Ball.*

Therefore, in employing the three-pronged *Lemon* test, we must do so mindful of the particular concerns that arise in the context of public elementary and secondary schools. We now turn to the evaluation of the Act under the *Lemon* test.

III

Lemon's first prong focuses on the purpose that animated adoption of the Act. "The purpose prong of the *Lemon* test asks whether government's actual purpose is to endorse or disapprove of religion." *Lynch* v. *Donnelly*. A governmental intention to promote religion is clear when the State enacts a law to serve a religious purpose. This intention may be evidenced by promotion of religion in general. See *Wallace* v. *Jaffree* (Establishment Clause protects individual freedom of conscience "to select any religious faith or none at all"), or by advancement of a particular religious belief, *e.g., Stone* v.*Graham* (invalidating requirement to post Ten Commandments, which are "undeniably a sacred text in the Jewish and Christian faiths") (footnote omitted); *Epperson* v. *Arkansas* (holding that banning the teaching of evolution in public schools violates the First Amendment since "teaching and learning" must not "be tailored to the principles or prohibitions of any religious sect or dogma"). If the law was enacted for the purpose of endorsing religion, "no consideration of the second or third criteria [of *Lemon*] is necessary." *Wallace* v. *Jaffree*. In this case, appellants have identified no clear secular purpose for the Louisiana Act.

True, the Act's stated purpose is to protect academic freedom. La. Rev. Stat. Ann. § 17:286.2. This phrase might, in common parlance, be understood as referring to enhancing the freedom of teachers to teach what they will. The Court of Appeals, however, correctly concluded that the Act was not designed to further that goal. We find no merit in the State's argument that the "legislature may not [have] use[d] the terms 'academic freedom' in the correct legal sense. They might have [had] in mind, instead, a basic concept of fairness; teaching all of the evidence." Tr. of Oral Arg. 60. Even if "academic freedom" is read to mean "teaching all of the evidence" with respect to the origin of human beings, the Act does not further this purpose. The goal of providing a more comprehensive science curriculum is not furthered either by outlawing the teaching of evolution or by requiring the teaching of creation science.

A

While the Court is normally deferential to a State's articulation of a secular purpose, it is required that the statement of such purpose be sincere and not a sham. See *Wallace* v. *Jaffree*. As JUSTICE O'CONNOR stated in *Wallace:* "It is not a trivial matter, however, to require that the legislature manifest a secular purpose and omit all sectarian endorsements from its laws. That requirement is precisely tailored to the Establishment Clause's purpose of assuring that Government not intentionally endorse religion or a religious practice."

It is clear from the legislative history that the purpose of the legislative sponsor, Senator Bill Keith, was to narrow the science curriculum. During the legislative hearings, Senator Keith stated: "My preference would be that neither [creationism nor evolution] be taught." Such a ban on teaching does not promote—indeed, it undermines—the provision of a comprehensive scientific education.

It is equally clear that requiring schools to teach creation science with evolution does not advance academic freedom. The Act does not grant teachers a flexibility that they did not already possess to supplant the present science curriculum with the presentation of theories, besides evolution, about the origin of life. Indeed, the Court of Appeals found that no law prohibited Louisiana public school teachers from teaching any scientific theory. As the president of the Louisiana Science Teachers Association testified, "[a]ny scientific concept that's based on established fact can be included in our curriculum already, and no legislation allowing this is necessary." The Act provides Louisiana schoolteachers with no new authority. Thus the stated purpose is not furthered by it.

The Alabama statute held unconstitutional in *Wallace* v. *Jaffree*, is analogous. In *Wallace*, the State characterized its new law as one designed to provide a 1-minute period for meditation. We rejected that stated purpose as insufficient, because a previously adopted Alabama law already provided for such a 1-minute period. Thus, in this case, as in *Wallace*, "[a]ppellants have not identified any secular purpose that was not fully served by [existing state law] before the enactment of [the statute in question]."

Furthermore, the goal of basic "fairness" is hardly furthered by the Act's discriminatory preference for the teaching of creation science and against the teaching of evolution. While requiring that curriculum guides be developed for creation science, the Act says nothing of comparable guides for evolution. La. Rev. Stat. Ann. § 17:286.7A. Similarly, resource services are supplied for creation science but not for evolution. § 17:286.7B. Only "creation scientists" can serve on the panel that supplies the resource services. The Act forbids school boards to discriminate against anyone who "chooses to be a creation-scientist" or to teach "creationism," but fails to protect those who choose to teach evolution or any other noncreation science theory, or who refuse to teach creation science. § 17:286.4C.

If the Louisiana Legislature's purpose was solely to maximize the comprehensiveness and effectiveness of science instruction, it would have encouraged the teaching of all scientific theories about the origins of humankind. But under the Act's requirements, teachers who were once free to teach any and all facets of this subject are now unable to do so. Moreover, the Act fails even to ensure that creation science will be taught, but instead requires the teaching of this theory only when the theory of evolution is taught. Thus we agree with the Court of Appeals' conclusion that the Act does not serve to protect academic freedom, but has the distinctly different purpose of discrediting "evolution by counterbalancing its teaching at every turn with the teaching of creationism. . . ."

B

Stone v. *Graham* invalidated the State's requirement that the Ten Commandments be posted in public classrooms. "The Ten Commandments are undeniably a sacred text in the Jewish and Christian faiths, and no legislative recitation of a supposed secular purpose can blind us to that fact." As a result, the contention that the law was designed to provide instruction on a "fundamental legal code" was "not sufficient to avoid conflict with the First Amendment." Similarly *Abington School Dist.* v. *Schempp* held unconstitutional a statute "requiring the selection and reading at the opening of the school day of verses from the Holy Bible and the recitation of the Lord's Prayer by the students in unison," despite the proffer of such secular purposes as the "promotion of moral values, the contradiction to the materialistic trends of our times, the perpetuation of our institutions and the teaching of literature."

As in *Stone* and *Abington*, we need not be blind in this case to the legislature's preeminent religious purpose in enacting this statute. There is a historic and contemporaneous link between the teachings of certain religious denominations and the teaching of evolution. It was this link that concerned the Court in *Epperson* v. *Arkansas* (1968), which also involved a facial challenge to a statute regulating the teaching of evolution. In that case, the Court reviewed an Arkansas statute that made it unlawful for an instructor to teach evolution or to use a textbook that referred to this scientific theory. Although the Arkansas antievolution law did not explicitly state its predominate religious purpose, the Court could not ignore that "[t]he statute was a product of the upsurge of 'fundamentalist' religious fervor" that has long viewed this particular scientific theory as contradicting the literal interpretation of the Bible. After reviewing the history of antievolution statutes, the Court determined that "there can be no doubt that the motivation for the [Arkansas] law was the same [as other antievolution statutes]: to suppress the teaching of a theory which, it was thought, 'denied' the divine creation of man." The Court found that there can be no legitimate state interest in protecting particular religions from scientific views "distasteful to them," and concluded "that the First Amendment does not permit the State to require that teaching and learning must be tailored to the principles or prohibitions of any religious sect or dogma."

These same historic and contemporaneous antagonisms between the teachings of certain religious denominations and the teaching of evolution are present in this case. The preeminent purpose of the Louisiana Legislature was clearly to advance the religious viewpoint that a supernatural being created humankind. The term "creation science" was defined as embracing this particular religious doctrine by those responsible for the passage of the Creationism Act. Senator Keith's leading expert on creation science, Edward Boudreaux, testified at the legislative hearings that the theory of creation science included belief in the existence of a supernatural creator. Senator Keith also cited testimony from other experts to support the creation-science view that "a creator [was] responsible for the universe and everything in it." The legislative history therefore reveals that the term "creation science," as contemplated by the legislature that adopted this Act, embodies the religious belief that a supernatural creator was responsible for the creation of humankind.

Furthermore, it is not happenstance that the legislature required the teachings of a theory that coincided with this religious view. The legislative history documents that the Act's primary purpose was to change the science curriculum of public schools in order to provide persuasive advantage to a particular religious doctrine that rejects the factual basis of evolution in its entirety. The sponsor of the Creationism Act, Senator

Keith, explained during the legislative hearings that his disdain for the theory of evolution resulted from the support that evolution supplied to views contrary to his own religious beliefs. According to Senator Keith, the theory of evolution was consonant with the "cardinal principle[s] of religious humanism, secular humanism, theological liberalism, aetheistism [sic]." The state senator repeatedly stated that scientific evidence supporting his religious views should be included in the public school curriculum to redress the fact that the theory of evolution incidentally coincided with what he characterized as religious beliefs antithetical to his own. The legislation therefore sought to alter the science curriculum to reflect endorsement of a religious view that is antagonistic to the theory of evolution.

In this case, the purpose of the Creationism Act was to restructure the science curriculum to conform with a particular religious viewpoint. Out of many possible science subjects taught in the public schools, the legislature chose to affect the teaching of the one scientific theory that historically has been opposed by certain religious sects. As in *Epperson*, the legislature passed the Act to give preference to those religious groups which have as one of their tenets the creation of humankind by a divine creator. The "overriding fact" that confronted the Court in *Epperson* was "that Arkansas' law selects from the body of knowledge a particular segment which it proscribes for the sole reason that it is deemed to conflict with . . . a particular interpretation of the Book of Genesis by a particular religious group." Similarly, the Creationism Act is designed *either* to promote the theory of creation science which embodies a particular religious tenet by requiring that creation science be taught whenever evolution is taught *or* to prohibit the teaching of a scientific theory disfavored by certain religious sects by forbidding the teaching of evolution when creation science is not also taught. The Establishment Clause, however, "forbids *alike* the preference of a religious doctrine *or* the prohibition of theory which is deemed antagonistic to a particular dogma." Because the primary purpose of the Creationism Act is to advance a particular religious belief, the Act endorses religion in violation of the First Amendment.

We do not imply that a legislature could never require that scientific critiques of prevailing scientific theories be taught. Indeed, the Court acknowledged in *Stone* that its decision forbidding the posting of the Ten Commandments did not mean that no use could ever be made of the Ten Commandments, or that the Ten Commandments played an exclusively religious role in the history of Western Civilization. In a similar way, teaching a variety of scientific theories about the origins of humankind to schoolchildren might be validly done with the clear secular intent of enhancing the effectiveness of science instruction. But because the primary purpose of the Creationism Act is to endorse a particular religious doctrine, the Act furthers religion in violation of the Establishment Clause.

IV

Appellants contend that genuine issues of material fact remain in dispute, and therefore the District Court erred in granting summary judgment. Federal Rule of Civil Procedure 56(c) provides that summary judgment "shall be rendered forthwith if the pleadings, depositions, answers to interrogatories, and admissions on file, together with the affidavits, if any, show that there is no genuine issue as to any material fact and that the moving party is entitled to a judgment as a matter of law." A court's finding of improper purpose behind a statute is appropriately determined by the statute on its face, its legislative history, or its interpretation by a responsible administrative agency. See, *e.g., Wallace* v. *Jaffree.* The plain meaning of the statute's words, enlightened by their context and the contemporaneous legislative history, can control the determination of legislative purpose. See *Wallace* v. *Jaffree.* Moreover, in determining the legislative purpose of a statue, the Court has also considered the historical context of the statute, *e.g., Epperson* v. *Arkansas, supra,* and the specific sequence of events leading to passage of the statute, *e.g., Arlington Heights* v. *Metropolitan Housing Dev. Corp.* (1977).

In this case, appellees' motion for summary judgment rested on the plain language of the Creationism Act, the legislative history and historical context of the Act, the specific sequence of events leading to the passage of the Act, the State Board's report on a survey of school superintendents, and the correspondence between the Act's legislative sponsor and its key witnesses. Appellants contend that affidavits made by two scientists, two theologians, and an education administrator raise a genuine issue of material fact and that summary judgment was therefore barred. The affidavits define creation science as "origin through abrupt appearance in complex form" and allege that such a viewpoint constitutes a true scientific theory.

We agree with the lower courts that these affidavits do not raise a genuine issue of material fact. The existence of "uncontroverted affidavits" does not bar summary judgment. Moreover, the postenactment testimony of outside experts is of little use in determining the Louisiana Legislature's purpose in enacting this statute. The Louisiana Legislature did hear and rely on scientific experts in passing the bill, but none of the persons making the affidavits produced by the appellants participated in or contributed to the enactment of the law or its implementation. The District Court, in its discretion, properly concluded that a Monday-morning "battle of the experts" over possible technical meanings of terms in the statute would not illuminate the contemporaneous purpose of the Louisiana Legislature when it made the law. We therefore conclude that the District Court did not err in finding that appellants failed to raise a genuine issue of material fact, and in granting summary judgment.

V

The Louisiana Creationism Act advances a religious doctrine by requiring either the banishment of the theory of evolution from public school classrooms or the presentation of a religious viewpoint that rejects evolution in its entirety. The Act violates the Establishment Clause of the First Amendment because it seeks to employ the symbolic and financial support of government to achieve a religious purpose. The judgment of the Court of Appeals therefore is

Affirmed.

SHERBERT *v.* VERNER ET AL., MEMBERS OF SOUTH CAROLINA EMPLOYMENT SECURITY COMMISSION, ET AL.

APPEAL FROM THE SUPREME COURT OF SOUTH CAROLINA.

No. 526. Argued April 24, 1963.—Decided June 17, 1963.

Appellant, a member of the Seventh-Day Adventist Church, was discharged by her South Carolina employer because she would not work on Saturday, the Sabbath Day of her faith. She was unable to obtain other employment because she would not work on Saturday, and she filed a claim for unemployment compensation benefits under the South Carolina Unemployment Compensation Act, which provides that a claimant is ineligible for benefits if he has failed, without good cause, to accept available suitable work when offered him. The State Commission denied appellant's application on the ground that she would not accept suitable work when offered, and its action was sustained by the State Supreme Court. *Held:* As so applied, the South Carolina statute abridged appellant's right to the free exercise of her religion, in violation of the First Amendment, made applicable to the states by the Fourteenth Amendment.

(a) Disqualification of appellant for unemployment compensation benefits, solely because of her refusal to accept employment in which she would have to work on Saturday contrary to her religious belief, imposes an unconstitutional burden on the free exercise of her religion.

(b) there is no compelling state interest enforced in the eligibility provisions of the South Carolina statute which justifies the substantial infringement of appellant's right to religious freedom under the First Amendment.

(c) This decision does not foster the "establishment" of the Seventh-Day Adventist religion in South Carolina contrary to the First Amendment.

MR. JUSTICE BRENNAN delivered the opinion of the Court.

Appellant, a member of the Seventh-day Adventist Church, was discharged by her South Carolina employer because she would not work on Saturday, the Sabbath Day of her faith. When she was unable to obtain other employment because from conscientious scruples she would not take Saturday work she filed a claim for Unemployment Compensation benefits under the South Carolina Unemployment Compensation Act. That law provides that, to be eligible for benefits, a claimant must be "able to work and . . . available for work"; and, further, that a claimant is ineligible for benefits "[i]f . . . he has failed, without good cause . . . to accept available suitable work when offered him by the employment office or the employer. . . ." The appellee Employment Security Commission, in administrative proceedings under the statute, found that appellant's restriction upon her availability for Saturday work brought her within the provision disqualifying for benefits insured workers who fail, without good cause, to accept "suitable work when offered . . . by the employment office or the employer. . . ." The Commission's finding was sustained by the Court of Common Pleas for Spartanburg County. That court's judgment was in turn affirmed by the South Carolina Supreme Court, which rejected appellant's contention that, as applied to her, the disqualifying provisions of the South Carolina statute abridged her right to the free exercise of her religion secured under the Free Exercise Clause of the First Amendment through the Fourteenth Amendment. The State Supreme Court held specifically that appellant's ineligibility infringed no constitutional liberties because such a construction of the statute "places no restriction upon the appellant's freedom of religion nor does it in any way prevent her in the exercise of her right and freedom to observe her religious beliefs in accordance with the dictates of her conscience." We noted probable jurisdiction of appellant's appeal. We reverse the judgment of the South Carolina Supreme Court and remand for further proceedings not inconsistent with this opinion.

I

The door of the Free Exercise Clause stands tightly closed against any governmental regulation of religious *beliefs* as such, *Cantwell* v. *Connecticut.* Government may neither compel affirmation of a repugnant belief, *Torcaso* v. *Watkins*, nor penalize or discriminate against individuals or groups because they hold religious views abhorrent to the authorities, *Fowler* v. *Rhode Island*, nor employ the taxing power to inhibit the dissemination of particular religious views, *Murdock* v. *Pennsylvania.* On the other hand, the Court has rejected challenges under the Free Exercise Clause to governmental regulation of certain overt acts prompted by religious beliefs or principles, for "even when the action is in accord with one's religious convictions, [it] is not totally free from legislative restrictions." *Braunfeld* v. *Brown.* The conduct or actions so regulated have invariably posed some substantial threat to public safety, peace or order. See, *e.g., Reynolds* v. *United States.*

Plainly enough, appellant's conscientious objection to Saturday work constitutes no conduct prompted by religious principles of a kind within the reach of state legislation. If, therefore, the decision of the South Carolina Supreme Court is to withstand appellant's constitutional challenge, it must be either because her disqualification as a beneficiary represents no infringement by the State of her constitutional rights of free exercise, or because any incidental burden on the free exercise of appellant's religion may be justified by a "compelling state interest in the regulation of a subject within the State's constitutional power to regulate...." *NAACP* v. *Button.*

II

We turn first to the question whether the disqualification for benefits imposes any burden on the free exercise of appellant's religion. We think it is clear that it does. In a sense the consequences of such a disqualification to religious principles and practices may be only an indirect result of welfare legislation within the State's general competence to enact; it is true that no criminal sanctions directly compel appellant to work a six-day week. But this is only the beginning, not the end, of our inquiry. For "[i]f the purpose or effect of a law is to impede the observance of one or all religions or is to discriminate invidiously between religions, that law is constitutionally invalid even though the burden may be characterized as being only indirect." *Braunfeld* v. *Brown.* Here not only is it apparent that appellant's declared ineligibility for benefits derives solely from the practice of her religion, but the pressure upon her to forego that practice is unmistakable. The ruling forces her to choose between following the precepts of her religion and forfeiting benefits, on the one hand, and abandoning one of the precepts of her religion in order to accept work, on the other hand. Governmental imposition of such a choice puts the same kind of burden upon the free exercise of religion as would a fine imposed against appellant for her Saturday worship.

Nor may the South Carolina court's construction of the statute be saved from constitutional infirmity on the ground that unemployment compensation benefits are not appellant's "right" but merely a "privilege." It is too late in the day to doubt that the liberties of religion and expression may be infringed by the denial of or placing of conditions upon a benefit or privilege. *American Communications Assn.* v. *Douds.* For example in *Flemming* v. *Nestor*, the Court recognized with respect to Federal Social Security benefits that "[t]he interest of a covered employee under the Act is of sufficient substance to fall within the protection from arbitrary governmental action afforded by the Due Process Clause." In *Speiser* v. *Randall*, we emphasized that conditions upon public benefits cannot be sustained if they so operate, whatever their purpose, as to inhibit or deter the exercise of First Amendment freedoms. We there struck down a condition which limited the availability of a tax exemption to those members of the exempted class who affirmed their loyalty to the state government granting the exemption. While the State was surely under no obligation to afford such an exemption, we held that the imposition of such a condition upon even a gratuitous benefit inevitably deterred or discouraged the exercise of First Amendment rights of expression and thereby threatened to "produce a result which the State could not command directly." "To deny an exemption to claimants who engage in certain forms of speech is in effect to penalize them for such speech." Likewise, to condition the availability of benefits upon this appellant's willingness to violate a cardinal principle of her religious faith effectively penalizes the free exercise of her constitutional liberties.

Significantly South Carolina expressly saves the Sunday worshipper from having to make the kind of choice which we here hold infringes the Sabbatarian's religious liberty. When in times of "national emergency" the textile plants are authorized by the State Commissioner of Labor to operate on Sunday, "no employee shall be required to work on Sunday . . . who is conscientiously opposed to Sunday work; and if any employee should refuse to work on Sunday on account of conscientious . . . objections he or she shall not jeopardize his or her seniority by such refusal or be discriminated against in any other manner." S. C. Code, § 64–4. No question of the disqualification of a Sunday worshipper for benefits is likely to arise, since we cannot suppose that an employer will discharge him in violation of this statute. The unconstitutionality of the disqualification of the Sabbatarian is thus compounded by the religious discrimination which South Carolina's general statutory scheme necessarily effects.

III

We must next consider whether some compelling state interest enforced in the eligibility provisions of the South Carolina statute justifies the substantial infringement of appellant's First Amendment right. It is basic that no showing merely of a rational relationship to some colorable state interest would suffice; in this highly sensitive constitutional area, "[o]nly the gravest abuses, endangering paramount interests, give occasion for permissible limitation." *Thomas* v. *Collins*. No such abuse or danger has been advanced in the present case. The appellees suggest no more than a possibility that the filing of fraudulent claims by unscrupulous claimants feigning religious objections to Saturday work might not only dilute the unemployment compensation fund but also hinder the scheduling by employers of necessary Saturday work. But that possibility is not apposite here because no such objection appears to have

been made before the South Carolina Supreme Court, and we are unwilling to assess the importance of an asserted state interest without the
views of the state court. Nor, if the contention had been made below,
would the record appear to sustain it; there is no proof whatever to
warrant such fears of malingering or deceit as those which the respondents now advance. Even if consideration of such evidence is not foreclosed by the prohibition against judicial inquiry into the truth or falsity
of religious beliefs, *United States* v. *Ballard*, a question as to which
we intimate no view since it is not before us—it is highly doubtful
whether such evidence would be sufficient to warrant a substantial infringement of religious liberties. For even if the possibility of spurious
claims did threaten to dilute the fund and disrupt the scheduling of
work, it would plainly be incumbent upon the appellees to demonstrate
that no alternative forms of regulation would combat such abuses without infringing First Amendment rights. Cf. *Shelton* v. *Tucker*.

In these respects, then, the state interest asserted in the present case
is wholly dissimilar to the interests which were found to justify the less
direct burden upon religious practices in *Braunfeld* v. *Brown*. The Court
recognized that the Sunday closing law which that decision sustained
undoubtedly served "to make the practice of [the orthodox Jewish merchants'] . . . religious beliefs more expensive," but the statute was nevertheless saved by a countervailing factor which finds no equivalent in
the instant case—a strong state interest in providing one uniform day
of rest for all workers. That secular objective could be achieved, the
Court found, only by declaring Sunday to be that day of rest. Requiring
exemptions for Sabbatarians, while theoretically possible, appeared to
present an administrative problem of such magnitude, or to afford the
exempted class so great a competitive advantage, that such a requirement would have rendered the entire statutory scheme unworkable. In
the present case no such justifications underlie the determination of the
state court that appellant's religion makes her ineligible to receive
benefits.

IV

In holding as we do, plainly we are not fostering the "establishment"
of the Seventh-day Adventist religion in South Carolina, for the extension of unemployment benefits to Sabbatarians in common with Sunday
worshippers reflects nothing more than the governmental obligation of

neutrality in the face of religious differences, and does not represent that involvement of religious with secular institutions which it is the object of the Establishment Clause to forestall. See *School District of Abington Township* v. *Schempp*. Nor does the recognition of the appellant's right to unemployment benefits under the state statute serve to abridge any other person's religious liberties. Nor do we, by our decision today, declare the existence of a constitutional right to unemployment benefits on the part of all persons whose religious convictions are the cause of their unemployment. This is not a case in which an employee's religious convictions serve to make him a nonproductive member of society. Finally, nothing we say today constrains the States to adopt any particular form or scheme of unemployment compensation. Our holding today is only that South Carolina may not constitutionally apply the eligibility provisions so as to constrain a worker to abandon his religious convictions respecting the day of rest. This holding but reaffirms a principle that we announced a decade and a half ago, namely that no State may "exclude individual Catholics, Lutherans, Mohammedans, Baptists, Jews, Methodists, Non-believers, Presbyterians, or the members of any other faith, *because of their faith, or lack of it,* from receiving the benefits of public welfare legislation." *Everson* v. *Board of Education*.

In view of the result we have reached under the First and Fourteenth Amendments' guarantee of free exercise of religion, we have no occasion to consider appellant's claim that the denial of benefits also deprived her of the equal protection of the laws in violation of the Fourteenth Amendment.

The judgment of the South Carolina Supreme Court is reversed and the case is remanded for further proceedings not inconsistent with this opinion.

It is so ordered.

NEW YORK TIMES CO. *v.* SULLIVAN

Argued January 6, 1964—Decided March 9, 1964.

Respondent, an elected official in Montgomery, Alabama, brought suit in a state court alleging that he had been libeled by an advertisement in corporate petitioner's newspaper, the text of which appeared over the names of the four individual petitioners and many others. [The advertisement included statements, some of which were false, about police action allegedly directed against students who participated in a civil rights demonstration and against a leader of the civil rights movement; respondent claimed the statements referred to him because his duties included supervision of the police department.] The trial judge instructed the jury that such statements were "libelous per se," legal injury being implied without proof of actual damages, and that for the purpose of compensatory damage malice was presumed, so that such damages could be awarded against petitioners if the statements were found to have been published by them and to have related to respondent. As to punitive damages, the judge instructed that mere negligence was not evidence of actual malice and would not justify an award of punitive damages; he refused to instruct that actual intent to harm or recklessness had to be found before punitive damages could be awarded, or that a verdict for respondent should differentiate between compensatory and punitive damages. The jury found for respondent and the State Supreme Court affirmed. *Held:* A State cannot under the First and Fourteenth Amendments award damages to a public official for defamatory falsehood relating to his official conduct unless he proves "actual malice"—that the statement was made with knowledge of its falsity or with reckless disregard of whether it was true or false.

(a) Application by state courts of a rule of law, whether statutory or not, to award a judgment in a civil action, is "state action" under the Fourteenth Amendment.

(b) Expression does not lose constitutional protection to which it would otherwise be entitled because it appears in the form of a paid advertisement.

(c) Factual error, content defamatory of official reputation, or both, are insufficient to warrant an award of damages for false statements unless "actual malice"—knowledge that statements are false or in reckless disregard of the truth—is alleged and proved.

(d) State court judgment entered upon a general verdict which does not differentiate between punitive damages, as to which under state law actual malice must be proved, and general damages, as to which it is "presumed," precludes any determination as to the basis of the verdict and requires reversal, where presumption of malice is inconsistent with federal constitutional requirements.

(e) The evidence was constitutionally insufficient to support the judgment for respondent, since it failed to support a finding that the statements were made with actual malice or that they related to respondent.

Reversed and remanded.

MR. JUSTICE BRENNAN delivered the opinion of the Court.

We are required in this case to determine for the first time the extent to which the constitutional protections for speech and press limit a

State's power to award damages in a libel action brought by a public official against critics of his official conduct.

Respondent L. B. Sullivan is one of the three elected Commissioners of the City of Montgomery, Alabama. He testified that he was "Commissioner of Public Affairs and the duties are supervision of the Police Department, Fire Department, Department of Cemetery and Department of Scales." He brought this civil liberal action against the four individual petitioners, who are Negroes and Alabama clergymen, and against petitioner the New York Times Company, a New York corporation which publishes the *New York Times*, a daily newspaper. A jury in the Circuit Court of Montgomery County awarded him damages of $500,000, the full amount claimed, against all the petitioners, and the Supreme Court of Alabama affirmed.

Respondent's complaint alleged that he had been libeled by statements in a full-page advertisement that was carried in the *New York Times* on March 29, 1960. Entitled "Heed Their Rising Voices," the advertisement began by stating that "As the whole word knows by now, thousands of Southern Negro students are engaged in widespread non-violent demonstrations in positive affirmation to the right to live in human dignity as guaranteed by the U.S. Constitution and the Bill of Rights." It went on to charge that "in their efforts to uphold these guarantees, they are being met by an unprecedented wave of terror by those who would deny and negate that document which the whole world looks upon as setting the pattern for modern freedom. . . ." Succeeding paragraphs purported to illustrate the "wave of terror" by describing certain alleged events. The text concluded with an appeal for funds for three purposes: support of the student movement, "the struggle for the right-to-vote," and the legal defense of Dr. Martin Luther King, Jr., leader of the movement, against a perjury indictment then pending in Montgomery.

The text appeared over the names of 64 persons, many widely known for their activities in public affairs, religion, trade unions, and the performing arts. Below these names, and under a line reading "We in the south who are struggling daily for dignity and freedom warmly endorse this appeal," appeared the names of the four individual petitioners and of 16 other persons, all but two of whom were identified as clergymen in various Southern cities. The advertisement was signed at the bottom of the page by the "Committee to Defend Martin Luther King and the Struggle for Freedom in the South," and the officers of the Committee were listed.

Of the 10 paragraphs of text in the advertisement, the third and a portion of the sixth were the basis of respondent's claim of libel. They read as follows:

Third paragraph:

In Montgomery, Alabama, after students sang "My Country, 'Tis of Thee" on the State Capitol steps, their leaders were expelled from school, and truckloads of police armed with shotguns and tear-gas ringed the Alabama State College Campus. When the entire student body protested to state authorities by refusing to re-register, their dining hall was padlocked in an attempt to starve them into submission.

Sixth paragraph:

Again and again the Southern violators have answered Dr. King's peaceful protests with intimidation and violence. They have bombed his home almost killing his wife and child. They have assaulted his person. They have arrested him seven times—for "speeding," "loitering" and similar "offenses." And now they have charged him with "perjury"—a *felony* under which they could imprison him for *ten years.* . . .

Although neither of these statements mentions respondent by name, he contended that the word "police" in the third paragraph referred to him as the Montgomery Commissioner who supervised the Police Department, so that he was being accused of "ringing" the campus with police. He further claimed that the paragraph would be read as imputing to the police, and hence to him, the padlocking of the dining hall in order to starve the students into submission. As to the sixth paragraph, he contended that since arrests are ordinarily made by the police, the statement "They have arrested [Dr. King] seven times" would be read as referring to him; he further contended that the "They" who did the arresting would be equated with the "They" who committed the other described acts and with the "Southern violators." Thus, he argued, the paragraph would be read as accusing the Montgomery police, and hence him, of answering Dr. King's protests with "intimidation and violence," bombing his home, assaulting his person, and charging him with perjury. Respondent and six other Montgomery residents testified that they read some or all of the statements as referring to him in his capacity as Commissioner.

It is uncontroverted that some of the statements contained in the two paragraphs were not accurate descriptions of events which occurred in Montgomery. Although Negro students staged a demonstration on the State Capitol steps, they sang the National Anthem and not "My Country, 'Tis of Thee." Although nine students were expelled by the State Board of Education, this was not for leading the demonstration at the Capitol, but for demanding service at a lunch counter in the Montgomery County courthouse on another day. Not the entire student body, but most of it, had protested the expulsion, not by refusing to register, but by boycotting classes on a single day; virtually all the students did register for the ensuing semester. The campus dining hall was not padlocked on any occasion, and the only students who may have been barred from eating there were the few who had neither signed a preregistration application nor requested temporary meal tickets. Although the police were deployed near the campus in large numbers on three occasions, they did not at any time "ring" the campus, and they were not called to the campus in connection with the demonstration on the State Capitol steps, as the third paragraph implied. Dr. King had not been arrested seven times, but only four; and although he claimed to have been assaulted some years earlier in connection with his arrest for loitering outside a courtroom, one of the officers who made the arrest denied that there was such an assault.

On the premise that the charges in the sixth paragraph could be read as referring to him, respondent was allowed to prove that he had not participated in the events described. Although Dr. King's home had in fact been bombed twice when his wife and child were there, both of these occasions antedated respondent's tenure as Commissioner and the police were not only not implicated in the bombings, but had made every effort to apprehend those who were. Three of Dr. King's four arrests took place before respondent became Commissioner. Although Dr. King had in fact been indicted (he was subsequently acquitted) on two counts of perjury, each of which carried a possible five-year sentence, respondent had nothing to do with procuring the indictment.

Respondent made no effort to prove that he suffered actual pecuniary loss as a result of the alleged libel. One of his witnesses, a former employer, testified that if he had believed the statements, he doubted whether he "would want to be associated with anybody who would be a party to such things that are stated in that ad," and that he would not re-employ respondent if he believed "that he allowed the Police Department to do the things that the paper say he did." But neither this witness or any of the others testified that he had actually believed the statements in their supposed reference to respondent.

The cost of the advertisement was approximately $4800 and it was published by the *Times* upon an order from a New York advertising agency acting for the signatory Committee. The agency submitted the advertisement with a letter from A. Philip Randolph, Chairman of the Committee, certifying that the persons whose names appeared on the advertisement had given their permission. Mr. Randolph was known to the *Times'* Advertising Acceptability Department as a responsible person, and in accepting the letter as sufficient proof of authorization it followed its established practice. There was testimony that the copy of the advertisement which accompanied the letter listed only the 64 names appearing under the text, and that the statement, "We in the south . . . warmly endorse this appeal," and the list of names thereunder, which included those of the individual petitioners, were subsequently added when the first proof of the advertisement was received. Each of the individual petitioners testified that he had not authorized the use of his name, and that he had been unaware of its use until receipt of respondent's demand for a retraction. The manager of the Advertising Acceptability Department testified that he had approved the advertisement for publication because he knew nothing to cause him to believe that anything in it was false, and because it bore the endorsement of "a number of people who are well known and whose reputation" he "had no reason to question." Neither he nor anyone else at the *Times* made an effort to confirm the accuracy of the advertisement, either by checking it against recent *Times* news stories relating to some of the described events or by any other means.

Alabama law denies a public officer recovery of punitive damages in a libel action brought on account of a publication concerning his official conduct unless he first makes a written demand for a public retraction and the defendant fails or refuses to comply. Alabama Code, Tit. 7, §914. Respondent served such a demand upon each of the petitioners. None of the individual petitioners responded to the demand, primarily because each took the position that he had not authorized the use of his name on the advertisement and therefore had not published the statements that respondent alleged had libeled him. The *Times* did not publish a retraction in response to the demand, but wrote respondent a letter stating, among other things, that "we . . . are somewhat puzzled as to how you think the statements in any way reflect on you," and "you might, if you desire, let us know in what respect you claim that the statements in the advertisement reflect on you." Respondent filed this suit a few days later without answering the letter. The *Times* did, however, subsequently publish a retraction of the advertisement upon the demand of Governor John Patterson of Alabama, who asserted that the publication charged him with "grave misconduct and . . . improper actions and omissions as Governor of Alabama and Ex-Officio Chairman of the State Board of Education of Alabama." When asked to explain why there had been a retraction for the Governor but not for respondent, the Secretary of the *Times* testified: "We did that because we didn't want anything that was published by *The Times* to be a reflection on the State of Alabama and the Governor was, as far as we could see, the embodiment of the State of Alabama and the proper representative of the State and, furthermore, we had by that time learned more of the actual facts which the ad purported to recite and, finally, the ad did refer to the action of the State authorities and the Board of Education presumably of which the Governor is the ex-officio chairman. . . ." On the other hand, he testified that he did not think that "any of the language in there referred to Mr. Sullivan."

The trial judge submitted the case to the jury under instructions that the statements in the advertisement were "libelous *per se*" and were not privileged, so that petitioners might be held liable if the jury found that they had published the advertisement and that the statements were made "of and concerning" respondent. The jury was instructed that, because the statements were libelous *per se*, "the law . . . implies legal injury from the bare fact of publication itself," "falsity and malice are presumed," "general damages need not be alleged for proved but are presumed," and "punitive damages may be awarded by the jury even though the amount of actual damages is neither found nor shown." An award of punitive damages—as distinguished from "general" damages, which are compensatory in nature—apparently requires proof of actual malice under Alabama law, and the judge charged that "mere negligence or carelessness is not evidence of actual malice or malice in fact, and does not justify an award of exemplary or punitive damages." He refused to charge, however, that the jury must be "convinced" of malice, in the sense of "actual intent" to harm or "gross negligence and recklessness," to make such an award, and he also refused to require that a verdict for respondent differentiate between compensatory and punitive damages. The judge rejected petitioners' contention that his rulings abridged the freedoms of speech and of the press that are guaranteed by the First and Fourteenth Amendments.

In affirming the judgment, the Supreme Court of Alabama sustained the trial judge's rulings and instructions in all respects. It held that "where the words published tend to injure a person libeled by them in his reputation, profession, trade or business, or charge him with an indictable offense, or tend to bring the individual into public contempt," they are "libelous per se"; that "the matter complained of is, under the above doctrine, libelous per se, if it was published of and concerning the plaintiff"; and that it was actionable without "proof of pecuniary injury . . . such injury being implied." It approved the trial court's ruling that the jury could find the statements to have been made "of and concerning" respondent, stating: "We think it common knowledge that the average person knows that municipal agents, such as police and firemen, and others, are under the control and direction of the city governing body, and more particularly under the direction and control of a single commissioner. In measuring the performance or deficiencies of such groups, praise or criticism is usually attached to the official in complete control of the body." In sustaining the trial court's determination that the verdict was not excessive, the court said that malice could be inferred from the *Times*' "irresponsibility" in printing the advertisement while "the *Times* in its own files had articles already published which would have demonstrated the falsity of the allegations in the advertisement"; from the *Times*' failure to retract for respondent while retracting for the Governor, whereas the falsity of some of the allegations was then known to the *Times* and "the matter contained in the advertisement was equally false as to both parties"; and from the testimony of the *Times*' Secretary that, apart from the statement that the dining hall was padlocked, he thought the two paragraphs were "substantially correct." The court reaffirmed a statement in an earlier opinion that "There is no legal measure of damages in cases of this character." It rejected petitioners' constitutional contentions with the brief statements that "The First Amendment of the U.S. Constitution does not protect libelous publications" and "The Fourteenth Amendment is directed against State action and not private action."

Because of the importance of the constitutional issues involved, we granted the separate petitions for certiorari of the individual petitioners and of the *Times*. We reverse the judgment. We hold that the rule of law applied by the Alabama courts is constitutionally deficient for failure to provide the safeguards for freedom of speech and of the press that are required by the First and Fourteenth Amendments in a libel action brought by a public official against critics of his official conduct. We further hold that under the proper safeguards the evidence presented in this case is constitutionally insufficient to support the judgment for respondent.

I

We may dispose at the outset of two grounds asserted to insulate the judgment of the Alabama courts from constitutional scrutiny. The first is the proposition relied on by the State Supreme Court—that "The Fourteenth Amendment is directed against State action and not private action." That proposition has no application to this case. Although this is a civil lawsuit between private parties, the Alabama courts have applied a state rule of law which petitioners claim to impose invalid restrictions on their constitutional freedoms of speech and press. I matters not that that law has been applied in a civil action and that it is common law only, though supplemented by statute. The test is not the form in which state power has been applied but, whatever the form, whether such power has in fact been exercised. See *Ex parte Virginia*.

The second contention is that the constitutional guarantees of freedom of speech and of the press are inapplicable here, at least so far as the *Times* is concerned, because the allegedly libelous statements were published as part of a paid, "commercial" advertisement. The argument relies on *Valentine v. Chrestensen*, where the Court held that a city ordinance forbidding street distribution of commercial and business advertising matter did not abridge the First Amendment freedoms, even as applied to a handbill having a commercial message on one side but a protest against certain official action on the other. The reliance is wholly misplaced. The Court in *Chrestensen* reaffirmed the constitutional protection for "the freedom of communicating information and disseminating opinion"; its holding was based upon the factual conclusions that the handbill was "purely commercial advertising" and that the protest against official action had been added only to evade the ordinance.

The publication here was not a "commercial" advertisement in the sense in which the word was used in *Chrestensen*. It communicated information, expressed opinion, recited grievances, protested claimed abuses, and sought financial support on behalf of a movement whose existence and objectives are matters of the highest public interest and concern. See *N. A. A. C. P.* v. *Button.* That the *Times* was paid for publishing the advertisement is as immaterial in this connection as is the fact that newspapers and books are sold. *Smith* v. *California.* Any other conclusion would discharge newspapers from carrying "editorial advertisements" of this type, and so might shut off an important outlet for the promulgation of information and ideas by persons who do not themselves have access to publishing facilities—who wish to exercise their freedom of speech even though they are not members of the press. Cf. *Lovell* v. *Griffin.* The effect would be to shackle the First Amendment in its attempt to secure "the wildest possible dissemination of information from diverse and antagonistic sources." *Associated Press* v. *United States.* To avoid placing such a handicap upon the freedoms of expression, we hold that if the allegedly libelous statements would otherwise be constitutionally protected from the present judgment, they do not forfeit that protection because they were published in the form of a paid advertisement.

II

Under Alabama law as applied in this case, a publication is "libelous per se" if the words "tend to injure a person . . . in his reputation" or to "bring [him] into public office, or impute misconduct to him in his office, or want of official integrity, or want of fidelity to a public trust. . . ." The jury must find that the words were published "of and concerning" the plaintiff, but where the plaintiff is a public official his place in the governmental hierarchy is sufficient evidence to support a finding that his reputation has been affected by statements that reflect upon the agency of which he is in charge. Once "libel per se" has been established, the defendant has no defense as to stated facts unless he can persuade the jury that they were true in all their particulars. *Alabama Ride Co.* v. *Vance.* His privilege of "fair comment" for expressions of opinion depends on the truth of the facts upon which the comment is based. *Parsons* v. *Age—Herald Publishing Co.* (1913). Unless he can discharge the burden of proving truth, general damages are presumed, and may be awarded without proof of pecuniary injury. A showing of actual malice is apparently a prerequisite to recovery of punitive damages, and the defendant may in any event forestall a punitive award by a retraction meeting the statutory requirements. Good motives and belief in truth do not negate an inference of malice, but are relevant only in mitigation of punitive damages if the jury chooses to accord them weight. *Johnson Publishing Co.* v. Davis.

The question before us is whether this rule of liability, as applied to an action brought by a public official against critics of his official conduct, abridges the freedom of speech and of the press that is guaranteed by the First and Fourteenth Amendments.

Respondent relies heavily, as did the Alabama courts, on statements of this Court to the effect that the Constitution does not protect libelous publications. Those statements do not foreclose our inquiry here. None of the cases sustained the use of libel laws to impose sanctions upon expression critical of the official conduct of public officials. The dictum in *Pennekamp* v. *Florida* that "when the statements amount to defamation, a judge has such remedy in damages for libel as do other public servants," implied no view as to what remedy might constitutionally be afforded to public officials. In *Beauharnais* v. *Illinois* the Court sustained an Illinois criminal libel statute as applied to a publication held to be both defamatory of a racial group and "liable to cause violence and disorder." But the Court was careful to note that it "retains and exercises authority to nullify action which encroaches on freedom of utterance under the guise of punishing libel"; for "public men, are, as it were, public property," and "discussion cannot be denied and the right, as well as the duty, of criticism must not be stifled." In the only previous case that did present the question of constitutional limitations upon the power of award damages for libel of a public official, the Court was equally divided and the question was not decided. *Schenectady Union Pub. Co.* v. *Sweeney.* In deciding the question now, we are compelled by neither precedent nor policy to give any more weight to the epithet "libel" than we have to other "mere labels" of state law. *N. A. A. C. P.* v. *Button.* Like insurrection, contempt, advocacy of unlawful acts, breach of the peace, obscenity, solicitation of legal business, and the various other formulae for the repression of expression that have been challenged in this Court, libel can claim no talismanic immunity from constitutional limitations. It must be measured by standards that satisfy the First Amendment.

The general proposition that freedom of expression upon public questions is secured by the First Amendment has long been settled by our decisions. The constitutional safeguard, we have said, "was fashioned to assure unfettered interchange of ideas for the bringing about of political and social changes desired by the people." *Roth* v. *United States.*

"The maintenance of the opportunity for free political discussion to the end that government may be responsive to the will of the people and that changes may be obtained by lawful means, an opportunity essential to the security of the Republic, is a fundamental principle of our constitutional system." *Stromberg* v. *California.* "[I]t is a prized American privilege to speak one's mind, although not always with perfect good taste, on all public institutions," *Bridges* v. *California*, and this opportunity is to be afforded for "vigorous advocacy" no less than "abstract discussion." *N. A. A. C. P.* v. *Button.* The First Amendment, said Judge Learned Hand, "presupposes that right conclusions are more likely to be gathered out of a multitude of tongues, than through any kind of authoritative selection. To many this is, and always will be, folly; but we have staked upon it our all." *United States* v. *Associated Press* (D. C. S. D. N. Y. 1943). Mr. Justice Brandeis, in his concurring opinion in *Whitney* v. *California*, gave the principle its classic formulation:

> Those who won our independence believed . . . that public discussion is a political duty; and that this should be a fundamental principle of the American government. They recognized the risks to which all human institutions are subject. But they knew that order cannot be secured merely through fear of punishment for its infraction; that it is hazardous to discourage thought, hope and imagination; that fear breeds repression; that repression breeds hate; that hate menaces stable government; that the path of safety lies in the opportunity to discuss freely supposed grievances and proposed remedies; and that the fitting remedy for evil counsels is good ones. Believing in the power of reason as applied through public discussion, they eschewed silence coerced by law—the argument of force in its worst form. Recognizing the occasional tyrannies of governing majorities, they amended the Constitution so that free speech and assembly should be guaranteed.

Thus we consider this case against the background of a profound national commitment to the principle that debate on public issues should be uninhibited, robust, and wide-open, and that it may well include vehement, caustic, and sometimes unpleasantly sharp attacks on government and public officials. See *Terminiello* v. *Chicago.* The present advertisement, as an expression of grievance and protest on one of the major public issues of our time, would seem clearly to qualify for the constitutional protection. The question is whether it forfeits that protection by the falsity of some of its factual statements and by its alleged defamation of respondent.

Authoritative interpretations of the First Amendment guarantees have consistently refused to recognize an exception for any test of truth—whether administered by judges, juries, or administrative officials—and especially one that puts the burden of proving truth on the speaker. Cf. *Speiser* v. *Randall.* The constitutional protection does not turn upon "the truth, popularity, or social utility of the ideas and beliefs which are offered." *N. A. A. C. P.* v. *Button.* As Madison said, "Some degree of abuse is inseparable from the proper use of every thing; and in no instance is this more true than in that of the press." 4 Elliot's Debates on the Federal Constitution (1876). In *Cantwell* v. *Connecticut* the Court declared:

> In the realm of religious faith, and in that of political belief, sharp differences arise. In both fields the tenets of one man may seem the rankest error to his neighbor. To persuade others to his own point of view, the pleader, as we know, at times, resorts to exaggeration, to vilification of men who have been, or are, prominent in church or state, and even to false statement. But the people of this nation have ordained in the light of history, that, in spite of the probability of excesses and abuses, these liberties are, in the long view, essential to enlightened opinion and right conduct on the part of the citizens of a democracy.

That erroneous statement is inevitable in free debate, and that it must be protected if the freedoms of expression are to have the "breathing space" that they "need . . . to survive," *N. A. A. C. P.* v. *Button* was also recognized by the Court of Appeals for the District of Columbia Circuit in *Sweeney* v. *Patterson* (1942). Judge Edgerton spoke for a unanimous court which affirmed the dismissal of a Congressman's libel suit based upon a newspaper article charging him with anti-Semitism in opposing a judicial appointment. He said:

> Cases which impose liability for erroneous reports of the political conduct of officials reflect the obsolete doctrine that the governed must not criticize their governors. . . . The interest of the public here outweighs the interest of appellant or any other individual. The pro-

tection of the public requires not merely discussion, but information. Political conduct and views which some respectable people approve, and others condemn, are constantly imputed to Congressmen. Errors of fact, particularly in regard to a man's mental states and processes, are inevitable. . . . Whatever is added to the field of libel is taken from the field of free debate.

Injury to official reputation affords no more warrant for repressing speech that would otherwise be free than does factual error. Where judicial officers are involved, this Court has held that concern for the dignity and reputation of the courts does not justify the punishment as criminal contempt of criticism of the judge or his decision. *Bridges* v. *California.* This is true even though the utterance contains "half-truths" and "misinformation." *Pennekamp* v. *Florida.* Such repression can be justified, if at all, only by a clear and present danger of the obstruction of justice. See also *Craig* v. *Harney.* If judges are to be treated as "men of fortitude, able to thrive in a hardy climate," *Craig* v. *Harney,* surely the same must be true of other government officials, such as elected city commissioners. Criticism of their official conduct does not lose its constitutional protection merely because it is effective criticism and hence diminishes their official reputations.

If neither factual error nor defamatory content suffices to remove the constitutional shield from criticism of official conduct, the combination of the two elements is no less inadequate. This is the lesson to be drawn from the great controversy over the Sedition Act of 1798, 1 Stat. 596, which first crystallized a national awareness of the central meaning of the First Amendment. That statute made it a crime, punishable by a $5,000 fine and five years in prison, "if any person shall write, print, utter or publish . . . any false, scandalous and malicious writing or writings against the government of the United States, or either house of the Congress . . . or the President . . . with intent to defame . . . or to bring them, or either of them, into contempt to disrepute; or to excite against them, or either or any of them, the hatred of the good people of the United States." The Act allowed the defendant the defense of truth, and provided that the jury were to be judges both of the law and the facts. Despite these qualifications, the Act was vigorously condemned as unconstitutional in an attack joined in by Jefferson and Madison. In the famous Virginia Resolutions of 1798, the General Assembly of Virginia resolved that it doth particularly protest against the palpable and alarming infractions of the Constitution, in the two late cases of the "Alien and Sedition Acts," passed the last session of Congress .... [The Sedition Act] exercises ... a power not delegated by the Constitution, but on the contrary, expressly and positively forbidden by one of the amendments thereto—a power which, more than any other, ought to produce universal alarm, because it is levelled against the right of freely examining public characters and measures, and of free communication among the people thereon, which has ever been justly deemed the only effectual guardian of every other right. [4 Elliot's Debates]

Madison prepared the Report in support of the protest. His premise was that the Constitution created a form of government under which "The people, not the government, possess the absolute sovereignty." The structure of the government dispersed power in reflection of the people's distrust of concentrated power, and of power itself at all levels. This form of government was "altogether different" from the British form, under which the Crown was sovereign and the people were subjects. "Is it not natural and necessary, under such different circumstances," he said, "that a different degree of freedom in the use of the press should be contemplated?" Earlier, in a debate in the House of Representatives, Madison had said: "If we advert to the nature of Republican Government, we shall find that the censorial power is the people over the Government, and not in the Government over the people." Of the exercise of that power by the press, his Report said: "In every state, probably, in the Union, the press has exerted a freedom in canvassing the merits and measures of public men, of every description, which has not been confined to the strict limits of the common law. On this footing the freedom of the press has stood; on this foundation it yet stands ...." 4 Elliot's Debates. The right of free public discussion of the stewardship of public officials was thus, in Madison's view, a fundamental principle of the American form of government.

Although the Sedition Act was never tested in this Court, the attack upon its validity has carried the day in the court of history. Fines levied in its prosecution were repaid by Act of Congress on the ground that it was unconstitutional. Calhoun, reporting to the Senate on February 4, 1836, assumed that its validity was a matter "which no one now doubts." Jefferson, as President, pardoned those who had been convicted and sentenced under the Act and remitted their fines, stating: "I discharged every person under punishment or prosecution under the sedition law, because I considered, and now consider, that law to be a nullity, as absolute and as palpable as if Congress had ordered us to fall down and worship a golden image.'' The invalidity of the Act has also been assumed by Justices of this Court. These views reflect a broad consensus that the Act, because of the restraint it imposed upon criticism of government and public officials, was inconsistent with the First Amendment.

There is no force in respondent's argument that the constitutional limitations implicit in the history of the Sedition Act apply only to Congress and not to the States. It is true that the First Amendment was originally addressed only to action by the Federal Government, and that Jefferson, for one, while denying the power of Congress "to controul the freedom of the press,'' recognized such a power in the States. But this distinction was eliminated with the adoption of the Fourteenth Amendment and the application to the States of the First Amendment's restrictions. See, *e. g., Gitlow* v. *New York.*

What a State may not constitutionally bring about by means of a criminal statute is likewise beyond the reach of its civil law of libel. The fear of damage awards under a rule such as that invoked by the Alabama courts here may be markedly more inhibiting than the fear of prosecution under a criminal statute. See *City of Chicago* v. *Tribune Co.* (1923). Alabama, for example, has a criminal libel law which subjects to prosecution "any person who speaks, writes, or prints of and concerning another any accusation falsely and maliciously importing the commission by such person of a felony, or any other indictable offense involving moral turpitude,'' and which allows a punishment upon conviction of a fine not exceeding $500 and a prison sentence of six months. Alabama Code, Tit. 14, §350. Presumably a person charged with violation of this statute enjoys ordinary criminal-law safeguards such as the requirements of an indictment and of proof beyond a reasonable doubt. These safeguards are not available to the defendant in a civil action. The judgment awarded in this case—without the need for any proof of actual pecuniary loss—was one thousand times greater than the maximum fine provided by the Alabama criminal statute, and one hundred times greater than that provided by the Sedition Act. And since there is no double-jeopardy limitation applicable to civil lawsuits, this is not the only judgment that may be awarded against petitioners for the same publication. Whether or not a newspaper can survive a succession of such judgments, the pall of fear and timidity imposed upon those who would give voice to public criticism in an atmosphere in which the

First Amendment freedoms cannot survive. Plainly the Alabama law of civil libel is "a form of regulation that creates hazards to protected freedoms markedly greater than those that attend reliance upon the criminal law." *Bantam Books, Inc., v. Sullivan.*

The state rule of law is not saved by its allowance of the defense of truth. A defense of erroneous statements honestly made is no less essential here than was the requirement of proof of guilty knowledge which, in *Smith* v. *California*, we held indispensable to a valid conviction of a bookseller for possessing obscene writings for sale. We said:

> For if the bookseller is criminally liable without knowledge of the contents, . . . he will tend to restrict the books he sells to those he has inspected; and thus the State will have imposed a restriction upon the distribution of constitutionally protected as well as obscene literature. . . . And the bookseller's burden would become the public's burden, for by restricting him the public's access to reading matter would be restricted. . . . [H]is timidity in the face of his absolute criminal liability, thus would tend to restrict the public's access to forms of the printed word which the State could not constitutionally suppress directly. The bookseller's self-censorship, compelled by the State, would be a censorship affecting the whole public, hardly less virulent for being privately administered. Through it, the distribution of all books, both obscene and not obscene, would be impeded.

A rule compelling the critic of official conduct to guarantee the truth of all his factual assertions—and to do so on pain of libel judgments virtually unlimited in amount—leads to a comparable "self-censorship." Allowance of the defense of truth, with the burden of proving it on the defendant, does not mean that only false speech will be deterred. Even courts accepting this defense as an adequate safeguard have recognized the difficulties of adducing legal proofs that the alleged libel was true in all its factual particulars. See *e.g., Post Publishing Co.* v. *Hallam* (C. A. 6th Cir. 1893). Under such a rule, would-be critics of official conduct may be deterred from voicing their criticism, even though it is believed to be true and even though it is in fact true, because of doubt whether it can be proved in court or fear of the expense of having to do so. They tend to make only statements which "steer far wider of the unlawful zone." *Speiser* v. *Randall*. The rule thus dampens the vigor and limits the variety of public debate. It is inconsistent with the First and Fourteenth Amendments.

The constitutional guarantees require, we think, a federal rule that prohibits a public official from recovering damages for a defamatory falsehood relating to his official conduct unless he proves that the statement was made with "actual malice"—that is, with knowledge that it was false or with reckless disregard of whether it was false or not. An oft-cited statement of a like rule, which has been adopted by a number of state courts is found in the Kansas case of *Coleman* v. *MacLennan* (1908). The State Attorney General, a candidate for re-election and a member of the commission charged with the management and control of the state school fund, sued a newspaper publisher for alleged libel in an article purporting to state facts relating to his official conduct in connection with a school-fund transaction. The defendant pleaded privilege and the trial judge, over the plaintiff's objection, instructed the jury that

> where an article is published and circulated among voters for the sole purpose of giving what the defendant believes to be truthful information concerning a candidate for public office and for the purpose of enabling such voters to cast their ballot more intelligently, and the whole thing is done in good faith and without malice, the article is privileged, although the principal matters contained in the article may be untrue in fact and derogatory to the character of the plaintiff; and in such a case the burden is on the plaintiff to show actual malice in the publication of the article.

In answer to a special question, the jury found that the plaintiff had not proved actual malice, and a general verdict was returned for the defendant. On appeal the Supreme Court of Kansas in an opinion by Justice Burch, reasoned as follows.

> It is of the utmost consequence that the people should discuss the character and qualifications of candidates for their suffrages. The importance to the state and to society of such discussions is so vast, and the advantages derived are so great, that they more than counterbalance the inconvenience of private persons whose conduct may be involved, and occasional injury to the reputations of individuals must yield to the public welfare, although at times such injury may be great. The public benefit from publicity is so great, and the chance of injury to private character so small, that such discussion must be privileged.

The court thus sustained the trial court's instruction as a correct state-ment of the law, saying:

> In such a case the occasion gives rise to a privilege, qualified to this extent: any one claiming to be defamed by the communication must show actual malice or go remediless. This privilege extends to a great variety of subjects, and includes matters of public concern, public men, and candidates for office.

Such a privilege for criticism of official conduct is appropriately analogous to the protection accorded a public official when *he* is sued for libel by a private citizen. In *Barr* v. *Matteo* this Court held the utterance of a federal official to be absolutely privileged if made "within the outer perimeter" of his duties. The States accord the same immunity to statements of their highest officers, although some differen-tiate their lesser officials and qualify the privilege they enjoy. But all hold that all officials are protected unless actual malice can be proved. The reason for the official privilege is said to be that the threat of damage suits would otherwise "inhibit the fearless, vigorous, and effec-tive administration of policies of government" and "dampen the ardor of all but the most resolute, or the most irresponsible, in the unflinching discharge of their duties." *Barr* v. *Matteo.* Analogous considerations support the privilege for the citizen-critic of government. It is as much his duty to criticize as it is the official's duty to administer. See *Whitney* v. *California.* As Madison said, see "the censorial power is in the people over the Government, and not in the Government over the peo-ple." It would give public servants an unjustified preference over the public they serve, if critics of official conduct did not have a fair equiva-lent of the immunity granted to the officials themselves.

We concluded that such a privilege is required by the First and Four-teenth Amendments.

III

We hold today that the Constitution delimits a State's power to award damages for libel in actions brought by public officials against critics of their official conduct. Since this is such an action, the rule requiring proof of actual malice is applicable. While Alabama law apparently requires proof of actual malice for an award of punitive damages, where general damages are concerned malice is "presumed." Such a presumption is inconsistent with the federal rule. "The power to create presumptions is not a means of escape from constitutional restrictions," *Bailey* v. *Alabama*; "the showing of malice required for the forfeiture of the privilege is not presumed but is a matter for proof by the plaintiff. . . ." *Lawrence* v. *Fox* (1959). Since the trial judge did not instruct the jury to differentiate between general and punitive damages, it may be that the verdict was wholly an award of one or the other. But it is impossible to know, in view of the general verdict returned. Because of this uncertainty, the judgment must be reversed and the case remanded. *Stromberg* v. *California.*

Since respondent may seek a new trial, we deem that considerations of effective judicial administration require us to review the evidence in the present record to determine whether it could constitutionally support a judgment for respondent. This Court's duty is not limited to the elaboration of constitutional principles; we must also in proper cases review the evidence to make certain that those principles have been constitutionally applied. This is such a case, particularly since the question is one of alleged trespass across "the line between speech unconditionally guaranteed and speech which may legitimately be regulated." *Speiser* v. *Randall.* In cases where that line must be drawn, the rule is that we "examine for ourselves the statements in issue and the circumstances under which they were made to see . . . whether they are of a character which the principles of the First Amendment, as adopted by the Due Process Clause of the Fourteenth Amendment, protect." *Pennekamp* v. *Florida.* We must "make an independent examination of the whole record," *Edwards* v. *South Carolina*, so as to assure ourselves that the judgment does not constitute a forbidden intrusion on the field of free expression.

Applying these standards, we consider that the proof presented to show actual malice lacks the convincing clarity which the constitutional standard demands, and hence that it would not constitutionally sustain the judgment for respondent under the proper rule of law. The case of the individual petitioners requires little discussion. Even assuming that they could constitutionally be found to have authorized the use of their names on the advertisement, there was no evidence whatever that they were aware of any erroneous statements or were in any way reckless in that regard. The judgment against them is thus without constitutional support.

As to the *Times,* we similarly conclude that the facts do not support a finding of actual malice. The statement by the *Times*' Secretary that, apart from the padlocking allegation, he thought the advertisement was "substantially correct," affords no constitutional warrant for the Alabama Supreme Court's conclusion that it was a "cavalier ignoring of the falsity of the advertisement [from which] the jury could not have but been impressed with the bad faith of *The Times*, and its maliciousness inferable therefrom." The statement does not indicate malice at the time of the publication; even if the advertisement was not "substantially correct"—although respondent's own proofs tend to show that it was— that opinion was at least a reasonable one, and there was no evidence to impeach the witness' good faith in holding it. *The Times*' failure to retract upon respondent's demand, although it later retracted upon the demand of Governor Patterson, is likewise not adequate evidence of malice for constitutional purposes. Whether or not a failure to retract may ever constitute such evidence, there are two reasons why it does not here. *First*, the letter written by the *Times* reflected a reasonable doubt on its part as to whether the advertisement could reasonably be taken to refer to respondent at all. *Second*, it was not a final refusal, since it asked for an explanation on this point—a request that respondent chose to ignore. Nor does the retraction upon the demand of the Governor supply the necessary proof. It may be doubted that a failure to retract which is not itself evidence of malice can retroactively become such by virtue of a retraction subsequently made to another party. But in any event that did not happen here, since the explanation given by the *Times*' Secretary for the distinction drawn between respondent and the Governor was a reasonable one, the good faith of which was not impeached.

Finally, there is evidence that the *Times* published the advertisement without checking its accuracy against the news stories in *Time*'s own files. The mere presence of these stories in the files does not, of course, establish that the *Times* "knew" the advertisement was false, since the state of mind required for actual malice would have to be brought home to the persons in the *Times*' organization having responsibility for the publication of the advertisement. With respect of the failure of those persons to make the check, the record shows that they relied upon their knowledge of the good reputation of many of those whose names were listed as sponsors of the advertisement, and upon the letter from A. Philip Randolph, known to them as a responsible individual, certifying that the use of the names was authorized. There was testimony that the persons handling the advertisement saw nothing in it that would render it unacceptable under the Times' policy of rejecting advertisements containing "attacks of a personal character"; their failure to reject it on this ground was not unreasonable. We think the evidence against the *Times* supports at most a finding of negligence in failing to discover the misstatements, and is constitutionally insufficient to show the recklessness that is required for a finding of actual malice. Cf. *Charles Parker Co.* v. *Silver City Crystal Co.* (1955).

We also think the evidence was constitutionally defective in another respect: it was incapable of supporting the jury's finding that the allegedly libelous statements were made "of and concerning" respondent. Respondent relies on the words of the advertisement and the testimony of six witnesses to establish a connection between it and himself. Thus, in his brief to this Court, he states:

> The reference to respondent as police commissioner is clear from the ad. In addition, the jury heard the testimony of a newspaper editor . . .; a real estate and insurance man . . .; the sales manager of a men's clothing store . . .; a food equipment man . . . a service station operator . . .; and the operator of a truck line for whom respondent had formerly worked. . . . Each of these witnesses stated that he associated the statements with respondent. . . .

There was no reference to respondent in the advertisement, either by name or official position. A number of the allegedly libelous statements—the charges that the dining hall was padlocked and that Dr. King's home was bombed, his person assaulted, and a perjury prosecution instituted against him—did not even concern the police; despite the ingenuity of the arguments which would attach this significance to the word "They," it is plain that these statements could not reasonably be read as accusing respondent of personal involvement in the acts in question. The statements upon which respondent principally relies as referring to him are the two allegations that did concern the police or police functions: that "truckloads of police . . . ringed the Alabama State College Campus" after the demonstration on the State Capitol steps, and that Dr. King had been "arrested . . . seven times." These statements were false only in that the police had been "deployed near" the campus but had not actually "ringed" it and had not gone there in connection with the State Capitol demonstration, and in that Dr. King had been arrested only four times. The ruling that these discrepancies between what was true and what was asserted were sufficient to injure respondent's reputation may itself raise constitutional problems, but we need not consider them here. Although the statements may be taken as referring to the police, they did not on their face make even an oblique reference to respondent as an individual. Support for the asserted reference must, therefore, be sought in the testimony of respondent's witnesses. But none of them suggested any basis for the belief that respondent himself was attacked in the advertisement beyond the bare fact that he was in overall charge of the Police Department and thus bore official responsibility for police conduct; to the extent that some of the witnesses thought respondent to have been charged with ordering or approving the conduct or otherwise being personally involved in it, they based this notion not on any statements in the advertisement, and not on any evidence that he had in fact been so involved, but solely on the unsupported assumption that, because of his official position, he must have been. This reliance on the bare fact of respondent's official position was made explicit by the Supreme Court of Alabama. That court, in holding that the trial court "did not err in overruling the demurrer [of the *Times*] in the aspect that the libelous matter was not of and concerning the [plaintiff]," based its ruling on the proposition that:

We think it common knowledge that the average person knows that municipal agents, such as police and firemen, and others, are under the control and direction of the city governing body, and more particularly under the direction and control of a single commissioner. In measuring the performance or deficiencies of such groups, praise or criticism is usually attached to the official in complete control of the body.

This proposition has disquieting implications for criticism of governmental conduct. For good reason, "no court of last resort in this country has ever held, or even suggested, that prosecutions for libel on government have any place in the American system of jurisprudence." *City of Chicago* v. *Tribune Co.* (1923). The present proposition would sidestep this obstacle by transmitting criticism of government, however impersonal it may seem on its face, into personal criticism, and hence potential libel, of the officials of whom the government is composed. There is no legal alchemy by which a State may thus create the cause of action that would otherwise be denied for a publication which, as respondent himself said of the advertisement, "reflects not only on me but on the other Commissioners and the community." Raising as it does the possibility that a good-faith critic of government will be penalized for his criticism, the proposition relied on by the Alabama courts strikes at the very center of the constitutionally protected area of free expression. We hold that such a proposition may not constitutionally be utilized to establish that an otherwise impersonal attack on governmental operations was a libel of an official responsible for those operations. Since it was relied on exclusively here, and there was no other evidence to connect the statements with respondent, the evidence was constitutionally insufficient to support a finding that the statements referred to respondent.

The judgment of the Supreme Court of Alabama is reversed and the case is remanded to that court for further proceedings not inconsistent with this opinion.

Reversed and remanded.

PARIS ADULT THEATRE I et al. *v.* SLATON,
DISTRICT ATTORNEY, et al.

Argued October 19, 1972—Denied June 21, 1973

Respondents sued under Georgia civil law to enjoin the exhibiting by petitioners of two allegedly obscene films. There was no prior restraint. In a jury-waived trial, the trial court (which did not require "expert" affirmative evidence of obscenity) viewed the films and thereafter dismissed the complaints on the ground that the display of the films in commercial theaters to consenting adult audiences (reasonable precautions having been taken to exclude minors) was "constitutionally permissible." The Georgia Supreme Court reversed, holding that the films constituted "hard core" pornography not within the protection of the First Amendment. *Held*:

1. Obscene material is not speech entitled to First Amendment protection. *Miller* v. *California*.

2. The Georgia civil procedure followed here (assuming use of a constitutionally acceptable standard for determining what is unprotected by the First Amendment) comported with the standards of *Teitel Film Corp.* v. *Cusack*.

3. It was not error to fail to require expert affirmative evidence of the films' obscenity, since the films (which were the best evidence of what they depicted) were themselves placed in evidence.

4. States have a legitimate interest in regulating commerce in obscene material and its exhibition in places of public accommodation, including "adult" theaters.

(a) There is a proper state concern with safeguarding against crime and the other arguably ill effects of obscenity by prohibiting the public or commercial exhibition of obscene material. Though conclusive proof is lacking, the States may reasonably determine that a nexus does or might exist between antisocial behavior and obscene material, just as States have acted on unprovable assumptions in other areas of public control.

(b) Though States are free to adopt a laissez-faire policy toward commercialized obscenity, they are not constitutionally obliged to do so.

(c) Exhibition of obscene material in places of public accommodation is not protected by any constitutional doctrine of privacy. A commercial theater cannot be equated with a private home; nor is there here a privacy right arising from a special relationship, such as marriage. *Stanley* v. *Georgia.* Nor can the privacy of the home be equated with a "zone" of "privacy" that follows a consumer of obscene materials wherever he goes. *United States* v. *Orito.*

(d) Preventing the unlimited display of obscene material is not thought control.

(e) Not all conduct directly involving "consenting adults" only has a claim to constitutional protection.

5. The Georgia obscenity laws involved herein should now be re-evaluated in the light of the First Amendment standards newly enunciated by the Court in *Miller* v. *California.*

BURGER, C. J., delivered the opinion of the Court, in which WHITE BLACKMUN, POWELL, and REHNQUIST, J.J., joined. DOUGLAS, J., filed a dissenting opinion, BRENNAN, J., filed a dissenting opinion.

MR. JUSTICE BRENNAN, with whom MR. JUSTICE STEWART and MR. JUSTICE MARSHALL join, dissenting.

This case requires the Court to confront once again the vexing problem of reconciling state efforts to suppress sexually oriented expression with the protections of the First Amendment, as applied to the States through the Fourteenth Amendment. No other aspect of the First Amendment has, in recent years, demanded so substantial a commitment of our time, generated such disharmony of views, and remained so resistant to the formulation of stable and manageable standards. I am convinced that the approach initiated 16 years ago in *Roth* v. *United States*, (1957), and culminating in the Court's decision today, cannot bring stability to this area of the law without jeopardizing fundamental First Amendment values, and I have concluded that the time has come to make a significant departure from that approach.

In this civil action in the Superior Court of Fulton County, the State of Georgia sought to enjoin the showing of two motion pictures, It All Comes Out In The End, and Magic Mirror, at the Paris Adult Theatres (I and II) in Atlanta, Georgia. The State alleged that the films were obscene under the standards set forth in Georgia Code Ann. §26-2101. The trial court denied injunctive relief, holding that even though the films could be considered obscene, their commercial presentation could not constitutionally be barred in the absence of proof that they were shown to minors or unconsenting adults. Reversing, the Supreme Court of Georgia found the films obscene, and held that the care taken to avoid exposure to minors and unconsenting adults was without constitutional significance.

I

The Paris Adult Theatres are two commercial cinemas, linked by a common box office and lobby, on Peachtree Street in Atlanta, Georgia. On December 28, 1970, investigators employed by the Criminal Court of Fulton County entered the theaters as paying customers and viewed each of the films which are the subject of this action. Thereafter, two separate complaints, one for each of the two films, were filed in the Superior Court seeking a declaration that the films were obscene and an injunction against their continued presentation to the public. The complaints alleged that the films were "a flagrant violation of Georgia Code Section 26-2101 in that the sole and dominant theme[s] of the said motion picture film[s] considered as a whole and applying contemporary community standards [appeal] to the prurient interest in sex, nudity and excretion, and that the said motion picture film[s are] utterly and absolutely without any redeeming social value whatsoever, and [transgress]) beyond the customary limits of candor in describing and discussing sexual matters." App. 20, 39.

Although the language of the complaints roughly tracked the language of §26-2101, which imposes criminal penalties on persons who knowingly distribute obscene materials,[2] this proceeding was not brought pursuant to that statute. Instead, the State initiated a nonstatutory civil proceeding to determine the obscenity of the films and to enjoin their exhibition. While the parties waived jury trial and stipulated that the decision of the trial court would be final on the issue of obscenity, the State has not indicated whether it intends to bring a criminal action under the statute in the event that it succeeds in proving the films obscene.

Upon the filing of the complaints, the trial court scheduled a hearing for January 13, 1971, and entered an order temporarily restraining the defendants from concealing, destroying, altering, or removing the films from the jurisdiction, but not from exhibiting the films to the public *pendente lite*. In addition to viewing the films at the hearing, the trial court heard the testimony of witnesses and admitted into evidence photographs that were stipulated to depict accurately the facade of the theater. The witnesses testified that the exterior of the theater was adorned with prominent signs reading "Adults Only," "You Must Be 21 and Able to Prove It," and "If the Nude Body Offends You, Do Not Enter." Nothing on the outside of the theater described the films with specificity. Nor were pictures displayed on the outside of the theater to draw the attention of passersby to the contents of the films. The admission charge to the theater was $3. The trial court heard no evidence that minors had ever entered the theater, but also heard no evidence that petitioners had enforced a systematic policy of screening out minors (apart from the posting of the notices referred to above).

On the basis of the evidence submitted, the trial court concluded, that the films could fairly be considered obscene, "[a]ssuming that obscenity is established by a finding that the actors cavorted about in the nude indiscriminately," but held, nonetheless, that "the display of these films in a commercial theatre, when surrounded by requisite notice to the public of their nature and by reasonable protection against the exposure of these films to minors, is constitutionally permissible. Since the issue did not arise in statutory proceeding, the trial court was not required to pass upon the constitutionality of any state statute, on its face or as applied, in denying the injunction sought by the State.

The Supreme Court of Georgia unanimously reversed, reasoning that the lower court's reliance on *Stanley* v. *Georgia* (1969) was misplaced in view of our subsequent decision in *United States* v. *Reidel*, (1971):

In [*Reidel*] the Supreme Court expressly held that the government could constitutionally prohibit the distribution of obscene materials through the mails, even though the distribution be limited to willing recipients who state that they are adults, and, further, that the constitutional right of a person to possess obscene material in the privacy of his own home, as expressed in the *Stanley* case, does not carry with it the right to sell and deliver such material. . . . Those who choose to pass through the front door of the defendant's theater and purchase a ticket to view the films and who certify thereby that they are more than 21 years of age are willing recipients of the material in the same legal sense as were those in the *Reidel* case, who, after reading the newspaper advertisements of the material, mailed an order to the defendant accepting his solicitation to sell them to the obscene booklet there. That case clearly establishes once and for all that the scale and delivery of obscene material to willing adults is not protected under the first amendment. [228 Ga. 343, 346 (1971)].

The decision of the Georgia Supreme Court rested squarely on its conclusion that the State could constitutionally suppress these films even if they were displayed only to persons over the age of 21 who were aware of the nature of their contents and who had consented to viewing them. For the reasons set forth in this opinion, I am convinced of the invalidity of that conclusion of law, and I would therefore vacate the judgment of the Georgia Supreme Court. I have no occasion to consider the extent of state power to regulate the distribution of sexually oriented materials to juveniles or to unconsenting adults. Nor am I required, for the purposes of this review, to consider whether or not these petitioners had, in fact, taken precautions to avoid exposure of films to minors or unconsenting adults.

II

In *Roth* v. *United States* (1957), the Court held that obscenity, although expression, falls outside the area of speech or press constitutionally protected under the First and Fourteenth Amendments against state or federal infringement. But at the same time we emphasized in *Roth* that "sex and obscenity are not synonymous" and that matter which is sexually oriented but not obscene is fully protected by the Constitution. For we recognized that "[s]ex, a great and mysterious motive force in human life, has indisputably been a subject of absorbing interest to mankind through the ages; it is one of the vital problems of human interest and public concern." *Roth* rested, in other words, on what has been termed a two-level approach to the question of obscenity. While much criticized, that approach has been endorsed by all but two members of this Court who have addressed the question since *Roth.* Yet our efforts to implement that approach demonstrate that agreement on the existence of something called "obscenity" is still a long and painful step from agreement on a workable definition of the term.

Recognizing that "the freedoms of expression . . . are vulnerable to gravely damaging yet barely visible encroachments," *Bantam Books, Inc.* v. *Sullivan* (1963) we have demanded that "sensitive tools" be used to carry out the "separation of legitimate from illegitimate speech." *Speiser* v. *Randall* (1958). The essence of our problem in the obscenity area is that we have been unable to provide "sensitive tools" to separate obscenity from other sexually oriented but constitutionally protected speech, so that efforts to suppress the former do not spill over into the suppression of the latter. The attempt, as the late Mr. Justice Harlan observed, has only "produced a variety of views among the members of the Court unmatched in any other course of constitutional abjudication." *Interstate Circuit, Inc.* v. *Dallas.* (1968)

To be sure, five members of the Court did agree in *Roth* that obscenity could be determined by asking "whether to the average person, applying contemporary community standards, the dominant theme of the material taken as a whole appeals to prurient interest." But agreement on that test—achieved in the abstract and without reference to the particular material before the Court, was, to say the least, short lived. By 1967 the following views had emerged: Mr. Justice Black and MR. JUSTICE DOUGLAS consistently maintained that government is wholly powerless to regulate any sexually oriented matter on the ground of its obscenity. See, *e.g., Ginzburg* v. *United States* (1966) Mr. Justice Harlan, on the other hand, believed that the Federal Government in the exercise of its enumerated powers could control the distribution of "hard core" pornography, while the States were afforded more latitude to "[ban] any material which, taken as a whole, has been reasonably found in state judicial proceedings to treat with sex in a fundamentally offensive manner, under rationally established criteria for judging such material." *Jacobellis* v. *Ohio.* MR. JUSTICE STEWART regarded "hard core" pornography as the limit of both federal and state power. See *e.g., Ginzburg* v. *United States.*

The view that, until today, enjoyed the most, but not majority, support was an interpretation of *Roth* (and not, as the Court suggests, a veering "sharply away from the *Roth* concept" and the articulation of "a new test of obscenity," *Miller* v. *California*) adopted by Mr. Chief Justice Warren, Mr. Justice Fortas, and the author of this opinion in *Memoirs* v. *Massachusetts* (1966). We expressed the view that Federal or State Governments could control the distribution of material where "three elements ... coalesce: it must be established that (a) the dominant theme of the material taken as a whole appeals to a prurient interest in sex; (b) the material is patently offensive because it affronts contemporary community standards relating to the description or representation of sexual matters; and (c) the material is utterly without redeeming social value." Even this formulation, however, concealed differences of opinion. Compare *Jacobellis* v. *Ohio*. Moreover, it did not provide a definition covering all situations. See *Mishkin* v. *New York* (1966) (prurient appeal defined in terms of a deviant sexual group); *Ginzburg* v. *United States* ("pandering" probative evidence of obscenity in close cases). Nor, finally, did it ever command a majority of the Court. Aside from the other views described above, Mr. Justice Clark believed that "social importance" could only "be considered together with evidence that the material in question appeals to prurient interest and is patently offensive." *Memoirs* v. *Massachusetts* (dissenting opinion). Similarly, MR. JUSTICE WHITE regarded "a publication to be obscene if its predominant theme appeals to the prurient interest in a manner exceeding customary limits of candor."

In the face of this divergence of opinion the Court began the practice in *Redrup* v. *New York* (1967) of *per curiam* reversals of convictions for the dissemination of materials that at least five members of the Court, applying their separate tests, deemed not to be obscene. This approach capped the attempt in *Roth* to separate all forms of sexually oriented expression in two categories—the one subject to full governmental suppression and the other beyond the reach of governmental regulation to the same extent as any other protected form of speech or press. Today a majority of the Court offers a slightly altered formulation of the basic *Roth* test, while leaving entirely unchanged the underlying approach.

III

Our experience with the *Roth* approach has certainly taught us that the outright suppression of obscenity cannot be reconciled with the fundamental principles of the First and Fourteenth Amendments. For we have failed to formulate a standard that sharply distinguishes protected from unprotected speech, and out of necessity, we have resorted to the *Redrup* approach, which resolves cases as between the parties, but offers only the most obscure guidance to legislation, abjudication by other courts, and primary conduct. By disposing of cases through summary reversal or denial of certiorari we have deliberately and effectively obscured the rationale underlying the decisions. It comes as no surprise that judicial attempts to follow our lead conscientiously have often ended in hopeless confusion.

Of course, the vagueness problem would be largely of our own creation if it stemmed primarily from our failure to reach a consensus on any one standard. But after 16 years of experimentation and debate I am reluctantly forced to the conclusion that none of the available formulas, including the one announced today, can reduce the vagueness to a tolerable level while at the same time striking an acceptable balance between the protections of the First and Fourteenth Amendments, on the one hand, and on the other the asserted state interest in regulating the dissemination of certain sexually oriented materials. Any effort to draw a constitutionally acceptable boundary on state power must resort to such indefinite concepts as "prurient interest," "patent offensiveness," "serious literary value," and the like. The meaning of these concepts necessarily varies with the experience, outlook, and even idiosyncrasies of the person defining them. Although we have assumed that obscenity does exist and that we "know it when [we] see it," *Jacobellis* v. *Ohio*, we are manifestly unable to describe it in advance except by reference to concepts so elusive that they fail to distinguish clearly between protected and unprotected speech.

We have more than once previously acknowledged that "constitutionally protected expression . . . is often separated from obscenity only by a dim and uncertain line." *Bantam Books, Inc.* v. *Sullivan.* Added to the "perhaps inherent residual vagueness" of each of the current multitude of standards, *Ginzburg* v. *United States*, is the further complication that the obscenity of any particular item may depend upon nuances of presentation and the context of its dissemination. *Redrup* itself suggested that obtrusive exposure to unwilling individuals, distribution to juveniles, and "pandering" may also bear upon the determination of obscenity. See *Redrup* v. *New York.* As Mr. Chief Justice Warren stated in a related vein, obscenity is a function of the circumstances of its dissemination:

It is not the book that is on trial; it is a person. The conduct of the defendant is the central issue, not the obscenity of a book or picture. The nature of the materials is, of course, relevant as an attribute of the defendant's conduct, but the materials are thus placed in context from which they draw color and character. [*Roth*]

I need hardly point out that the factors which must be taken into account are judgmental and can only be applied on "a case-by-case, sight-by-sight" basis. *Mishkin* v. *New York*. These considerations suggest that no one definition, no matter how precisely or narrowly drawn, can possibly suffice for all situations, or carve out fully suppressible expression from all media without also creating a substantial risk of encroachment upon the guarantees of the Due Process Clause and the First Amendment.

The vagueness of the standards in the obscenity area produced a number of separate problems, and any improvement must rest on an understanding that the problems are to some extent distinct. First, a vague statute fails to provide adequate notice to persons who are engaged in the type of conduct that the statute could be thought to proscribe. The Due Process Clause of the Fourteenth Amendment requires that all criminal laws provide fair notice of "what the State commands or forbids." *Lanzetta* v. *New Jersey* (1939); In the service of this general principle we have repeatedly held that the definition of obscenity must provide adequate notice of exactly what is prohibited from dissemination. See *e.g., Rabe* v. *Washington* (1972); while various tests have been upheld under the Due Process Clause, see *Ginsberg* v. *New York*. I have grave doubts that any of those tests could be sustained today. For I know of no satisfactory answer to the assertion by Mr. Justice Black, "after the fourteen separate opinions handed down" in the trilogy of cases decided in 1966, that "no person, not even the most learned judge much less a layman, is capable of knowing in advance of an ultimate decision in his particular case by this Court whether certain material comes within the area of 'obscenity' . . ." *Ginzburg* v. *United States*. As Mr. Chief Justice Warren pointed out, "[t]he constitutional requirement of definiteness is violated by a criminal statute that fails to give a person of ordinary intelligence fair notice that his contemplated conduct is forbidden by the statute. The underlying principle is that no man shall be held criminally responsible for conduct which he could not reasonably understand to be proscribed." *Untied States* v. *Harriss* (1954). In this context, even the most painstaking efforts to determine in advance whether certain sexually oriented expression is obscene must inevitably prove unavailing. For the insufficiency of the notice compels persons to guess not only whether their conduct is covered by a criminal statute, but also whether their conduct falls within the constitutionally permissible reach of the statute. The resulting level of uncertainty is utterly intolerable, not alone because it makes "[b]ook-selling . . . a hazardous profession," *Ginsberg* v. *New York*, but as well because it invites arbitrary and erratic enforcement of the law. See *e.g., Papachristou* v. *City of Jacksonville* (1972).

In addition to problems that arise when any criminal statute fails to afford fair notice of what it forbids, a vague statute in the areas of speech and press creates a second level of difficulty. We have indicated that "stricter standards of permissible statutory vagueness may be applied to a statute having a potentially inhibiting effect on speech; a man may the less be required to act at his peril here, because the free dissemination of ideas may be the loser." *Smith* v. *California* (1959). That proposition draws its strength from our recognition that

> [t]he fundamental freedoms of speech and press have contributed greatly to the development and well-being of our free society and are indispensable to its continued growth. Ceaseless vigilance is the watchword to prevent their erosion by Congress or by the States. The door barring federal and state intrusion into this area cannot be left ajar. . . . [*Roth*]

To implement this general principle, and recognizing the inherent vagueness of any definition of obscenity, we have held that the definition of obscenity must be drawn as narrowly as possible so as to minimize the interference with protected expression. Thus, in *Roth* we rejected the test of *Regina* v. *Hicklin* [1868] that "[judged] obscenity by the effect of isolated passages upon the most susceptible persons." That test, we held in *Roth*, "might well encompass material legitimately treating with sex. . . ." *Ibid.* Cf. *Mishkin* v. *New York.* And we have supplemented the *Roth* standard with additional tests in an effort to hold in check the corrosive effect of vagueness on the guarantees of the First Amendment. We have held, for example, that "a State is not free to adopt whatever procedures it pleases for dealing with obscenity. . . ." *Marcus* v. *Search Warrant* (1961). "Rather, the First Amendment requires that procedures be incorporated that 'ensure against the curtailment of constitutionally protected expression. . . .' " *Blount* v. *Rizzi* (1971), quoting from *Bantam Books, Inc.,* v. *Sullivan.*

Similarly, we have held that a State cannot impose criminal sanctions for the possession of obscene material absent proof that the possessor

had knowledge of the contents of the material. *Smith* v. *California.*
"Proof of scienter" is necessary "to avoid the hazard of self-censorship
of constitutionally protected material and to compensate for the ambigu-
ities inherent in the definition of obscenity." *Mishkin* v. *New York.*

> [t]he objectionable quality of vagueness and overbreadth ... [is] the
> danger of tolerating, in the area of First Amendment freedoms, the
> existence of a penal statute susceptible of sweeping and improper
> application. Cf. *Marcus* v. *Search Warrant.* These freedoms are deli-
> cate and vulnerable, as well as supremely precious in our society.
> The threat of sanctions may deter their exercise almost as potently
> as the actual application of sanctions. Cf. *Smith* v. *California.* Be-
> cause First Amendment freedoms need breathing space to survive,
> government may regulate in the area only with narrow specificity.
> [*Cantwell* v. *Connecticut*]

The problems of fair notice and chilling protected speech are very
grave standing alone. But it does not detract from their importance to
recognize that a vague statute in this area creates a third, although
admittedly more subtle, set of problems. These problems concern the
institutional stress that inevitably results where the line separating protected from unprotected speech is excessively vague. In *Roth* we conceded that "there may be marginal cases in which it is difficult to
determine the side of the line on which a particular fact situation
falls...." Our subsequent experience demonstrates that almost every
case is "marginal." And since the "margin" marks the point of separation between protected and unprotected speech, we are left with a system in which almost every obscenity case presents a constitutional
question of exceptional difficulty. "The suppression of a particular writing or other tangible form of expression is ... an *individual* matter,
and in the nature of things every such suppression raises an individual
constitutional problem, in which a reviewing court must determine for
itself whether the attacked expression is suppressible within constitutional standards." *Roth.*

Examining the rationale, both explicit and implicit, of our vagueness
decisions, one commentator has viewed these decisions as an attempt
by the Court to establish an "insulating buffer zone of added protection
at the peripheries of several of the Bill of Rights freedoms." Note, The
Void-for-Vagueness Doctrine in the Supreme Court 109. U. Pa. L. Rev.
67, 75 (1960). The buffer zone enables the Court to fend off legislative

attempts "to pass to the courts—and ultimately to the Supreme Court—
the awesome task of making case by case at once the criminal and the
constitutional law." Thus,

> [b]ecause of the Court's limited power to reexamine fact on a cold
> record, what appears to be going on in the administration of the law
> must be forced, by restrictive procedures, to reflect what is really
> going on; and because of the impossibility, through sheer volume of
> cases, of the Court's effectively policing law administration case by
> case, those procedures must be framed to assure, as well as proce-
> dures can assure, a certain overall *probability* of regularity.

As a result of our failure to define standards with predictable application to any given piece of material, there is no probability of regularity
in obscenity decisions by state and lower federal courts. That is not to
say that these courts have performed badly in this area or paid insufficient attention to the principles we have established. The problem is,
rather, that one cannot say with certainty that material is obscene until
at least five members of this Court, applying inevitably obscure standards, have pronounced it so. The number of obscenity cases on our
docket gives ample testimony to the burden that has been placed upon
this Court.

But the sheer number of the cases does not define the full extent of
the institutional problem. For, quite apart from the number of cases
involved and the need to make a fresh constitutional determination in
each case, we are tied to the "absurd business of perusing and viewing
the miserable stuff that pours into the Court. . . ." *Interstate Circuit,
Inc.* v. *Dallas.* While the material may have varying degrees of social
importance, it is hardly a source of edification to the members of this
Court who are compelled to view it before passing on its obscenity.
Cf. *Mishkin* v. *New York.*

Moreover, we have managed the burden of deciding scores of obscenity cases by relying on *per curiam* reversals or denials of certiorari—a
practice which conceals the rationale of decision and gives at least the
appearance of arbitrary action by this Court. See *Bloss* v. *Dykema*
(1970). More important, no less than the procedural schemes struck
down in such cases as *Blount* v. *Rizzi*, and *Freedman* v. *Maryland*, the
practice effectively censors protected expression by leaving lower court
determinations of obscenity intact even though the status of the alleg-

edly obscene material is entirely unsettled until final review here. In addition, the uncertainty of the standards creates a continuing source of tension between state and federal courts, since the need for an independent determination by this Court seems to render superfluous even the most conscientious analysis by state tribunals. And our inability to justify our decisions with a persuasive rationale—or indeed, any rationale at all—necessarily creates the impression that we are merely second-guessing state court judges.

The severe problems arising from the lack of fair notice, from the chill on protected expression, and from the stress impressed on the state and federal judicial machinery persuade me that a significant change in direction is urgently required. I turn, therefore, to the alternatives that are now open.

IV

1. The approach requiring the smallest deviation from our present course would be to draw a new line between protected and unprotected speech, still permitting the States to suppress all material on the unprotected side of the line. In my view, clarity cannot be obtained pursuant to this approach except by drawing a line that resolves all doubt in favor of state power and against the guarantees of the First Amendment. We could hold, for example, that any depiction or description of human sexual organs, irrespective of the manner or purpose of the portrayal, is outside the protection of the First Amendment and therefore open to suppression by the States. That formula would, no doubt, offer much fairer notice of the reach of any state statute drawn at the boundary of the State's constitutional power. And it would also, in all likelihood, give rise to a substantial probability of regularity in most judicial determinations under the standard. But such a standard would be appallingly overboard, permitting the suppression of a vast range of literary, scientific, and artistic masterpieces. Neither the First Amendment nor any free community could possibly tolerate such a standard. Yet short of that extreme it is hard to see how any choice of words could reduce the vagueness problem to tolerable proportions, so long as we remain committed to the view that some class of materials is subject to outright suppression by the State.

2. The alternative adopted by the Court today recognizes that a prohibition against any depiction or description of human sexual organs could

not be reconciled with the guarantees of the First Amendment. But the Court does retain the view that certain sexually oriented material can be considered obscene and therefore unprotected by the First and Fourteenth Amendments. To describe that unprotected class of expression, the Court adopts a restatement of the *Roth-Memoirs* definition of obscenity: "The basic guidelines for the trier of fact must be: (a) whether 'the average person, applying contemporary community standards' would find that the work, taken as a whole, appeals to the prurient interest . . . (b) whether the work depicts or describes, in a patently offensive way, sexual conduct specifically defined by the applicable state law, and (c) whether the work, taken as a whole, lacks serious literary, artistic, political, or scientific value." *Miller* v. *California.* In apparent illustration of "sexual conduct," as that term is used in the tests's second element, the Court identifies "(a) Patently offensive representations or descriptions of ultimate sexual acts, normal or perverted, actual or simulated," and "(b) Patently offensive representations or descriptions of masturbation, excretory functions, and lewd exhibition of the genitals."

The differences between this formulation and the three-pronged *Memoirs* test are, for the most part, academic. The first element of the Court's test is virtually identical to the *Memoirs* requirement that "the dominant theme of the material taken as a whole [must appeal] to a prurient interest in sex." Whereas the second prong of the *Memoirs* test demanded that the material be "patently offensive because it affronts contemporary community standards relating to the description or representation of sexual matters," the test adopted today requires that the material describe, "in a patently offensive way, sexual conduct specifically defined by the applicable state law." *Miller* v. *California.* The third component of the *Memoirs* test is that the material must be "utterly without redeeming social value." The court's rephrasing requires that the work, taken as a whole, must be proved to lack "serious literary, artistic, political, or scientific value." *Miller.*

The Court evidently recognizes that difficulties with the *Roth* approach necessitate a significant change of direction. But the Court does not describe its understanding of those difficulties, nor does it indicate how the restatement of the *Memoirs* test is in any way responsive to the problems that have arisen. In my view, the restatement leaves unresolved the very difficulties that compel our rejection of the underlying *Roth* approach, while at the same time contributing substantial difficulties of its own. The modification of the *Memoirs* test may prove sufficient to jeopardize the analytic underpinnings of the entire scheme. And today's restatement will likely have the effect, whether or not intended, of permitting far more sweeping suppression of sexually oriented expression, including expression that would almost surely be held protected under our current formulation.

Although the Court's restatement substantially tracks the three-part test announced in *Memoirs* v. *Massachusetts, supra*, it does purport to modify the "social value" component of the test. Instead of requiring, as did *Roth* and *Memoirs*, that state suppression be limited to materials utterly lacking in social value, the Court today permits suppression if the government can prove that the materials lack "*serious* literary, artistic, political or scientific value." But the definition of "obscenity" as expression utterly lacking in social importance is the key to the conceptual basis of *Roth* and our subsequent opinions. In *Roth* we held that certain expression is obscene, and thus outside the protection of the First Amendment, precisely *because* it lacks even the slightest redeeming social value. See *Roth* v. *United States.* The Court's approach necessarily assumes that some works will be deemed obscene—even though they clearly have *some* social value—because the State was able to prove that the value, measured by some unspecified standard, was not sufficiently "serious" to warrant constitutional protection. That result is not merely inconsistent with our holding in *Roth*; it is nothing less than a rejection of the fundamental First Amendment premises to widespread suppression of sexually oriented speech. Before today, the protections of the First Amendment have never been thought limited to expressions of *serious* literary or political value. See *Gooding* v. *Wilson* (1972).

Although the Court concedes that "*Roth* presumed 'obscenity' to be 'utterly without redeeming social importance,' " it argues that *Memoirs* produced "a drastically altered test that called on the prosecution to prove a negative *i.e.,* that the material was 'utterly without redeeming social value'—a burden virtually impossible to discharge under our criminal standards of proof." One should hardly need to point out that under the third component of the Court's test the prosecution is still required to "prove a negative"—*i.e.,* that the material lacks serious literary, artistic, political, or scientific value. Whether it will be easier to prove that material lacks "serious" value than to prove that it lacks any value at all remains, of course, to be seen.

In any case, even if the Court's approach left undamaged the conceptual framework of *Roth*, and even if it clearly barred the suppression of works with at least some social value, I would nevertheless be compelled to reject it. For it is beyond dispute that the approach can have no ameliorative impact on the cluster of problems that grow out of the vagueness of our current standards. Indeed, even the Court makes no argument that the reformulation will provide fairer notice to booksellers, theater owners, and the reading and viewing public. Nor does the Court contend that the approach will provide clearer guidance to law enforcement officials or reduce the chill on protected expression. Nor, finally, does the Court suggest that the approach will mitigate to the slightest degree the institutional problems that have plagued this Court and the state and federal judiciary as a direct result of the uncertainty inherent in any definition of obscenity.

Of course, the Court's restated *Roth* test does limit the definition of obscenity to depictions of physical conduct and explicit sexual acts. And that limitation may seem, at first glance, a welcome and clarifying addition to the *Roth-Memoirs* formula. But, just as the agreement in *Roth* on an abstract definition of obscenity gave little hint of the extreme difficulty that was to follow in attempting to apply that definition to specific material, the mere formulation of a "physical conduct" test is no assurance that it can be applied with any greater facility. The Court does not indicate how it would apply its test to the materials involved in *Miller* v. *California*, and we can only speculate as to its application. But even a confirmed optimist could find little realistic comfort in the adoption of such a test. Indeed, the valiant attempt of one lower federal court to draw the constitutional line at depictions of explicit sexual conduct seems to belie any suggestion that this approach marks the road to clarity. The Court surely demonstrates little sensitivity to our own institutional problems, much less the other vagueness-related difficulties, in establishing a system that requires us to consider whether a description of human genitals is sufficiently "lewd" to deprive it of constitutional protection; whether a sexual act is "ultimate"; whether the conduct depicted in materials before us fits within one of the categories of conduct whose depiction the State and Federal Governments have attempted to suppress; and a host of equally pointless inquiries. In addition, adoption of such a test does not, presumably, obviate the need for consideration of the nuances of presentation of sexually oriented material, yet it hardly clarifies the application of those opaque but important factors.

If the application of the "physical conduct" test to pictorial material is fraught with difficulty, its application to textual material carries the potential for extraordinary abuse. Surely we have passed the point where the mere written description of sexual conduct is deprived of First Amendment protection. Yet the test offers no guidance to us, or anyone else, in determining which written descriptions of sexual conduct are protected, and which are not.

Ultimately, the reformulation must fail because it still leaves in this Court the responsibility of determining in each case whether the materials are protected by the First Amendment. The Court concedes that even under its restated formulation, the First Amendment interests at stake require "appellate courts to conduct an independent review of constitutional claims when necessary," *Miller* v. *California*, citing Mr. Justice Harlan's opinion in *Roth*, where he stated, "I do not understand how the Court can resolve the constitutional problems now before it without making its own independent judgment upon the character of the material upon which these convictions were based." Thus, the Court's new formulation will not relieve us of "the awesome task of making case by case at once the criminal and the constitutional law." And the careful efforts of state and lower federal courts to apply the standard will remain an essentially pointless exercise, in view of the need for an ultimate decision by this Court. In addition, since the status of sexually oriented material will necessarily remain in doubt until final decision by this Court, the new approach will not diminish the chill on protected expression that derives from the uncertainty of the underlying standard. I am convinced that a definition of obscenity in terms of physical conduct cannot provide sufficient clarity to afford fair notice, to avoid a chill on protected expression, and to minimize the institutional stress, so long as that definition is used to justify the outright suppression of any material that is asserted to fall within its terms.

3. I have also considered the possibility of reducing our own role, and the role of appellate courts generally, in determining whether particular matter is obscene. Thus, we might conclude that juries are best suited to determine obscenity *vel non* and that jury verdicts in this area should not be set aside except in cases of extreme departure from prevailing standards. Or, more generally, we might adopt the position that where a lower federal or state court has conscientiously applied the constitutional standard, its finding of obscenity will be no more vulnerable to reveal by this Court than any finding of fact. Cf. *Interstate Circuit, Inc.* v. *Dallas*. While the point was not clearly resolved prior to our decision in *Redrup* v. *New York* (1967), it is implicit in that decision that the First Amendment requires an independent review by appellate courts of the constitutional fact of obscenity. That result is

required by principles applicable to the obscenity issue no less than to any other area involving free expression, see, *e.g., New York Times Co.* v. *Sullivan,* or other constitutional right. In any event, even if the Constitution would permit us to refrain from judging for ourselves the alleged obscenity of particular materials, that approach would solve at best only a small part of our problem. For while it would mitigate the institutional stress produced by the *Roth* approach, it would neither offer nor produce any cure for the other vices of vagueness. Far from providing a clearer guide to permissible primary conduct, the approach would inevitably lead to even greater uncertainty and the consequent due process problems of fair notice. And the approach would expose much protected, sexually oriented expression to the vagaries of jury determinations. Cf. *Herndon* v. *Lowry* (1937). Plainly, the institutional gain would be more than offset by the unprecedented infringement of First Amendment rights.

4. Finally, I have considered the view, urged so forcefully since 1957 by our brothers Black and DOUGLAS, that the First Amendment bars the suppression of any sexually oriented expression. That position would effect a sharp reduction, although perhaps not a total elimination, of the uncertainty that surrounds our current approach. Nevertheless, I am convinced that it would achieve that desirable goal only by stripping the States of power to an extent that cannot be justified by the commands of the Constitution, at least so long as there is available an alternative approach that strikes a better balance between the guarantee of free expression and the States' legitimate interests.

V

Our experience since *Roth* requires us not only to abandon the effort to pick out obscene materials on a case-by-case basis, but also to reconsider a fundamental postulate of *Roth:* that there exists a definable class of sexually oriented expression that may be totally suppressed by the Federal and State Governments. Assuming that such a class of expression does in fact exist, I am forced to conclude that the concept of "obscenity" cannot be defined with sufficient specificity and clarity to provide fair notice to persons who create and distribute sexually oriented materials, to prevent substantial erosion of protected speech as a byproduct of the attempt to suppress unprotected speech, and to avoid very costly institutional harms. Given these inevitable side effects of state efforts to suppress what is assumed to be *unprotected* speech, we must scrutinize with care the state interest that is asserted to justify the suppression. For in the absence of some very substantial interest in suppressing such speech, we can hardly condone the ill effects that seem to flow inevitably from the effort.

Obscenity laws have a long history in this country. Most of the States that had ratified the Constitution by 1792 punished the related crime of blasphemy or profanity despite the guarantees of free expression in their constitutions, and Massachusetts expressly prohibited the "Composing, Writing, Printing or Publishing, of any Filthy Obscene or Prophane Song, Pamphlet, Libel or Mock-Sermon, in Imitation or in Mimicking of Preaching, or any other part of Divine Worship." Acts and laws of Massachusetts Bay Colony (1726). In 1815 the first reported obscenity conviction was obtained under the common law of Pennsylvania. See *Commonwealth* v. *Sharpless*, 2 S. & R. 91. A conviction in Massachusetts under its common law and colonial statute followed six years later. See *Commonwealth* v. *Holmes* (1821). In 1821 Vermont passed the first state law proscribing the publication or sale of "lewd or obscene" material, Laws of Vermont, 1824 c. XXXII, No. 1, §23, and federal legislation barring the importation of similar matter appeared in 1842. See Tariff Act of 1842, § 28, 5 State. 566. Although the number of early obscenity laws was small and their enforcement exceedingly lax, the situation significantly changed after about 1870 when Federal and State Governments, mainly as a result of the efforts of Anthony Comstock, took an active interest in the suppression of obscenity. By the end of the 19th century at least 30 States had some type of general prohibition on the dissemination of obscene materials, and by the time of our decision in *Roth* no State was without some provision on the subject. The Federal Government meanwhile had enacted no fewer than 20 obscenity laws between 1842 and 1956. See *Roth* v. *United States.*

This history caused us to conclude in *Roth* "that the unconditional phrasing of the First Amendment [that 'Congress shall make no law . . . abridging the freedom of speech, or of the press . . .'] was not intended to protect every utterance." It also caused us to hold, as numerous prior decisions of this Court had assumed, that obscenity could be denied the protection of the First Amendment and hence suppressed because it is a form of expression "utterly without redeeming social importance," as "mirrored in the universal judgment that [it] should be restrained. . . ."

Because we assumed—incorrectly, as experience has proved—that obscenity could be separated from other sexually oriented expression without significant costs either to the First Amendment or to the judicial machinery charged with the task of safeguarding First Amendment freedoms, we had no occasion in *Roth* to probe the asserted state interest in curtailing unprotected, sexually oriented speech. Yet, as we have increasingly come to appreciate the vagueness of the concept of obscenity, we have begun to recognize and articulate the state interests at stake. Significantly, in *Redrup* v. *New York*, (1967), where we set aside findings of obscenity with regard to three sets of material, we pointed out that

> [i]n none of the cases was there a claim that the statute in question reflected a specific and limited state concern for juveniles. See *Prince* v. *Massachusetts*, 321 U.S. 158; cf. *Butler* v. *Michigan*, 352 U.S. 380. In none was there any suggestion of an assault upon individual privacy by publication in a manner so obtrusive as to make it impossible for an unwilling individual to avoid exposure to it. Cf. *Breard* v. *Alexandria*. And in none was there evidence of the sort of "pandering" which the Court found significant in *Ginzburg* v. *United States*.

The opinions in *Redrup* and *Stanley* reflected our emerging view that the state interests in protecting children and in protecting unconsenting adults may stand on a different footing from the other asserted state interests. It may well be, as one commentator has argued, that "exposure to [erotic material] is for some persons an intense emotional experience. A communication of this nature, imposed upon a person contrary to his wishes, has all the characteristics of a physical assault . . . [And it] constitutes an invasion of his privacy. . . ." But cf. *Cohen* v. *California*. Similarly, if children are "not possessed of that full capacity for individual choice which is the presupposition of the First Amendment guarantees," *Ginsberg* v. *New York*, then the State may have a substantial interest in precluding the flow of obscene materials even to consenting juveniles.

But, whatever the strength of the state interests in protecting juveniles and unconsenting adults from exposure to sexually oriented materials, those interests cannot be asserted in defense of the holding of the Georgia Supreme Court in this case. That court assumed for the purpose of its decision that the films in issue were exhibited only to persons over the age of 21 who viewed them willingly and with prior knowledge of the nature of their contents. And on that assumption the state court held that the films could still be suppressed. The justification of the suppression must be found, therefore, in some independent interest in regulating the reading and viewing habits of consenting adults.

At the outset it should be noted that virtually all of the interests that might be asserted in defense of suppression, laying aside the special interests associated with distribution to juveniles and unconsenting adults, were also posited in *Stanley* v. *Georgia*, where we held that the State could not make the "mere private possession of obscene material a crime." That decision presages the conclusions I reach here today.

In *Stanley* we pointed out that "[t]here appears to be little empirical basis for" the assertion that "exposure to obscene materials may lead to deviant sexual behavior or crimes of sexual violence." In any event, we added that "if the State is only concerned about printed or filmed materials inducing antisocial conduct, we believe that in the context of private consumption of ideas and information we should adhere to the view that '[a]mong free men, the deterrents ordinarily to be applied to prevent crime are education and punishment for violations of the law. . . .' *Whitney* v. California."

Moreover, in *Stanley* we rejected as "wholly inconsistent with the philosophy of the First Amendment," the notion that there is a legitimate state concern in the "control [of] the moral content of a person's thoughts," and we held that a State "cannot constitutionally premise legislation on the desirability of controlling a person's private thoughts." That is not to say, of course, that a State must remain utterly indifferent to—and take no action bearing on—the morality of the community. The traditional description of state police power does embrace the regulation of morals as well as the health, safety, and general welfare of the citizenry. See *e.g., Village of Euclid* v. *Ambler Realty Co.* (1926). And much legislation—compulsory public education laws, civil rights laws, even the abolition of capital punishment—is grounded, at least in part, on a concern with the morality of the community. But the State's interest in regulating morality by suppressing obscenity, while often asserted, remains essentially unfocused and ill defined. And, since the attempt to curtail unprotected speech necessarily spills over into the area of protected speech, the effort to serve this speculative interest through the suppression of obscene material must tread heavily on rights protected by the First Amendment.

In *Roe* v. *Wade* (1973) we held constitutionally invalid a state abortion law, even though we were aware of the sensitive and emotional nature of the abortion controversy, of the vigorous opposing views, even among physicians, and of the deep and seemingly absolute convictions that the subject inspires. One's philosophy, one's experiences, one's exposure to the raw edges of human existence, one's religious training, one's attitudes toward life and family and their values, and the moral standards one establishes and seeks to observe, are all likely to influence and to color one's thinking and conclusions about abortion.

Like the proscription of abortions, the effort to suppress obscenity is predicated on unprovable, although strongly held, assumptions about human behavior, morality, sex and religion. The existence of these assumptions cannot validate a statute that substantially undermines the guarantees of the First Amendment, any more than the existence of similar assumptions on the issue of abortion can validate a statute that infringes the constitutionally protected privacy interests of a pregnant woman.

If, as the Court today assumes, "a state legislature may . . . act on the . . . assumption that commerce in obscene books, or public exhibitions focused on obscene conduct, have a tendency to exert a corrupting and debasing impact leading to antisocial behavior," then it is hard to see how state-ordered regimentation of our minds can ever be forestalled. For if a State, in an effort to maintain or create a particular moral tone, may prescribe what its citizens cannot read or cannot see, then it would seem to follow that in pursuit of that same objective a State could decree that its citizens must read certain books or must view certain films. Cf. *United States* v. *Roth* (CA2 1956) (Frank J., concurring). However laudable its goal—and that is obviously a question on which reasonable minds may differ—the State cannot proceed by means that violate the Constitution. The precise point was established a half century ago in *Meyer* v. *Nebraska* (1923).

That the State may do much, go very far, indeed, in order to improve the quality of its citizens, physically, mentally and morally, is clear; but the individual has certain fundamental rights which must be respected. The protection of the Constitution extends to all, to those who speak other languages as well as to those born with English on the tongue. Perhaps it would be highly advantageous if all had ready understanding of our ordinary speech, but this cannot be coerced by methods which conflict with the Constitution—a desirable end cannot be promoted by prohibited means.

For the welfare of his Ideal Commonwealth, Plato suggested a law which should provide: "That the wives of our guardians are to be common, and their children are to be common, and no parent is to know his own child, nor any child his parent. . . . The proper officers will take the offspring of the good parents to the pen or fold, and there they will deposit them with certain nurses who dwell in a separate quarter; but the offspring of the inferior, or of the better when they chance to be deformed, will be put away in some mysterious, unknown place, as they should be." In order to submerge the individual and develop ideal citizens, Sparta assembled the males at seven into barracks and intrusted their subsequent education and training to official guardians. Although such measures have been deliberately approved by men of great genius, their ideas touching the relation between individual and State were wholly different from those upon which our institutions rest; and it hardly will be affirmed that any legislature could impose such restrictions upon the people of a State without doing violence to both letter and spirit of the Constitution.

Recognizing these principles, we have held that so-called thematic obscenity—obscenity which might persuade the viewer or reader to engage in "obscene" conduct—is not outside the protection of the First Amendment:

> It is contended that the State's action was justified because the motion picture attractively portrays a relationship which is contrary to the moral standards, the religious precepts, and the legal code of its citizenry. This argument misconceives what it is that the Constitution protects. Its guarantee is not confined to the expression of ideas that are conventional or shared by a majority. It protects advocacy of the opinion that adultery may sometimes be proper, no less than advocacy of socialism or the single tax. And in the realm of ideas it protects expression which is eloquent no less than that which is unconvincing. [*Kingsley Pictures Corp.* v. *Regents* (1959)].

Even a legitimate, sharply focused state concern for the morality of the community cannot, in other words, justify an assault on the protections of the First Amendment. Cf. *Griswold* v. *Connecticut* (1965).

Where the state interest in regulation of morality is vague and ill defined, interference with the guarantees of the First Amendment is even more difficult to justify.

In short, while I cannot say that the interests of the State—apart from the question of juveniles and unconsenting adults—are trivial or nonexistent, I am compelled to conclude that these interests cannot justify the substantial damage to constitutional rights and to this Nation's judicial machinery that inevitably results from state efforts to bar the distribution even of unprotected material to consenting adults. *NAACP* v. *Alabama* (1964); I would hold, therefore, that at least in the absence of distribution to juveniles or obtrusive exposure to unconsenting adults, the First and Fourteenth Amendments prohibit the State and Federal Governments from attempting wholly to suppress sexually oriented materials on the basis of their allegedly "obscene" contents. Nothing in this approach precludes those governments from taking action to serve what may be strong and legitimate interests through regulation of the manner of distribution of sexually oriented material.

VI

Two Terms ago we noted that

> There is developing sentiment that adults should have complete freedom to produce, deal in, possess and consume whatever communicative materials may appeal to them and that the law's involvement with obscenity should be limited to those situations where children are involved or where it is necessary to prevent imposition on unwilling recipients of whatever age. The concepts involved are said to be so elusive and the laws so inherently unenforceable without extravagant expenditures of time and effort by enforcement officers and the courts that basic reassessment is not only wise but essential. [*United States* v. *Reidel*]

Nevertheless, we concluded that "the task of restructuring the obscenity laws lies with those who pass, repeal, and amend statutes and ordinances." But the law of obscenity has been fashioned by this Court— and necessarily so under our duty to enforce the Constitution. It is surely the duty of this court, as expounder of the Constitution, to provide a remedy for the present unsatisfactory state of affairs. I do not pretend to have found a complete and infallible answer to what Mr. Justice Harlan called "the intractable obscenity problem." *Interstate Circuit, Inc.* v. *Dallas.* Difficult questions must still be faced, notably in the areas of distribution to juveniles and offensive exposure to unconsenting adults. Whatever the extent of state power to regulate in those areas, it should be clear that the view I espouse today would introduce a large measure of clarity to this troubled area, would reduce the institutional pressure on this Court and the rest of the State and Federal Judiciary, and would guarantee fuller freedom of expression while leaving room for the protection of legitimate governmental interests. Since the Supreme Court of Georgia erroneously concluded that the State has power to suppress sexually oriented material even in the absence of distribution to juveniles or exposure to unconsenting adults, I would reverse that judgment and remand the case to that court for further proceedings not inconsistent with this opinion.

NEBRASKA PRESS ASSN. ET AL. V. STUART, JUDGE, ET AL.

Argued April 19, 1976—Decided June 20, 1976

Respondent Nebraska state trial judge, in anticipation of a trial for a multiple murder which had attracted widespread news coverage, entered an order which, as modified by the Nebraska Supreme Court, restrained petitioner newspapers, broadcasters, journalists, news media associations, and national newswire services from publishing broadcasting accounts of confessions or admissions made by the accused to law enforcement officers or third parties, except members of the press, and other facts "strongly implicative" of the accused. The modification of the order had occurred in the course of an action by petitioners, which had sought a stay of the trial court's original order and in which the accused and the State of Nebraska intervened. This Court granted certiorari to determine whether the order violated the constitutional guarantee of freedom of the press. The order expired by its own terms when the jury was impaneled. Respondent was convicted; his appeal is pending in the Nebraska Supreme Court. *Held:*

    1. The case is not moot simply because the order has expired, since the controversy between the parties is "capable of repetition, yet evading review."

    2. While the guarantees of freedom of expression are not an absolute prohibition under all circumstances, the barriers to prior restraint remain

high and the presumption against its use continues intact. Although it is unnecessary to establish a priority between First Amendment rights and the Sixth Amendment right to a fair trial under all circumstances, as the authors of the Bill of Rights themselves declined to do, the protection against prior restraint should have particular force as applied to reporting of criminal proceedings.

3. The heavy burden imposed as a condition to securing a prior restraint was not met in this case.

(a) On the pretrial record the trial judge was justified in concluding that there would be intense and pervasive pretrial publicity concerning the case, and he could also reasonably conclude, based on common human experience, that publicity might impair the accused's right to a fair trial. His conclusion as to the impact of such publicity on prospective jurors was of necessity speculative, however, dealing as he was with factors unknown and unknowable.

(b) There is no finding that measures short of prior restraint on the press and speech would not have protected the accused's rights; the Nebraska Supreme Court no more than implied that alternative measures might not suffice, and the record lacks evidence that would support such a finding.

(c) It is not clear that prior restraint on publication would have effectively protected the accused's rights, in view of such practical problems as the limited territorial jurisdiction of the trial court issuing the restraining order, the difficulties inherent in predicting what information will in fact undermine the jurors' impartiality, the problem of drafting an order that will effectively keep prejudicial information from prospective jurors, and the fact that in this case the events occurred in a small community where rumors would travel swiftly by word of mouth.

(d) To the extent that the order prohibited the reporting of evidence adduced at the open preliminary hearing held to determine whether the accused should be bound over for trial, it violated the settled principle that "there is nothing that proscribes the press from reporting events that transpire in the courtroom," *Sheppard* v. *Maxwell,* 384 U.S. 333, 362–363, and the portion of the order restraining publication of other facts "strongly implicative" of the accused is too vague and too broad to survive the scrutiny given to restraints on First Amendment rights.

Reversed.

BURGER, C. J., delivered the opinion of the Court, in which WHITE, BLACKMUN, POWELL, and REHNQUIST, JJ., joined. WHITE, J., *post,* p. 570, and POWELL, J., *post,* p. 571, filed concurring opinions. BRENNAN, J., filed an opinion concurring in the judgment, in which STEWART and

MARSHALL, JJ., joined, *post,* p. 572. STEVENS, J., filed an opinion concurring in the judgment, *post,* p. 617.

MR. JUSTICE BRENNAN, with whom MR. JUSTICE STEWART and MR. JUSTICE MARSHALL join, concurring in the judgment.

The question presented in this case is whether, consistently with the First Amendment, a court may enjoin the press, in advance of publication, from reporting or commenting on information acquired from public court proceedings, public court records, or other sources about pending judicial proceedings. The Nebraska Supreme Court upheld such a direct prior restraint on the press, issued by the judge presiding over a sensational state murder trial, on the ground that there existed a "clear and present danger that pretrial publicity could substantially impair the right of the defendant [in the murder trial] to a trial by an impartial jury unless restraints were imposed." *State* v. *Simants,* (1975). The right to a fair trial by a jury of one's peers is unquestionably one of the most precious and sacred safeguards enshrined in the Bill of Rights. I would hold, however, that resorting to prior restraints on the freedom of the press is a constitutionally impermissible method for enforcing that right; judges have at their disposal a broad spectrum of devices for ensuring that fundamental fairness is accorded the accused without necessitating so drastic an incursion on the equally fundamental and salutary constitutional mandate that discussion of public affairs in a free society cannot depend on the preliminary grace of judicial censors.

I

The history of the current litigation highlights many of the dangers inherent in allowing any prior restraint on press reporting and commentary concerning the operations of the criminal justice system.

This action arose out of events surrounding the prosecution of respondent-intervenor Simants for the premeditated mass murder of the six members of the Kellie family in Sutherland, Neb., on October 18, 1975. Shortly after the crimes occurred, the community of 850 was alerted by a special announcement over the local television station. Residents were requested by the police to stay off the streets and exercise caution as to whom they admitted into their houses, and rumors quickly spread that a sniper was loose in Sutherland. When an investigation implicated Simants as a suspect, his name and description were provided to the press and then disseminated to the public.

Simants was apprehended on the morning of October 19, charged with six counts of premeditated murder, and arraigned before the County Court of Lincoln County, Neb. Because several journalists were in attendance and "proof concerning bail . . . would be prejudicial to the rights of the defendant to later obtain a fair trial," App. 7, a portion of the bail hearing was closed, over Simants' objection, pursuant to the request of the Lincoln County Attorney. At the hearing, counsel was appointed for Simants, bail was denied, and October 22 was set as the date for a preliminary hearing to determine whether Simants should be bound over for trial in the District Court of Lincoln County, Neb. News of Simants' apprehension, which was broadcast over radio and television and reported in the press, relieved much of the tension that had built up during the night. During the period from October 19 until the first restrictive order was entered three days later, representatives of the press made accurate factual reports of the events that transpired, including reports of incriminating statements made by Simants to various relatives.

On the evening of October 21, the prosecution filed a motion that the County Court issue a restrictive order enjoining the press from reporting significant aspects of the case. The motion, filed without further evidentiary support, stated:

> The State of Nebraska hereby represents unto the Court that *by reason of the nature of the above-captioned case,* there has been, and no doubt there will continue to be, mass coverage by news media not only locally but nationally as well; that a preliminary hearing on the charges has been set to commence at 9:00 A.M. on October 22, 1975; and there is *a reasonable likelihood of prejudicial news which would make difficult, if not impossible, the impaneling of an impartial jury* and tend to prevent a fair trial should the defendant be bound over to trial in the District Court if testimony of witnesses at the preliminary hearing is reported to the public.
>
> Wherefore the State of Nebraska moves that the Court forthwith enter a Restrictive Order setting forth the matters that may or may not be publicly reported or disclosed to the public with reference to said case or with reference to the preliminary hearing thereon, and to whom said order shall apply.
> [App. 8 (Emphasis supplied.)]

Half an hour later, the County Court Judge heard argument on the prosecution motion. Defense counsel joined in urging imposition of a restrictive order, and further moved that the preliminary hearing be closed to both the press and the public. No representatives of the media were notified of or called to testify at the hearing, and no evidence of any kind was introduced.

On October 22, when the autopsy results were completed, the County Attorney filed an amended complaint charging that the six premeditated murders had been committed by Simants in conjunction with the perpetration of or attempt to perpetrate a sexual assault. About the same time, at the commencement of the preliminary hearing, the County Court entered a restrictive order premised on its finding that there was "a reasonable likelihood of prejudicial news which would make difficult, if not impossible, the impaneling of an impartial jury in the event that the defendant is bound over to the District Court for trial. . . ." Amended Pet. for Cert. 1a. Accordingly, the County Court ordered that all parties to the case, attorneys court personnel, public officials, law enforcement officials, witnesses, and "any other person present in Court" during the preliminary hearing, were not to "release or authorize the release for public dissemination in any form or manner whatsoever any testimony given or evidence adduced during the preliminary hearing." The court further ordered that no law enforcement official, public officer, attorney, witness, or "news media" "disseminate any information concerning this matter apart from the preliminary hearing other than as set forth in the Nebraska Bar-Press Guidelines for Disclosure and Reporting of Information Relating to Imminent or Pending Criminal Litigation." The order was to remain in effect "'until modified or rescinded by a higher court or until the defendant is ordered released from these charges." The court also denied the defense request to close the preliminary hearing, and an open hearing was then held, at which time various witnesses testified, disclosing significant factual information concerning the events surrounding the alleged crimes. Upon completion of the hearing, the County Court bound the defendant over for trial in the District Court, since it found that the offenses charged in the indictment had been committed, and that there was probable cause to believe that Simants had committed them.

The next day, petitioners—Nebraska newspapers publishers, broadcasters, journalists, and media associations, and national newswire services that report from and to Nebraska—sought leave from the District Court to intervene in the criminal case and vacation of the County Court's restrictive order as repugnant to the First and Sixth Amendments to the United States Constitution as well as relevant provisions of the Nebraska Constitution. Simants' attorney moved that the order be continued and that future pretrial hearings in the case be closed. The District Court then held an evidentiary hearing, after which it denied the motion to close any hearings, granted petitioners' motion to intervene, and adopted on an interim basis the County Court's restrictive order. The only testimony adduced at the hearing with respect to the need for the restrictive order was that of the County Court Judge, who stated that he had premised his order on his awareness of media publicity, "[c]onversation around the courthouse," and "statements of counsel." App. 64, 65. In addition, several newspaper clippings pertaining to the case were introduced as exhibits before the District Court.

Without any further hearings, the District Court on October 27 terminated the County Court's order and substituted its own. The court found that *"because of the nature of the crimes charged* in the complaint . . . there is a *clear and present danger* that pre-trial publicity *could impinge upon the defendant's right to a fair trial* and that an order setting forth the limitations of pre-trial publicity is appropriate. . . .'' Amended Pet. for Cert. 9a (emphasis supplied). Respondent Stuart, the District Court Judge, then "adopted" as his order the Nebraska Bar-Press Guidelines as "clarified" by him in certain respects.

On October 1, petitioners sought a stay of the order from the District Court and immediate relief from the Nebraska Supreme Court by way of mandamus, stay, or expedited appeal. When neither the District Court nor the Nebraska Supreme Court acted on these motions, petitioners on November 5 applied to MR. JUSTICE BLACKMUN, as Circuit Justice, for a stay of the District Court's order. Five days later, the Nebraska Supreme Court issued a *per curiam* statement that to avoid being put in the position of "exercising parallel jurisdiction with the Supreme Court of the United States," it would continue the matter until this Court "made known whether or not it will accept jurisdiction in the matter."

On November 13, MR. JUSTICE BLACKMUN filed an in-chambers opinion in which he declined to act on the stay "at least for the immediate present." He observed: "[I]f no action on the [petitioners'] application to the Supreme Court of Nebraska could be anticipated before December 1, [as was indicated by a communication from that court's clerk before the court issued the *per curiam* statement], . . . a definitive decision by the State's highest court on an issue of profound constitutional implications, demanding immediate resolution, would be delayed for a period so long that the very day-to-day duration of that delay would constitute and aggravate a deprival of such constitutional rights, if any, that the [petitioners] possess and may properly assert. Under those circumstances, I would not hesitate promptly to act." However, since the Nebraska Supreme Court had indicated in its *per curiam* statement that it was only declining to act because of uncertainty as to what this Court would do, and since it was deemed appropriate for the state court to pass initially on the validity of the restrictive order, MR. JUSTICE BLACKMUN, "without prejudice to the [petitioners] to reapply to me should prompt action not be forthcoming," denied the stay "[o]n the expectation ... that the Supreme Court of Nebraska, forthwith and without delay will entertain the [petitioners'] application made to it, and will promptly decide it in the full consciousness that 'time is of the essence.' "

When, on November 18, the Supreme Court of Nebraska set November 25 as the date to hear arguments on petitioners' motions, petitioners reapplied to MR. JUSTICE BLACKMUN for relief. On November 20, MR. JUSTICE BLACKMUN, concluding that each passing day constituted an irreparable infringement on First Amendment values and that the state courts had declared adjudication of petitioners' claims beyond "tolerable limits," granted a partial stay of the District Court's order. First, the "wholesale incorporation" of the Nebraska Bar-Press Guidelines was stayed on the ground that they "constitute a 'voluntary code' which was not intended to be mandatory" and which was "sufficiently riddled with vague and indefinite admonitions—understandably so in view of the basic nature of 'guidelines,' " that they did "not provide the substance of a permissible court order in the First Amendment area." However, the state courts could "reimpose particular provisions included in the Guidelines so long as they are deemed pertinent to the facts of this particular case and so long as they are adequately specific and in keeping with the remainder of this order." Second, the portion of the District Court order prohibiting reporting of the details of the crimes, the identities of the victims, and the pathologist's testimony at the preliminary hearing was stayed because there was "[n]o persuasive justifications" for the restraint; such "facts in themselves do not implicate a particular putative defendant," and "until the bare facts concerning the crimes are related to a particular accused.... their being reported in the media [does not appear to] irreparably infringe the accused's right to a fair trial of the issue as to whether he was the one who committed the crimes." Third, believing that prior restraints of this kind "are not necessarily and in all cases invalid," MR. JUSTICE BLACKMUN concluded that "certain facts that strongly implicate an accused may be restrained from publication by the media prior to his trial. A confession or statement against interest is the paradigm,'' and other such facts would include ''those associated with the circumstances of his arrest,'' those ''that are not necessarily implicative, but that are highly prejudicial, as, for example, facts associated with the accused's criminal record, if he has one,'' and ''statements as to the accused's guilt by those associated with the prosecution.'' Finally, the restrictive order's limitation on disclosure of the nature of the limitations themselves was stayed ''to the same extent'' as the limitations.

The following day petitioners filed a motion that the Court vacate MR. JUSTICE BLACKMUN'S order to the extent it permitted the imposition of any prior restraint on publication. Meanwhile, on November 25, the Supreme Court of Nebraska heard oral argument as scheduled, and on December 1 filed a *per curiam* opinion. Initially, the court held that it was improper for petitioners or any other third party to intervene in a criminal case, and that the appeal from the case must therefore be denied. However, the court concluded that it had jurisdiction over petitioners' mandamus action against respondent Stuart, and that respondents Simants and State of Nebraska had properly intervened in that action. Addressing the merits of the prior restraint issued by the District Court, the Nebraska Supreme Court acknowledged that this Court ''has not yet had occasion to speak definitively where a clash between these two preferred rights [the First Amendment freedom of speech and of the press and the Sixth Amendment right to trial by an impartial jury] was sought to be accommodated by a prior restraint on freedom of the press.'' However, relying on dictum in *Branzburg* v. *Hayes* (1972), and our statement in *New York Times Co.* v. *United States,* (1971), that a prior restraint on the media bears '' 'a heavy presumption against its constitutional validity,' '' the court discerned an ''implication'' ''that if there is only a presumption of unconstitutionality then there must be some circumstances under which prior restraints may be constitutional for otherwise there is no need for a mere presumption.'' The court then concluded that there was evidence ''to overcome the heavy presumption'' in that the State's obligation to accord Simants an impartial jury trial ''may be impaired'' by pretrial publicity and that pretrial publicity ''might make it difficult or impossible'' to accord Simants a fair trial. Accordingly, the court held,

[T]he order of the District Court of October 27, 1975, is void insofar as it incorporates the voluntary guidelines and in certain other aspects in that it impinges too greatly upon freedom of the press. The guidelines were not intended to be contractual and cannot be enforced as if they were.

The order of the District Court of October 27, 1975, is vacated and is modified and reinstated in the following respects: It shall be effective only as to events which have occurred prior to the filing of this opinion, and only as it applies to the relators herein, and only insofar as it restricts publication of the existence or content of the following, if any such there be: (1) Confessions or admissions against interest made by the accused to law enforcement officials. (2) Confessions or admissions against interest, oral or written, if any, made by the accused to third parties, excepting any statements, if any, made by the accused to representatives of the news media. (3) Other information strongly implicative of the accused as the perpetrator of the slayings.

On December 4 petitioners applied to this Court for a stay of that order and moved that their previously filed papers be treated as a petition for a writ of certiorari. On December 8, we granted the latter motion and deferred consideration of the petition for a writ and application for a stay pending responses from respondents on the close of business the following day. On December 12, we granted the petition for a writ of certiorari, denied the motion to expedite, and denied the application for a stay.

II

A

The Sixth Amendment to the United States Constitution guarantees that "[i]n all criminal prosecutions, the accused shall enjoy the right to a speedy and public trial, by an impartial jury of the State and district wherein the crime shall have been committed. . . ." The right to a jury trial, applicable to the States through the Due Process Clause of the Fourteenth Amendment, see, *e.g., Duncan* v. *Louisiana* (1968), is essentially the right to a "fair trial by a panel of impartial, 'indifferent' jurors," *Irvin* v. *Dowd* (1961), jurors who are " 'indifferent as [they] stand unsworn.' " *Reynolds* v. *United States* (1879), quoting E. Coke, A Commentary upon Littleton 155*b* (19th ed. 1832). So basic to our jurisprudence is the right to a fair trial that it has been called "the most fundamental of all freedoms." *Estes* v. *Texas* (1965). It is a right essential to the preservation and enjoyment of all other rights, providing a necessary means of safeguarding personal liberties against government oppression. See, *e.g., Rideau* v. *Louisiana.*

The First Amendment to the United States Constitution, however, secures rights equally fundamental in our jurisprudence, and its ringing proclamation that "Congress shall make no law . . . abridging the freedom of speech, or of the press . . ." has been both applied through the Fourteenth Amendment to invalidate restraints on freedom of the press imposed by the States, see, *e.g., Miami Herald Publishing Co.* v. *Tornillo* (1974), and interpreted to interdict such restraints imposed by the courts, see, *e.g., New York Times Co.* v. *United States* (1971). Indeed, it has been correctly perceived that a "responsible press has always been regarded as the handmaiden of effective judicial administration, especially in the criminal field. . . . The press does not simply publish information about trials but guards against the miscarriage of justice by subjecting the police, prosecutors, and judicial processes to extensive public scrutiny and criticism." *Sheppard* v. *Maxwell* (1966). Commentary and reporting on the criminal justice system is at the core of First Amendment values, for the operation and integrity of that system is of crucial import to citizens concerned with the administration of government. Secrecy of judicial action can only breed ignorance and distrust of courts and suspicion concerning the competence and impartiality of judges; free and robust reporting, criticism, and debate can contribute to public understanding of the rule of law and to comprehension of the functioning of the entire criminal justice system, as well as improve the quality of that system by subjecting it to the cleansing effects of exposure and public accountability. See, *e.g., In re Oliver.*

No one can seriously doubt, however, that uninhibited prejudicial pretrial publicity may destroy the fairness of a criminal trial, see, *e.g., Sheppard* v. *Maxwell,* and the past decade has witnessed substantial debate, colloquially known as the Free Press/Fair Trial controversy, concerning this interface of First and Sixth Amendment rights. In effect, we are now told by respondents that the two rights can no longer coexist when the press possesses and seeks to publish "confessions or admissions against interest" and other information "strongly implicative" of a criminal defendant as the perpetrator of a crime, and that one or the other right must therefore be subordinated. I disagree. Settled case law concerning the impropriety and constitutional invalidity of prior restraints on the press compels the conclusion that there can be no prohibition on the publication by the press of any information pertaining to pending judicial proceedings or the operation of the criminal justice system, no matter how shabby the means by which the information is obtained. This does not imply, however, any subordination of Sixth Amendment rights, for an accused's right to a fair trial may be adequately assured through methods that do not infringe First Amendment values.

B

"[I]t has been generally, if not universally, considered that it is the chief purpose of the [First Amendment's] guaranty to prevent previous restraints upon publication." *Near* v. *Minnesota ex rel. Olson.* Prior restraints are "the essence of censorship," *Near* v. *Minnesota ex rel. Olson,* and "[o]ur distaste for censorship—reflecting the natural distaste of a free people—is deep-written in our law." *Southeastern Promotions, Ltd.* v. *Conrad* (1975). The First Amendment thus accords greater protection against prior restraints than it does against subsequent punishment for a particular speech, see, *e.g., Carroll* v. *Princess Anne* (1968); "a free society prefers to punish the few who abuse rights of speech *after* they break the law than to throttle them and all others beforehand. It is always difficult to know in advance what an individual will say, and the line between legitimate and illegitimate speech is often so finely drawn that the risks of free-wheeling censorship are formidable." *Southeastern Promotions, Ltd.* v. *Conrad.* A commentator has cogently summarized many of the reasons for this deep-seated American hostility to prior restraints:

A system of prior restraint is in many ways more inhibiting than a system of subsequent punishment: It is likely to bring under government scrutiny a far wider range of expression; it shuts off communication before it takes place; suppression by a stroke of the pen is more likely to be applied than suppression through a criminal process; the procedures do not require attention to the safeguards of the criminal process; the system allows less opportunity for public appraisal and criticism; the dynamics of the system drive toward excesses, as the history of all censorship shows. [T. Emerson, The System of Freedom of Expression 506 (1970)].

Respondents correctly contend that "the [First Amendment] protection even as to previous restraint is not absolutely unlimited." *Near* v. *Minnesota ex rel. Olson.* However, the exceptions to the rule have been confined to "exceptional cases." *Ibid.* The Court in *Near,* the first case in which we were faced with a prior restraint against the press, delimited three such possible exceptional circumstances. The first two exceptions were that "the primary requirements of decency may be enforced against obscene publications," and that "[t]he security of the community life may be protected against incitements to acts of violence and the overthrow by force of orderly government [for] [t]he constitutional guaranty of free speech does not 'protect a man from an injunction against uttering words that may have all the effect of force. . . . ' " These exceptions have since come to be interpreted as situations in which the "speech" involved is not encompassed within the meaning of the First Amendment. See, *e.g., Roth* v. *United States* (1957). And even in these situations, adequate and timely procedures are mandated to protect against any restraint of speech that does come within the ambit of the First Amendment. See, *e.g., Southeastern Promotions, Ltd.* v. *Conrad.* Thus, only the third category in *Near* contemplated the possibility that speech meriting and entitled to constitutional protection might nevertheless be suppressed before publication in the interest of some overriding countervailing interest:

> "When a nation is at war many things that might be said in time of peace are such a hindrance to its effort that their utterance will not be endured so long as men fight and that no Court could regard them as protected by any constitutional right." *Schenck* v. *United States.* No one would question but that a government might prevent actual obstruction to its recruiting service or the publication of the sailing dates of transports or the number and location of troops.

Even this third category, however, has only been adverted to in dictum and has never served as the basis for actually upholding a prior restraint against the publication of constitutionally protected materials. In *New York Times Co.* v. *United States* we specifically addressed the scope of the "military security" exception alluded to in *Near* and held that there could be no prior restraint on publication of the "Pentagon Papers" despite the fact that a majority of the Court believed that release of the documents, which were classified "Top Secret—Sensitive" and which were obtained surreptitiously, would be harmful to the

Nation and might even be prosecuted after publication as a violation of various espionage statutes. To be sure, our brief *per curiam* declared that " '[a]ny system of prior restraints of expression comes to this Court bearing a heavy presumption against its constitutional validity,' " quoting *Bantam Books, Inc.* v. *Sullivan,* and that the "Government 'thus carries a heavy burden of showing justification for the imposition of such a restraint,' " quoting *Organization for a Better Austin* v. *Keefe* (1971). This does not mean, as the Nebraska Supreme Court assumed, that prior restraints can be justified on an *ad hoc* balancing approach that concludes that the "presumption" must be overcome in light of some perceived "justification." Rather, this language refers to the fact that, as a matter of procedural safeguards and burden of proof, prior restraints even within a recognized exception to the rule against prior restraints will be extremely difficult to justify; but as an initial matter, the purpose for which a prior restraint is sought to be imposed "must fit within one of the narrowly defined exceptions to the prohibition against prior restraints." *Southeastern Promotions, Ltd.* v. *Conrad.* Indeed, two Justices in *New York Times* apparently controverted the existence of even a limited "military security" exception to the rule against prior restraints on the publication of otherwise protected material. And a majority of the other Justices who expressed their views on the merits made it clear that they would take cognizance only of a "single, extremely narrow class of cases in which the First Amendment's ban on prior judicial restraint may be overridden." Although variously expressed, it was evident that even the exception was to be construed very, very narrowly: when disclosure "will *surely result in direct, immediate, and irreparable damage* to our Nation or its people," or when there is "governmental allegation and proof that publication must *inevitably, directly, and immediately* cause the occurrence of an event kindred to imperiling the safety of a transport already at sea. . . . [But] [i]n no event may mere conclusions be sufficient." It is thus clear that even within the sole possible exception to the prohibition against prior restraints on publication of constitutionally protected materials, the obstacles to issuance of such an injunction are formidable. What respondents urge upon us, however, is the creation of a new, potentially pervasive exception to this settled rule of virtually blanket prohibition of prior restraints.

I would decline this invitation. In addition to the almost insuperable presumption against the constitutionality of prior restraints even under a recognized exception, and however laudable the State's motivation for imposing restraints in this case, there are compelling reasons for not carving out a new exception to the rule against prior censorship of publication.

1

Much of the information that the Nebraska courts enjoined petitioners from publishing was already in the public domain, having been revealed in open court proceedings or through public documents. Our prior cases have foreclosed any serious contention that further disclosure of such information can be suppressed before publication or even punished after publication. "A trial is a public event. What transpires in the court room is public property. . . . Those who see and hear what transpired can report it with impunity. There is no special perquisite of the judiciary which enables it, as distinguished from other institutions of democratic government, to suppress, edit, or censor events which transpire in proceedings before it." *Craig* v. *Harney*. Similarly, *Estes* v. *Texas*, a case involving the Sixth Amendment right to a fair trial, observed: "[R]eporters of all media . . . are plainly free to report whatever occurs in open court through their respective media. This was settled in *Bridges* v. *California*, (1941), which we reaffirm." And *Sheppard* v. *Maxwell*, a case that detailed numerous devices that could be employed for ensuring fair trials, explicitly reiterated that "[o]f course, there is nothing that proscribes the press from reporting events that transpire in the courtroom." See also *Stroble* v. *California* (1952). The continuing vitality of these statements was reaffirmed only last Term in *Cox Broadcasting Corp.* v. *Cohn*, a case involving a suit for damages brought after publication under state law recognizing the privacy interest of its citizens. In holding that a "State may [not] impose sanctions on the accurate publication of the name of a rape victim obtained from public records," we observed:

[I]n a society in which each individual has but limited time and resources with which to observe at first hand the operations of his government, he relies necessarily upon the press to bring to him in convenient form the facts of those operations. *Great responsibility is accordingly placed upon the news media to report fully and accurately the proceedings of government, and official records and documents open to the public are the basic data of governmental operations.* Without the information provided by the press most of us and many of our representatives would be unable to vote intelligently or to register opinions on the administration of government generally. *With respect to judicial proceedings in particular, the function of the press serves to guarantee the fairness of trials and to bring to bear the beneficial effects of public scrutiny upon the administration of justice.* See *Sheppard* v. *Maxwell* (1966).

Appellee has claimed in this litigation that the efforts of the press have infringed his right to privacy by broadcasting to the world the fact that his daughter was a rape victim. *The commission of crime, prosecutions resulting from it, and judicial proceedings arising from the prosecutions, however, are without question events of legitimate concern to the public and consequently fall within the responsibility of the press to report the operations of government.*

The special protected nature of accurate reports of judicial proceedings has repeatedly been recognized. [emphasis supplied].

By placing the information in the public domain on official court records, the State must be presumed to have concluded that the public interest was thereby being served. *Public records by their very nature are of interest to those concerned with the administration of government, and a public benefit is performed by the reporting of the true contents of the records by the media. The freedom of the press to publish that information appears to us to be of critical importance to our type of government in which the citizenry is the final judge of the proper conduct of public business.* In preserving that form of government the First and Fourteenth Amendments command nothing less than that the States may not impose sanctions on the publication of truthful information contained in official court records open to public inspection.

Prior restraints are particularly anathematic to the First Amendment, and any immunity from punishment subsequent to publication of given material applies *a fortiori* to immunity from suppression of that material before publication. Thus, in light of *Craig,* which involved a contempt citation for a threat to the administration of justice, and *Cox Broadcasting,* which similarly involved an attempt to establish civil liability after publication, it should be clear that no injunction against the reporting of such information can be permissible.

2

The order of the Nebraska Supreme Court also applied, of course, to "confessions" and other information "strongly implicative" of the accused which were obtained from sources other than official records or open court proceedings. But for the reasons that follow—reasons equally applicable to information obtained by the press from official records or public court proceedings—I believe that the same rule against prior restraints governs *any* information pertaining to the criminal justice system, even if derived from nonpublic sources and regardless of the means employed by the press in its acquisition.

The only exception that has thus far been recognized even in dictum to the blanket prohibition against prior restraints against publication of material which would otherwise be constitutionally shielded was the "military security" situation addressed in *New York Times Co.* v. *United States.* But unlike the virtually certain, direct, and immediate harm required for such a restraint under *Near* and *New York Times,* the harm to a fair trial that might otherwise eventuate from publications which are suppressed pursuant to orders such as that under review must inherently remain speculative.

A judge importuned to issue a prior restraint in the pretrial context will be unable to predict the manner in which the potentially prejudicial information would be published, the frequency with which it would be repeated or the emphasis it would be given, the context in which or purpose for which it would be reported, the scope of the audience that would be exposed to the information, or the impact, evaluated in terms of current standards for assessing juror impartiality, the information would have on that audience. These considerations would render speculative the prospective impact on a fair trial of reporting even an alleged confession or other information "strongly implicative" of the accused. Moreover, we can take judicial notice of the fact that given the prevalence of plea bargaining, few criminal cases proceed to trial, and the judge would thus have to predict what the likelihood was that a jury would even have to be impaneled. Indeed, even in cases that do proceed to trial, the material sought to be suppressed before trial will often be admissible and may be admitted in any event. And, more basically, there are adequate devices for screening from jury duty those individuals who have in fact been exposed to prejudicial pretrial publicity.

Initially, it is important to note that once the jury is impaneled, the techniques of sequestration of jurors and control over the courtroom and conduct of trial should prevent prejudicial publicity from infecting the fairness of judicial proceedings. Similarly, judges may stem much of the flow of prejudicial publicity at its source, before it is obtained by representatives of the press. But even if the press nevertheless obtains potentially prejudicial information and decides to publish that information, the Sixth Amendment rights of the accused may still be adequately protected. In particular, the trial judge should employ the *voir dire* to probe fully into the effect of publicity. The judge should broadly explore such matters as the extent to which prospective jurors had read particular news accounts or whether they had heard about incriminating data such as an alleged confession or statements by purportedly reliable sources concerning the defendant's guilt. See, *e.g., Ham* v. *South Carolina* (1973). Particularly in cases of extensive publicity, defense counsel should be accorded more latitude in personally asking or tendering searching questions that might root out indications of bias, both to facilitate intelligent exercise of peremptory challenges and to help uncover factors that would dictate disqualification for cause. Indeed, it may sometimes be necessary to question on *voir dire* prospective jurors individually or in small groups, both to maximize the likelihood that members of the venire will respond honestly to the questions concerning bias, and to avoid contaminating unbiased members of the venire when other members disclose prior knowledge of prejudicial information. Moreover, *voir dire* may indicate the need to grant a brief continuance or to grant a change of venue, techniques that can effectively mitigate any publicity at a particular time or in a particular locale. Finally, if the trial court fails or refuses to utilize these devices effectively, there are the "palliatives" of reversals on appeal and directions for a new trial. *Sheppard* v. *Maxwell.* We have indicated that even in a case involving outrageous publicity and a "carnival atmosphere" in the courtroom, "these procedures would have been sufficient to guarantee [the defendant] a fair trial. . . ." For this reason, the one thing *Sheppard* did not approve was "any direct limitations on the freedom traditionally exercised by the news media." Indeed, the traditional techniques approved in *Sheppard* for ensuring fair trials would have been adequate in every case in which we have found that a new trial was required due to lack of fundamental fairness to the accused.

For these reasons alone I would reject the contention that speculative deprivation of an accused's Sixth Amendment right to an impartial jury is comparable to the damage to the Nation or its people that *Near* and *New York Times* would have found sufficient to justify a prior restraint on reporting. Damage to that Sixth Amendment right could never be considered so direct, immediate and irreparable, and based on such proof rather than speculation, that prior restraints on the press could be justified on this basis.

C

There are additional, practical reasons for not starting down the path urged by respondents. The exception to the prohibition of prior restraints adumbrated in *Near* and *New York Times* involves no judicial weighing of the countervailing public interest in receiving the suppressed information; the direct, immediate, and irreparable harm that would result from disclosure is simply deemed to outweigh the public's interest in knowing, for example, the specific details of troop movements during wartime. As the Supreme Court of Nebraska itself admitted, however, any attempt to impose a prior restraint on the reporting of information concerning the operation of the criminal justice system will inevitably involve the courts in an *ad hoc* evaluation of the need for the public to receive particular information that might nevertheless implicate the accused as the perpetrator of a crime. For example, disclosure of the circumstances surrounding the obtaining of an involuntary confession or the conduct of an illegal search resulting in incriminating fruits may be the necessary predicate for a movement to reform police methods, pass regulatory statutes, or remove judges who do not adequately oversee law enforcement activity; publication of facts surrounding particular plea-bargaining proceedings or the practice of plea bargaining generally may provoke substantial public concern as to the operations of the judiciary or the fairness of prosecutorial decisions; reporting the details of the confession of one accused may reveal that it may implicate others as well, and the public may rightly demand to know what actions are being taken by law enforcement personnel to bring those other individuals to justice; commentary on the fact that there is strong evidence implicating a government official in criminal activity goes to the very core of matters of public concern, and even a brief delay in reporting that information shortly before an election may have a decisive impact on the outcome of the democratic process, see *Carroll* v. *Princess Anne*; dissemination of the fact that indicted individuals who had been accused of similar misdeeds in the past had not been prosecuted or had received only mild sentences may generate crucial debate on the functioning of the criminal justice system; revelation of the fact that despite apparently overwhelming evidence of guilt, prosecutions were dropped or never commenced against large campaign contributors or members of special interest groups may indicate possible corruption among government officials; and disclosure of the fact that a suspect has been apprehended as the perpetrator of a heinous crime may be necessary to calm community fears that the actual perpetrator is still at large. Cf. *Times-Picayune Pub. Corp.* v. *Schulingkamp.* In all of these situations, judges would be forced to evaluate whether the public interest in receiving the information outweighed the speculative impact on Sixth Amendment rights.

These are obviously some examples of the problems that plainly would recur, not in the almost theoretical situation of suppressing disclosure of the location of troops during wartime, but on a regular basis throughout the courts of the land. Recognition of any judicial authority to impose prior restraints on the basis of harm to the Sixth Amendment rights of particular defendants, especially since that harm must remain speculative, will thus inevitably interject judges at all levels into censorship roles that are simply inappropriate and impermissible under the First Amendment. Indeed, the potential for arbitrary and excessive judicial utilization of any such power would be exacerbated by the fact that judges and committing magistrates might in some cases be determining the propriety of publishing information that reflects on their competence, integrity, or general performance on the bench.

There would be, in addition, almost intractable procedural difficulties associated with any attempt to impose prior restraints on publication of information relating to pending criminal proceedings, and the ramifications of these procedural difficulties would accentuate the burden on First Amendment rights. The incentives and dynamics of the system of prior restraints would inevitably lead to overemployment of the technique. In order to minimize pretrial publicity against his clients and pre-empt ineffective-assistance-of-counsel claims, counsel for defendants might routinely seek such restrictive orders. Prosecutors would often acquiesce in such motions to avoid jeopardizing a conviction on appeal. And although judges could readily reject many such claims as frivolous, there would be a significant danger that judges would nevertheless be predisposed to grant the motions, both to ease their task of ensuring fair proceedings and to insulate their conduct in the criminal proceeding from reversal. We need not raise any specter of floodgates of litigation or drain on judicial resources to note that the litigation with respect to these motions will substantially burden the media. For to bind the media, they would have to be notified and accorded an opportunity to be heard. See, *e.g., Carroll* v. *Princess Anne, supra; McKinney* v. *Alabama* (1976). This would at least entail the possibility of restraint proceedings collateral to every criminal case before the courts, and there would be a significant financial drain on the media involuntarily made parties to these proceedings. Indeed, small news organs on the margin of economic viability might choose not to contest even blatantly unconstitutional restraints or to avoid all crime coverage, with concomitant harm to the public's right to be informed of such proceedings. Such acquiescence might also mean that significant erroneous precedents will remain unchallenged, to be relied on for even broader restraints in the future. Moreover, these collateral restraint proceedings would be unlikely to result in equal treatment of all organs of the media and, even if all the press could be brought into the proceeding, would often be ineffective, since disclosure of incriminating material may transpire before an effective restraint could be imposed.

To be sure, because the decision to impose such restraints even on the disclosure of supposedly narrow categories of information would depend on the facts of each case, and because precious First Amendment rights are at stake, those who could afford the substantial costs would seek appellate review. But that review is often inadequate, since delay inherent in judicial proceedings could itself destroy the contemporary news value of the information the press seeks to disseminate. As one commentator has observed:

> Prior restraints fall on speech with a brutality and a finality all their own. Even if they are ultimately lifted they cause irremediable loss—a loss in the immediacy, the impact, of speech. . . . Indeed it is the hypothesis of the First Amendment that injury is inflicted on our society when we stifle the immediacy of speech. [A. Bickel, The Morality of Consent 61 (1975)].

And, as noted, given the significant financial disincentives, particularly on the smaller organs of the media, to challenge any restrictive orders once they are imposed by trial judges, there is the distinct possibility that many erroneous impositions would remain uncorrected.

III

I unreservedly agree with Mr. Justice Black that ''free speech and fair trials are two of the most cherished policies of our civilization, and it would be a trying task to choose between them.'' *Bridges* v. *California*. But I would reject the notion that a choice is necessary, that there is an inherent conflict that cannot be resolved without essentially abrogating one right or the other. To hold that courts cannot impose any prior restraints on the reporting of or commentary upon information revealed in open court proceedings, disclosed in public documents, or divulged by other sources with respect to the criminal justice system is not, I must emphasize, to countenance the sacrifice of precious Sixth Amendment rights on the altar of the First Amendment. For although there may in some instances be tension between uninhibited and robust reporting by the press and fair trials for criminal defendants, judges possess adequate tools short of injunctions against reporting for relieving that tension. To be sure, these alternatives may require greater sensitivity and effort on the part of judges conducting criminal trials than would the stifling of publicity through the simple expedient of issuing a restrictive order on the press; but that sensitivity and effort is required in order to ensure the full enjoyment and proper accommodation of both First and Sixth Amendment rights.

There is, beyond peradventure, a clear and substantial damage to freedom of the press whenever even a temporary restraint is imposed on reporting of material concerning the operations of the criminal justice system, an institution of such pervasive influence in our constitutional scheme. And the necessary impact of reporting even confessions can never be so direct, immediate, and irreparable that I would give credence to any notion that prior restraints may be imposed on that rationale. It may be that such incriminating material would be of such slight news value or so inflammatory in particular cases that responsible organs of the media, in an exercise of self-restraint, would choose not to publicize that material, and not make the judicial task of safeguarding precious rights of criminal defendants more difficult. Voluntary codes such as the Nebraska Bar-Press Guidelines are a commendable acknowledgment by the media that constitutional prerogatives bring enormous responsibilities, and I would encourage continuation of such voluntary cooperative efforts between the bar and the media. However, the press may be arrogant, tyrannical, abusive, and sensationalist, just as it may be incisive, probing, and informative. But at least in the context of prior restraints on publication, the decision of what, when, and how to publish is for editors, not judges. See, *e.g., Near* v. *Minnesota ex rel. Olson.* Every restrictive order imposed on the press in this case was accordingly an unconstitutional prior restraint on the freedom of the press, and I would therefore reverse the judgment of the Nebraska Supreme Court and remand for further proceedings not inconsistent with this opinion.

APPENDIX TO OPINION OF BRENNAN, J., CONCURRING IN JUDGMENT

NEBRASKA BAR-PRESS GUIDELINES FOR DISCLOSURE AND REPORTING OF INFORMATION RELATING TO IMMINENT OR PENDING CRIMINAL LITIGATION

These voluntary guidelines reflect standards which bar and news media representatives believe are a reasonable means of accommodating, on a voluntary basis, the correlative constitutional rights of free speech and free press with the right of an accused to a fair trial. They are not intended to prevent the news media from inquiring into and reporting on the integrity, fairness, efficiency and effectiveness of law enforcement, the administration of justice, or political or governmental questions whenever involved in the judicial process.

As a voluntary code, these guidelines do not necessarily reflect in all respects what the members of the bar or the news media believe would be permitted or required by law.

Information Generally Appropriate for Disclosure, Reporting

Generally, it is appropriate to disclose and report the following information:

1. The arrested person's name, age, residence, employment, marital status and similar biographical information.

2. The charge, its text, any amendments thereto, and, if applicable, the identity of the complainant.

3. The amount of conditions of bail.

4. The identity or and biographical information concerning the complaining party and victim, and, if a death is involved, the apparent

cause of death unless it appears that the cause of death may be a contested issue.

5. The identity of the investigating and arresting agencies and the length of the investigation.

6. The circumstances of arrest, including time, place, resistance, pursuit, possession of and all weapons used, and a description of the items seized at the time of arrest. It is appropriate to disclose and report at the time of seizure the description of physical evidence subsequently seized other than a confession, admission or statement. It is appropriate to disclose and report the subsequent finding of weapons, bodies, contraband, stolen property and similar physical items if, in view of the time and other circumstances, such disclosure and reporting are not likely to interfere with a fair trial.

7. Information disclosed by the public records, including all testimony and other evidence adduced at the trial.

Information Generally Not Appropriate for Disclosure, Reporting

Generally, it is not appropriate to disclose or report the following information because of the risk of prejudice to the right of an accused to a fair trial:

1. The existence or contents of any confession, admission or statement given by the accused, except it may be stated that the accused denies the charges made against him. This paragraph is not intended to apply to statements made by the accused to representatives of the news media or to the public.

2. Opinions concerning the guilt, the innocence or the character of the accused.

3. Statements predicting or influencing the outcome of the trial.

4. Results of any examination or tests or the accused's refusal or failure to submit to an examination or test.

5. Statements or opinions concerning the credibility or anticipated testimony of prospective witnesses.

6. Statements made in the judicial proceedings outside the presence of the jury relating to confessions or other matters which, if reported, would likely interfere with a fair trial.

Prior Criminal Records

Lawyers and law enforcement personnel should not volunteer the prior criminal records of an accused except to aid in his apprehension or to warn the public of any dangers he presents. The news media can obtain prior criminal records from the public records of the courts, police agencies and other governmental agencies and from their own files. The news media acknowledge, however, that publication or broadcast of an individual's criminal record can be prejudicial, and its publication or broadcast should be considered very carefully, particularly after the filing of formal charges and as the time of the trial approaches, and such publication or broadcast should generally be avoided because readers, viewers and listeners are potential jurors and an accused is presumed innocent until proven guilty.

Photographs

1. Generally, it is not appropriate for law enforcement personnel to deliberately pose a person in custody for photographing or televising by representatives of the news media.
2. Unposed photographing and televising of an accused outside the courtroom is generally appropriate, and law enforcement personnel should not interfere with such photographing or televising except in compliance with an order of the court or unless such photographing or televising would interfere with their official duties.
3. It is appropriate for law enforcement personnel to release to representatives of the news media photographs of a suspect or an accused. Before publication of any such photographs, the news media should eliminate any portions of the photographs that would indicate a prior criminal offense or police record.

Continuing Committee for Cooperation

The members of the bar and the news media recognize the desirability of continued joint efforts in attempting to resolve any areas of differences that may arise in their mutual objective of assuring to all Americans both the correlative constitutional rights to freedom of speech and press and to a fair trial. The bar and the news media, through their respective associations, have determined to establish a permanent committee to revise these guidelines whenever this appears necessary or appropriate, to issue opinions as to their application to specific situations, to receive, evaluate and make recommendations with respect to complaints and to seek to effect through educational and other voluntary means a proper accommodation of the constitutional correlative rights of free speech, free press and fair trial.

June, 1970

UNITED STATES v. WADE

Argued February 16, 1967.—Decided June 12, 1967.

Several weeks after respondent's indictment for robbery of a federally insured bank and for conspiracy, respondent, without notice to his appointed counsel, was placed in a lineup in which each person wore strips of tape on his face, as the robber allegedly had done, and on direction repeated words like those the robber allegedly had used. Two bank employees identified respondent as the robber. At the trial when asked if the robber was in the courtroom, they identified respondent. The prior lineup identifications were elicited on cross-examination. Urging that the conduct of the lineup violated his Fifth Amendment privilege against self-incrimination and his Sixth Amendment right to counsel, respondent filed a motion for judgment of acquittal or, alternatively, to strike the courtroom identifications. The trial court denied the motions and respondent was convicted. The Court of Appeals reversed, holding that though there was no Fifth Amendment deprivation the absence of counsel at the lineup denied respondent his right to counsel under the Sixth Amendment and required the grant of a new trial at which the in-court identifications of those who had made lineup identifications would be excluded. *Held:*

1. Neither lineup itself nor anything required therein violated respondent's Fifth Amendment privilege against self-incrimination since merely exhibiting his person for observation by witnesses and using his voice as an identifying physical characteristic involved no compulsion of the accused to give evidence of a testimonial nature against himself which is prohibited by that Amendment.

2. The Sixth Amendment guarantees an accused the right to counsel not only at his trial but at any critical confrontation by the prosecution at pretrial proceedings where the results might well determine his fate and where the absence of counsel might derogate from his right to a fair trial.

3. The post-indictment lineup (unlike such preparatory steps as analyzing

fingerprints and blood samples) was a critical prosecutive stage at which respondent was entitled to the aid of counsel.

(a) There is a great possibility of unfairness to the accused at that point, (1) because of the manner in which confrontations for identification are frequently conducted, (2) because of dangers inherent in eyewitness identification and suggestibility inherent in the context of the confrontations, and (3) because of the likelihood that the accused will often be precluded from reconstructing what occurred and thereby obtaining a full hearing on the identification issue at trial.

(b) This case illustrates the potential for improper influence on witnesses through the lineup procedure, since the bank employees were allowed to see respondent in the custody of FBI agents before the lineup began.

(c) The presence of counsel at the lineup will significantly promote fairness at the confrontation and a full hearing at trial on the issue of identification.

4. In-court identification by a witness to whom the accused was exhibited before trial in the absence of counsel must be excluded unless it can be established that such evidence had an independent origin or that error in its admission was harmless. Since it is not clear that the Court of Appeals applied the prescribed rule of exclusion, and since the nature of the in-court identifications here was not an issue in the trial and cannot be determined on the record, the case must be remanded to the District Court for resolution of these issues.

Vacated and remanded.

MR. JUSTICE BRENNAN delivered the opinion of the Court.

The question here is whether courtroom identifications of an accused at trial are to be excluded from evidence because the accused was exhibited to the witnesses before trial at a post-indictment lineup conducted for identification purposes without notice to and in the absence of the accused's appointed counsel.

The federally insured bank in Eustace, Texas, was robbed on September 21, 1964. A man with a small strip of tape on each side of his face entered the bank, pointed a pistol at the female cashier and the vice president, the only persons in the bank at the time, and forced them to fill a pillowcase with the bank's money. The man then drove away with an accomplice who had been waiting in a stolen car outside the bank. On March 23, 1965, an indictment was returned against respondent, Wade, and two others for conspiring to rob the bank, and against Wade and the accomplice for the robbery itself. Wade was arrested or April 2, and counsel was appointed to represent him on April 26. Fifteen days later an FBI agent, without notice to Wade's lawyer, arranged to have the two bank employees observe a lineup made up of Wade and five or six other prisoners and conducted in a courtroom of the local county courthouse. Each person in the line wore strips of tape such as allegedly worn by the robber and upon direction each said something like "put the money in the bag," the words allegedly uttered by the robber. Both bank employees identified Wade in the lineup as the bank robber.

At trial, the two employees, when asked on direct examination if the robber was in the courtroom, pointed to Wade. The prior lineup identification was then elicited from both employees on cross-examination. At the close of testimony, Wade's counsel moved for a judgment of acquittal or, alternatively, to strike the bank officials' courtroom identifications on the ground that conduct of the lineup, without notice to and in the absence of his appointed counsel, violated his Fifth Amendment privilege against self-incrimination and his Sixth Amendment right to the assistance of counsel. The motion was denied, and Wade was convicted. The Court of Appeals for the Fifth Circuit reversed the conviction and ordered a new trial at which the in-court identification evidence was to be excluded, holding that, though the lineup did not violate Wade's Fifth Amendment rights, "the lineup, held as it was, in the absence of counsel, already chosen to represent appellant, was a violation of his Sixth Amendment rights. . . ." We granted certiorari, and set the case for oral argument. We reverse the judgment of the Court of Appeals and remand to that court with direction to enter a new judgment vacating the conviction and remanding the case to the District Court for further proceedings consistent with this opinion.

I

Neither the lineup itself nor anything shown by this record that Wade was required to do in the lineup violated his privilege against self-incrimination. We have only recently reaffirmed that the privilege "protects an accused only from being compelled to testify against himself, or otherwise provide the State with evidence of a testimonial or communicative nature. . . ." *Schmerber* v. *California.* We there held that compelling a suspect to submit to a withdrawal of a sample of his blood for analysis for alcohol content and the admission in evidence of the analysis report were not compulsion to those ends. That holding was supported by the opinion in *Holt* v. *United States,* in which case a question arose as to whether a blouse belonged to the defendant. A witness testified at trial that the defendant put on the blouse and it had fit him. The defendant argued that the admission of the testimony was error because compelling him to put on the blouse was a violation of his privilege. The Court rejected the claim as "an extravagant extension of the Fifth Amendment," Mr. Justice Holmes saying for the Court:

> [T]he prohibition of compelling a man in a criminal court to be witness against himself is a prohibition of the use of physical or moral compulsion to extort communications from him, not an exclusion of his body as evidence when it may be material.

The Court in *Holt,* however, put aside any constitutional questions which might be involved in compelling an accused, as here, to exhibit himself before victims of or witnesses to an alleged crime; the Court stated "we need not consider how far a court would go in compelling a man to exhibit himself."

We have no doubt that compelling the accused merely to exhibit his person for observation by a prosecution witness prior to trial involves no compulsion of the accused to give evidence having testimonial significance. It is compulsion of the accused to exhibit his physical characteristics, not compulsion to disclose any knowledge he might have. It is no different from compelling Schmerber to provide a blood sample or Holt to wear the blouse, and, as in those instances, is not within the cover of the privilege. Similarly, compelling Wade to speak within hearing distance of the witnesses, even to utter words purportedly uttered by the robber, was not compulsion to utter statements of a "testimonial" nature; he was required to use his voice as an identifying physical characteristic, not to speak his guilt. We held in *Schmerber,* that the distinction to be drawn under the Fifth Amendment privilege against self-incrimination is one between an accused's "communications" in whatever form, vocal or physical, and "compulsion which makes a suspect or accused the source of 'real or physical evidence.'" We recognized that "both federal and state courts have usually held that . . . [the privilege] offers no protection against compulsion to submit to fingerprinting, photography, or measurements, to write or speak for identification, to appear in court, to stand, to assume a stance, to walk, or to make a particular gesture." None of these activities becomes testimonial within the scope of the privilege because required of the accused in a pretrial lineup.

Moreover, it deserves emphasis that this case presents no question of the admissibility in evidence of anything Wade said or did at the lineup which implicates his privilege. The Government offered no such evidence as part of its case, and what came out about the lineup proceedings on Wade's cross-examination of the bank employees involved no violation of Wade's privilege.

II

The fact that the lineup involved no violation of Wade's privilege against self-incrimination does not, however, dispose of his contention that the courtroom identifications should have been excluded because the lineup was conducted without notice to and in the absence of his counsel. Our rejection of the right to counsel claim in *Schmerber* rested on our conclusion in that case that "[n]o issue of counsel's ability to assist petitioner in respect of any rights he did possess is presented." In contrast, in this case it is urged that the assistance of counsel at the lineup was indispensable to protect Wade's most basic right as a criminal defendant—his right to a fair trial at which the witnesses against him might be meaningfully cross-examined.

The Framers of the Bill of Rights envisaged a broader role for counsel than under the practice then prevailing in England of merely advising his client in "matters of law," and eschewing any responsibility for "matters of fact." The constitutions in at least 11 of the 13 States expressly or impliedly abolished this distinction. *Powell* v. *Alabama,* (1964). "Though the colonial provisions about counsel were in accord on few things, they agreed on the necessity of abolishing the facts-law distinction; the colonists appreciated that if a defendant were forced to stand alone against the state, his case was foredoomed." 73 Yale L. J., *supra,* at 1033–1034. This background is reflected in the scope given by our decisions to the Sixth Amendment's guarantee to an accused of the assistance of counsel for his defense. When the Bill of Rights was adopted, there were no organized police forces as we know them today. The accused confronted the prosecutor and the witnesses against him, and the evidence was marshalled, largely at the trial itself. In contrast, today's law enforcement machinery involves critical confrontations of the accused by the prosecution at pretrial proceedings where the results might well settle the accused's fate and reduce the trial itself to a mere formality. In recognition of these realities of modern criminal prosecution, our cases have construed the Sixth Amendment guarantee to apply to "critical" stages of the proceedings. The guarantee reads: "In all criminal prosecutions, the accused shall enjoy the right . . . to have the Assistance of Counsel *for his defence.*" (Emphasis supplied.) The plain wording of this guarantee thus encompasses counsel's assistance whenever necessary to assure a meaningful "defence."

As early as *Powell* v. *Alabama, supra,* we recognized that the period from arraignment to trial was "perhaps the most critical period of the proceedings . . . ," during which the accused "requires the guiding hand of counsel . . . ," if the guarantee is not to prove an empty right. That principle has since been applied to require the assistance of counsel at the type of arraignment—for example, that provided by Alabama— where certain rights might be sacrificed or lost: "What happens there may affect the whole trial. Available defenses may be irretrievably lost, if not then and there asserted. . . ." *Hamilton* v. *Alabama.* The principle was also applied in *Massiah* v. *United States,* where we held that incriminating statements of the defendant should have been excluded from evidence when it appeared that they were overheard by federal agents who, without notice to the defendant's lawyer, arranged a meeting between the defendant and an accomplice turned informant. We said, quoting a concurring opinion in *Spano* v. *New York,* that "[a]nything less . . . might deny a defendant 'effective representation by counsel at the only stage when legal aid and advice would help him.' "

In *Escobedo* v. *Illinois* we drew upon the rationale of *Hamilton* and *Massiah* in holding that the right to counsel was guaranteed at the point where the accused, prior to arraignment, was subjected to secret interrogation despite repeated requests to see his lawyer. We again noted the necessity of counsel's presence if the accused was to have a fair opportunity to present a defense at the trial itself:

> the rule sought by the State here, however, would make the trial no more than an appeal from the interrogation; and the "right to use counsel at the formal trial [would be] a very hollow thing [if], for all practical purposes, the conviction is already assured by pretrial examination. . . . One can imagine a cynical prosecutor saying: "Let them have the most illustrious counsel, now. They can't escape the noose. There is nothing that counsel can do for them at the trial.' "

Finally in *Miranda* v. *Arizona,* the rules established for custodial interrogation included the right to the presence of counsel. The result was rested on our finding that this and the other rules were necessary to safeguard the privilege against self-incrimination from being jeopardized by such interrogation.

Of course, nothing decided or said in the opinions in the cited cases links the right to counsel only to protection of Fifth Amendment rights. Rather those decisions "no more than reflect a constitutional principle established as long ago as *Powell* v. *Alabama. . . .*" *Massiah* v. *United States.* It is central to that principle that in addition to counsel's presence at trial, the accused is guaranteed that he need not stand alone against the State at any stage of the prosecution, formal or informal, in court or out, where counsel's absence might derogate from the accused's right to a fair trial. The security of that right is as much the aim of the right to counsel as it is of the other guarantees of the Sixth Amendment— the right of the accused to a speedy and public trial by an impartial jury, his right to be informed of the nature and cause of the accusation, and his right to be confronted with the witnesses against him and to have compulsory process for obtaining witnesses in his favor. The presence of counsel at such critical confrontations, as at the trial itself, operates to assure that the accused's interests will be protected consistently with our adversary theory of criminal prosecution. Cf. *Pointer* v. *Texas.*

In sum, the principle of *Powell* v. *Alabama* and succeeding cases requires that we scrutinize *any* pretrial confrontation of the accused to determine whether the presence of his counsel is necessary to preserve the defendant's basic right to a fair trial as affected by his right meaningfully to cross-examine the witnesses against him and to have effective assistance of counsel at the trial itself. It calls upon us to analyze whether potential substantial prejudice to defendant's rights inheres in the particular confrontation and the ability of counsel to help avoid that prejudice.

III

The Government characterizes the lineup as a mere preparatory step in the gathering of the prosecution's evidence, not different—for Sixth Amendment purposes—from various other preparatory steps, such as systematized or scientific analyzing of the accused's fingerprints, blood sample, clothing, hair, and the like. We think there are differences which preclude such stages being characterized as critical stages at which the accused has the right to the presence of his counsel. Knowledge of the techniques of science and technology is sufficiently available, and the variables in techniques few enough, that the accused has the opportunity for a meaningful confrontation of the Government's case at trial through the ordinary processes of cross-examination of the Government's expert witnesses and the presentation of the evidence of his own experts. The denial of a right to have his counsel present at such analysis does not therefore violate the Sixth Amendment; they are not critical stages since there is minimal risk that his counsel's absence at such stages might derogate from his right to a fair trial.

IV

But the confrontation compelled by the State between the accused and the victim or witnesses to a crime to elicit identification evidence is peculiarly riddled with innumerable dangers and variable factors which might seriously, even crucially, derogate from a fair trial. The vagaries of eyewitness identification are well-known; the annals of criminal law are rife with instances of mistaken identification. Mr. Justice Frankfurter once said: "What is the worth of identification testimony even when uncontradicted? The identification of strangers if proverbially untrustworthy. The hazards of such testimony are established by a formidable number of instances in the records of English and American trials. These instances are recent—not due to the brutalities of ancient criminal procedure." The Case of Sacco and Vanzetti 30 (1927). A major factor contributing to the high incidence of miscarriage of justice from mistaken identification has been the degree of suggestion inherent in the manner in which the prosecution presents the suspect to witnesses for pretrial identification. A commentator has observed that "[t]he influence of improper suggestion upon identifying witnesses probably accounts for more miscarriages of justice than any other single factor— perhaps it is responsible for more such errors than all other factors combined." Wall, Eye-Witness Identification in Criminal Cases 26. Suggestion can be created intentionally or unintentionally in many subtle ways. And the dangers for the suspect are particularly grave when the witness' opportunity for observation was insubstantial, and thus his susceptibility to suggestion the greatest.

Moreover, "[i]t is a matter of common experience that, once a witness has picked out the accused at the lineup, he is not likely to go back on his word later on, so that in practice the issue of identity may (in the absence of other relevant evidence) for all practical purposes be determined there and then, before the trial."

The pretrial confrontation for purpose of identification may take the form of a lineup, also known as an "identification parade" or "showup," as in the present case, or presentation of the suspect alone to the witness, as in *Stovall* v. *Denno*. It is obvious that risks of suggestion attend either form of confrontation and increase the dangers inhering in eyewitness identification. But as is the case with secret interrogations, there is serious difficulty in depicting what transpires at lineups and other forms of identification confrontations. "Privacy results in secrecy and this in turn results in a gap in our knowledge as to what in fact goes on. . . ." *Miranda* v. *Arizona*. For the same reasons, the defense can seldom reconstruct the manner and mode of lineup identification for judge or jury at trial. Those participating in a lineup with the accused may often be police officers; in any event, the participants' names are rarely recorded or divulged at trial. The impediments to an objective observation are increased when the victim is the witness. Lineups are prevalent in rape and robbery prosecutions and present a particular hazard that a victim's understandable outrage may excite vengeful or spiteful motives. In any event, neither witnesses nor lineup participants are apt to be alert for conditions prejudicial to the suspect. And if they were, it would likely be of scant benefit to the suspect since neither witnesses nor lineup participants are likely to be schooled in the detection of suggestive influences. Improper influences may go undetected by a suspect, guilty or not, who experiences the emotional tension which we might expect in one being confronted with potential accusers. Even when he does observe abuse, if he has a criminal record he may be reluctant to take the stand and open up the admission of prior convictions. Moreover, any protestations by the suspect of the fairness of the lineup made at trial are likely to be in vain; the jury's choice is between the accused's unsupported version and that of the police officers present. In short, the accused's inability effectively to reconstruct at trial any unfairness that occurred at the lineup may deprive him of his only opportunity meaningfully to attack the credibility of the witness' courtroom identification.

What facts have been disclosed in specific cases about the conduct of pretrial confrontations for identification illustrate both the potential for substantial prejudice to the accused at that stage and the need for its revelation at trial. A commentator provides some striking examples:

> In a Canadian case . . . the defendant had been picked out of a lineup of six men, of which he was the only Oriental. In other cases, a black-haired suspect was placed among a group of light-haired persons, tall suspects have been made to stand with short non-suspects, and, in a case where the perpetrator of the crime was known to be a youth, a suspect under twenty was placed in a line-up with five other persons, all of whom were forty or over.

Similarly state reports, in the course of describing prior identifications admitted as evidence of guilt, reveal numerous instances of suggestive procedures, for example, that all in the lineup but the suspect were known to the identifying witness, that the other participants in a lineup were grossly dissimilar in appearance to the suspect, that only the suspect was required to wear distinctive clothing which the culprit allegedly wore, that the witness is told by the police that they have caught the culprit after which the defendant is brought before the witness alone or is viewed in jail, that the suspect is pointed out before or during a lineup, and that the participants in the lineup are asked to try on an article of clothing which fits only the suspect.

The potential for improper influence is illustrated by the circumstances, insofar as they appear, surrounding the prior identifications in the three cases we decide today. In the present case, the testimony of the identifying witnesses elicited on cross-examination revealed that those witnesses were taken to the courthouse and seated in the courtroom to await assembly of the lineup. The courtroom faced on a hallway observable to the witnesses through an open door. The cashier testified that she saw Wade "standing in the hall" within sight of an FBI agent. Five or six other prisoners later appeared in the hall. The vice president testified that he saw a person in the hall in the custody of the agent who "resembled the person that we identified as the one that had entered the bank."

The lineup in *Gilbert, supra,* was conducted in an auditorium in which some 100 witnesses to several alleged state and federal robberies charged to Gilbert made wholesale identifications of Gilbert as the robber in each other's presence, a procedure said to be fraught with dangers of suggestion. And the vice of suggestion created by the identification in *Stovall* was the presentation to the witness of the suspect alone handcuffed to police officers. It is hard to imagine a situation more clearly conveying the suggestion to the witness that the one presented is believed guilty by the police.

The few cases that have surfaced therefore reveal the existence of a process attended with hazards of serious unfairness to the criminal accused and strongly suggest the plight of the more numerous defendants who are unable to ferret out suggestive influences in the secrecy of the confrontation. We do not assume that these risks are the result of police procedures intentionally designed to prejudice an accused. Rather we assume they derive from the dangers inherent in eyewitness identification and the suggestibility inherent in the context of the pretrial identification. Williams & Hammelmann, in one of the most comprehensive studies of such forms of identification, said, "[T]he fact that the police themselves have, in a given case, little or no doubt that the man put up for identification has committed the offense, and that their chief preoccupation is with the problem of getting sufficient proof, because he has not 'come clean,' involves a danger that this persuasion may communicate itself even in a doubtful case to the witness in some way. . . ."

Insofar as the accused's conviction may rest on a courtroom identification in fact the fruit of a suspect pretrial identification which the accused is helpless to subject to effective scrutiny at trial, the accused is deprived of that right of cross-examination which is an essential safeguard to his right to confront the witnesses against him *Pointer* v. *Texas*. And even though cross-examination is a precious safeguard to a fair trial, it cannot be viewed as an absolute assurance of accuracy and reliability. Thus in the present context, where so many variables and pitfalls exist, the first line of defense must be the prevention of unfairness and the lessening of the hazards of eyewitness identification at the lineup itself. The trial which might determine the accused's fate may well not be that in the courtroom but that at the pretrial confrontation, with the State alignment against the accused, the witness the sole jury, and the accused unprotected against the overreaching, intentional or unintentional, and with little or no effective appeal from the judgment there rendered by the witness—"that's the man."

Since it appears that there is grave potential for prejudice, intentional or not, in the pretrial lineup, which may not be capable of reconstruction at trial, and since presence of counsel itself can often avert prejudice and assure a meaningful confrontation at trial, there can be little doubt that for Wade the post-indictment lineup was a critical stage of the prosecution at which he was "as much entitled to such aid [of counsel]

... as at the trial itself." *Powell* v. *Alabama.* Thus both Wade and his counsel should have been notified of the impending lineup, and counsel's presence should have been a requisite to conduct of the lineup, absent an "intelligent waiver." See *Carnley* v. *Cochran.* No substantial countervailing policy considerations have been advanced against the requirement of the presence of counsel. Concern is expressed that the requirement will forestall prompt identifications and result in obstruction of the confrontations. As for the first, we note that in the two cases in which the right to counsel is today held to apply, counsel had already been appointed and no argument is made in either case that notice to counsel would have prejudicially delayed the confrontations. Moreover, we leave open the question whether the presence of substitute counsel might not suffice where notification and presence of the suspect's own counsel would result in prejudicial delay. And to refuse to recognize the right to counsel for fear that counsel will obstruct the course of justice is contrary to the basic assumptions upon which this Court has operated in Sixth Amendment cases. We rejected similar logic in *Miranda* v. *Arizona* concerning presence of counsel during custodial interrogation.

> [A]n attorney is merely exercising the good professional judgment he has been taught. This is not cause for considering the attorney a menace to law enforcement. He is merely carrying out what he is sworn to do under his oath—to protect to the extent of his ability the rights of his client. In fulfilling this responsibility the attorney plays a vital role in the administration of criminal justice under our Constitution.

In our view counsel can hardly impede legitimate law enforcement; on the contrary, for the reasons expressed, law enforcement may be assisted by preventing the infiltration of taint in the prosecution's identification evidence. That result cannot help the guilty avoid conviction but can only help assure that the right man has been brought to justice.

Legislative or other regulations, such as those of local police departments, which eliminate the risks of abuse and unintentional suggestion at lineup proceedings and the impediments to meaningful confrontation at trial may also remove the basis for regarding the stage as "critical." But neither Congress nor the federal authorities have seen fit to provide a solution. What we hold today "in no way creates a constitutional straightjacket which will handicap sound efforts at reform, nor is it intended to have this effect.'' *Miranda* v. *Arizona.*

V

We come now to the question whether the denial of Wade's motion to strike the courtroom identification by the bank witnesses at trial because of the absence of his counsel at the lineup required, as the Court of Appeals held, the grant of a new trial at which such evidence is to be excluded. We do not think this disposition can be justified without first giving the Government the opportunity to establish by clear and convincing evidence that the in-court identifications were based upon observations of the suspect other than the lineup identification. See *Murphy* v. *Waterfront Commission.* Where, as here, the admissibility of evidence of the lineup identification itself is not involved, a *per se* rule of exclusion of courtroom identification would be unjustified. See *Nardone* v. *United States.* A rule limited solely to the exclusion of testimony concerning identification at the lineup itself, without regard to admissibility of the courtroom identification, would render the right to counsel an empty one. The lineup is most often used, as in the present case, to crystallize the witnesses' identification of the defendant for future reference. We have already noted that the lineup identification will have that effect. The State may then rest upon the witnesses' unequivocal courtroom identification, and not mention the pretrial identification as part of the State's case at trial. Counsel is then in the predicament in which Wade's counsel found himself—realizing that possible unfairness at the lineup may be the sole means of attack upon the unequivocal courtroom identification, and having to probe in the dark in an attempt to discover and reveal unfairness, while bolstering the government witness' courtroom identification by bringing out and dwelling upon his prior identification. Since counsel's presence at the lineup would equip him to attack not only the lineup identification but the courtroom identification as well, limiting the impact of violation of the right to counsel to exclusion of evidence only of identification at the lineup itself disregards a critical element of that right.

We think it follows that the proper test to be applied in these situations is that quoted in *Wong Sun* v. *United States,* " '[W]hether, granting establishment of the primary illegality, the evidence to which instant objections made has been come at by exploitation of that illegality or instead by means sufficiently distinguishable to be purged of the primary taint.' Maguire, Evidence of Guilt 221 (1959)." See also *Hoffa* v. *United States*. Application of this test in the present context requires consideration of various factors; for example, the prior opportunity to observe the alleged criminal act, the existence of any discrepancy between any pre-lineup description and the defendant's actual description, any identification prior to lineup of another person, the identification by picture of the defendant prior to the lineup, failure to identify the defendant on a prior occasion, and the lapse of time between the alleged act and the lineup identification. It is also relevant to consider those facts which, despite the absence of counsel, are disclosed concerning the conduct of the lineup.

We doubt that the Court of Appeals applied the proper test for exclusion of the in-court identification of the two witnesses. The court stated that "it cannot be said with any certainty that they would have recognized appellant at the time of trial if this intervening lineup had not occurred," and that the testimony of the two witnesses "may well have been colored by the illegal procedure [and] was prejudicial." Moreover, the court was persuaded, in part, by the "compulsory verbal responses made by Wade at the instance of the Special Agent." This implies the erroneous holding that Wade's privilege against self-incrimination was violated so that the denial of counsel required exclusion.

On the record now before us we cannot make the determination whether the in-court identifications had an independent origin. This was not an issue at trial, although there is some evidence relevant to a determination. That inquiry is most properly made in the District Court. We therefore think the appropriate procedure to be followed is to vacate the conviction pending a hearing to determine whether the in-court identifications had an independent source, or whether, in any event, the introduction of the evidence was harmless error, *Chapman* v. *California*, and for the District Court to reinstate the conviction or order a new trial, as may be proper. See *United States* v. *Shotwell Mfg. Co.*

The judgment of the Court of Appeals is vacated and the case is remanded to that court with direction to enter a new judgment vacating the conviction and remanding the case to the District Court for further proceedings consistent with this opinion.

It is so ordered.

McCLESKEY v. KEMP, SUPERINTENDENT, GEORGIA DIAGNOS-
TIC AND CLASSIFICATION CENTER

Argued October 15, 1986—Decided April 22, 1987

In 1978, petitioner, a black man, was convicted in a Georgia trial court of
armed robbery and murder, arising from the killing of a white police officer
during the robbery of a store. Pursuant to Georgia statutes, the jury at the
penalty hearing considered the mitigating and aggravating circumstances of
petitioner's conduct and recommended the death penalty on the murder
charge. The trial court followed the recommendation, and the Georgia Supreme Court affirmed. After unsuccessfully seeking postconviction relief in
state courts, petitioner sought habeas corpus relief in Federal District Court.
His petition included a claim that the Georgia capital sentencing process
was administered in a racially discriminatory manner in violation of the
Eighth and Fourteenth Amendments. In support of the claim, petitioner proffered a statistical study (the Baldus study) that purports to show a disparity
in the imposition of the death sentence in Georgia based on the murder
victim's race and, to a lesser extent, the defendant's race. The study is based
on over 2,000 murder cases that occurred in Georgia during the 1970's, and
involves data relating to the victim's race, the defendant's race, and the
various combinations of such persons' races. The study indicates that black
defendants who killed white victims have the greatest likelihood of receiving
the death penalty. Rejecting petitioner's constitutional claims, the court denied his petition insofar as it was based on the Baldus study, and the Court
of Appeals affirmed the District Court's decision on this issue. It assumed
the validity of the Baldus study but found the statistics insufficient to demonstrate unconstitutional discrimination in the Fourteenth Amendment context
or to show irrationality, arbitrariness, and capriciousness under Eighth
Amendment analysis.

Held:

1. The Baldus study does not establish that the administration of the
Georgia capital punishment system violates the Equal Protection Clause.

(a) To prevail under that Clause, petitioner must prove that the decisionmakers in *his* case acted with discriminatory purpose. Petitioner offered
no evidence specific to his own case that would support an inference that
racial considerations played a part in his sentence, and the Baldus study is
insufficient to support an inference that any of the decisionmakers in his
case acted with discriminatory purpose. This Court has accepted statistics
as proof of intent to discriminate in the context of a State's selection of the
jury venire and in the context of statutory violations under Title VII of the
Civil Rights Act of 1964. However, the nature of the capital sentencing
decision and the relationship of the statistics to that decision are fundamen-

tally different from the corresponding elements in the venire-selection or Title VII cases. Petitioner's statistical proffer must be viewed in the context of his challenge to decisions at the heart of the State's criminal justice system. Because discretion is essential to the criminal justice process, exceptionally clear proof is required before this Court will infer that the discretion has been abused.

(b) There is no merit to petitioner's argument that the Baldus study proves that the State has violated the Equal Protection Clause by adopting the capital punishment statute and allowing it to remain in force despite its allegedly discriminatory application. For this claim to prevail, petitioner would have to prove that the Georgia Legislature enacted or maintained the death penalty statute *because of* an anticipated racially discriminatory effect. There is no evidence that the legislature either enacted the statute to further a racially discriminatory purpose, or maintained the statute because of the racially disproportionate impact suggested by the Baldus study.

2. Petitioner's argument that the Baldus study demonstrates that the Georgia capital sentencing system violates the Eighth Amendment's prohibition of cruel and unusual punishment must be analyzed in the light of this Court's prior decisions under that Amendment. Decisions since *Furman* v. *Georgia,* have identified a constitutional permissible range of discretion in imposing the death penalty. First, there is a required threshold below which the death penalty cannot be imposed, and the State must establish rational criteria that narrow the decisionmaker's judgment as to whether the circumstances of a particular defendant's case meet the threshold. Second, States cannot limit the sentencer's consideration of any relevant circumstance that could cause it to decline to impose the death penalty. In this respect, the State cannot channel the sentencer's discretion, but must allow it to consider any relevant information offered by the defendant.

3. The Baldus study does not demonstrate that the Georgia capital sentencing system violates the Eighth Amendment.

(a) Petitioner cannot successfully argue that the sentence in his case is disproportionate to the sentences in other murder cases. On the one hand, he cannot base a constitutional claim on an argument that his case differs from other cases in which defendants *did* receive the death penalty. The Georgia Supreme Court found that his death sentence was not disproportionate to other death sentences imposed in the State. On the other hand, absent a showing that the Georgia capital punishment system operates in an arbitrary and capricious manner, petitioner cannot prove a constitutional violation by demonstrating that other defendants who may be similarly situated did *not* receive the death penalty. The opportunities for discretionary leniency under state law do not render the capital sentences imposed arbitrary and capricious. Because petitioner's sentence was imposed under Georgia sentencing procedures that focus discretion ''on the particularized nature of the crime and the particularized characteristics of the individual defendant,'' it may be presumed that his death sentence was not ''wantonly and freakishly'' imposed, and thus that the sentence is not disproportionate within any recognized meaning under the Eighth Amendment. *Gregg* v. *Georgia.*

(b) There is no merit to the contention that the Baldus study shows that Georgia's capital punishment system is arbitrary and capricious in *application.* The statistics do not *prove* that race enters into any capital sentencing decisions or that race was a factor in petitioner's case. The likelihood of racial prejudice allegedly shown by the study does not constitute the constitutional measure of an unacceptable risk of racial prejudice. The inherent lack of predictability of jury decisions does not justify their condemnation. On the contrary, it is the jury's function to make the difficult and uniquely human judgments that defy codification and that build discretion, equity, and flexibility into the legal system.

(c) At most, the Baldus study indicates a discrepancy that appears to correlate with race, but this discrepancy does not constitute a major systemic defect. Any mode for determining guilt or punishment has its weaknesses and the potential for misuse. Despite such imperfections, constitutional guarantees are met when the mode for determining guilt or punishment has been surrounded with safeguards to make it as fair as possible.

4. Petitioner's claim, taken to its logical conclusion, throws into serious question the principles that underlie the entire criminal justice system. His claim easily could be extended to apply to other types of penalties and to claims based on unexplained discrepancies correlating to membership in other minority groups and even to gender. The Constitution does not require that a State eliminate any demonstrable disparity that correlates with a potentially irrelevant factor in order to operate a criminal justice system that includes capital punishment. Petitioner's arguments are best presented to the legislative bodies, not the courts.

Affirmed.

POWELL, J., delivered the opinion of the Court, in which REHNQUIST, C. J., and WHITE, O'CONNOR, and SCALIA, JJ., joined. BRENNAN, J., filed a dissenting opinion.

JUSTICE BRENNAN, with whom JUSTICE MARSHALL joins, and with whom JUSTICE BLACKMUN and JUSTICE STEVENS join in all but Part I, dissenting.

I

Adhering to my view that the death penalty is in all circumstances cruel and unusual punishment forbidden by the Eighth and Fourteenth

Amendments, I would vacate the decision below insofar as it left undisturbed the death sentence imposed in this case. *Gregg* v. *Georgia* (1976) (BRENNAN, J., dissenting). The Court observes that "[t]he *Gregg*-type statute imposes unprecedented safeguards in the special context of capital punishment," which "ensure a degree of care in the imposition of the death penalty that can be described only as unique." Notwithstanding these efforts, murder defendants in Georgia with white victims are more than four times as likely to receive the death sentence as are defendants with black victims. Petitioner's Exhibit DB 82. Nothing could convey more powerfully the intractable reality of the death penalty: "that the effort to eliminate arbitrariness in the infliction of that ultimate sanction is so plainly doomed to failure that it—and the death penalty—must be abandoned altogether." *Godfrey* v. *Georgia* (1980) (MARSHALL, J., concurring in judgment).

Even if I did not hold this position, however, I would reverse the Court of Appeals, for petitioner McCleskey has clearly demonstrated that his death sentence was imposed in violation of the Eighth and Fourteenth Amendments. While I join Parts I through IV–A of JUSTICE BLACKMUN's dissenting opinion discussing petitioner's Fourteenth Amendment claim, I write separately to emphasize how conclusively McCleskey has also demonstrated precisely the type of risk of irrationality in sentencing that we have consistently condemned in our Eighth Amendment jurisprudence.

II

At some point in this case, Warren McCleskey doubtless asked his lawyer whether a jury was likely to sentence him to die. A candid reply to this question would have been disturbing. First, counsel would have to tell McCleskey that few of the details of the crime or of McCleskey's past criminal conduct were more important than the fact that his victim was white. Petitioner's Supplemental Exhibits (Supp. Exh.) 50. Furthermore, counsel would feel bound to tell McCleskey that defendants charged with killing white victims in Georgia are 4.3 times as likely to be sentenced to death as defendants charged with killing blacks. Petitioner's Exhibit DB 82. In addition, frankness would compel the disclosure that it was more likely than not that the race of McCleskey's victim would determine whether he received a death sentence: 6 of every 11 defendants convicted of killing a white person would not have received the death penalty if their victims had been black, Supp. Exh. 51, while, among defendants with aggravating and mitigating factors comparable to McCleskey's, 20 of every 34 would not have been sentenced to die if their victims had been black. Finally, the assessment would not be complete without the information that cases involving black defendants and white victims are more likely to result in a death sentence than cases featuring any other racial combination of defendant and victim. The story could be told in a variety of ways, but McCleskey could not fail to grasp its essential narrative line: there was a significant chance that race would play a prominent role in determining if he lived or died.

The Court today holds that Warren McCleskey's sentence was constitutionally imposed. It finds no fault in a system in which lawyers must tell their clients that race casts a large shadow on the capital sentencing process. The Court arrives at this conclusion by stating that the Baldus study cannot "*prove* that race enters into any capital sentencing decisions or that race was a factor in McCleskey's particular case." Since, according to Professor Baldus, we cannot say "to a moral certainty that race influenced a decision, we can identify only "a likelihood that a particular factor entered into some decisions," and "a discrepancy that appears to correlate with race." This "likelihood" and "discrepancy," holds the Court, is insufficient to establish a constitutional violation. The Court reaches this conclusion by placing four factors on the scales opposite McCleskey's evidence: the desire to encourage sentencing discretion, the existence of "statutory safeguards" in the Georgia scheme, the fear of encouraging widespread challenges to other sentencing decisions, and the limits of the judicial role. The Court's evaluation of the significance of petitioner's evidence is fundamentally at odds with our consistent concern for rationality in capital sentencing, and the considerations that the majority invokes to discount that evidence cannot justify ignoring its force.

III

A

It is important to emphasize at the outset that the Court's observation that McCleskey cannot prove the influence of race on any particular sentencing decision is irrelevant in evaluating his Eighth Amendment claim. Since *Furman* v. *Georgia* (1972), the Court has been concerned with the *risk* of the imposition of an arbitrary sentence, rather than the proven fact of one. *Furman* held that the death penalty "may not be imposed under sentencing procedures that create a substantial risk that the punishment will be inflicted in an arbitrary and capricious manner." *Godfrey* v. *Georgia.* As JUSTICE O'CONNOR observed in *Caldwell* v. *Mississippi* (1985), a death sentence must be struck down when the circumstances under which it has been imposed "creat[e] an unacceptable *risk* that 'the death penalty [may have been] meted out arbitrarily or capriciously' or through 'whim or mistake' " (emphasis added) (quoting *California* v. *Ramos* [1983]). This emphasis on risk acknowledges the difficulty of divining the jury's motivation in an individual case. In addition, it reflects the fact that concern for arbitrariness focuses on the rationality of the system as a whole, and that a system that features a significant probability that sentencing decisions are influenced by impermissible considerations cannot be regarded as rational. As we said in *Gregg* v. *Georgia,* "the petitioner looks to the sentencing system as a whole (as the Court did in *Furman* and we do today)": a constitutional violation is established if a plaintiff demonstrates a "*pattern* of arbitrary and capricious sentencing."

As a result, our inquiry under the Eighth Amendment has not been directed to the validity of the individual sentences before us. In *Godfrey,* for instance, the Court struck down the petitioner's sentence because the vagueness of the statutory definition of heinous crimes created a *risk* that prejudice or other impermissible influences *might have infected* the sentencing decision. In vacating the sentence, we did not ask whether it was likely that Godfrey's own sentence reflected the operation of irrational considerations. Nor did we demand a demonstration that such considerations had actually entered into other sentencing decisions involving heinous crimes. Similarly, in *Roberts* v. *Louisiana* (1976) and *Woodson* v. *North Carolina,* (1976), we struck down death sentences in part because mandatory imposition of the death penalty created the *risk* that a jury *might* rely on arbitrary considerations in deciding which persons should be convicted of capital crimes. Such a risk would arise, we said, because of the likelihood that jurors reluctant to impose capital punishment on a particular defendant would refuse to return a conviction, so that the effect of mandatory sentencing would be to recreate the unbounded sentencing discretion condemned in*Furman.* We did not ask whether the death sentences in the cases before us could have reflected the jury's rational consideration and rejection of mitigating factors. Nor did we require proof that juries had actually acted irrationally in other cases.

Defendants challenging their death sentences thus never have had to prove that impermissible considerations have actually infected sentencing decisions. We have required instead that they establish that the system under which they were sentenced posed a significant risk of such an occurrence. McCleskey's claim does differ, however, in one respect from these earlier cases: it is the first to base a challenge not on speculation about how a system *might* operate, but on empirical documentation of how it *does* operate.

The Court assumes the statistical validity of the Baldus study, and acknowledges that McCleskey has demonstrated a risk that racial prejudice plays a role in capital sentencing in Georgia. Nonetheless, it finds the probability of prejudice insufficient to create constitutional concern. Close analysis of the Baldus study, however, in light of both statistical principles and human experience, reveals that the risk that race influenced McCleskey's sentence is intolerable by any imaginable standard.

B

The Baldus study indicates that, after taking into account some 230 nonracial factors that might legitimately influence a sentencer, the jury *more likely than not* would have spared McCleskey's life had his victim been black. The study distinguishes between those cases in which (1) the jury exercises virtually no discretion because the strength or weakness of aggravating factors usually suggests that only one outcome is appropriate; and (2) cases reflecting an "intermediate" level of aggravation, in which the jury has considerable discretion in choosing a sentence. McCleskey's case falls into the intermediate range. In such cases, death is imposed in 34% of white-victim crimes and 14% of black-victim crimes, a difference of 139% in the rate of imposition of the death penalty. Supp. Exh. 54. In other words, just under 59%—almost 6 in 10—defendants comparable to McCleskey would not have received the death penalty if their victims had been black.

Furthermore, even examination of the sentencing system as a whole, factoring in those cases in which the jury exercises little discretion, indicates the influence of race on capital sentencing. For the Georgia system as a whole, race accounts for a six percentage point difference in the rate at which capital punishment is imposed. Since death is imposed in 11% of all white-victim cases, the rate in comparably aggra-vated black-victim cases is 5%. The rate of capital sentencing in a white-victim case is thus 120% greater than the rate in a black-victim case. Put another way, over half—55%—of defendants in white-victim crimes in Georgia would not have been sentenced to die if their victims had been black. Of the more than 200 variables potentially relevant to a sentencing decision, race of the victim is a powerful explanation for variation in death sentence rates—as powerful as nonracial aggravating factors such as a prior murder conviction or acting as the principal planner of the homicide.

These adjusted figures are only the most conservative indication of the risk that race will influence the death sentences of defendants in Georgia. Data unadjusted for the mitigating or aggravating effect of other factors show an even more pronounced disparity by race. The capital sentencing rate for all white-victim cases was almost *11 times* greater than the rate for black-victim cases. Supp. Exh. 47. Furthermore, blacks who kill whites are sentenced to death at nearly *22 times* the rate of blacks who kill blacks, and more than *7 times* the rate of whites who kill blacks. *Ibid.* In addition, prosecutors seek the death penalty for 70% of black defendants with white victims, but for only 15% of black defendants with black victims, and only 19% of white defendants with black victims. *Id.,* at 56. Since our decision upholding the Georgia capital sentencing system in *Gregg,* the State has executed seven per-sons. All of the seven were convicted of killing whites, and six of the seven executed were black. Such execution figures are especially strik-ing in light of the fact that, during the period encompassed by the Baldus study, only 9.2% of Georgia homicides involved black defen-dants and white victims, while 60.7% involved black victims.

McCleskey's statistics have particular force because most of them are the product of sophisticated multiple-regression analysis. Such anal-ysis is designed precisely to identify patterns in the aggregate, even though we may not be able to reconstitute with certainty any individual decision that goes to make up that pattern. Multiple-regression analysis is particularly well suited to identify the influence of impermissible considerations in sentencing, since it is able to control for permissible factors that may explain an apparent arbitrary pattern. While the deci-sionmaking process of a body such as a jury may be complex, the Baldus study provides a massive compilation of the details that are most relevant to that decision. As we held in the context of Title VII of the Civil Rights Act of 1964 last Term in*Bazemore* v. *Friday* (1986), a multiple-regression analysis need not include every conceivable variable to establish a party's case, as long as it includes those variables that account for the major factors that are likely to influence decisions. In this case, Professor Baldus in fact conducted additional regression analyses in response to criticisms and suggestions by the District Court, all of which confirmed, and some of which even strengthened, the study's original conclusions.

The statistical evidence in this case thus relentlessly documents the risk that McCleskey's sentence was influenced by racial considerations. This evidence shows that there is a better than even chance in Georgia that race will influence the decision to impose the death penalty: a majority of defendants in white-victim crimes would not have been sentenced to die if their victims had been black. In determining whether this risk is acceptable, our judgment must be shaped by the awareness that "[t]he risk of racial prejudice infecting a capital sentencing proceeding is especially serious in light of the complete finality of the death sentence," *Turner* v. *Murray* (1986), and that "[i]t is of vital importance to the defendant and to the community that any decision to impose the death sentence be, and appear to be, based on reason rather than caprice or emotion," *Gardner* v. *Florida* (1977). In determining the guilt of a defendant, a State must prove its case beyond a reasonable doubt. That is, we refuse to convict if the chance of error is simply less likely than not. Surely, we should not be willing to take a person's life if the chance that his death sentence was irrationally imposed is *more* likely than not. In light of the gravity of the interest at stake, petitioner's statistics on their face are a powerful demonstration of the type of risk that our Eighth Amendment jurisprudence has consistently condemned.

C

Evaluation of McCleskey's evidence cannot rest solely on the numbers themselves. We must also ask whether the conclusion suggested by those numbers is consonant with our understanding of history and human experience. Georgia's legacy of a race-conscious criminal justice system, as well as this Court's own recognition of the persistent danger that racial attitudes may affect criminal proceedings, indicates that McCleskey's claim is not a fanciful product of mere statistical artifice.

For many years, Georgia operated openly and formally precisely the type of dual system the evidence shows is still effectively in place. The criminal law expressly differentiated between crimes committed by and against blacks and whites, distinctions whose lineage traced back to the time of slavery. During the colonial period, black slaves who killed whites in Georgia, regardless of whether in self-defense or in defense of another, were automatically executed.

By the time of the Civil War, a dual system of crime and punishment was well established in Georgia. See Ga. Penal Code (1861). The state criminal code contained separate sections for "Slaves and Free Persons of Color," Pt. 4, Tit. 3, Ch. 1, and for all other persons. The code provided, for instance, for an automatic death sentence for murder committed by blacks, but declared that anyone else convicted of murder might receive life imprisonment if the conviction were founded solely on circumstantial testimony *or* simply if the jury so recommended. The code established that the rape of a free white female by a black "shall be" punishable by death. However, rape by anyone else of a free white female was punishable by a prison term not less than 2 nor more than 20 years. The rape of *blacks* was punishable "by fine and imprisonment, at the discretion of the court." §4249. A black convicted of assaulting a free white person with intent to murder could be put to death at the discretion of the court, §4708, but the same offense committed against a black, slave or free, was classified as a "minor" offense whose punishment lay in the discretion of the court, as long as such punishment did not "extend to life, limb, or health." Art. III, §§4714, 4718. Assault with intent to murder by a white person was punishable by a prison term of from 2 to 10 years. While sufficient provocation could reduce a charge of murder to manslaughter, the code provided that "[o]bedience and submission being the duty of a slave, much greater provocation is necessary to reduce a homicide of a white person by him to voluntary manslaughter, than is prescribed for white persons." Art. II, §4711.

In more recent times, some 40 years ago, Gunnar Myrdal's epochal study of American race relations produced findings mirroring McCleskey's evidence:

> As long as only Negroes are concerned and no whites are disturbed, great leniency will be shown in most cases. . . . The sentences for even major crimes are ordinarily reduced when the victim is another Negro.
>
> For offenses which involve any actual or potential danger to whites, however, Negroes are punished more severely than whites.

On the other hand, it is quite common for a white criminal to be set free if his crime was against a Negro.

[G. Myrdal, An American Dilemma 551–553 (1944)].

This Court has invalidated portions of the Georgia capital sentencing system three times over the past 15 years. The specter of race discrimination was acknowledged by the Court in striking down the Georgia death penalty statute in *Furman*. Justice Douglas cited studies suggesting imposition of the death penalty in racially discriminatory fashion, and found the standardless statutes before the Court "pregnant with discrimination." JUSTICE MARSHALL pointed to statistics indicating that "Negroes [have been] executed far more often than whites in proportion to their percentage of the population. Studies indicate that while the higher rate of execution among Negroes is partially due to a higher rate of crime, there is evidence of racial discrimination." Although Justice Stewart declined to conclude that racial discrimination had been plainly proved, he stated that "[m]y concurring Brothers have demonstrated that, if any basis can be discerned for the selection of these few to be sentenced to die, it is the constitutionally impermissible basis of race." In dissent, Chief Justice Burger acknowledged that statistics "suggest, at least as a historical matter, that Negroes have been sentenced to death with greater frequency than whites in several States, particularly for the crime of interracial rape." Finally, also in dissent, JUSTICE POWELL intimated that an Equal Protection Clause argument would be available for a black "who could demonstrate that members of his race were being singled out for more severe punishment than others charged with the same offense." He noted that although the Eighth Circuit had rejected a claim of discrimination in *Maxwell* v. *Bishop* (1968), vacated and remanded on other grounds (1970), the statistical evidence in that case "tend[ed] to show a pronounced disproportion in the number of Negroes receiving death sentences for rape in parts of Arkansas and elsewhere in the South." It is clear that the Court regarded the opportunity for the operation of racial prejudice a particularly troublesome aspect of the unbounded discretion afforded by the Georgia sentencing scheme.

Five years later, the Court struck down the imposition of the death penalty in Georgia for the crime of rape. *Coker* v. *Georgia* (1977). Although the Court did not explicitly mention race, the decision had to have been informed by the specific observations on rape by both the Chief Justice and JUSTICE POWELL in *Furman*. Furthermore, evidence submitted to the Court indicated that black men who committed rape, particularly of white women, were considerably more likely to be sentenced to death than white rapists. For instance, by 1977 Georgia had executed 62 men for rape since the Federal Government began compiling statistics in 1930. Of these men, 58 were black and 4 were white.

Three years later, the Court in *Godfrey* found one of the State's statutory aggravating factors unconstitutionally vague, since it resulted in "standardless and unchanneled imposition of death sentences in the uncontrolled discretion of a basically uninstructed jury. . . ." JUSTICE MARSHALL, concurring in the judgment, noted that "[t]he disgraceful distorting effects of racial discrimination and poverty continue to be painfully visible in the imposition of death sentences."

This historical review of Georgia criminal law is not intended as a bill of indictment calling the State to account for past transgressions. Citation of past practices does not justify the automatic condemnation of current ones. But it would be unrealistic to ignore the influence of history in assessing the plausible implications of McCleskey's evidence. "[A]mericans share a historical experience that has resulted in individuals within the culture ubiquitously attaching a significance to race that is irrational and often outside their awareness." Lawrence, The Id, The Ego, and Equal Protection: Reckoning With Unconscious Racism, 39 Stan. L. Rev. 327 (1987). As we said in *Rose* v. *Mitchell* (1979):

> [W]e . . . cannot deny that, 114 years after the close of the War Between the States and nearly 100 years after *Strauder,* racial and other forms of discrimination still remain a fact of life, in the administration of justice as in our society as a whole. Perhaps today that discrimination takes a form more subtle than before. But it is not less real or pernicious.

The ongoing influence of history is acknowledged, as the majority observes, by our " 'uneasing efforts' to eradicate racial prejudice from our criminal justice system." (*Batson* v. *Kentucky,* [1986]). These efforts, however, signify not the elimination of the problem but its persistence. Our cases reflect a realization of the myriad of opportunities for racial considerations to influence criminal proceedings: in the exercise of peremptory challenges, *Batson* v. *Kentucky;* in the selection of the grand jury, *Vasquez* v. *Hillery* (1986); in the selection of the petit jury, *Whitus* v. *Georgia* (1967); in the exercise of prosecutorial discretion, *Wayte* v. *United States* (1985); in the conduct of argument, *Donnelly*

v. *DeChristoforo* (1974); and in the conscious or unconscious bias of jurors, *Turner* v. *Murray* (1986), *Ristaino* v. *Ross* (1976).

The discretion afforded prosecutors and jurors in the Georgia capital sentencing system creates such opportunities. No guidelines govern prosecutorial decisions to seek the death penalty, and Georgia provides juries with no list of aggravating and mitigating factors, nor any standard for balancing them against one another. Once a jury identifies one aggravating factor, it has complete discretion in choosing life or death, and need not articulate its basis for selecting life imprisonment. The Georgia sentencing system therefore provides considerable opportunity for racial considerations, however subtle and unconscious, to influence charging and sentencing decisions.

History and its continuing legacy thus buttress the probative force of McCleskey's statistics. Formal dual criminal laws may no longer be in effect, and intentional discrimination may no longer be prominent. Nonetheless, as we acknowledged in*Turner,* "subtle, less consciously held racial attitudes" continue to be of concern, and the Georgia system gives such attitudes considerable room to operate. The conclusions drawn from McCleskey's statistical evidence are therefore consistent with the lessons of social experience.

The majority thus misreads our Eighth Amendment jurisprudence in concluding that McCleskey has not demonstrated a degree of risk sufficient to raise constitutional concern. The determination of the significance of his evidence is at its core an exercise in human moral judgment, not a mechanical statistical analysis. It must first and foremost be informed by awareness of the fact that death is irrevocable, and that as a result "the qualitative difference of death from all other punishments requires a greater degree of scrutiny of the capital sentencing determination." *California* v. *Ramos*. For this reason, we have demanded a uniquely high degree of rationality in imposing the death penalty. A capital sentencing system in which race more likely than not plays a role does not meet this standard. It is true that every nuance of decision cannot be statistically captured, nor can any individual judgment be plumbed with absolute certainty. Yet the fact that we must always act without the illumination of complete knowledge cannot induce paralysis when we confront what is literally an issue of life and death. Sentencing data, history, and experience all counsel that Georgia has provided insufficient assurance of the heightened rationality we have required in order to take a human life.

IV

The Court cites four reasons for shrinking from the implications of McCleskey's evidence: the desirability of discretion for actors in the criminal justice system, the existence of statutory safeguards against abuse of that discretion, the potential consequences for broader challenges to criminal sentencing, and an understanding of the contours of the judicial role. While these concerns underscore the need for sober deliberation, they do not justify rejecting evidence as convincing as McCleskey has presented.

The Court maintains that petitioner's claim "is antithetical to the fundamental role of discretion in our criminal justice system." It states that "[w]here the discretion that is fundamental to our criminal process is involved, we decline to assume that what is unexplained is invidious."

Reliance on race in imposing capital punishment, however, is antithetical to the very rationale for granting sentencing discretion. Discretion is a means, not an end. It is bestowed in order to permit the sentencer to "trea[t] each defendant in a capital case with that degree of respect due the uniqueness of the individual." *Lockett* v. *Ohio* (1978). The decision to impose the punishment of death must be based on a "particularized consideration of relevant aspects of the character and record of each convicted defendant." *Woodson* v. *North Carolina.* Failure to conduct such an individualized moral inquiry "treats all persons convicted of a designated offense not as unique individual human beings, but as members of a faceless, undifferentiated mass to be subjected to the blind infliction of the penalty of death."

Considering the race of a defendant or victim in deciding if the death penalty should be imposed is completely at odds with this concern that an individual be evaluated as a unique human being. Decisions influenced by race rest in part on a categorical assessment of the worth of human beings according to color, insensitive to whatever qualities the individuals in question may possess. Enhanced willingness to impose the death sentence on black defendants, or diminished willingness to render such a sentence when blacks are victims, reflects a devaluation of the lives of black persons. When confronted with evidence that race more likely than not plays such a role in a capital sentencing system, it is plainly insufficient to say that the importance of discretion demands that the risk be higher before we will act—for in such a case the very end that discretion is designed to serve is being undermined.

Our desire for individualized moral judgments may lead us to accept some inconsistencies in sentencing outcomes. Since such decisions are not reducible to mathematical formulae, we are willing to assume that a certain degree of variation reflects the fact that no two defendants are completely alike. There is thus a presumption that actors in the criminal justice system exercise their discretion in responsible fashion, and we do not automatically infer that sentencing patterns that do not comport with ideal rationality are suspect.

As we made clear in *Batson* v. *Kentucky* (1986), however, that presumption is rebuttable. *Batson* dealt with another arena in which considerable discretion traditionally has been afforded, the exercise of peremptory challenges. Those challenges are normally exercised without any indication whatsoever of the grounds for doing so. The rationale for this deference has been a belief that the unique characteristics of particular prospective jurors may raise concern on the part of the prosecution or defense, despite the fact that counsel may not be able to articulate that concern in a manner sufficient to support exclusion for cause. As with sentencing, therefore, peremptory challenges are justified as an occasion for particularized determinations related to specific individuals, and, as with sentencing, we presume that such challenges normally are not made on the basis of a factor such as race. As we said in *Batson,* however, such features do not justify imposing a "crippling burden of proof," in order to rebut that presumption. The Court in this case apparently seeks to do just that. On the basis of the need for individualized decisions, it rejects evidence, drawn from the most sophisticated capital sentencing analysis ever performed, that reveals that race more likely than not infects capital sentencing decisions. The Court's position converts a rebuttable presumption into a virtually conclusive one.

The Court also declines to find McCleskey's evidence sufficient in view of "the safeguards designed to minimize racial bias in the [capital sentencing] process." *Gregg* v. *Georgia,* upheld the Georgia capital sentencing statute against a facial challenge which JUSTICE WHITE described in his concurring opinion as based on "simply an assertion of lack of faith" that the system could operate in a fair manner (opinion concurring in judgment). JUSTICE WHITE observed that the claim that prosecutors might act in an arbitrary fashion was "unsupported by any facts," and that prosecutors must be assumed to exercise their charging duties properly "[a]bsent facts to the contrary." It is clear that *Gregg* bestowed no permanent approval on the Georgia system. It simply held that the State's statutory safeguards were assumed sufficient to channel discretion without evidence otherwise.

It has now been over 13 years since Georgia adopted the provisions upheld in *Gregg*. Professor Baldus and his colleagues have compiled data on almost 2,500 homicides committed during the period 1973–1979. They have taken into account the influence of 230 nonracial variables, using a multitude of data from the State itself, and have produced striking evidence that the odds of being sentenced to death are significantly greater than average if a defendant is black or his or her victim is white. The challenge to the Georgia system is not speculative or theoretical; it is empirical. As a result, the Court cannot rely on the statutory safeguards in discounting McCleskey's evidence, for it is the very effectiveness of those safeguards that such evidence calls into question. While we may hope that a model of procedural fairness will curb the influence of race on sentencing, "we cannot simply assume that the model works as intended; we must critique its performance in terms of its results." Hubbard, "Reasonable Levels of Arbitrariness" in Death Sentencing Patterns: A Tragic Perspective on Capital Punishment, 18 U. C. D. L. Rev. 1113, 1162 (1985).

The Court next states that its unwillingness to regard petitioner's evidence as sufficient is based in part on the fear that recognition of McCleskey's claim would open the door to widespread challenges to all aspects of criminal sentencing. Taken on its face, such a statement seems to suggest a fear of too much justice. Yet surely the majority would acknowledge that if striking evidence indicated that other minority groups, or women, or even persons with blond hair, were disproportionately sentenced to death, such a state of affairs would be repugnant to deeply rooted conceptions of fairness. The prospect that there may be more widespread abuse than McCleskey documents may be dismaying, but it does not justify complete abdication of our judicial role. The Constitution was framed fundamentally as a bulwark against government power, and preventing the arbitrary administration of punishment is a basic ideal of any society that purports to be governed by the rule of law.

In fairness, the Court's fear that McCleskey's claim is an invitation to descend a slippery slope also rests on the realization that any humanly imposed system of penalties will exhibit some imperfection. Yet to reject McCleskey's powerful evidence on this basis is to ignore both the qualitatively different character of the death penalty and the particular repugnance of racial discrimination, considerations which may properly be taken into account in determining whether various punishments are "cruel and unusual." Furthermore, it fails to take account of the unprecedented refinement and strength of the Baldus study.

It hardly needs reiteration that this Court has consistently acknowledged the uniqueness of the punishment of death. "Death, in its finality, differs more from life imprisonment than a 100-year prison term differs from one of only a year or two. Because of that qualitative difference, there is a corresponding difference in the need for reliability in the determination that death is the appropriate punishment." *Woodson.* Furthermore, the relative interests of the state and the defendant differ dramatically in the death penalty context. The marginal benefits accruing to the state from obtaining the death penalty rather than life imprisonment are considerably less than the marginal difference to the defendant between death and life in prison. Such a disparity is an additional reason for tolerating scant arbitrariness in capital sentencing. Even those who believe that society can impose the death penalty in a manner sufficiently rational to justify its continuation must acknowledge that the level of rationality that *is* considered satisfactory must be *uniquely* high. As a result, the degree of arbitrariness that may be adequate to render the death penalty "cruel and unusual" punishment may not be adequate to invalidate lesser penalties. What these relative degrees of arbitrariness might be in other cases need not concern us here; the point is that the majority's fear of wholesale invalidation of criminal sentences is unfounded.

The Court also maintains that accepting McCleskey's claim would pose a threat to all sentencing because of the prospect that a correlation might be demonstrated between sentencing outcomes and other personal characteristics. Again, such a view is indifferent to the considerations that enter into a determination whether punishment is "cruel and unusual." Race is a consideration whose influence is expressly constitutionally proscribed. We have expressed a moral commitment, as embodied in our fundamental law, that this specific characteristic should not be the basis for allotting burdens and benefits. Three constitutional amendments, and numerous statutes, have been prompted specifically by the desire to address the effects of racism. "Over the years, this Court has consistently repudiated '[d]istinctions between citizens solely because of their ancestry' as being 'odious to a free people whose institutions are founded upon the doctrine of equality.' " *Loving* v. *Virginia,* (1967) (quoting *Hirabayashi* v. *United States* [1943]). Furthermore, we have explicitly acknowledged the illegitimacy of race as a consideration in capital sentencing, *Zant* v. *Stephens* (1983). That a decision to impose the death penalty could be influenced by *race* is thus a particularly repugnant prospect, and evidence that race may play even a modest role in levying a death sentence should be enough to characterize that sentence as "cruel and unusual."

Certainly, a factor that we would regard as morally irrelevant, such as hair color, at least theoretically could be associated with sentencing results to such an extent that we would regard as arbitrary a system in which that factor played a significant role. As I have said above, how ever, the evaluation of evidence suggesting such a correlation must be informed not merely by statistics, but by history and experience. One could hardly contend that this Nation has on the basis of hair color inflicted upon persons deprivation comparable to that imposed on the basis of race. Recognition of this fact would necessarily influence the evaluation of data suggesting the influence of hair color on sentencing, and would require evidence of statistical correlation even more powerful than that presented by the Baldus study.

Furthermore, the Court's fear of the expansive ramifications of a holding for McCleskey in this case is unfounded because it fails to recognize the uniquely sophisticated nature of the Baldus study. McCleskey presents evidence that is far and away the most refined data ever assembled on any system of punishment, data not readily replicated through casual effort. Moreover, that evidence depicts not merely arguable tendencies, but striking correlations, all the more powerful because nonracial explanations have been eliminated. Acceptance of petitioner's evidence would therefore establish a remarkably stringent standard of statistical evidence unlikely to be satisfied with any frequency.

The Court's projection of apocalyptic consequences for criminal sentencing is thus greatly exaggerated. The Court can indulge in such speculation only by ignoring its own jurisprudence demanding the highest scrutiny on issues of death and race. As a reuslt, it fails to do justice to a claim in which both those elements are intertwined—an occasion calling for the most sensitive inquiry a court can conduct. Despite its acceptance of the validity of Warren McCleskey's evidence, the Court is willing to let his death sentence stand because it fears that we cannot successfully define a different standard for lesser punishments. This fear is baseless.

Finally, the Court justifies its rejection of McCleskey's claim by cautioning against usurpation of the legislatures' role in devising and monitoring criminal punishment. The Court is, of course, correct to emphasize the gravity of constitutional intervention and the importance that it be sparingly employed. The fact that "[c]apital punishment is now the law in more than two thirds of our States," however, does not diminish the fact that capital punishment is the most awesome act that a State can perform. The judiciary's role in this society counts for little if the use of governmental power to extinguish life does not elicit close scrutiny. It is true that society has a legitimate interest in punishment. Yet, as Alexander Bickel wrote:

It is a premise we deduce not merely from the fact of a written constitution but from the history of the race, and ultimately as a moral judgment of the good society, that government should serve not only what we conceive from time to time to be our immediate material needs but also certain enduring values. This in part is what is meant by government under law. [The Least Dangerous Branch 24 (1962)].

Our commitment to these values requires fidelity to them even when there is temptation to ignore them. Such temptation is especially apt to arise in criminal matters, for those granted constitutional protection in this context are those whom society finds most menacing and opprobrious. Even less sympathetic are those we consider for the sentence of death, for execution "is a way of saying, 'You are not fit for this world, take your chance elsewhere.' " *Furman.*

For these reasons, "[t]he methods we employ in the enforcement of our criminal law have aptly been called the measures by which the quality of our civilization may be judged." *Coppedge* v. *United States* (1962). Those whom we would banish from society or from the human community itself often speak in too faint a voice to be heard above society's demand for punishment. It is the particular role of courts to hear these voices, for the Constitution declares that the majoritarian chorus may not alone dictate the conditions of social life. The Court thus fulfills, rather than disrupts, the scheme of separation of powers by closely scrutinizing the imposition of the death penalty, for no decision of a society is more deserving of "sober second thought," Stone, The Common Law in the United States, 50 Harv. L. Rev. 4, 25 (1936).

V

At the time our Constitution was framed 200 years ago this year, blacks "had for more than a century before been regarded as beings of an inferior order, and altogether unfit to associate with the white race, either in social or political relations; and so far inferior, that they had no rights which the white man was bound to respect." *Dred Scott* v. *Sandford* (1857). Only 130 years ago, this Court relied on those observations to deny American citizenship to blacks. A mere three generations ago, this Court sanctioned racial segregation, stating that "[i]f one race be inferior to the other socially, the Constitution of the United States cannot put them upon the same plane." *Plessy* v. *Ferguson* (1896).

In more recent times, we have sought to free ourselves from the burden of this history. Yet it has been scarcely a generation since this Court's first decision striking down racial segregation, and barely two decades since the legislative prohibition of racial discrimination in major domains of national life. These have been honorable steps, but we cannot pretend that in three decades we have completely escaped the grip of a historical legacy spanning centuries. Warren McCleskey's evidence confronts us with the subtle and persistent influence of the past. His message is a disturbing one to a society that has formally repudiated racism, and a frustrating one to a Nation accustomed to regarding its destiny as the product of its own will. Nonetheless, we ignore him at our peril, for we remain imprisoned by the past as long as we deny its influence in the present.

It is tempting to pretend that minorities on death row share a fate in no way connected to our own, that our treatment of them sounds no echoes beyond the chambers in which they die. Such an illusion is ultimately corrosive, for the reverberations of injustice are not so easily confined. "The destinies of the two races in this country are indissolubly linked together," and the way in which we choose those who will die reveals the depth of moral commitment among the living.

The Court's decision today will not change what attorneys in Georgia tell other Warren McCleskeys about their chances of execution. Nothing will soften the harsh message they must convey, nor alter the prospect that race undoubtedly will continue to be a topic of discussion. McCleskey's evidence will not have obtained judicial acceptance, but that will not affect what is said on death row. However many criticisms of today's decision may be rendered, these painful conversations will serve as the most eloquent dissents of all.

Index

BIO   Goldman, Roger L.
BRENNAN
           Justice William J.
           Brennan, Jr.

                              36401000040491

$24.95

DATE			